The third volume of the remarkable A WALK IN
THE DARK SERIES.

The Lord Regent, Sulakon, is trying to draw the
rebel lords to his standard in order to raise an army
against 'the witch' – Aleizon Ailix Ayndra.

Meanwhile, Ayndra, in her attempt to reunite the
empire has many other hazards and adversities to
contend with: she is kidnapped by the evil Lord
Sandar, who has developed a lustful passion for
her; there are plots against her life; and the ghost of
Ailixond seems to have returned to the world . . .

The New Empire

THE STREETS OF THE CITY

Book Three of
A WALK IN THE DARK

◆————————————◆————————————◆

SPEDDING

UNWIN
PAPERBACKS

LONDON SYDNEY WELLINGTON

First published in Great Britain by Unwin ® Paperbacks, an imprint of
Unwin Hyman Limited, in 1988

UNWIN HYMAN LIMITED
15–17 Broadwick Street, London W1V 1FP

Allen & Unwin Australia Pty Ltd
8 Napier Street, North Sydney, NSW 2060, Australia

Unwin Paperbacks with the Port Nicholson Press
60 Cambridge Terrace, Wellington, New Zealand

British Library Cataloguing in Publication Data

Spedding
    The streets of the city.
I. Title   II. Series
823'.914[F]
ISBN 0–04–440148–5

Set in 10 on 11 point Sabon by Computape (Pickering) Ltd, N. Yorkshire
and printed in Great Britain by Cox and Wyman Ltd, Reading.

Prologue

THE ROAD AND THE HILLS:

Book One of *A Walk in the Dark*

In the Fourth Month of the four hundred and sixty-first year of the city, the Grand Army of Lord Ailixond, King of Safi, was marching north from Mirkitya into Biit-Yiakarak, when a scruffy youth named Aleizon Ailix Ayndra enlisted in the artillery. His exotic name and habits gained him some note among the other catapult men, but only his catapult-master Ogo discovered that he was in fact a young woman in disguise. Ogo kept his own counsel on the matter, though women were forbidden by rule to remain in the soldiers' camp, until the Army was besieging Raq'min, capital of the northern kingdom of Haramin. Aleizon Ailix Ayndra confected a stuff she called *powderfire*, which she packed into fused boxes and fired from the catapult, to explode on impact – or earlier. It was on the day she chose to demonstrate them that the King came to inspect the catapult battery; when Ailixond stood too close to the machine for safety, she threw him down in the mud for his own protection. After this piece of lèse-majesté he ordered her to leave the battery and follow his entourage. Ogo expected that he would order her executed, and him cashiered for keeping a woman in the camp. In fact he offered her a captain's commission, and did not withdraw it when she announced her sex to him. Her appointment was received as a nine-days'-wonder among the noble lords who accompanied the King, who expected that she would shortly be dismissed, dead, or pregnant. When she failed to fall in battle, defended herself against the advances of Lord Polem, and brought herself further to the attention of the King, her shameless behaviour and lack of respect for convention provoked much opposition among the more traditional members of the nobility. After the great victory of Palagar at the end of 462, her love affair with Ailixond became public knowledge. The King's cousin Sulakon was the chief of those who demanded that he should either regularise his union with her or expel her altogether. Sulakon was absent on a mission to quell rebels in the recently conquered Seaward Plains when the lords opposed to Ailixond's insatiable desire for new conquest rose to an attempt on his life. Those responsible were soon arrested, but with the army divided only nine lords remained beside the accused, and the law demanded a jury of ten peers for justice. Ailixond resorted to the scandalous expedient of creating his mistress a lord – an honour which the King was free to bestow on any Safic citizen born of full marriage rather than concubinage or common-law union, but which was usually extended to those who were not sons or heiress daughters of lords only as a very special reward for services. This only drew their affair into greater prominence, and when Ailixond's wife Othanë arrived, he felt compelled to ask Aleizon Ailix Ayndra to marry him. Shocked by her refusal, he struck her, and they parted. When, shortly afterward, Ailixond encountered Setha, the daughter of a petty prince who was as renowned for her pride in rejecting suitors as she was famed for her beauty, he demanded and received her hand. He ordered Aleizon Ailix Ayndra to prepare the wedding feast. She ruined the bridal soup, insisted in taking part in the procession to put the bridegroom to bed, and in a drunken state in the small hours she challenged Lord Lakkannar to a duel. Ailixond woke from his marriage bed to see her standing over Lakkannar's prostrate body in the yard outside his window. She was punished for contravening the ban on duels within the Army with banishment from court and sent to govern the province of Haramin. The Grand Army continued its march westward, while Setha bore Ailixond a son, Paraki-son, in 464 – a cause of great rejoicing, since his fourteen-year-old marriage to Othanë continued childless. Aleizon Ailix Ayndra, whose mother came from Haramin, was well established at the head of the province when Polem was sent to put down a rebellion in the mountains of Pirramin. When he fell into a trap laid for him by the rebels, she led the army of Haramin to rescue him; and returned to find a peremptory summons from Ailixond, instructing her to join him at the city of New Hope which he had founded, far out in the

vi

plains of the northwest. He gave no reason for the order, and when she arrived, he sent her on an embassy to a group of wild nomads who blinded the other envoy and flogged her half to death before the Grand Army reached them.

In the spring, Ailixond proposed further advances into the unknown west, and the army mutinied, demanding a return to Safi. Aleizon Ailix Ayndra was the only one of the lords who offered to follow him onward, but when they set out southward, ostensibly to return to Safi, she remained in the outer circle of his associates. She discovered that Ailixond had deceived the army as to their route, and they were in reality travelling toward the matrilineal kingdom of S'Thurrulass, where she had spent some years in the household of one Lady Ylureen and learnt, among other things, the art of making powderfire. She helped him to make the whole appear a plot by their guides when the rest of the army discovered the truth, but she could do nothing to restore the flagging enthusiasm of the mass of soldiery. The S'Thurrulans avoided battle and drew them deeper into the country; when they finally made a stand in the city of Merultine, Ailixond's fervour was hardly able to get his men to attack, until he received a yard-long arrow in his side as he led the assault on the citadel. The Grand Army believed him dead and went on the rampage, burning the lower city to the ground. The King and Queen in Suthine sent Lady Ylureen as ambassador to sue for peace, offering hospitality, a free passage through S'Thurrulass and an annual tribute if Ailixond would abandon their country. Alive, but disabled by his wound, Ailixond accepted their terms, and was received with great pomp in the splendid court of Suthine. Ylureen solicited Aleizon Ailix Ayndra's permanent appointment as Ambassador of Safi to Suthine, but she preferred to follow Ailixond when, late in 466, the Grand Army set out on the march to Safi, with the best part of a year still to go before they reached home. Ailixond had been given out as fully recovered, but his continuing debility and the colossal administrative burden of his New Empire drew him into greater dependence on those around him as the summer passed, and the bond between him and Aleizon Ailix Ayndra deepened. Setha, secure as the mother of his son, no longer welcomed his advances, but Othanë was at last expecting a child, while the King was possessed with feverish energy as he felt his vitality ebbing away. As they drew closer to Safi, he summoned the Lord Regent Meraptar and his son Sandar to report on the state of the capital, while the Army encamped in an old half-ruined summer palace among the hills. It was during a banquet to honour the guests before they departed that Ailixond collapsed and was carried from the hall unconscious. It was clear to all that he would not live much longer. He finally declared himself to Aleizon Ailix Ayndra and in his last days they were reunited, while the rest of the Grand Army was already searching out the alliances they would pursue as soon as he was dead. His last act was to call Aleizon Ailix Ayndra to him, pull the Royal Ring from his hand and give it to her, before he died.

A CLOUD OVER WATER

Book Two of *A Walk in the Dark*

A Cloud Over Water opens in the Fifth Month of the four hundred and sixty-seventh year of the city, just after the King's death.

After the death of Lord Ailixond, the regency was put to election. Sulakon was elected by a large majority to act as Lord Regent until the Little King, Parakison, came of age. By various subterfuges, Ayndra managed to avoid relinquishing the Royal Ring to Sulakon, and used the Royal Seal to forge a letter to Lord Garadon to return from the province of Haramin, where news of Ailixond's death had not yet filtered, to Safi. She left Safi by the back door, and was welcomed back to Haramin as Governor.

Meanwhile, Sulakon led the remnants of the Grand Army against rebel Lords Sandar and Lakkanar. On the fifteenth day of Second Month, in the four hundred and seventieth year of the city, Lord Sulakon promulgated the Edict against Immorality. Firumin, former Steward of the Royal Household, sold his possessions, packed two small bags and went over to Haramin.

Aleizon Ailix Ayndra declared her intent to restore the united Empire, starting by marching into Lakkanar's domains, annexing Yiakarak on the way. During the battle, which had gone badly for him, Lakkanar left the field, leaving victory to Ayndra. On the third day of pursuit, she caught up with Lakkanar on the river, where he suggested parley. But Lakkanar's ploy was treacherous: in his attempt to murder her, Ayndra fell overboard, and was believed drowned. She was, however, far from dead and made her way successfully in disguise back to Haramin. This miraculous-seeming survival started a rumour that Aleizon Ailix Ayndra was a witch. She then confiscated a wagonload of back-taxes collected by Sulakon. This was in various denominations and included some debased coinage that Sulakon had minted himself. Ayndra decided to mint her own, in pure metal bearing Ailixond's head.

Ayndra then attacked Sulakon's army, and took his camp. He, however, took hers. Her mercenaries, led by Hagan, decided to betray her to the enemy. They knocked her out and took her to Sulakon, offering to trade her for their families and possessions. Sulakon accepted their offer. Ayndra was committed for trial in Safi for accepting creation as a lord without proffering the necessary proof of eligibility; impersonating a lord on this illegal basis for many years; stealing the Royal Seal; forging the royal signature; assuming the governorship of Haramin; raising an army; initiating hostilities; conducting a civil war; abducting an army; abducting royal taxes; coining money; rebelling against the King in the person of the Lord Regent; harbouring criminals; conducting negotiations with foreign states; conspiring with S'Thurrulass; murdering Lady Othanë; stealing the Royal Ring; promoting a life of vice; committing adultery; being a blasphemer and an atheist; being a witch; performing necromancy; drug-trafficking; bringing the nobility into disrepute.

By ingenious argument, and with the help of a document that proved Sulakon was her half-brother (a great shock to Sulakon, and everyone else) and therefore unable to judge her, Ayndra escaped the death penalty, but was sentenced to life imprisonment. She had her hair shorn, and was paraded around the city. With aid from Lady Sumakas, she engineered her escape, sought refuge with Lord Polem, and finally returned to Haramin. There she examined the state of her army and finances and decided to recruit the best she could afford, two mercenary captains, Daior-deor and Hanno, recently in the service of Lord Sandar.

She then set about encapturing Raq'min, with a tiny band of followers, and in the process took revenge on the traitors Atho and Hagan. Once more she assumed the governorship of Haramin, and announced an alliance with S'Thurrulass, whence arrived Lady Ylureen. With her allies, Ayndra's army seized Shgal'min in the spring. People from a dozen nations flocked to the banners of Haramin. Veterans said it was like the return of the Grand Army. The army was joined by the fleet Suthine, and together they took Lakkanar's capital of Magarrla: the lord of the city she killed in a duel.

During celebrations Daior-deor stumbled upon my lord of Haramin and the Lady Ylureen in a compromising situation and was considerably shocked.

The army continued on its progress and took Purrllum in the Needle's Eye. Shortly after taking the city Ayndra rode out alone into the surrounding woods, where assailants fell upon her . . .

CAST OF CHARACTERS in alphabetical order

AGRIANO officer in Sulakon's army

AILISSA Lord Ailixond's sister, wife of Sulakon

AILIXOND eighth of that name, Most Serene Lord and King of Safi; the conqueror of the New Empire, now dead

ALEIZON AILIX AYNDRA an adventurer of disreputable origins, created a lord of Safi by Ailixond

ALEIZON AILIX AYNDRA known as small Aleizon, Ylureen's daughter

AMIA senior wife of Parakison seventh

AMURRET miner and military engineer

ANDALDA Selanor's mistress

ANDALË mother of Rinahar

ANKO, COARAN, PASDAR mercenaries in Daior-deor's troop

ANTINAR son of Ditarris and Arpalond

ANUARL noblewoman of Haramin, daughter of King Yourcen

ARPALOND lord of Safi and amateur historian

ATHO mercenary enlisted with Aleizon Ailix Ayndra

CADINSHA friend of Sumakas

CAHILAR lord of Safi

CAIBLIN physician to Ailixond

CALABAT Haraminharn pirate, admiral of Ayndra's fleet

CANIHA a herbalist

CARLEN a false name used by Aleizon Ailix Ayndra after her supposed drowning

CASIK created a lord of Safi by Ailixond

CHAGEL, LIA, TIKKIDI, SELANË, THIO some of Polem's bastards

CHAMARIN mercenary

COSMAR captain in Casik's army

COTHIR herald to Golaron

DAIKET a Safic officer

DAIOR-DEOR mercenary from a merchant family in Thaless, Hanno's partner

DARRIN, AKUZ, the sons of Akuz and others: Safic moneylenders, Sulakon's creditors

DEREZHAID nobleman of line Gika, husband of Siriane

DIAMOON a witch, member of the Guild of Fire Witches, Polem's sometime mistress

DIBBRO Sulakon's commander in Yiakarak

DITARRIS wife of Arpalond

DOMAR lord of Safi

ELLAKON lord of Safi

ESALDAR lord of Safi, Ailixond's governor in the Needle's Eye

ESAS'THI client slave of line Pilith

FARACALN nobleman of line Ukasheti, admiral of the fleet sent by Suthine to Haramin

FIRUMIN Steward of the Royal Household under Ailixond

GALLARIA wife of Sandar

GALLIAN clerk in the government of Haramin

GARADON lord of Safi, Ailixond's governor in Haramin

GARGET a war cripple, once an artilleryman under Ogo

GATALIN Ayndra's trumpeter

GATRIN Safic commander in Raq'min

GERRIN Ayndra's cavalry captain

GETALEEN commoner of the line Ukasheti, officer in the army of Suthine

GILMIS nurse of the child Parakison

GISHIIN nobleman of the line Barrami, husband of Ylureen

GOLARON lord created by Parakison seventh

GULDAN officer in the army of Haramin

HAELIS one of the few female lords of Safi

HAGAN mercenary enlisted with Aleizon Ailix Ayndra

HAHHNI Ylureen's mute chattel slave

HALDIN bastard son of Polem

HALIGON lord of Safi

HANNO Safic mercenary of peasant origin

HAPPET bodyguard to Aleizon Ailix Ayndra

HARESOND lord of Safi, son of Golaron

HASMON lord of Safi, adherent to the traditional faction

HOREN client slave of the line Ukasheti, loaned to Polem as housekeeper

HOURISHAY Haraminharn officer

HURIGO Haraminharn officer

IADAGON lord of Safi, Sulakon's governor in Haramin

IKINDUR Haraminharn scout commander

SARGOND lord of Safi, Ailixond's governor in Lysmal

SASSAFRANGE a mercenary, from S'Thurrulass but employed in Safic dominions

SELANOR captain in the Grand Army

SENKUR Daior-deor's Haraminharn summoner

SERANNIN portrait painter

SETHA Ailixond's second wife, from Haridt in Pirramin, mother of Parakison

SHANRINË wife of Irailond

SIRIANE noblewoman of line Pilith, ambassador of Suthine to the court of Lord Ailixond

SISTRI, HISTRI twin slaves from Haridt; lifelong attendants on Setha

S'THIRIAIDI noblewoman of line Ukasheti

SULAKON lord of Safi, Ailixond's first cousin and ardent traditionalist

SUMAKAS Dowager Queen of Safi, widow of Parakison seventh and mother of Ailixond

TAKAREM oldest son of Sulakon and Ailissa

TELI madam of a brothel on the Street of Dreams

TENNAT Ailixond's secretary

THIRO, TOBIN army officers

TIBBAT agent of Sandar

TIKKATI grass plains nomad, slave to Ogo

TIRIS petty nobleman, lord of Gingito

TISSAMË daughter of Oborenë and Haligon

YARANO Safic clerk chosen by Setha to teach Parakison

YLUREEN rich noblewoman of Suthine, future head of the line Pilith

YUNNIL Ayndra's slave, purchased after the sack of Raq'min in 462

The men clustered around the body drew apart as they heard a horse approaching. One ran to take its head as the rider dismounted. He sauntered up to the crumpled figure on the ground and stood with his hands on his hips. Aleizon Ailix Ayndra was sprawled as she had fallen, face pressed into the mould; blood matted the curls at the back of her head. 'Turn her over,' Tibbat said. He nodded as the long nose came up spangled with pine needles under the mop of blonde hair.

'She breathes, master,' said the man who held her arm.

'I can see that. How many followed her?'

'Nary a soul, master, I swear it.'

'Bind her legs and bring her to the stream. Be sure that you leave nothing here. We shall ride on as soon as I have dosed her.' He whistled through the gap in his teeth as he mounted his horse. His underlings picked up their axes and foresters' hats.

'What shall we do with the horse?'

'Take it with us. Worth a few sols, I should say.'

'Are you sure? Have you had a good look at it? It's her black one, is it not? I heard tell she rides a horse with five toes on each foot and the same number of teeth as a man.'

'Do you believe every tale-teller you meet in this market? Let's have a look at its feet, then.'

'Look you, do not approach it like that, see, it's ready to—'

'Oey! Ai! Woreson bitch of a horse!'

'As vicious as its god-cursed mistress!'

'Can we not tie her on its back?'

'He said, on no account is she to have her own horse. I'll put her across mine.'

'Untie it from the tree, then.'

The man shuffled cautiously forward. Tarap rolled his eyes and pranced. When the man reached out for his reins he reared up as far as they allowed and struck out with his steelshod forefeet. The soldier ducked out of range. 'The damned beast is vicious. Who'd buy a horse like that?'

'It's a demon in horse's shape. Look at its eyes!'

'Ah, slash the reins and let it go. We have not the time to bother with it. Drive it away, and let us be going.'

Tarap thundered down the aisles of the forest, twice as

1

fast now he had no rider. He hardly slackened his pace even when he came to the city gate; people scattered like the gobs of foam he cast, flying into the stableyard he had been led from earlier in the day. Haldin and the head groom were filling buckets at the pump; they paused in amazement as the stallion entered. Tarap careered once round the yard and came to a shuddering halt. Two women came rushing in after him.

'Is that your horse? What think you you're at, letting it run around the streets so! It ran right over my sister-in-law here—'

'It's my lord's horse,' said Haldin. 'What have they done to the reins?' He skirted Tarap patiently, making calming noises, until the horse let him come close enough to touch the slashed ends of the leather. The groom was trying to mollify the angry woman, offering her some liniment for her sister-in-law's bruises. 'Did someone take him out for exercise?' he said to the slave who mucked out the stalls.

'My lord took him out, sir.'

'What? Do you know when?'

'Janko came for him—three hours ago, it might have been.'

Haldin examined the damaged reins again. Apart from his harness Tarap wore only a regulation-issue saddlecloth, without saddlebags or insignia. His black coat was soaked and reeking with sweat. 'I think I must go and find my father,' Haldin said.

She woke up lying face down on a rough saddlecloth. Someone was kneeling at her left side, sponging the back of her head with warm liquid. Lukewarm drops trickled over her neck and ears. It was daylight, but a fire was burning to her right, and she heard men and horses near. The one who was sponging her spoke.

'Hold on to her feet. Let's see if she wakes yet.'

Hands gripped her ankles; other hands gripped hanks of hair on either side of her head and raised her by them on to her knees. The pain was excruciating; she could not resist a grimace. She opened her eyes.

He was dressed like a woodcutter, but his hair was cropped like an infantryman's. When he grinned two front teeth showed missing. 'Beaten us to it,' he said.

2

'Indeed? I should think it was you who had beaten me,' she replied. She looked into his green eyes. He grinned more widely but did not release his grip on her hair.

'First we search you. Then we give you something to drink. You'll not try to fight us while we search you.' As he spoke, other men were gathering round the fire, a mixture of common soldiers and workmen it seemed. Some had faces that seemed to recall streets in Kedikot. She went on looking at the green eyes while two of his party took her arms and raised her to standing and another sauntered up and prepared to run his hands over her. He called over his shoulder, 'Shall we search her for witch's marks, then?'

'Search her for weapons. He says she carries knives. The rest you leave. He wants her untouched.'

'Untouched? The Whore of Haramin?' He laughed. Aleizon Ailix Ayndra transferred her reptilian gaze to him.

'Untouched,' the leader repeated impassively behind him.

Laugh he might; but the searcher wiped his palms on his breeches twice before he put his hands on her shoulders, and his touch was forceful but careless. He soon found the two knives at her waist, and knelt down to check her legs.

'Take her boots off. Give them to me. Leave hold of her now and let her sit down ... what's with you, Master Aleizon Ailix Ayndra? Do you not wish to sit down?'

'I'll stand for the time being,' she said. 'Do you work for yourself, or is someone paying you for me?'

'Someone will pay me for you in the end, no doubt,' he said. 'Is the drink ready?'

'Are we going to stay here this night?' she asked.

'You ask too many questions. There, give it to her.'

The drink steamed in a small drinking-horn; it smelt medicinal. She took it and sniffed its fumes without sipping. 'Will you not take the first mouthful?'

'If it were poison, do you think we'd feed it to you so openly? An you'll not swallow it yourself, we must feed it to you. Drink it.'

She tasted a drop. 'Poppy-syrup!'

'Drink it,' the green-eyed man repeated. She looked at the dark liquid. 'I haven't tasted poppy-syrup since I tried ... Ailixond's medicine ... where are you taking me?'

'I think you know,' he said.

3

'I think I'll not know anything an I drink this. Why, it must be laced with it. I tasted it at once. Do you want me asleep for days?'

Before she had finished speaking, she was flat on her back on the ground with a grimy hand pinching her nose shut. The heavily-flavoured tisane slopped into her mouth, and she had to swallow some to breathe. There was something like strong wine in it beside opium; she was already dizzy when they tied her hands and feet together and carried her to the packhorse.

'And what proof d'you have that she lives?' Casik hawked and spat on the floor. 'Some two-quarit sorceress who looks into pools of ink—'

Diamoon stood up. 'My lord,' she said clearly, 'I will show you what I have seen an you do not believe it.'

Casik looked at her with barely-disguised contempt; Polem took his arm. 'My lord, you must understand; the lady never lies. And you know it is not wise to think that my lord of Haramin is dead, for do you not remember how Lakkanar drowned her in a river and then she sprang up again? No, we must believe she lives.'

Casik grunted. 'Firumin, fetch us some more wine,' Polem said.

Ylureen had been standing by the window, hands clasped behind her back. She turned to face the Safeen. 'My lords. We marsh straight Purrllum an' bing San'ar surren'er.'

'Now?' said Casik. 'And who is to lead us in this?'

'I lead,' said Ylureen.

'Lady! I beg your pardon!' he said.

'Pardon?' echoed Ylureen.

'My lady, with all honour to your birth, you have never commanded an army in the field, and Purrllum is one of the greatest strongholds of the New Empire; whereas I have more than twenty-five years' knowledge of war, and much of it spent fighting over these very same lands. I must urge you to restrain your concern for my lord of Haramin and allow the campaign to be directed by one whose judgement is not clouded by the weakness and inexperience of your sex.'

'What you say?' shrieked Ylureen.

4

'I put myself forward as commander of the army,' said Casik.

'Well, now,' said Polem, sitting up, but he was interrupted by Ylureen. 'There two comman'er of army! Two! Myself an' my lord Aleizon Ailix Ayndra. Foul villain San'ar taker away an' I comman'. Wass you saying comman'? You man!'

'Lady,' said Casik grimly. 'We must have a man at the head of our army.'

'Surely we do not have a sole commander in any case,' said Polem. 'We will all decide together.' Ylureen was shaking her head; she tried several phrases in broken Safic, and then beckoned Siriane to interpret.

'My lord,' Siriane said for her. 'This is a folly of the Safic people, that they will always put a man in command; from this springs all disorder. There will be no order until the men of Safi have learnt to listen to the words of the women, for out of the mouths of women comes wisdom. For there are two mouths in the world, the mouth of teeth and the mouth of lips. The mouth of teeth is the mouth of the man: it consumes and gives forth lying speech. The mouth of lips is the mouth of the woman, that gives forth life and does not lie. The man speaks of the little things, the things of the day, but when he wishes to know the great things he must ask of a woman, for only the woman can speak the truth. In our country the men listen to the words of the women and peace, prosperity and victory come to us. Lady Ylureen has no wish, my lord Casik, to take your place at the head of your troops, nor does she decry your knowledge of the art of war. She listens to your counsel and honours it. We shall gather together our wisdom and hand it to my lady and she will instruct us. Then we shall go forth with banners and prevail over Sandar. You understand, my lord, that such will be the best for all of us.'

'I am not sure I understand anything at all,' said Casik. 'Mouths?'

'It is as Lady Ylureen says; two heads are better than one,' said Polem.

'We do not even know she is not dead,' Casik repeated.

Polem sighed. 'My lord,' he said, 'considerable as your forces are, this is the army of Haramin. An we let out to the

5

men that their lord is dead, what will we do then? Let us say that she is alive in Purrllum and in this way incite them to help us take the Needle's Eye. That done, an she lives we have saved her, and should she have died – which the gods forbid! – we shall at least have the Needle's Eye.'

Casik grunted. Siriane spoke for Ylureen again.

'We shall make a lightning campaign, just as in the time of Lord Ailixond. Within two days we shall march, carrying no more than weapons. If Sandar has my lord of Haramin, we must not delay.'

'If Sandar has her, he will murder her,' said Casik.

'Then 'e shall not 'aver,' said Ylureen to herself, her changeable eyes stony pale in their rims of sooty pigment.

'With an army we cannot hope to come to Purrllum in less than a twelveday,' he went on, 'while they, mounted as they must be, will be there in six; less, even.'

Ylureen struck the table with her fist. 'We are mounted same as they! No slow. My lord, you aren' wan' Needle's Eye perhaps? Sandar pay you stay us here, perhaps? Too fright to fight, even, perhaps? Eh?'

Casik kicked his chair back. 'Lady. An you were a man, I would challenge you to a duel of honour for those words. As it is I think I cannot sit with one who, having no honour at all, dares to impugn mine!' He flung out of the room. Polem excused himself and ran after him. In an hourtenth he was back.

'He says that he will come with his officers to the army council this evening.'

'Very well.' Ylureen was smiling. She called Sabraid to her and spoke to him in their own tongue; he bowed and ran off. She turned to Polem. 'We call our Captain Daiordeor, the Captain Selanor too, you call them, know their nem; then we all talk, de-cide. This day night we all know and Casik, he can' say. Then we all go Purrllum an' rescue my lord Aleizon Ailix Ayndra. Yes?'

'Of course,' said Polem. 'Only tell me, lady, and I will do anything you say.'

Her scraped and blistered feet stumbled over flagstones, steps, smooth glazed tiles and then a soft wool covering. Hands pushed her into a chair and undid the blindfold,

6

while others hacked the wooden slave-collar from her neck. She looked up blinking into Sandar's face. In his eagerness he had risen and as she raised her head his hand struck at her throat. Other hands clamped her down in the chair. But Sandar only groped for the gold chain he had glimpsed among her filthy linen, and pulled it out of her shirt; only to find nothing on the end of it. The expectation turned foggy in his eyes. A broad smile spread across Aleizon Ailix Ayndra's face.

'You did not think I took it with me on excursions like this?' she said.

Sandar let go the chain and moved back; hands on hips, he surveyed her out of pouched eyes. She flicked her greasy tresses back off her face. 'Sit down! Let us converse as equals!' She burst out laughing. Sandar glared at the men who had brought her and told them to go and report to Lobiak and then return to wait for him. He followed them into the lobby and made sure that no one remained there before he passed back through the inner door. Aleizon Ailix Ayndra was sitting where he had left her.

'A fine way you have of inviting me to your councils,' she said. 'Beaten unconscious, drugged, put in a slave-collar and made to walk barefoot – and what do you expect now? The Royal Ring of Safi?'

Sandar propped his buttocks on the table and folded his arms over his paunch. 'It was said that you wore it always, awake and asleep.'

'Perhaps when I am at home I do,' she replied. 'I have looked forward to meeting you, Sandar, I thought that perhaps you could tell me what Ylureen is doing; those men of yours were of no use at all, but I am sure you are informed of all these matters.' She giggled behind her hand. 'Ay! Perhaps I comprehend now why Ailixond was so sanguine in his last days.' Sandar merely went on gazing at her. She rubbed her nose, then turned up one foot and began picking dirt from between its toes. It seemed an engrossing enough task to occupy her for hours. When she eventually looked up Sandar was still gazing at her. 'Stand up,' he said.

She got to her feet and stood poised with her hands clasped behind her back, taut as a bow ready to shoot.

Sandar shuffled ponderously up to her; he was only a hand's breadth taller, but twice as broad. His shoulders were like a strongman's in a travelling air. He stared into her eyes. She stared back. 'Why have you brought me here?' she said. Her eyes glowed with aggression in their net of fine wrinkles.

Sandar's glance roved over her, scrutinising the form of her body in its stiff and dirty wrappings. His tongue delicately traced the line of his upper lip. 'There is no reason why we should work against each other,' he said.

'What do you mean, work against each other? I work for myself. Do you want me to work for you, I'll not do it. If you—'

'This is what I mean.' Sandar's arms leapt round her, hands digging into her buttocks and pulling her tightly against him; his mouth sought ravenously for hers. She slipped one arm up backwards out of his embrace and jerked her knee up between his thighs at the same time as she delivered a stinging slap to the side of his face. He grunted in pain and doubled over; she danced in front of the window, her hands slicing the air as she spoke. 'Ha! Is that what you think? What will you offer me, concubine marriage? Will you give me command of all your armies and the keys to your treasury? Will you offer me a treaty of alliance with my own body written into the conditions? Will you offer me to share a bed with you, with your— !' Her gestures encompassed him from head to foot and threw him away with the same contemptuous disgust as a young gallant faced with an ancient and poxshotten whore.

'It cost the lives of two men to bring you here.' Sandar stood massaging his abused genitals; his usually pale face had coloured and his eyes shone.

'Those creatures? Do you care about them?'

'They were faithful to me, in their fashion.'

'And you find it hard to make people faithful to you, is that it?'

Sandar let the taunt pass in silence. He opened the flap of his breeches to let his hand work there more easily. Aleizon Ailix Ayndra looked out of the window, but it gave on a sheer wall falling for three storeys before it met a muddy street; nevertheless, from such a height one could see over the rooftops to the walls of the city and beyond: green and yellow moors, patches of knotted scrub in sheltered hollows, the rust-brown ribbon of the main road; it was such a clear day that one could even see some snow peaks, and the road, rising and falling as it ... she leant out of the casement to see better. 'What's that, coming along the road? It looks as if– ' Her last words were lost in a forcible gasp as she was spun round and thrust against the wall by the window. Sandar pinned her arms and used his bulk to keep her in place. 'It will do you no good to scream,' he said, 'we are used to that in Purrllum.' He tried to kiss her again, but she writhed like a snake and clamped her legs together ... Sandar freed one hand and attempted to prise her thighs apart, but she twisted out of his weakened grip and was on the other side of the room again. He sighed in frustration but did not appear at all unhappy. 'Why are you so reluctant to sell your favours?'

'I do not sell anything,' she said.

Sandar laughed. 'You sold yourself to Lady Ylureen in exchange for the fleet of S'Thurrulass. You sold yourself to our late lamented Lord Ailixond in exchange for a pair of lord's bracelets and the revenues of Haramin. You sold yourself to half the street scum of Safi to get a few coppers to feed yourself and your fatherless brat. You see? – I too can make enquiries about the past. There's a woman called Fat Mari worked on the Street of Dreams before your supposed half-brother drove her out. She has a house in Purrllum now. I think there cannot have been two climbapoles of the same barbarous name in the city. She says you were a cheap whore; there was nothing they could train you to do; they used to send you to the fish porters of the market, is that not so?'

Aleizon Ailix Ayndra's face had gone stony blank. She said in a high voice, 'The woman who did those things is dead.'

'O, come,' said Sandar, smiling; his face had turned quite jocular and rubicund. 'I recognise that you think yourself a courtesan these days. I do not offer you the market slut's price. You give me the ring and you can be my consort, an you like it. You can even ride your stallion in front of the troops, whatever gives you pleasure.'

'What gives me pleasure,' said Aleizon Ailix Ayndra, 'is to be second to no one.'

Sandar, shaking his head, approached her. She backed away, speaking rapidly. 'Is that how you approach your allies? Then it's no wonder that you have none you can trust. You sit here calculating how you'll come to dip your wick while Golaron has overrun all the Timerill and your officers are double-crossing you in Kedikot– '

'I was waiting for you.' He put his hand out to stroke her hair and she jumped out of reach. He smiled even more broadly. 'I had thought that I should show you some of my machines, to affright you. But now I see what it is that you're truly frightened of.'

'O yes?'

'You are a woman. You've been under a man and you know you'll be under one again, be you never so sprightly in a pair of breeches, have you never so many foreign witches slobbering between your thighs. You surround yourself with clerks and half-men, like that dwarf mercenary captain of mine, and besotted fools who've not yet woken up to Lord Ailixond's death, and female perverts who've found so few men in their own country that they cannot tell a whore in breeches from the real thing. And the only court you know is that slew of lace-trimmed queans who used to follow our scented King on his ridiculous travels. Our King! – whose greatest dream was to receive Lord Polem's steam-ing rod up his back passage! – but then, I need not tell you about Lord Polem's rod, need I?'

'Why do you hate him so much?'

'Things you would not understand. His mother used to wait on the customers in her father's bodega. He looked more like her than he ever did old Lord Parakison. That's why she had to do away with the other Ailixond, in order to get her bastard the throne, after she'd slain the old man when she knew he'd never do her will. He was nothing but his mother's son, Ailixond. Why think you he had to wait till he found a slut disguised as a boy before he took himself a mistress? I do not doubt that he told you he'd waited for you all his life, nor that he was telling the truth!' Sandar laughed merrily. Aleizon Ailix Ayndra looked mutinous, her upper lip drawn back over her teeth. 'Ah!' he said. 'Now you will find out what it is to have a true noble lord.'

'Never,' she said. Sandar laughed some more. He pulled

10

one of several embroidered strips that hung upon the wall, and looked at her with unexpectedly soft eyes. 'Your response is touching. You must have believed all the stories he told you.'

'I was more touched by the sight of Ylureen's banners,' she replied. 'They cannot be so far from the walls. What will you do then?'

'Having lost her military commander, I should not imagine that your merchant princess will overwhelm this city in any short time. I shall wait. In due course you will explain a sensible course of action to her, and we shall proceed toward Safi, which is, after all, where you wish to go.' He chucked her under the chin like a child. She knocked his hand away. 'You can do what you like! I'll never give you the ring.' A couple of soft raps sounded on the door by which she had entered. 'We shall see,' said Sandar as he unlocked it to admit four men in household livery. They bowed to him, and looked at her with eager eyes. 'This is the Witch of Haramin,' he said. 'I want that you should take her to the empty bear's pen in the basement of the circus wing. When she has entered the pen, strip her of every article of clothing she possesses, and leave her there. Report that she is safely penned, and order the animal keepers to watch her; I will send guards shortly. But beware of her tricks as you take her there, and listen to nothing that she says. O yes; and leave her her lord's bracelets. I shall enjoy her more with them on.' His laughter seemed to follow them for miles.

All the way out of the camp Hanno was very silent, and followed Daior-deor without asking where they went; but then he had crossed and recrossed these slopes as many times himself. It was fully light by the time they reached a place that gave them a comprehensive view of the city. Hanno sat down and took out his flask. When he had drunk he wiped the mouth on his sleeve and handed the bottle to Daior-deor.

'One day I knew I'd come to see those walls from siege-lines,' he said.

'Rough and ready siege-lines, to be sure,' said Daior-deor, still standing.

11

'Never thought that we'd come up here so fast. A miracle, what we have done. Golaron would have been a month to do the same – ay, and then we'd have siege-towers and a house of women and a menagerie, too.'

'Selanor says that Lord Ailixond could have done no better.'

'Ay, give me that bottle back – Lord Ailixond! You spend too much time with them, Daior, you start to speak as they do. Lord Ailixond! Lord Ailixond! I know not why they have not all joined his religion. D'you recall how those noddleaddle priests ran into the fire to save his picture? People say my lord has one hung up over her bed so she can look up at him while she enjoys herself– '

'What?' said Daior-deor.

Hanno repeated the story, with details.

'I think it's not true,' said Daior-deor.

'Do you not know?'

'Now, how should I know?'

'I thought you were accepted in all the councils of the great these days.'

'Not that accepted,' said Daior-deor.

'What about Lady Ylureen and that . . . what is his name . . . Savride?'

'Sabraid. What about him?'

'Well . . . people say . . .'

'Tell me what they say.' Daior-deor sat down beside Hanno. 'For God's sake, Hanno, you're my friend, the only one I have here. No matter how many councils I enter. If you'll not speak to me honestly, then who will?'

'Since this Lady Ylureen took a fancy to you, it has been as if you were all of a sudden commander of the half of the army. And I still riding turnabout in the vanguard – Daior, I'd not mean to say that you should'a sought me a place. But I wonder – you know what they say goes on with my lord and Lady Ylureen. And now, with her and this, this Sabraid – and he's good for nothing, is he not? More feeble than a girl.'

Daior-deor's eyes widened. 'You'd not mean that I– ?'

'I know not what any of it means,' said Hanno. He pointed out at the city. 'Think you that she's alive in there?'

'I know the witch says that she is. But beside, would she

12

not be of more use to Sandar alive than dead? You know what we may expect from him soon.'

'He will send Lady Ylureen her finger in a box.'

'Or her hand, with the lord's bracelet still on it.'

'I'd not like to be a powerful man, and his prisoner,' said Hanno. 'You know the witch as well, do you not?'

'Mistress Diamoon?'

'Is she not a lady, then? She goes about and lets people call her my lady.'

'She's not Lord Polem's wife. She has twice the wits he has, beside; I think he would do nothing she did not tell him to.'

'Do you suppose her foretellings are true, then?'

'In faith, she believes them,' said Daior-deor. 'I do not believe that she's a charlatan. She says spirits talk to her, and I'm not one to judge whether spirits lie or not.'

Hanno grunted and sipped some more firewater, rolling it round and round in his mouth before he swallowed. 'I was talking to a captain in the artillery yesterday,' he said. 'They took some catapults to pieces and brought them up on mules. He said they have an idea to throw that powder-fire stuff into the city. I said, it'll be a good while before the walls fall down, doing that, and then I thought myself, why do you and I not go into Purrllum and bring her out? Given that she's in there.'

'You mean, rescue my lord?'

Hanno was grinning broadly. 'Your star's high, Daior. Do this, and we'll be shining in daylight. Let them throw their powderfire! We'll show'em.'

'But we have not the least idea where she is – O, I know we could ask Mistress Diamoon to divine it, but– '

'Ask her, then – but we need no foretellings. We know all the cellars and dungeons where he keeps his prisoners, do we not? And all the manners of his people. Maishis' mound, I think I even have my old livery tunic still. I'd not like to see her finger in a box, either. An anyone could do it, Daior, it's you and I. What d'you say?'

'I'd say that you should come to the Inner Council with me, this morning, and we'll argue it together. We should tell them what we know about what Sandar does to his prisoners, too, and that the longer he keeps her, the worse things he will do – unless she gives in to him.'

'She would roast before she gave in,' Hanno declared. Descending the hill, he was silent again, but clearly filled with happy speculations. Daior-deor asked him what he was laughing about.

'I'd not mind to be a provincial governor one day,' he replied.

'I'd not pitch your hopes too high. What an we cannot find her?'

'Ah! They'll make songs about us for this one, Daior. You wait and see.'

The bear's pen had more space and air than was ever granted to single human prisoners, but being sited beneath the level of the earth it was a dank and stony place. A low earth platform in one corner had a heap of straw on it, and a runnel of fresh water bisected the floor; they said it had to be fresh water, for the animals sickened from dirty water sooner than human prisoners did. The animal keepers came to watch the guards stripping the witch naked, commenting in surprise that she was a woman like any other under her clothes. They remained, peering through the heavy grating of the door, after the guards had locked them out and gone about their duties. The witch walked over to the heap of straw and kicked it about, making sounds of disgust at how damp and mouldy it was. She came back to the door and stood facing them, hands on hips, no shame at all. 'Do your animals not even get dry bedding?'

There was a good deal of shuffling and throat-clearing before a voice replied, 'Key's gone, mistress, we cannot open the door.'

'What is that up in the ceiling, then, I swear you'll have some way to put things in here when the beast is too fierce to open the door on it. Let me a bale of straw down through that trapdoor.'

Much discussion followed, until one ordered the others to go, and she was left in silence. She squatted down by the runnel and scooped up water to drink from her hand, then put the edge of her left hand in her mouth and fell into a reverie. From time to time feet passed in the corridor outside, dogs barked, and once some large animal roared, but the dimly filtered light hardly changed. After the third

14

passage of the guard, bumps and grinds sounded about the ceiling, and the trapdoor groaned upwards. She scrambled out of the way of it, and an untidy bundle of straw tumbled through; the trap shut again. She pulled the bale to the bed platform and set about picking the thistles and burdocks out of it; it was tied with a couple of cords. She put them aside, then picked them up again, tried their strength, and hid them under the straw. The next passage of the guard was marked by the glow of a lamp that waxed and faded between the door-bars. When that had gone, in the last dregs of the day, she squatted with her back to the door and plunged three fingers up between her legs, fished for purchase a little while, and pulled. It came free with a soft glutinous cluck; she put it in her mouth and licked it very thoroughly. When she took it out to look at it it was almost too dark to see; the great diamond was as lifeless as a lump of quartz. She took a long time knotting the cord on to the shank of the ring, working by the blind touch of her fingers; when the guards' lamp approached, she curled up in the musty straw until it had gone. With such poor bedding and no clothes, it was too cold to sleep deeply; for much of the night she walked up and down the pen, teeth chattering, or sat and tossed the cord with its precious weight round her outstretched foot, caught the ring in her other hand, and jerked in opposite directions, pulling the cord tight. She did this over and over again, until she could do it perfectly, in the dark, every time. When day came she slept. No one brought her food. She roused again around nightfall, and commenced pacing for warmth. She did not know if it was the night or the growing exhaustion of her body that made her hear so many more sounds in this period of darkness: horses coming and going, troops of men passing, strange distant thumps and bangs as though there was a thunderstorm passing at a distance, yet never a drop of rain nor a sight of a lightning flash. Her shivers grew more and more violent, but it had been hours since a guard last passed whom she could have pleaded with for bedding. Finally, after she had perceived the first grey harbingers of dawn her deliverance, Sandar came to her.

Daior-deor had expected some grand performance with music and trances, but all Diamoon did was to burn some herbs in a brazier and ask him a multitude of questions about the streets and buildings of Purrllum, while she poured some white sand in a circle on a piece of leather and scratched lines in it with a stick. The herbs made the air thick and sweet, and the lapses between her questions and his replies grew longer and longer. Then she threw something else onto the coals and red flames leapt up, filling the tent with bloody light. 'Now I see it,' she said. 'You must enter by the place where he keeps his animals. Here.' She showed him on the sketch plan she had drawn in the sand. 'I think you will not have to go far . . . but tell your friend he should act with care. It will be better if you go first while you are in Sandar's houses. You should leave at about fourth hour of this next morning, so that you climb over the walls in the darkness and enter the building in the first light of dawn.'

'And will we find her?'

Diamoon put her index fingers to her temples and closed her eyes for a while. 'I see two people– ' She was interrupted by a couple of explosions from the direction of the city. 'What a barbarous method of war!' she exclaimed.

'Two people, not three?' asked Daior-deor.

Diamoon shrugged. 'The future is not a still pool, to see clear reflections in it,' she said. 'Perhaps what I see is you and your friend entering the city. But I have foretold my lord's life before now, and I never saw her dying in a place like this – has she told you my prophecy?'

'No, I never knew that there was one.'

'Only a short prophecy.' Diamoon recited:

'Your rise began with powderfire
With death and death you'll rise yet higher
Through many battles, unscathed in all
Except the last; in blood you'll fall.'

'O,' said Daior-deor.

'You expected something more exciting? But you should go and sleep now, captain; if you can in this hellish racket. I will not ask you for any money for this. Count it as a gift to my lord of Haramin.'

'Ask you for money for that? I should think not! She has told you nothing you'd not be able to fish out of your own head,' said Hanno when Daior-deor went to tell him of the foretelling. 'Nor am I going to sleep, if we're to be leaving at fourth hour. I should rather go and watch this attack. They have put all sorts of stuff to make the fire coloured in with the powder, have you seen? You would never think it was a weapon of war, to watch it. Come with me and we'll buy a flask of lifewater and sit it out–' A colossal bang drowned his words.

'I swear that one came from their side,' said Daior-deor. 'Do you suppose that Sandar has learnt how to make it too?'

'Who knows? Let us go and put Sandar's livery on under our cloaks. then we can do as we will until it's morning.'

Sandar made sure that the entire basement of the animals' wing was empty of human witnesses before he unlocked the door of the bear pen. He wore a thick hooded cloak and carried a lantern and a long staff, as though he were a shepherd going to tend his flock. The first thing he did was to lock the door behind him; then he reached up with the staff and pulled down a chain from the high ceiling – high enough that a full-grown bear standing on its hind legs could not possibly reach it. He opened the shades of the lantern so that it shed maximum light, hung it on the chain and hoisted it up to illuminate the pen. His prisoner watched him do it, crouched among the straw, without moving. He thrust the staff between the bars and out of the pen, unfastened his cloak and spread it out on the floor. His bulky shadow wavered like cuttlefish ink between his spread legs. 'Come into the light,' he said.

Aleizon Ailix Ayndra stood up. She did not fold her arms, either in an attempt at modesty or in search of warmth, but she could not stop herself from shivering. Sandar beckoned her with two fingers, smiling. 'Into the light.'

She halted about three yards away from him, brushing her hair back from her eyes. Despite the goose pimples and the grime, it was clear that her body had aged far better than her face. Sandar smiled more broadly, then made a courtly bow, inviting her to the spread cloak. She looked at it with dull arrogance.

'You'll need to do better than that,' she said hoarsely.

'You never asked more of Lord Ailixond, the first time.'

She put one hand up to her forehead. 'Where do you pick up all these horrible tales?'

'Intelligence is always worth more than gold.' He moved towards her. Her face creased up with suspicious fear and she shuffled backwards; Sandar began to run, she ran too, they were chasing each other round the pen, round and round and round while his breathing grew ever more stertorous and his face reddened, but not with lust. At last he came to a stop and stood there puffing.

She laughed. 'You should take more exercise.'

Sandar waited to get his breath back, and when he spoke, it was in a pleasant voice. 'Let us leave off this mockery. You know what I ask of you. Give me that, and I'll put away my wife for you. You can be Queen of Safi. If you fight, it will only end up the worse for you.' He turned his hip to her to show the short sword strapped there. 'If you continue to resist, I shall have to put you to the machines as I would any common prisoner.' He showed her the cloak again. 'In half an hour you can be in a hot bath with clean silks and linen to dress in.'

'Why do you not give me the bath first? I smell like the animals you've penned me with.'

'I never minded a little rankness in a bitch,' Sandar replied. His eyes were feasting on her body. He licked his lips and gave a little shuddering sigh; with his left hand he was undoing his breeches. Aleizon Ailix Ayndra spoke in surprise. 'You truly want me, do you not?'

Several soft crumps resounded, somewhere in the paling distance, as Sandar spoke. 'Yes,' he said, his voice thickening with the honey of anticipation. She raised her arms from her sides, but before she could complete the gesture he had embraced her. One arm pulled her against him, the other went round her shoulders and tipped her head back to let him have free play in her mouth. She reached for the hilt of his short sword, but he felt her and slapped her hand down even while his tongue probed between her resisting lips. At that she let her mouth spread wide and his tongue leaped down her throat. Then she bit. Sandar howled with pain and staggered backwards, spitting gouts of bloody saliva over the silken lining of his cloak; he put his fingers in his mouth, feeling for his tongue, unable even to curse. Aleizon

18

Ailix Ayndra burst out laughing. 'You damned fool! Do you think I want to be Queen of Safi? I could have been Queen of Safi ten years ago if I had wanted it.'

She had retreated to the bed platform and crouched there, a hand buried in the straw. Sandar shook his head. Making sure that he always faced her, he sidled up to the runnel and scooped water into his mouth. After several rinses he could speak indistinctly. 'If that is what you want,' he said, 'you'll get it.' He drew his sword and moved towards her. She remained still, but her eyes were like two live coals. She saw him rise onto the balls of his feet just before he threw himself at her, and then she flew. He was too heavy to turn as fast as she could, and he did not realise what it was that flashed past his vision till the cord was tightening round his throat; he tumbled backwards, scrabbling for it as he choked and the early daylight faded black.

Aleizon Ailix Ayndra wormed out from under his warm bulk and, very carefully, pulled the cord free and wound it up into her hand. The victim's face hardly seemed discoloured, but his tongue protruded swollen and bloody from his open mouth and his eyes stared like half-eaten suckets. She looked from side to side, saw and heard nothing; she looked at the corpse, and with shaking hands fumbled at the buckle of his sword-belt, then undid his tunic and pulled it off the unresisting form. When she put it on the sleeves hung over her hands and even when she kilted it up with the belt, it sagged open at the front, made to contain a belly she did not possess; she looked at Sandar's ruffled shirt, then shrugged, put the sword back in its sheath and went to try his keys in the door. Her hands were trembling so much it took her three or four tries to fit each one into the keyhole. Eventually the door swung open. She drew the sword again and advanced into the corridor.

It took only a few moments to scale the crumbling bastion, when the sentries had passed; as the sky had begun to lighten, so the bombardment from both sides had increased, and there was no need to worry about noise. They used the rope to slither down the inside of the wall and left it hanging as they made off into the alleys. Daior-deor was in the lead, but when they came to the gateway of the palace stableyards, Hanno dashed in front of him. 'I know the way. Down here, into the cellars, they go through into the dungeons. Quick!' There were some other men in livery on the far side of the yard, but they paid them no heed.

'Do not run so,' hissed Daior-deor.

'Be calm, be calm. Everyone is in a hurry, we are under siege.' Hanno chuckled as he hastened down the stairs into the basement. 'Let us run now, the sooner we get there the better. Say "Urgent business!" if anyone pass.'

'Hanno, I know,' said Daior-deor, exasperated, but Hanno was off. At least he had enough sense to skirt the wall instead of running down the middle of the corridor as if he were late for a parade. Fortunately, there was no one else around; presumably they had all gone to see the circus at the main gate. The passage ran straight for a while between the barred doors of the pens, then turned a right-angle. Daior-deor had almost caught up with Hanno as he bounded round the corner and screamed. He crumpled forward onto the person who had run him through; the blade tore up through his guts as it was pulled loose; the assailant had tangled the weapon in them, could not get it free in time, as Daior-deor leapt round Hanno's other side and threw himself at the killer's throat, knocking them back against the wall with the point of his sword going up under the chin – and then he saw who he was about to slaughter. It was as if the world split open and he had seen all its torn innards in her eyes. He dropped his sword.

'Pick that up!' She was wiping her sword on Hanno's back; she wore nothing but a russet wool tunic that gaped open to show her breasts in front and rode up over her buttocks behind, and her face and hair were so wild and dirty she might have been a charcoal-burner. Daior-deor dropped to his knees, retrieving his weapon. 'Hanno,' he said.

'Hanno? Is he here? Did you come in that way? Which is the best way– '

'This is Hanno.' Daior-deor lifted his friend's head onto his knees. He heard Aleizon Ailix Ayndra gasp but he could not look at the mess she had made of the lower body. 'Hanno? Hanno, can you hear me?'

The eyelids fluttered over half-moons of white. Daior-deor had seen enough belly wounds to know what came of them. He put the dying man's head on the ground and held up his sword hilt to what he thought was the west. 'Bless me, Hanno, and I shall see you on – on– '

'The other side of the curtain,' said Aynodra's voice, unexpectedly shrill, behind him. Daior-deor let the sword fall, but he did not stay to look at his work; he knew by the sound and the feel of the blow that it was clean. Aleizon Ailix Ayndra snatched his free hand and pulled him after her. 'Run!'

'Had we been Sandar's men now, you would be dead!' he said.

'Do you think I don't know it? Only, come away! How did you get in here?'

'We came over the walls – on a rope, I think it's still there– ' They were at the stair leading up into the yard. 'Let me go up first!' he said. 'If they see you– '

'Then let us run away to hide, but anywhere, anywhere but here, before they come to look for him– '

'For Hanno?' he exclaimed.

'For Sandar!' Daior-deor looked astonished; Ayndra threw up her hands. 'Why ever d'you think I'm dressed like this?'

Daior-deor looked her up and down. 'God only knows!' he said.

She let out a shriek. 'I've killed him! I strangled him! He lies dead in there, they must come after him soon, he sent the guards away – and what is all that noise outside? Is Ylureen using powderfire? You do not plan an escalade?'

'You killed Sandar?'

'Did I not say so? – but let us go, Daior, let us go!' She bounded up the steps, but he was ahead of her, and when she turned the wrong way, he snatched her sleeve. 'Follow!' She followed so closely that she fell on him when he halted in the corner of a house, to creep up unseen on the place where the rope was. His caution was justified; two or three people were debating at the foot of it. As he watched, someone on the wall-walk threw the other end down to them and they started to coil it up. 'We cannot go that way. Let us get out of sight while we think what to do next.' It was a miracle that no one had given chase to them thus far;

but then it was not so odd that a man in Sandar's livery led a filthy half-naked woman about the streets, and from what little they had seen most people seemed preoccupied with the bombardment on the east side of the city. And in Purrllum it never paid to ask many questions. He knew the quarter, its warehouses and workshops; it was still too early for many people to be at work, and they easily found a loft with a couple of pallets in it where they could bolt the door from the inside and look out in three directions. Aleizon Ailix Ayndra tried to see where the firing was coming from. Daior-deor sat down with his eyes closed. He heard her leave the dormer and shuffle about among the tattered coverings on the pallets. 'Apprentices must sleep here in ordinary time.'

'Apprentices sleep in the master's house. They put the carters and muleteers up here, when they bring the load in. Or porters, if they have their own.' He looked round; she was trying to wrap herself in a piece of frieze as an improvised cloak. Underneath the grime she looked very sick. 'They brought me here the day before yesterday, in the morning, and ever since I have been in that place, the animal pen, with no clothes, and no food. I think you must have got here later the same day, is that not so? Very fast. Is Ylureen in command? You must tell me what has happened, for days I was wandering in the woods, I escaped but they caught me again: I had very bad luck – what will they do when they find Sandar is dead? He sent all the guards away, he hates them to watch him.'

'Fight among themselves, I should think,' said Daior-deor. 'I know not who is at whose throat these days – you slew him? Just now?'

'I had let myself out of the pen just the moment before you – found me. Not half an hour ago. They took away everything I had so I made this.' She flicked the plaited cord at him.

Daior-deor caught the weight at the end of it, then brought it up close for a look. 'What kind of stone is this?'

'It's a diamond, but never cut. It's supposed to be the same it was as when Ailixond first picked it up on the beach where he decided to found the city.' She was on hands and knees, head joined to his over the white eye of the ring. 'It's

22

the only thing he ever gave me,' she said. 'The same age as the city.'

'You had it round your neck at the ... when Ylureen ...'

'Yes. I always have it,' she added. 'No end of people have wanted to take it away – but why do I talk about this? You must explain to me what the battle is.'

'I hardly know how it is myself, for they were firing all night but it was not until it was almost morning that Sandar brought out his new machine, and then we had to go, only I heard a great noise from it, and screaming, but then we began to throw powderfire at them as soon as the night came – it was red and green and gold– '

'Whose idea was that?'

'S'Thiraidi. She said it would affright the barbarians more.'

Aleizon Ailix Ayndra laughed. 'And did it?'

'I cannot say; certainly a multitude of them came out to watch, and half our camp too. The sky was full of coloured lights– '

'Ay! just like a festival in Suthine. But did not many of these people have fireboxes landing on them as they watched?'

'They did, and some of the boxes had in them potshards, or old nails, all kind of things, but one could not see in the dark what became of them. But our people were still watching, and we saw them setting up catapults on the gate towers, and then all of a sudden fireboxes began to land among our people also, and they had to get out of the way, and after that it was back and forth all night, until our lookouts said that they were preparing something, but I never saw what it was – do they fire still?'

'It seems so – I never knew that we had so much powder, let alone to drag it up here in this wet! Ylureen is a very miracle. Did she send you here?'

'No,' said Daior-deor, 'we – it was Hanno's idea. Perhaps it was ill-considered – we should not have left the rope there like that, and you, you seem to have rescued yourself – but he's paid for it now! And you – if it had been anyone else but you, my lord, then – you'd be dead by now!'

She had turned round to stare in his eyes, and this time he

23

did not give way to her. She said, her gaze fixed on him, 'I understand what it is that you've done for me. I know not what I owe you for it, but when I do, I'll give it you.' Another artificial thunderclap finished her sentence, as if giving the agreement of god. When she spoke again her voice had shifted up a span of tones. 'But all I want now is to be out of this city!'

'In a little while, when they find out that Sandar is dead, there'll be an end to order, at least among the mercenaries – and each of his high officers was always so ambitious for his place, no one of them will give in to the others, and beside, everyone will want to rob the treasury . . .'

'And will our people try an escalade? These walls must be easy for an escalade, they are crumbling in every part; a child of five could go over them – lords above! How much powder do they have? Have they blown up the gate perhaps?'

'Perhaps they have begun an escalade already. We had not planned it, but who knows? Lady Ylureen says that only fools think that because they have once made a plan they have to stick to it.'

Both tried to look out of the windows, and saw only a lot of smoke and activity in the quarters down towards the main eastward gate. 'I think our best hope is to go out on the street, and run,' said Aleizon Ailix Ayndra, knotting the corners of a blanket under her chin, and pulling up the ornate belt studded with agates which was the only thing rendering her plundered tunic even remotely decent. Daiordeor began to say, 'I think it's not wise– ' but she silenced him. 'If you were going to be wise in your life, Daior, you would have gone into trade as your father told you to. Let us go!'

Sandar's new machines fired for the first time at dawn.

The besiegers had seen them being set up along with the catapults, but no one knew then what they were for: gross stubby cast-iron cylinders, open at one end and closed in the form of a hemisphere at the other. A number of stone balls, each larger than a man's head, were brought up on wooden litters and stacked beside the mysterious artefacts on the walls. When the grey light of morning was added to the intermittent and ghastly illumination of the exploding fireboxes, the observers in Ylureen's command post – high up where Hanno and Daior-deor had gone to look at the city – could see liveried soldiers packing something into the closed end of the irons, then rolling one of the balls in on top of it; they seemed to have been made to fit exactly the diameter of the opening. After that the men all disappeared from the walls, except for one who put a taper to the end of the iron thing, waited for a few moments until the sputtering flame had gone out of sight down some concealed hole, and then ran after his friends. The bang when it came was colossal; smoke poured across the gateway; then came faint screams and clamour from the section of the camp which the machine had been directed towards. There were four of them, and they fired one after the other. Ylureen was so moved that she started to curse. 'Siriane! Send to the commander of archers that his best men should set themselves to picking off the men who are serving those, those devils' organs– ' She abandoned her cup of hot chabe to go forward to get a better view of the scene. 'My mother's skirt! Has anyone ever seen such a device?'

'Never in my life, lady. Has this Lord Sandar invented it? Who would have thought the barbarians could show such cleverness?' said Derezhaid.

'A clever barbarian is far more dangerous than a civilised person,' Ylureen said grimly. 'I think it would be better an this Lord Sandar did not survive the siege of his city.'

'Those devices are not half so clever, for my mind, as our fireboxes with nails in them,' said Derezhaid. 'Simple, yet deadly – and attractive too! – while those machines, why look at them, the trouble they go to to throw one stone through the air, why they might as well have a catapult– ' He was interrupted by Lord Polem, scarlet as his tunic, and so out of breath it was many moments before he could speak.

Ylureen sent Derezhaid to bring a chair and some chabe for him. 'Ah!' he said, one hand on his heart. 'I've not run so far in years.'

'What is the matter? Here, sit down.'

'Casik – ah, thank you – Casik is going to lead an escalade.'

'A what?' said Ylureen.

'An escalade. You know, with siege ladders, over the wall. Did you not do the same at Yiakarak? Captain Kadaron said that you did—'

'Eskerladd,' said Ylureen. 'When?'

'I think now, this very moment. I tried to stop him, or at least tell him to wait, to consult the allied commanders, but he said he was subject to no damned council of women – o, excuse me, lady, but that's what he said – anyway, he said that he was going to lead his men, because Purrllum was his by rights anyway, and he was not going to sit on his arse while a group of witches – excuse me again, lady – while they made coloured lights in the sky and held a sabbath on the mountain. He had all the officers from his troops there, and they were all armed. But I think it would be easy to escalade here, lady, you should not look so worried. I've been in an escalade many times, and this wall, being in such bad repair, it will not be at all difficult, though Shumar knows where he got the ladders from. Why, we'd spend a sixday making ladders before the assault – but that's as may be. I could not find any messengers so I thought I should run up here to inform you. I must say, though, all these fireboxes, and now those what-you-may-call-its on the walls, there's a lot of destruction down there, perhaps an escalade is no bad thing . . .'

In half an hour it was clear to the eye what Casik was doing: his troops had crossed to the western approaches of the city, on the opposite side from the bombardment, and were scrambling up the walls on a variety of ropes, cords and improvised ladders. It was at about the same time that one of Sandar's metal stonethrowers emitted an exceptionally loud bang and swathed the entire gateway in clouds of bitter smoke; when they cleared it could be seen lying there, burst open like a blooming lily, with assorted scarlet scraps around it that had once been part of human beings; all the other devices had been deserted. The catapults fired a few more shots, but then their crews too disappeared. Derezhaid brought out his seeing-glass and with its aid Ylureen was able to discern a great deal of fighting within the city, and not only in the part where Casik's men were entering;

26

columns of smoke were belching from the Governor's house and all the private dwellings seemed to have closed shutters and barred doors, while men in Sandar's dark blue livery were running through the streets carrying all sorts of items, not only weapons but furnishings, swatches of cloth, boxes, jars and loaded sacks. Selanor and Karadon argued strongly for another assault by escalade, saying that Casik would establish himself in command of the city and they would find it difficult after that to dislodge him, but in the face of Ylureen's adamance they gave in and did as she ordered: deployed the forces of Haramin and S'Thurrulass in a cordon right round the city, so that even if they opened the gates no one could leave, and waited.

Smoke thickened over the Governor's dwelling and a soft grey rain came filtering from the south, veiling the chaos within the walls; as the wind tore holes in the curtain, so Casik's banner of a blue eagle on a white ground could be seen planted on the walls where his men had made the assault. Polem was filled with excitement; he took Derez-haid out to the windswept edge of the prominence and stood there clasping at his arm and pointing all over the city, howling a detailed commentary on what he saw all mixed up with scores of sieges under Ailixond into the teeth of the wind. Ylureen remained in shelter and asked every messenger who came up whether they had seen Captain Daior-deor and Hanno, before they even had a chance to greet her. The seeing-glass was useless in the murk, but eyes made plain that there was fighting on both sides of the city, round the main east gate and to the west with Casik, and plenty of disturbance round Sandar's house, while no one showed any interest in firing at the besiegers any more. People began to crowd up on the walls at the east gate, and some let themselves down on ropes, or started to lower bundles; others slashed the ropes from below and fled towards Ylureen's lines with the goods, or threw the owners into the ditch and hauled the bundle back up again. A whole series of scuffles developed on the wall walk. Then the gate was flung open from within, and the riot burst out into the open. Some continued to fight among themselves, others made to flee, only to discover that the besiegers surrounded them on all sides, and they had to join those who tentatively

27

approached them. A couple of greenish rags on poles appeared in the gateway, and a party of men marched out behind them, carrying reversed half-pikes and the swords sheathed on their shoulders. The other refugees hurried away from their blue tunics and gathered in no man's land. Too far away to hear a word, yet it was clear that the leader of the party asked to speak to an officer, and in a few moments a man in a red cloak was addressing them. After some hesitation, they laid down their weapons and allowed a Haraminharn escort to close in round them, while the man in the red cloak stepped forward to summon the other refugees.

'Captain Selanor reports, lady. Sixty-five mercenaries of Lord Sandar's pay offer you their surrender on the usual terms. A Captain Lobiak leads them. He claims that he was the head of Sandar's house of clandestine reports. He says that Sandar was murdered at dawn and that the city mob broke loose in the streets at the news, before Casik even went over the wall, and commends himself to your service. My captain adds: Lobiak and his men were hated and feared by the rest of Sandar's people, and my captain thinks that this is why they have surrendered, for fear that without Sandar's protection they will be murdered by the many people they have abused. Captain Selanor says, my lady, he thinks it best to keep Lobiak and his men in safe custody and promise nothing until the city is ours. He begs for any further advice you may give him.'

'Sandar is murdered? Who is it who murders him?'

'No one knows, lady; at least, this Lobiak said that they found him strangled in the animal pens of the palace, and no sign of who had done it.'

'And what of my lord Aleizon Ailix Ayndra? You have ask this man if Sandar has her, where she is?'

'He says that she was captured and brought to Purrllum two days ago, and Sandar took her away, but no one knew where, for it was for his own . . . my lady . . .'

'What has he say? Tell me!'

'Lady, I cannot tell. Forgive me, I know only what my captain told me.'

Ylureen indicated that he should leave. She ordered another of her aides. 'Tell Captain Selanor that he pen up all those leave the city, like they were sell them slave, he knows? But this Lobiak, send him with guard to me, so I question him.'

'Whatever you wish, my lady.' The man, a straw-haired barbarian from Haramin, bowed and ran on his way. Ylureen snapped her fingers for another cup of chabe. Sabraid brought it to her. She loosened the high collar of her tunic. He understood immediately, came forward and began to massage the tight muscles of her neck. She moaned as his trained fingers dissipated the knots of a sleepless night. 'Sabraid. What a comfort you are to me.'

Sabraid shook his head and bent over to kiss her cheek. He retreated silently to the back of the shelter when he saw the soldiers coming.

Lobiak, when offered a private conference with Ylureen, seemed overjoyed; she walked with him a distance up the hill, so that her people could see but not hear them, until she started screaming at him with such fury that even he cowered, and stood there like a milkfaced loon as she struck him across the face. She came down the slope in a storm of mantles while Lobiak's guards ran to recapture their dazed charge; only Sabraid dared go after her. In a little while he was back in the smoke-filled angle under the tarpaulin where the stove was, asking for more chabe. 'He said that Sandar took her off the way he did the ones he wanted for his own playthings, making sure that no one else knew. In ordinary times it would soon have been known all the same, but what with the siege. Then she asked him what Sandar did with the ones for his own playthings, and he started to tell her, saying he had helped sometimes. That was when she began to scream at him.'

'So no one knows where my lord of Haramin is?'

'No one knows.'

'But the lord Sandar could have done . . ?'

Sabraid shuddered. 'Horrible things!' The chabe was ready; Esas'thi wrapped the cup in a warm cloth. 'With love to my lady,' she said.

Ylureen was not where he had left her; she had returned to the shelter and was addressing a knot of barbarians in their own tongue. Derezhaid told him what she was saying. 'That they should go forward and capture the gate, why

29

have they not done so already? . . . that all our army will march into the city . . . that she will come and proclaim that the allied army has captured it, before Casik can do so . . .'

Six Haraminharn drummers walked in the lead, swags of black cloth decorating drums and sticks, beating the rhythm of slow march. A company of archers followed them, then Ylureen on her high horse, flanked by Selanor, Kadaron and their officers; a hundred pikemen with upright sarissas backed them. The streets were lined by troops of Haramin and Suthine and an entire regiment of phalanx was drawn up in the largest plaza. Flagpoles had been hastily erected behind the auctioneers' dais: blue waves on white in the middle, plain black to the right and black spiral on red to the left. A small crowd of townspeople had been permitted to gather on the far side. Blood still stained the paving stones and bitter smoke tainted the winter air. The monotonous thump of the drums resounded like a sick heart in the narrow streets.

Ylureen stood at the edge of the dais and read from a paper which Selanor handed to her. 'I, Lady Ylureen of Pilith, Royal Ambassador of S'Thurrulass to Safi, speak in the name of Suthine and in the name of Lord Aleizon Ailix Ayndra of Haramin and Safi. By virtue of the royal authorities vested in us, and finding this our city of Purrllum without a head by reason of the decease of its governor, Sandar lord of Safi, we have entered here in full force of arms, our intention being—'

Safic war trumpets burst into a chaotic fanfare from the west side of the square. Ylureen paused angrily in her recitation, and snapped at her entourage; a mounted officer trotted out from behind the dais, but Casik's banners were already in sight with the lord himself at the head of five or six horsemen, pushing their way through the allied infantry. Casik reined his stallion in brutally at the foot of the dais; the horse pranced and snorted as he spoke. 'My lady! Has it escaped your notice that we of Cambar hold this city?' he roared.

'We commend the bravery of your men,' Ylureen said smoothly. She consulted another part of the paper. 'We assume the rule of this city in the name of the allied army of

30

Suthine, Haramin and Cambar, until such time as the commanders of the army shall find—'

Casik tore the paper from her hand, crumpled it up and flung it on the ground. Ylureen's eyes widened. 'My lord,' she said, catching Casik's eye and pointing at the troops arrayed in the plaza. Casik stared stonily at her. 'I hold this city,' he said sullenly. 'Where is Lord Ayndra? You, lady, are a foreigner, no matter how noble, how then do you seek to take office here? And what proof do you have that Lord Sandar is dead? As a lord of Safi created in due form by Lord Ailixond himself, I am by rights Governor of this city, if, as you say, Sandar is dead.'

'We are decide later who is the Governor of the city,' said Ylureen. She told one of her staff to go and retrieve the paper. 'For now, my lord, we make the proclamation. Will you come up with us here? We are allies.' Casik's horse had quietened, and eyes were drawn off to another turmoil in the cordon of soldiers. Someone cried, 'Do you not know me? Anko, you blind fool!' and a shrill yell went up: 'Ylureen!'

A short figure in Sandar's blue appeared, pulling off a leather cap to show bright copper hair; a scarecrow sprang out beside it and ran out into the open, bare white legs flashing above mudspattered feet. Ylureen cried out and vaulted down from the dais, ignoring the hooves of Casik's warhorse. She walked forward with her hands held out. Aleizon Ailix Ayndra slowed down and made to approach her in a formal manner, taking her hands and looking at her face; suddenly dropped her hands, flung her arms round her and buried her face in Ylureen's neck. Ylureen burst into tears. Ayndra broke her embrace; she stood back a little, lifted up a corner of her blanket mantle to dab at smeared paint, spoke to her in S'Thurrulan. They did not look at Casik until he was right beside them, and then both turned at once. The drummers had begun of their own accord to tap out a rapid beat and the soldiers were clapping and stamping in time to it. Aleizon Ailix Ayndra looked around her and up at Casik with a wide white smile and raised her hand to him in salute. 'You have done well!' she said.

'My lord,' said Casik, scanning her up and down, appalled.

'Congratulate me on escaping from Sandar's prisons, Casik. Let us go up on the dais, Ylureen, and make a proclamation. What is this one you have? O, no good at all.'

'Sandar's prisons? Then where is Sandar?' Casik urged his horse on beside them.

'Dead,' Ayndra said cheerfully.

'How did he die?'

She swung her thumb at her own chest, grinning widely; looked over her shoulder and beckoned. 'Daior-deor!'

'Captain!' Ylureen kissed him. 'Where is Hanno?'

'Dead, lady.'

Ylureen exclaimed and hugged Daior-deor. Ayndra was climbing the steps to the dais; people crowded to meet her at the top. She waved to Casik. 'Come up here with us!' Seeing the way things were going, he was already dismounting. 'Put your banner there,' he said, pointing to the left of the flag of S'Thurrulass. 'Selanor! Old friend! But first this proclamation! There's no need of a written one, I can make one as I stand, but have we any clerks here? And who are those people? Surely we want to proclaim ourselves to the townspeople, not merely our own men . . .'

City of many masters, Purrllum became immediately peaceful when it became clear that it had acquired a new one – or rather a set of new ones. By the end of the day people were coming forward offering the services of their hot-shops or wine cellars for the expected celebration, and no one seemed to remember the name Sandar; except for Lobiak and his men, shivering under protective custody in improvised tents away from the city. The business of moving a garrison into the city took most of the day, and Daior-deor was grateful for it; he could not endure the jubilation of all those not actually on duty. No one spoke to him except to discuss the task in hand. When he could find no more excuses to stay away, he went up to the governor's house where the banquet was erupting all over the building. A line of S'Thurrulan women were selling chabe with slugs of lifewater in it, and bottles of the precious fluid to those prepared to pay. He did not bother to haggle over the price she asked, but took the cheap ceramic flask round to the back of the kitchens and sat down there to drink it. He was already quite drunk by the time that Selanor found him.

'Captain! You must join us, sir, you are a neglected hero – why do you hide away here? This is no time to be modest. Would you care for some of this?'

This was a highly spiritous fruit punch. 'Here, take this flask,' said Selanor. 'You deserve it. You and Hanno. Where is Hanno?'

Daior-deor shook his head. 'I have not seen him all day,' said Selanor. Then he noticed Daior-deor's expression. 'Shumar! God curse me for a fool. How did it happen? God save me, I thought we were on separate duties.'

'She did it,' said Daior-deor. 'An accident.'

'What! How did it happen?'

Daior-deor swallowed some punch. 'I would rather not talk about it,' he said.

'Where is his body?'

'I have not been back. Still where he left it.'

'Do you want to go and take it up? I will get some blankets and come with you.'

'Thank you,' Daior-deor said, too dull to show his surprise. 'Do you not have to be . . . in there . . .'

'No more than you do,' said Selanor. 'Wait here for me.'

'I am not about to leave,' said Daior-deor, drinking.

When Selanor came back with blankets, ropes and a carrying pole, he followed him mutely, speaking only to direct his steps and tell him to bring a lantern. Only when they were moving along the actual corridor was he moved to words. 'Here. He was running along here, like this, and she was coming round the corner. He didn't see. He . . .' His hands in the lamplight showed how the short sword had ripped Hanno's belly; the oval of light slid over rough ground, blackish stains and came to rest on the original wound. 'I almost killed her,' said Daior-deor.

Selanor knelt beside the body. 'Why did you not?'

'I could not,' said Daior-deor. The corridor stank of cold stone and blood and animals. He leant over the corpse. 'The dogs have been at him.'

'Cover him up now. I think there are dogs in here still. Was there much fighting here?'

'In here? I think not. We ran straight out again. Perhaps afterwards . . .'

'Stay here a moment.' Selanor had another swig from the flask, picked up the stout pole and lantern to go down the further corridor. He disappeared into the black maw of an open door; a chorus of yaps and snarls broke out, he could be heard striking out and swearing. A couple of mangy mongrels burst out of the doorway and fled past Daior-deor. Selanor followed them with a couple of articles in his hand. He showed them to Daior-deor. 'Lord's bracelets. It must be Lord Sandar dead in there, though you could never tell now from the face. Was she penned in here?'

'I never asked her.'

Selanor looked at Hanno's shrouded body, weighing the bracelets in his hand. He looked at Daior-deor. 'You worked with him.'

'He was my friend.'

'Why could you not kill her?'

Daior-deor looked up at him. 'Why? Because she looked at me, because it was an accident – I do not know why! Do you say I should have done it?'

'No,' Selanor said softly. 'I do not think I would have done it either. But I thought you were perhaps less of a fool for her than I am.' He knelt down to bind the corpse's feet together. 'Let us sling him on the pole, then, and we will take him to the burning-ground.'

They drank more on the way to the burning-ground; they gave generously in drink and money to the priest whom they found there offering to chant prayers for the dead all night; they drank more on the way back to the Governor's house. By the time they entered the hall there Daior-deor found that he could walk unassisted only with a great deal of concentration. Lights and faces swung about him as though they were riding at anchor in a high sea. He disengaged himself from Selanor. 'Sit here. Rest for a while.'

'Are you well?'

'Very well. Only sit down for a while.' He propped his back against the wall and closed his eyes, but that made it worse so he opened them again. The noise was terrific; people coming and going were forever treading on his feet or tripping over his legs. He pushed himself upright and staggered outdoors. To his surprise he found that the lifewater bottle was still in his hand, and it slopped when he shook it. There was a colonnaded passage running down one side of the hall, plunged in shadow at this hour; he tottered into it and found a place where he could sprawl in peace. Now and then soldiers with heavily perfumed women would weave past arm in arm, on their way to deeper shadows and deserted rooms in other parts of the building, but they paid him no heed, not even to ask for a mouthful of drink. The tiled roof over the colonnade was decaying; when he looked up where lost tiles had been he saw a couple of stars, pale and steady in the inky sky. When someone came towards him from the back of the hall he ignored them till they crept right up beside him and called out his name – 'Daior-de-e-or!' as though it were some S'Thurrulan ditty. He tried to sit up and in doing so knocked over the bottle. 'God curse it!' It was almost empty when he picked it up.

'No worry. I'll get you some more,' said Aleizon Ailix Ayndra behind him in a peculiar sing-song voice.

'I need no more,' he said.

'I could not find you,' she said. 'Are you going to leave?'

'Leave?' he said. 'Why should I leave? I have nowhere to go. With Hanno . . . I could have gone anywhere! And now . . . I am nothing. Where, where should I go?'

'I thought you'd gone away,' she said, 'for what I'd done – sweet heaven! What is it? O, do not cry – I wanted to tell you, Daior, you are free to leave, whenever, but for what you did this day, I swear to you, so long as I ever have money, it will be yours – o, what is it?' Daior-deor shook his head mutely; tears like vinegar filled his eyes. She put her hands on his shoulders. 'You can go where I go,' she said. Daior-deor found himself sobbing with his cheek crushing the ruffles of her clean shirt, too drunk to remember what he had meant to say to her let alone enunciate it. It was the last thing he remembered of the night.

'Extraordinarily lucky,' said Aleizon Ailix Ayndra happily. 'Ay! I believed I was dead for sure. O! how fine it is to be in your bed again.' She rolled over, laughing, in a cocoon of blankets.

Ylureen smiled at her reflection in the mirror which Hahhni held for her. 'I believed that Lord Sandar had been too clever at last for you,' she said.

'Ha! He was betrayed by lust and blinded by desire. For that he did not act as cleverly as he should.'

'And what would that have been?'

'Cut my head off.' Ayndra writhed till her hands were free and made a rolling gesture at Hahhni. The slave pointed to a marquetry box beside the bed, and she squirmed over to take a smokestick from it.

'Surely he believed you more valuable to him as a live hostage than as a dead body.'

'Surely he did; but he was wrong.'

'It seems that most of your opponents have been wrong so far, else you'd not be here now.'

'Lakkanar tried to kill me, and would have done so if he had had me in his power so much as a half-hour. But I do not think that anyone will make Sandar's mistake again.' She sat up with the covers crumpled round her waist, dragging thoughtfully on the smokestick. 'I do not intend that they will have the chance to make it, either.'

'Then you will listen to what I say.' Ylureen bent over to let Hahhni drop her nightshift over her head. The slave knelt down to pull off her trousers underneath it, added them to the pile of discarded clothes, and padded away to take them to be laundered. Ylureen sat down on the bed and reached for the smokestick.

'I always listen to what you say, Ylureen. Well . . . as much as I listen to anyone.'

Ylureen made a sign of disgust. Aleizon Ailix Ayndra lay back on the heaped pillows, picking up the Royal Ring, restored to the chain round her neck; she turned it back and forth, trying to trap the light within the rough diamond. 'Let me see,' said Ylureen, leaning over. She examined the jewel in silence while Ayndra gazed up into her face. 'Who wears this?'

'The King,' said Ayndra softly. 'The King of Safi.'

'And Sandar let you keep it.'

'Only because he did not find it. He wanted it. He asked me to give it to him.'

'What did you say?'

'O, I told him it was elsewhere . . . he had not let his men search me properly because he wanted to save that liberty for himself.'

'They all know that you have it, then.'

'O, of course they do. Half of them were there when Ailixond gave it to me.' She offered her palm, and Ylureen dropped the ring into it. 'Sulakon asked me to give it to him, after he was chosen Regent.'

'And?'

'I ran away.' She grinned foolishly into the pillow.

'Will you keep it for ever?'

'O no. When there is a king in Safi again, then I shall surrender it.'

'Are you sure?' said Ylureen.

'I would give it to Parakison, when he is eighteen.'

'But if the next king is not Parakison?'

'It will be Parakison.'

'It may not – how old is he now?'

'Eight? Nine? Some such age.'

'What if he does not live to be eighteen? Or proves altogether foolish?'

Ayndra grinned more widely. 'Then we shall see. Take your shift off, Ylureen.'

Parro greets his beloved father Lord Polem and Diamoon and everyone else. Father, I pray that this letter reach you, I have to send it secretly because a most dreadful thing has befallen us here. Last sixday I had gone out hunting when Lord Hasmon came to the city with troops of soldiers and a whole horde of people and a letter from Lord Sulakon saying that you were a rebel and Drimmanë belonged to him. When I came back they were already in the city, the soldiers seized me at the gate and dragged me into the house and there was Lord Hasmon sitting in your chair and a whole crowd of merchants and clerks and people around him. He showed me the letter and I could not say anything, he spoke on and on saying you had run away to the Witch of Haramin and the Empire opposed the forces of evil, I could not follow it all and there was nothing I could do anyway. Since then he has been governing here and the merchants and clerks he has brought with him have been going around collecting taxes in every part, saying that we owe them for all the taxes since Lord Ailixond died and that everyone must pay now, even though it is not yet spring and the people have hardly any food let alone any money. You would not believe the things that are in the market now, all the horses and oxen and jewellery, a multitude of things and all very cheap and Sulakon's people buying them. I told him that he was doing a bad thing but he called me a bastard and said that if I did not shut my mouth I would never open it again. All sorts of moneylenders have come with him too and are taking the money away to Safi. People came from the country to see me and said that Sulakon's people would have been taking all their things, not just the taxes, the women too, and what would you do? Would you come home and save them? I cannot tell what I should do, father, I could not say to them that I did not know where you had gone so I told them not to give the money to Hasmon if they did not want to. You never told me what I should do if something like this happened. Please write to me! Please come home too if you can. Chagel and Lia and Tikkidi and Selanë and Little Thio and the others all ask for you. We fear that Hasmon may take us away, he says he will put us in prison if we do not make the people pay, but how can we? We can do nothing, and besides, no one has any money anyway, we cannot get blood from a stone. Please write to me, it is very urgent. I am sending this letter with my friend Garag to take it as fast as he can. Given in Master Tennat's hand, the twenty-fifth day of Fifth Month in the four hundred and seventy-third year of the city, in the city and province of Drimmanë.

'What shall I do? What shall I do? What shall I do?'

'There is nothing you can do,' said Aleizon Ailix Ayndra.

'I shall leave! I shall go back there tomorrow!' Polem swung round. 'Will you give me a company?'

'A company! Polem, we know not how many men Hasmon has with him. Will you retake Drimmanë with a company?'

'You captured Raq'min with less!'

She regarded him in a monitorial fashion. He waved the

letter. 'Are you sure that you want a company?' she said. 'I would ask for volunteers.'

'No, I am not sure,' said Polem. He stopped in his pacing. 'What can I do?'

'Ask this man Garag for everything he can tell. Not just how many they are, but everything that he can remember that they have done since they arrived and what he thinks they will have done since. Go and talk to him and Diamoon, she will remember it all. Then I will come and we will all talk together. Very likely there is nothing we can do.' She picked up her hat from the table and looked into the small glass mirror hanging on the wall as she put it on; she looked enormously pleased with herself.

'Where are you going?' Polem asked.

'To attend as the people dispense justice.'

'You mean to judge.'

'No,' she said. 'The people will dispense justice. I hope to do no more than keep order in the debate. Will you come? Lobiak and his followers are to be tried – but you will need a strong stomach; what I know of their crimes is not sweet, and I think that this day we will hear worse. Sandar was not loved, and they carried out Sandar's orders.'

'What are you going to do with them? Will you put them to death?'

'I shall do nothing to them. The people whose kin they have tortured and slain will do all that is needed.'

'What? But are you not going to give them a trial?'

'Why?' she said.

Polem fished for a reason. 'They . . . everyone deserves a trial, do they not?'

'This will be a trial.'

'But a trial – are you not going to be the judge? And the lawyers– '

'Judges, lawyers!' She flung her cloak round her shoulders.

'But in Safi– '

She laughed. 'When I am in Safi, Polem, everything will change! Will you come with me? Or will you speak with Garag?'

'I had better . . . I am very worried, after all, it says here they will put all of them in prison – all my children! Except

39

Haldin of course— ' She took his arm and led him out of the room still talking.

When Lobiak's men saw that they were to be handed over to the people whom they had extorted and whose kin they had abducted or slowly killed, their tongues were loosened and their loyalty to one another melted away; they fell over one another to recite lists of crimes and delicts by everyone but the speaker, the details of Sandar's machines and the secrets of his government. Before she let the mob have them, Aleizon Ailix Ayndra learnt much about the devices in the cellars of the Governor's house, and discovered three secret treasuries where Sandar had stored coin, apart from the one rifled during the sack of the city, as well as numerous small hoards which would have kept their owners in comfortable retirement but proved insufficient to buy their freedom. Selanor collected their testimonies, and the monetary proceeds had been sequestered for the army of Haramin before the other allied commanders knew that they existed. Extensive lists recorded the names of Sandar's agents in every city of the Empire, including Raq'min; sealed orders were sent to Ayndra's officers in the lands she governed to remove these paid traitors. The only question she could not answer was the whereabouts of Sandar's family. His wife, Lady Gallaria, had lived in the strictest seclusion, while concubines accompanied him in public; her eldest son, named Meraptar in a concession to the pride of his noble line rather than an expression of Sandar's love for his father, would have been made a lord a year ago if there were a king in Safi, and Sandar presented him everywhere as his heir. There had been four other children, boys and girls, and a daughter who had gone to Lysmal to marry Golaron's grandson, four years ago at a time when the two lords had been friends. Their rooms in the palace were all deserted, and though the clothes and furnishings remained, the jewels and valuables had been efficiently removed in a way that suggested an orderly flight rather than rapine or abduction. Sandar must have planned for their safety in such secrecy that not even his chief lieutenants knew where they might flee or who was charged with protecting them; and, while they did not appear in the city, people were already saying that Lord Ayndra had slain them in the same way as their lord and master. She contented herself with posting spoken and written proclamations asking for their whereabouts and promising them safe conduct; but she did not much expect to see them answered; the governance of the city pressed her more than a few evil rumours.

The allied commanders managed to agree that the circuit of watches should be divided into three parts, with Haramin taking one part, Cambar the second and S'Thurrulass the third; but that that was the only decision they were able simply to take. For the first six days, Casik and Aleizon Ailix Ayndra bickered constantly, but masked their divisions in public. The quarrel really began when messengers arrived from Lord Golaron, carrying letters addressed to 'Lord Aleizon Ailix Ayndra, supreme commander of the army of Haramin and its allies of Cambar and S'Thurrulass'. Golaron praised her for capturing the stronghold of the Needle's Eye, and proposed that they should join forces in order to expel Sulakon from Safi and restore good government to the Empire. He said that he was leaving Caoni to go eastwards and suggested that they meet at Yahloish, the town at the lowest bridging point on the Shulion river. It was a couple of days' ride north of the place where Sargond, Ailixond's governor in Lysmal, had been murdered by his mutinous troops in the first year of the wars, at about the same time as Casik had abandoned Sulakon to attach himself to Golaron for a while. Golaron enclosed a letter full of prolix greetings but with no more meat in it than his principal missive, addressed to Lady Ylureen, but he did not flatter Casik by thus singling him out. In private, Casik raved against this insult, and though in public he affected unconcern, his rage smouldered and grew like the heat in the heart of a midden. He sat silent through all the meetings to make arrangements for the march into Lysmal and let it be taken for granted that he would follow. Only when it came time to decide who would be left to hold Purrllum for the allies did he speak up.

'The jurisdiction of this city is mine by right of territory and right of capture both. Clearly we must leave a military governor here, even an you set up your citizens' council.'

'No one denies that we need a military governor,' Ayndra

said placidly. 'But we sit here in one of the lynchpins of the Empire. You yourself know, my lord, how easy it is for any who hold Purrllum to cast away their allegiance to rulers either side of them. I think it better that we do not give such a prize into the hands of any one governor, however loyal, nor leave any great concentration of arms here.'

'But of course we must leave arms here! The pass must be defended—'

'Who is it to be defended against?' Ayndra idly tilted her chair back.

'The wild Mirkits – rebels—'

'We are the rebels!' She laughed. Casik saw that the path he was on took him nowhere. He leant forward with his arms on the table. 'A city such as this cannot be left in the hands of a passel of merchants. There must be some one sole commander whose word can override their chattering when danger approaches. Captain Cosmar is a courageous man who has fought over this region since the King died. I say we should leave him as governor here.' He did not add that Cosmar had also served Golaron, until he decided to secede along with Casik, and had been one of his chief aides ever since; instead he signed to him to stand up where he sat on the officers' benches. Cosmar bowed. 'My lords, gentlemen, I would be honoured to accept such a post. And as my lord says, I have considerable knowledge of these parts, even to the Lysmalish dialect.'

Ylureen said something in S'Thurrulan. 'They do not,' said Aleizon Ailix Ayndra.

Casik beat his fist on the table. 'May I plead that these councils be conducted in Safic? If my lady has a word, pray let us all hear it.'

'She said that they do not speak Lysmalish dialect in the Needle's Eye, but another tongue altogether,' Ayndra said.

'Lysmalish dialect is the common tongue of the merchants and the caravaneers,' Cosmar said.

'I would be the first to honour the Captain's record of valour,' said Selanor. 'So much so that I would regret the loss of his skills, were he to stay here when we march into Lysmal. As we approach Safi we can expect to meet the full resistance of the Lord Regent, and the hardest fights

42

we have yet seen. We cannot give up our experienced officers before we have won the city.'

Cosmar scowled, but he was not about to proclaim himself unfit to fight and so meet to be left behind. Getaleen stood up at the back of the officers' benches. 'I speak first, then Safic after.' She made a brief speech in her own tongue, then switched to the common language. 'Already with three armies we have well garrison this town. Issa good plan and work well. The merchant are wise and want peace for the trade. Can we not le'em have government while we in three garrison the town still, as do now? The citizen council they are very grateful to us for they are now a free city and Sandar gone; they want only the trade, they are not rise against us. We leave here soldiers to guard no more. My lord is right when she say not to leave one person, not only they are too much power but as we see now we are never choose one person only, because all want their own. Do you listen?'

Cosmar gave a minimal shrug in Casik's direction and sat down again. Casik raised his voice. 'And how is this council to be chosen?'

'We shall call all its members before us and select them in council as we are now, when the guild masters have sent their representatives. You may nominate any other citizen you choose for it,' said Ayndra with a smile.

In her own language S'Thiraidi said, 'But he will not see a one of them elected.'

Ylureen kicked her under the table. 'They are not all deaf to words! Keep your comments for later.'

It was Ayndra's turn to tap the table for order. 'I ask our noble friends to recall that some of us are ignorant of their speech. Let us decide now when we shall leave for the west, so that we can order the citizens to present themselves before us.'

Casik held his own council late that night, in a private room at the Sign of the Mule in Harness. His aides appeared one by one, as if they did not more than visit a second or third tavern; the witch's spies were everywhere. 'The woman is infernally clever my lord; she has the council on the back of her hand.'

'Better that we agree with her in front of others. It cannot

43

do us good an we stand up against her; it will only increase her suspicions.'

'She has suspicions in any case. It is the nature of sorceresses; they are so evil they can never believe that others are good,' said Casik sullenly. 'Maishis our mother! We have shed blood for this city, yet she recognises no claims but her own. Supreme Commander! Ha! She will think she is Lord Ailixond come again the next thing.'

'With respect, my lord, is it so important that we leave one of ours here? An we reach Safi, then we can have whatever we wish. Are we not better to go with her now?'

'When she has Safi her army will break up quarrelling, I swear it. Then we will have our chance. Let us go with her now and show all loyalty. It will bring us better fortune in the end.'

'God curse Golaron for a son of a whore.' Casik remained preoccupied with the slight on his honour. His officers sat patiently while he ranted, sent out for more wine, and began to propose the names of local notables who, if they gained seats on this citizens' council, would favour his interests against those of the witch.

In the mountains of the Needle's Eye, spring lagged behind; the sky was still shaking icy salt over Purrllum when flowers were invading the eroded hills of Lysmal. Sixth and Seventh Month were the dreariest times of the year in the highlands; the snow that whitened the moors melted in a few days in the town, but the damp got into every joint and people sickened of woodsmoke and poorly salted meats. Ylureen lamented having to travel at such a season; after she had sealed up all the draughty cracks in her rooms and even got a supply of hot water to the tiny bathhouse adjoining the House of Women, she did not want to have to go and live in wagons and tents again until it was summer, the proper time for such things.

'Why do you complain so much? I think it is very like the weather in Suthine here, except there are no fogs.' Aleizon Ailix Ayndra walked up to the large polished metal mirror on the wall opposite the bed and looked at herself in it. She was wearing nothing except one of Ylureen's embroidered bedgowns, though there were so many braziers in the room

44

that it was warm enough to sit about naked. The pattern of leaping flames round the hem undulated as it trailed behind her on the floor. 'Suthine is perfectly foul at this season,' said Ylureen.

'It's since you have been carrying that you feel the cold so much.' Ayndra pulled her hair into a bunch at the back of her head, then piled it up on her crown and frowned at her image.

'What?' said Ylureen. The reflection in the mirror gave her a long slow smile. 'How do you know?' said Ylureen.

Ayndra turned round, letting the blonde tresses fall down her back; she spread her hands. 'Look at you! You have never been thin since I knew you—'

'I should hope not!'

'But now, Ylureen . . .' She shrugged, running a hand through her hair so that it fell over her face. 'You're like a dish of fresh cream in a dairy.'

Ylureen lay back laughing. 'Then come and drink the buttermilk!'

Aleizon Ailix Ayndra crawled obediently into the welcoming circle of her arms. 'Besides,' she said, muffled, 'I know when your moon days are. Very likely no one else has even thought of it. Did you count your days wrongly while I was away?'

'I was so distressed for you that I forgot to count them at all.'

'Aaah!' For a while she lost her words in the landscape of flesh that surrounded her, then reared up suddenly. 'I hope you will do something about it. Soon.'

'What?' It was Ylureen's turn to rear up in surprise. 'What do you mean?'

'Well . . . it will have no father — I mean, I know that Sabraid, but . . .'

Ylureen widened her eyes. 'My husband is the father.'

'I know, but do you expect them to understand that?'

'Hah! An you expect me to kill my child, merely because I do not follow the witless customs of your people, customs which I have never noted that you held in very high repute, if—' Ayndra was semaphoring her into silence. She gave a snort of disgust. 'Never,' she said.

'We are going into the hottest lands of the Empire. You'll

be heavily laden in the worst heat of the year – when will it be born? Second Month? Third Month?'

'In your Second Month.'

'And how are you going to ride? And live in an armed camp? Heaven knows what battles we will encounter this summer.'

'I shall travel in a litter when I become uncomfortable on horseback. And I have never charged at the head of my troops. An we have to flee in disorder, then I shall be at a disadvantage; but I hardly expect that we shall have to flee in disorder. You are not going to tell me that the sight of so many swords will see my child born with a pointed head?'

'No, Ylureen,' said Ayndra. She twisted up her mouth and fidgeted.

Ylureen took her hands. 'You must understand, Aleizon, this is my last child. In a few more years it will be too late for me. I took no care with Sabraid and instructed him to take none because I thought I was already too old. If I were a woman of twenty-five I would discard it, for the inconvenience, but I cannot let this one go. For all I know the mothers may take it from me in a little while anyway. Can you not leave it up to their judgement?' As she spoke her hands wandered to the other woman's breasts and thighs, pushing the embroidered coat aside. 'And beside, why should you complain? I shall grow fat and placid and leave you to take over all my commands.'

Aleizon Ailix Ayndra could not maintain her displeasure. 'Fat, perhaps,' she said, and tumbled Ylureen over onto the bed.

The citizens' council decreed a magnificent send-off for the departing army, with musical bands and streamers decorating the main streets; it was true that most of the streamers were in Sandar's colours, but with a few black and white ones mixed in they could claim they represented the waves of Safi and the banner of Haramin. The councillors in their merchants' gowns were careful to pay marked honour to Lord Casik, as their lord of Haramin had instructed them to do; she did not even turn up for some while, and the foreign witches let him take the place of highest precedence in her absence. By the time she arrived his mood was so improved that he willingly exchanged the kiss of equals with her. She took his sleeve and drew him aside, indicating to Daiordeor that he should leave her for the time being. He went to pay his respects to Ylureen and her companions. S'Thiraidi offered him her hand to kiss and held on to his fingers. 'You are all in black still. Is it for following my lord of Haramin?'

'For Hanno, lady, mourning for my friend,' said Daiordeor.

'But the funeral is passed, is it not? I am told the Safeen wear black only until the funeral.'

'In Thaless an a brother dies we wear black for half a year after. Hanno was like my brother, lady, and I know not where the rest of his family is. He came from south Safi, in the country, and his elder brother threw him out when his father died and he inherited the land. I think there is no one else to mourn for him, and I owe him that at least.'

'Iss good, very good,' she said, releasing him; she watched him as he went behind the group of S'Thurrulans to a place where he could overhear Lord Ayndra and Casik. With his winter-pale white skin and copper hair he looked spectacular in black. S'Thiraidi smiled sadly to herself. Aleizon Ailix Ayndra was looking up into Casik's eyes and dispensing enough charm to unnerve anyone who knew her. Fragments of her conversation drifted over: '. . . interests lie on the same road . . . in Lysmal Golaron will certainly . . . when we reach Safi . . . for both our fortunes we have decided to work together. What merit it then that we oppose one another within this our allied army? Casik, let us be friends!'

'I have desired the government of Purrllum—' Casik began.

'We have all desired the government of Purrllum. Would you rather have seen it given into the hands of Lady Ylureen?'

'Of course not!' Casik exclaimed, so loudly that Ylureen herself turned her head. He rapidly modulated his tones, and the listeners could not hear the rest of the conversation, muffled as it was by the clatter of their horses being brought into the courtyard and the approaching noise of massed musicians. Whatever it had been, it left Casik grinning all over his face when the time came to mount.

'What lies did you tell him this time?' Ylureen said in her own tongue to Aleizon Ailix Ayndra.

'I never tell lies, Ylureen!' Ayndra burst out laughing and urged Tarap to the head of the procession; Casik on his bay stallion rode out of the gate at her side.

'And it is not true, what she told you was in the treasury at Purrllum, nothing; true, the big treasury that his villains knew was there was ransacked, and she took you to see it; but we have found that there were three other treasuries where Sandar kept his secret monies, and where are these?'

'In the treasury of Haramin,' said Ylureen despairingly.

'True, my lady.' S'Thiraidi bowed to make a gracious offer of her pipe. Ylureen took it, but was too distracted to draw. 'That woman's avarice is beyond all reason!' Siriane could not help but grin. 'The pigsty says the privy stinks,' she murmured to Derezhaid. Ylureen was going on: 'I shall have to be more watchful . . . it is no good to leave all to her these military activities, we shall have to send more of our people— '

'But who shall we send?' said S'Thiraidi. 'I beg to say, my lady, that you will not have to throw yourself into the fray with a crowd of barbarians rabid as dogs. I hardly think we can expect our people . . .' Hahhni padded up with a lighted splint and held it over the bowl of the pipe; Ylureen paused to suck on it. Someone clapped their hands outside the doorway of the tent; Siriane went to see who it was. S'Thiraidi raised her voice, hoping to cover fear with volume. 'Surely, my lady, it were best to, ah, to ask my lord of Haramin for a more equitable division of the spoils.'

Ylureen turned round. S'Thiraidi kept her forearms on her knees and maintained a wavering gaze. Derezhaid acted as if he were somewhere else altogether. 'You think that I am the one to ask this concession from her. You think that I will not dare lose face before you by admitting that I cannot make her do what I wish, thus I will close my mouth and cease to criticise you for having failed to find out her falsehoods until they are all dead herrings. Yes?'

'My intelligencers cannot find out events before they take place, lady,' said S'Thiraidi.

'But you come to me with news of events months old. No

48

doubt she has burnt every paper which confirms the receipt of these monies. Think you she shares her politics with me as easily as she shares my bed?'

'Lady, I would not dare to presume upon the details of your private life!'

'Then do not do so. I see no value in challenging her over old graves. Instead let us consider how we shall avoid these failings in the future.'

Siriane came back into the tent and stood there looking full of news. 'Yes?' said Ylureen.

'Lady, we hear that Lord Polem's children have arrived. It seems that there is a great uprising to the north — all the peasants have thrown off their masters — and they have fled away here for safety. But lady, there are fourteen of them as well as the oldest, and two more who are children of the eldest himself, and all out of different mothers! Yet Polem has brought them all to his line! Will you credit it?'

'How many? Fourteen?'

'Sixteen of them by Lord Polem, with Master Haldin — he is the second oldest — down to carry-babies even! They have brought the smallest ones in panniers on the backs of mules.'

'And the mothers?'

'There is not a single mother with them, lady. Lord Polem's children, no more.'

'This I must see! Where are they?'

'Just down where my lord of Haramin has her tent, lady.'

Hahhni ran up with Ylureen's mantle. S'Thiraidi's shoulders slackened with relief.

The hubbub surrounding the new arrivals was visible from a distance, a sea of heads and shoulders around a circle of torches blowing out flat in the wind. Ylureen's guards ran ahead, calling out, and cleared a way through for her. She did not see Aleizon Ailix Ayndra at first, but Polem's oldest son was visible at a glance, a juvenile copy of his father, slender and with all his hair. The two of them were standing arm in arm, with Haldin hanging on at their side, in the middle of a whirlpool of children, from youths to a wailing three-year-old. Boys and girls both were dressed in scruffy breeches and patched cloaks; some looked like Polem, some not, there were blond and black

49

and brown among them, and they were all clamouring. Another blonde head ducked round Polem's broad shoulders and forged through the horde toward them; several of the brats clung on to her clothes and were dragged with her as she saluted Ylureen. Ayndra reached up to kiss her on the cheek, but Ylureen was fascinated by the scene and ignored it. 'Astonishing!' she said. 'Are they all . . . how has he done this?'

'You mean, how has he fathered so many? Well, he has been about twenty-five years at it—'

'I knew that your Ailixond had two wives, but Siriane says – sixteen!'

'What do you mean, sixteen? Polem has not any wives at all.' Ayndra looked down at the child she towed on her arm; it was staring up at them with the ingenuous eyes of a baby seal and its face was running with snot.

'You mean he is not married to any of their mothers?'

'No, not a one. Here.' She pulled a large handkerchief from her sleeve and showed the child what it should do with it. It said something to her in babyish Safic. 'Later,' she said in the same language.

'But then how are they his?' cried Ylureen.

Aleizon Ailix Ayndra laughed. 'Why, Ylureen, you know how they are his. The same way as yours is Sabraid's.'

Ylureen automatically put her hand on her stomach. 'But it is not Sabraid's – even were I to die it would not go to him! No. Are the mothers of all these dead? Siriane said they were all out of different mothers.'

'Except for the two of them that are twins, I believe so. Come, we shall have to get them all fed and bedded.' She offered her free arm to Ylureen and they went towards the family group. 'Say that Polem is rich and noble, while the mothers are mostly poor and without honour; is that not a reason why they should let him have the upbringing of the children?'

'Then all these will be noble?'

'No, none; they are all bastards: bastards cannot be noble.'

'But you trace the line through the father. Then they must be noble, are they not?'

'No, as I told you, they're bastards every one.'

'But you proved your nobility when you showed that paper saying your father was Lord, what was it, Lord something or other—'

'It would not have mattered were he named as Lord of Misrule, so long as he married my mother in proper form. I thought always it was an excess of Diamoon's to put Lord Takarem's name on that paper.'

'Chiiska! I shall never see the reasons behind your customs.'

'You find this difficult, Ylureen? I have not yet told them about yours; I know not how I shall ever bring them to understand that Gishiin is the father when you have not seen him for more than a year.' She switched deftly into Safic and addressed Parro. 'Let me introduce to you, Parro, my lady Ylureen, commander of the army Suthine has sent to aid us.'

Parro took Ylureen's hand and greeted her with such grace that it was clear that he had been educated in the best company, whatever his origins. A trio of servants, in tunics of unbleached wool with a black square on chest and back, were rounding up the children. 'My lord, Master Firumin says that the food is ready.'

'Then let us go in and eat it. Parro, I say again, I am astounded that you should all have come safely through such a great distance – and with the countryside in flames as well!'

'That was only round Drimmanë, my lord, where Hasmon's tax collectors had gone. When we came to Thaless we found no trouble there, and Sulakon's officers did not think to ask who we were.'

'And are they treating the people well in Thaless?'

'O no; we heard nothing but complaints, indeed, and whenever we saw a patrol on the highway good men and women told us to hide, saying that they would demand our money be we never so honest.'

'So think you – but you wish to eat. You must come to me next day after we have struck camp and explain to me all this. I am most interested to know what the peasants are doing.'

'But I am very ignorant, my lord – ignorant, and a fool and a weakling! Father left me in charge of Drimmanë, and

51

what have I done but lost it all? I have saved nothing beyond our own bodies!'

'But did you not say that the peasants were marching on the city?'

'It was after we had escaped, we heard that they were going to surround it and murder Hasmon. And we did see many of them marching in armed bands.'

Aleizon Ailix Ayndra rubbed her palms together. 'I think you have not done ill at all, Parro. We shall talk about all this next day. Now let us sup.'

Aleizon Ailix Ayndra, lord of Safi, Governor of Haramin, greets Golaron, lord of Safi, Governor of Lysmal and her honourable ally. Golaron, you will excuse me an I tell you news which you already know; however, it concerns the province of Drimmanë, a region which until now we have had no reason to concern ourselves with, so I think that you may find this novel. You know that Polem left Drimmanë in the hands of his eldest son Parro and departed last summer to join me in the Land-beyond-the-Mountains. Sulakon being informed of this, he sent Hasmon to seize the territory and restore it to the allegiance of Safi. Since Polem had left Parro no arms, Hasmon was able to march in peacefully, but at his back came all the hounds of debt to whom Sulakon owes money, determined to appropriate the fruits of the new lands. They applied threats to all and sundry, collected several years' taxes in one and engaged in all kinds of extortion beside. In a few months they had provoked the people to the point of armed resistance. Polem's family, whom he had left behind, were placed under threat of imprisonment an they did not quell the rising, but the people were already beyond all command. Parro gathered together his half-siblings and escaped from the city, having just now joined us on the road to Yahloish. As he left he saw many bands of peasants, armed with sticks, scythes, billhooks and the few proper weapons they could summon, marching on the city with the intention of putting Hasmon to death. This was at the end of Sixth Month. Since then merchants coming out of Thaless have told us that Drimmanë is besieged and the entire province in disorder; by now the city has most likely fallen, but we have been able to *get no news, in itself a sign that all authority in that region has collapsed. Sulakon's men are out in force in Thaless, fearing that the disorder will soon spread to that province, if not to Safi itself; all these regions have groaned under the yoke of his taxation for years, and the people hate the Regency on which they blame all their ills. As I write I am at most two sixdays from Yahloish and will make all speed to arrive there. I hope that we will then unite our forces and proceed to Kemmyss, where we can better study the situation. I think this uprising the best thing we could have hoped to befall us. I know not who leads it, or if it have any leaders at all, but clearly they as much as we wish to see Sulakon removed and a more equitable government in his place. I am sure that this popular resentment can be turned to our account. I shall be most gratified an you know any more concerning it. I await with eagerness our meeting in Yahloish. Given in my own hand, the eleventh day of Eighth Month, in the four hundred and seventy-third year of the city.*

Late winter in the Timerill was as warm as a cool northern summer. The hills flowered before the heat of year's end came to dry them up; the nights were long and liquid under purple skies. The camp followers multiplied now that it was possible to sleep in a blanket among the sprouting grass; the army was more sprawling and noisy every day. The S'Thurrulans pitched tents in a compact huddle in the middle of the Haraminharn column, with Ylureen's double striped tent in the middle of it. Some days they went to the trouble of putting up her giant pavilion in its place, even though they would have to disassemble the great thing to move off next morning; on those nights their camp throbbed with the beat of multiple drums and the sound of women's voices, and Derezhaid and the rest of their men hung around on the outskirts or went to carouse with foreign companions, while it seemed that even the poorest women among their camp followers went to the festival. Daior-deor would see them all coming and going in the course of his patrols. He asked Getaleen why they had this new custom of dancing every eight days, and why the men did not go to it.

'Issa chadas'thua matter,' she said. 'The men are on the

outside of chadas'thua; they do not go. Also I, I have very little chadas'thua, as you see; I do not go presently. Come the full moon I shall go.'

'But we have only just passed the full moon.'

'O no! Issn' that moon. Weer on' in the small moon now. Af'er half moon more go, and af'er the full moon all, even I. The eight days, you see, iss five time the one moon, but the sky moon. We have the mother moon for the dances.'

'The dances are for children?' Daior-deor found no illumination in her remarks.

'O, yes, yes. Thass why the men don' go. Is my lord of Haramin tell you about it?' Getaleen looked suspicious.

'I know that she attends,' said Daior-deor, 'but she says nothing of what you do there; I wondered an you could tell me.'

For some reason Getaleen looked affronted at this. 'Sir! Issa godly thing, drum dances; no part of the men in it. Even I don' go, on'y in the full moon. Your lord of Haramin go for Lady Ylureen, she's no chadas'thuata, no! I hear she do the knife dance. Ha! Inna full moon, then she see the knife dance.' One of her archers clapped his hands outside, and she called him in the tent and they chattered in their own tongue. Getaleen looked over her shoulder to tell Daior-deor, 'An' you aren' ask more question the dances, sir, yes?' and went out. The man sat down in her place, but he had no more than a dozen words of market Safic. Daior-deor excused himself and went to inspect the guard patrols, until Coaran came to take the next watch. There were lights and music in Selanor's tent, and, when he looked in, half a dozen of them with flasks of firewater. He tried to ask Selanor, since he spent so much time with their allies, if he knew what *chadas'thua* was, but when he explained that it was to do with the drum dances, Selanor brushed the enquiry aside. 'You were better to talk to the men, Captain; Ikarrange told me that the women have a religion of their own, and men are not permitted to know of it. In truth the men do know, but they dare not spy upon the women's ceremonies all the same, for if the women catch them they will cut them; Ikarrange pointed out to me a man who had suffered it. Better you do not ask their women about it.'

'But Getaleen answered me; though I understood not a

54

word. Something about the full moon. Is it moon worship, perhaps?'

'More likely Captain Getaleen was making mock of your ignorance in a secret way. I have noted that they are fond on that; have another drink, Daior, and sing a Thaless song for the harpist. I am sick of his weary tunes.'

'Is Lady Ylureen going to bear a child?'

'What?'

Daior-deor repeated his question.

'What do you think?' said Selanor.

'Well, I would say . . . on a woman like my lady, it does not show for a while.'

'Save to those who have eyes to see.' Selanor filled both their cups to overflowing. 'But until it become plain to all, it is a sensitive matter. Until then you were better to talk about the full moon, like our friend Getaleen. Your health!' He tossed the liquor down his throat in one gulp and reached for more, before addressing the men with flute and flattanharp. 'In the mode of Thaless. Captain Daior-deor is going to sing us a song.'

'Has it a chorus? Teach us the chorus.'

'It is in Thaless dialect.'

'I come from Thaless,' said one of the drinkers, a phalanx captain.

'Do you so? I never knew we were countrymen! Where is your home?'

When he next went outside, the stars showed that it was past midnight. Two had drunk themselves sick and left, but Selanor might have been drinking water for all the difference it seemed to make to him; no doubt he had learnt to drink firewater from the many nights he had spent with Lord Faracaln. The other three were riotous. 'Ay! Let us send out for some food. A spiced pasty. No, a tub of pork crackling . . .'

They were arguing over what to have when Aleizon Ailix Ayndra walked in. 'Drunken animals!' she said. Selanor and she made faces at one another. Two of the drunkards tried to bow and the third fell over. She giggled. 'O, do not stand on ceremony, an you can stand at all! Selanor, have you a seat for me, and a little cup of chabe before I go to bed? Carry on, gentlemen, I have been enjoying your music

55

and singing from a distance. Daior-deor! I hear that you were asking about the drum dances.'

'News travels fast, my lord.'

'So it does.' She accepted a steaming bowl of chabe from Selanor's servant. 'Will you have some of this? People say that it moderates the effects of drunkenness. I hope that Getaleen illuminated you with her answers.'

'Not at all, my lord. She talked about the full moon and *chadas'thua* – whatever that may be; and now Captain Selanor tells me that it is all a secret from men in any case.'

'*Chadas'thua? Chadas'thuata*, that is what they say for a powerful woman in S'Thurrulass. I remember, at first I thought it meant a fat woman who had passed her middle years! *Chadas'thua*, it means . . . truly I do not know what it means in Safic; an I say to you that Ylureen says one can tell by looking at me that I have no *chadas'thua* at all, will you understand it a little?' She supped her hot drink and laughed.

'Getaleen spoke somewhat to that effect,' said Daior-deor.

'Did she, indeed? How envious she is! It is because I am a fighting woman like her. In S'Thurrulass the *chadas'thuata* are not fighting women. And they are all older sisters; while I do not know who my mother's mother was. Who am I to hold power, indeed?' She laughed like a drain; her eyes were so dilated the irises had nearly disappeared.

'You're the best lord in th'ole Empire!' interjected one of the drinkers; the others made a loyal chorus.

'Thank you, thank you!' she said. 'What was it Ailixond used to say – "While such men as you follow me / We never shall defeated be"? But as I speak, Selanor, Guldan came in just now with the hobilars, to say that Golaron is awaiting us already in Yahloish. Let us camp a little way outside the town next day, and then enter the next morning with banners and full state.'

'Like the entry into Suthine,' said Selanor. He was inclined to reminisce at length when drunk; indeed it was the principal index of his intoxication. Daior-deor, having no part in such memories, made his excuses and went to bed.

Golaron had come to Yahloish with his two middle-aged sons, five grown grandsons and three thousand fighting

56

men. He declared that he wished only to see peace restored in the Empire so that he could hand Lysmal to his son Haresond and retire at last. He greeted Casik warmly, with no reference to their former differences, and the latter seemed to have forgotten his rancour for the time being. Aleizon Ailix Ayndra found herself unchallenged as supreme commander of their united forces. She dictated the brief proclamation to which they all appended their seals.

We, lords of Safi, the lords of Haramin, of Yiakarak, of the Land-beyond-the-Mountains, of Cambar, of the Needle's Eye, of Lysmal, of Drimmanë, address Sulakon, lord of Safi and Lord Regent of the New Empire. We declare that you have lost the allegiance of these our provinces; that, furthermore, in those lands which you still claim, the people are in ferment against you and that you hold them in check only by tyrannous measures; that in consequence of this bad government and the decay into which you have brought the Empire, you have forfeited the trust laid upon you by the lords of Safi in Council and thus lost all right to the Regency. We demand that you freely abdicate and surrender to us the keys of Safi-the-city, that a new Lord Regent may be put in your place and unity restored to the Empire. An you do not freely do so, we shall surround the city and exact the keys by force of arms. We further declare that any who take up arms against you or your officers are our allies in the struggle, and that any such rebels who join us in our march to Safi will be welcomed without question. We declare finally that this proclamation will be read out in all the cities of our jurisdictions so that all the people know of our intent. Given this twenty-sixth day of Seventh Month in the four hundred and seventy-third year of the city.

'Should it not have the place where we are on it?' asked Haresond.

'Why tell him that? Let him find it out for himself.'

'Our ally, Lady Ylureen,' Golaron said. 'You do not name her here at all.'

'This is a matter among the lords of Safi. I have contracted a private alliance with Ylureen.' Ayndra allowed herself a faint smirk as she went on. 'When we are in Safi, then we shall be able to contract a public alliance between the King in Safi and the King and Queen in Suthine. But presently this is no matter for Ylureen; therefore her name is omitted.'

'Hmmm,' rumbled Golaron; he said no more.

Half a troop of cavalry and a rag-tag and bob-tail of soldiers, clerks and money lenders on whatever poor mounts they had been able to procure were all of Hasmon's forces that escaped the sack of Drimmanë and survived the journey through the countryside. The stories they brought with them were tales of horror.

'They caught Captain Agriano and made him dance barefoot for them until he dropped – they beat him with whips every time he fell, till he could get up no more; and a band playing all the time, and dancing, men and women both, all drunk – for they'd ransacked all the wineshops, an the keepers did not give them drink for free. And then they stuffed earth in his mouth till he choked, saying that it was for the earth that was all his men had left them to eat. They would have done the same to me, the next day, they were forever telling me so, saying I should dance then to practise. But, gods bless, they were so drunk in the night that I escaped . . .'

'They seized all the money, my lord, and distributed it among themselves – I saw them all fighting over the gold, like animals, in the public square. I found some old clothes in the slaves' quarters, and my parents were country people, sir, I know their manner of speech, so I could slip away in the crowd. That was how I saw what they did to Master Darrin and the sons of Akuz.' It was one of the Akuz family's hired clerks who spoke; he twisted his hat in his hands.

'What did they do?' asked Sulakon. 'I am accustomed to atrocities in war. You need not be afraid of plain speaking.'

'They . . . put them face down over barrels and . . . made women out of them, my lord. Master Darrin was the first, when I came out they were just . . . finishing with him, and making the others ready for it. And readying themselves, my lord, opening their clothes and . . . doing things I've never seen the like of, my lord, not even at the harvest festival when people couple in the fields.'

58

'And these were men and women too?' Sulakon's face was stiff with disgust; lines furrowed his cheeks and brow like the tracks of a ploughshare.

'Men. All men, my lord. I think, even a peasant woman would shun such, such grossness.'

'But they did put them to death?'

'I saw them cut Darrin's throat, my lord. I did not stay to see what they did to the others. I think they slaughtered them too.'

Parhannon said, 'I thank the gods that Hasmon died defending the gate. Shumar knows what end he would have come to else.'

'And what of Lord Polem's bastard, and his brothers and sisters? When last we heard from Hasmon, he said that he held them under threat of imprisonment an they would not tell the people to obey him.'

'It was he that caused it,' said one of the cavalry captains.

'Indeed, my lord, for all of them escaped under our noses not a twelveday before the peasants were under our walls. And then I heard some of them saying that Lord Parro – so they called him, I know he is no more lord than a barrow-boy – said they need not pay their taxes an they would not. That was before they came at us armed; I thought naught of it at the time.'

'Indeed, my lord, without a doubt he had forewarning; he must have been sending them messages all the while.'

'Then where is he?' Sulakon had got up and started to pace around the room, tapping one hand on his chin. 'He is with them now, their leader?'

'I could not say, sir. An he was with them when they sacked the city, he kept himself secret.'

'He ran off with the whole bastard mob of them, what, twenty of them or more, and some of his own as well – little children, most of them.'

'You did not see any sign of them as you came here?'

'No, my lord, nothing.'

Sulakon commended them for their courage and fortitude in misfortune, and sent them away to where a meal had been prepared for them. He sat down at his desk and rested his head in his hands. 'And the witch already at the borders of Lysmal.'

'You cannot withdraw Cahilar from the frontier of Thaless,' said Parhannon. 'With this news, it is clear that his vigilance there is a thousand times more needful than we thought it was.'

'I know; yet you have seen the report which says that the witch intends to take Kemmyss, and that Golaron has offered her his aid.'

'Kemmyss is neutral ground,' Parhannon said hopefully, but Sulakon shook his head. 'She has no respect for such agreements.'

'Let us offer a reward for this Parro. Fifty gold sols for his head.'

'We were better to spend the money on mercenaries to defend our frontier. Would that I knew how far this damnable uprising has spread. I should never have allowed these bloodsuckers of merchants to go with Hasmon and collect their debts themselves. They have no knowledge of statecraft; all they think of is how best to line their pockets in the shortest time, and be hanged what may follow. The fate of our people is terrible, yet I knew that they were treating the peasants unfairly; I might have known that some such as this would follow.' He was pulling a quill pen to pieces as he spoke. 'Do not castigate yourself so,' said Parhannon. 'You are not a god, to know the future. At least those two brothers Akuz are dead – were they not our largest creditors?'

'Yes, but their father still lives, and now I have lost him his heirs as well as the best part of his funds.' Sulakon's hair spilled over his clenched hands like ashes. Parhannon stood by the window, silent. Flowers had been planted in stone troughs round the raised pool in the middle of the court-yard, rambling extravagantly over the tired stone; the air smelt of rain. 'An you want a commander to go into the field against the witch, I shall be glad to do it,' Parhannon said.

'I would do it myself. It was my folly, that I did not cut her head off when it was in my power to do so.'

'But an you leave here one moment, Sumakas will be out to hand the lock, stock and barrel over to the witch,' said Parhannon.

'But you are our admiral, Parhannon; the witch will bring her fleet up. It was in the same report that we had from

Caoni, that the harbour there was full already of ships from Suthine. You cannot leave. We have Cahilar in the field already, and I can send Ellakon if need be; beside, our officers– ' There was a triple knock on the door. 'Enter,' he called.

The door swung open and a sulky child was propelled into the room. A veiled woman showed herself briefly behind him. 'My lord Parakison, my lord, come for his lesson.' The door slammed behind her before Sulakon had a chance to thank her. Parakison was dressed in an immaculate blue woollen tunic and a shirt with carefully gauffered frills, his hair brushed to frame his heart-shaped face. He stood with his arms folded and his lip curled until it practically touched his nose. 'What are you going to teach me this day?' he said.

'Good day, Parakison,' Sulakon rose and offered his hand across his littered desk.

Parakison began to pick his nose. 'Gran'ma says you've lost Drimmanë to the rebels. They came from there just now.' He examined what he had found on the end of his finger and flicked it away. 'Where is Drimmanë? I never heard about it before now.'

'Parakison, you should greet your uncle when he welcomes you,' Parhannon said.

'I said, good day, Parakison.' Sulakon did not offer his hand to be kissed a second time.

Parakison gave a brief, correct nod. 'Good day, my lord uncle,' he said, and broke into a winning smile. 'You ought to kiss my hand, truly.'

'Parakison, you are not yet the King; when that day comes, I will defer to you. Until then, you must apply yourself to your books as you are ordered to. At your age your father could read a passage out of any book in the library. At your mother's insistence I have agreed to put aside some of my time in order to drill you in your letters. I am not Master Yarano, nor will I tolerate your tantrums as he did. Do you understand?' He turned to Parhannon. 'Will you excuse me, my lord?'

'Of course. Parakison, I wish you good day, and attend to what your uncle tells you.' Gratefully he closed the door on them.

'But is he here with her, the father of this child?'

'His name is Sabraid, he is one of her servants – but as I say, he is not the father as they understand it. Lord Gishiin is the father, but he is away in Suthine.'

'But he accepts the present state of affairs?'

'I am sure he will be delighted with it,' said Aleizon Ailix Ayndra in a tired whine. Golaron went on shaking his head. She flicked one hand in exasperation. 'As I have told you: all the children of a married woman are her husband's children, and that is an end of it.'

'Nevertheless, I– '

'So you may well consider it whoredom; but Golaron, there is naught we can do about it, so you may as well accept things as they are.'

'Lady Ylureen will of course have to retire from public life for the time being,' Casik said.

'No, why should she?'

'Why, because in a little while – well, you will excuse me, my lord, if I say that it is already – but in a little while it will be very evident.'

'So?' retorted Ayndra.

Daior-deor got up and edged quietly towards the door. Casik continued to protest. 'Frankly, my lord, no lady appears in public in such a condition. And besides – in an armed camp?'

'What about the camp women? You may see them going about big-bellied every time you set foot in the market.'

'But they are all whores– ' Casik said without thinking, and then stopped. Daior-deor closed the door as softly as possible against the storm which was about to break. He heard Ayndra exclaim in a voice like a knife, 'Will you say that again?'

Haldin was loitering in the courtyard outside. 'Daior-deor. Are you on duty? No? Let us go into town then.'

'Certainly. Where shall we go? Let us go to the Sea Serpent.'

The dusty streets of Kemmyss were seething with people, three times as many as in its best days as a mercenaries' mart; the taverns and hotshops had put tables outside for the overflowing custom, and street-stalls choked every alleyway. They found free seats on the end of a bench under a blue awning, painted with a giant and ferocious serpent raising its fanged mouth above triangular waves. A man with the creased face of one who had spent most of his life working in the fields slapped down two tankards of cheap wine and insisted that they pay before tasting. 'The last time I came here, it was with Sassafrange,' said Daior-deor. 'Someone started mocking his nose, and he threw a jug at them . . . I think it was when you and my lord were spying on us.'

'I remember it well.'

'And I . . . I hope we do not stay in this town too long. I remember too many things here. I should rather leave.'

'But we shall be going very soon, as soon as they have made sure that everyone has a full set of weapons.'

'That will take long enough. I could almost hope that we run into battle very soon; may be that it would put an end to all these quarrels.'

'My father says that Lord Ayndra is not very happy about it.'

'About what? God's teeth, she provokes half of it.'

'About Lady Ylureen.'

'I heard that you knocked Haresond down over that.'

Haldin shrugged. 'He said my lord was the father of it, that she – well, I told him not to be foul-mouthed, and he suggested . . . I punched him in the mouth. Father said that he dared not complain to Golaron that I beat him, for the shame of being beaten by a bastard young enough to be his son. But he says that my lord asked Lady Ylureen to do away with it, before it came to anything – after all, if Lady Ylureen has a child while she . . .'

'But they still keep company,' said Daior-deor.

'Yes, they do.'

'I have never spoken of these things with her. As gods are my witnesses, it was months before I suspected, fool that I am!' He laughed. 'Even now I would not dare open it with her.'

'No more would I, but she has been friends with my father for years and years.'

'But she denied him the troops he wanted to go to Drimmanë.'

'And very right she was!' said Haldin. 'What would it

serve, to take an army into Drimmanë? The rebels are on our side, they have driven out Sulakon's governor. Better we should go into Safi and recover our lands there. You know that father has seven different estates in Safi-the-land? When we went to Drimmanë Sulakon declared that we were rebels and seized all of them, save Samala that we rented to Lord Arpalond. I was born on our estate of Turu.'

'Will you inherit it?'

Haldin frowned. 'In law bastards cannot inherit land. I may inherit moveable goods, but the land is the family property.'

'But surely your father could make a will to gift it to you in spite of that.'

'That is what I hope,' said Haldin. 'Except that he will always favour Parro. I think it is because Parro favours him so greatly, while I favour my mother. But then Parro is no more legitimate than I am, and the estates are entailed to the lordship. Surely it must be possible to render us legitimate in the eyes of the law. I hope that he will see my prowess in this campaign and recognise that I should be his heir. I would not want all the patrimony, after all, I would be happy to receive Turu. Sometimes I curse him that he did not marry my mother before he got me. Anyone who likes may call me a bastard and I cannot stand up to them.'

'But your father is one of the highest nobles in Safi, is he not? I am told that there is hardly a lineage in the land as rich as he.'

'We have no riches now. Sulakon has taken them all.' Haldin buried his nose in his tankard. 'This is a dismal tavern,' said Daior-deor. 'Drink up, and let us go some-where more cheerful.'

The army wound like a river of dust into the valleys of Thaless. Each contingent marched under its own banners: red with a black spiral or a gold circle, white with blue waves, plain black, blue with the snarling gold head of a mountain cat, horsehair and skulls and coloured streamers on poles. Its outriders scattered through the countryside, proclaiming the end of Sulakon's rule and their goodwill towards the people; they did not even ask for taxes, but offered payment in coin in return for food and horses, although they were also happy to accept all manner of gifts from the frightened inhabitants of the towns. Fear grew as rumours filtered from the north: there had been a pitched battle in Jussi between Lord Cahilar's troops and bands of rebels; Cahilar had been driven back to the fortress of Mirries on the upper reaches of the Safi river; the rebels had surrounded Jussi town, set fire to the houses, and killed all the townspeople who did not join their forces. In many parts people were so frightened that they had not finished the spring planting, preferring to retire to some walled settlement and hoard the seed-corn for sale on a market driven wild by speculation and terror of the witch's army: they might come with peace in their mouths, but in Thaless people still remembered old Lord Parakison's wars twenty-five years ago: 'Trust a snake before a Safin,' they said to each other. Aleizon Ailix Ayndra told people everywhere she went that they should go on with their lives without fear, else they would be starving next winter; they listened, but however often she declared that Sulakon would be deposed, she still had to fight him. Those who tilled the land to feed themselves had gone ahead and planted anyway; on some of the deserted estates they had approved the opportunity to plant the landlords' fields as well. For the time being the lords did not concern themselves with such matters. On the midday of Eighth Month they met with rebels for the first time.

They stood in the middle of the road carrying green branches and weapons both; they did not retreat as the vanguard of the enormous cavalcade rolled down the broad hillside toward them. There were perhaps fifteen on horseback and another fifty surrounding them with improvised pikes. The cavalry of the vanguard surrounded them; they turned their pikes to all sides, but made not a sound. Captain Tobin pushed his horse to the front. 'Who are you? Who is your leader?'

'You are the lords who fight against Lord Sulakon,' said one horseman, in thick back-country Safic. Another went on: 'We come to lead you against his soldiers. We know where they are, we take you there.'

'Put your weapons down, and I shall take you to the lords,' Tobin said.

'We keep our weapons.'

'We'll not use them save in self-defence.'

'You'll not lay down your arms to take us there, will you, sir?'

The man who had spoken first told them to carry the pikes reversed. Tobin ordered his second to continue along the road, and detailed half the troop to act as escort for the visitors. He sent one of his message-riders off to fetch Lord Ayndra directly. They had hardly marshalled the rebels to wait at the side of the road, the cynosure of the advancing battalions, before she was on them, clinging to the reins of her lathered horse and hotly pursued by Daior-deor. 'My brothers! Where have you come from? Were you at Jussi?' She dismounted, thrust the reins at one of Tobin's men, and walked into the middle of the rebel group, offering her hand to them one after the other. In a few moments they were all talking at once. 'We were at Jussi – from Mirries – all the way from Drimmanë– '

'Daior-deor! Call Polem over here.'

'Lord Polem! Lord Polem, is he with you?'

'Yes, of course, where did you think he was? And Parro and all the rest of them. But tell me about Mirries – and Tobin, for gods' sake keep them marching on! This is not a travelling circus, to stop for every little spectacle.'

'Of course, my lord – and the other lords, will you have them informed as well?'

'They will be informed very shortly. Came you by your own notion from Mirries?'

'We chose to come, but Hircan sent us.'

'Hircan and Nain it was both.'

'All the people sent us,' declared a third.

'But you want us to go with you to Mirries.'

'Aye, sir, for it's a great fortress and we can do nothing with it, while you – do you not have machines, like Lord Ailixond used to?'

'O, machines, and soldiers, and every thing needful for an assault, no matter how strong the fortress.'

'Are you to siege Safi then, sir?'

'Very likely.'

As more and more of the army rolled into view, the rebels were distracted, staring at the panorama. They looked at

Aleizon Ailix Ayndra too, her black clothes like one bereaved, her flowing hair like an unmarried girl, her lined face and her radiant eyes. 'Sir,' said one, 'who commands all these? Whose men are they?'

She was tapping her thumbnail against her teeth; she stopped with a bright smile. 'Why, mine I suppose. Are they not splendid?'

'Yours, sir? My lord?'

'Indeed!' She put her hand on her heart and made a half bow. 'Lord Aleizon Ailix Ayndra, of Safi and Haramin, at your service. Most definitely at your service!' Now they were all staring at her. 'People call me the witch of Haramin, but it is a lie,' she said, 'I am no more a witch than you are. Do I look like a witch?'

'Who knows what a witch looks like?' responded the spokesman. He was interrupted by the shouts of those from Drimmanë, as Polem and Parro came galloping up.

Ayndra went back to Tarap, and one of the rebels made a stirrup of his hands to aid her in mounting without she even asked him. He said his name was Kereli; he was dressed like a peasant, but did not speak like one. She urged Tarap to the head of the group. 'Let us join the march, my brothers, and we shall talk.'

High Thaless, the eastern part of the country, was a stony, mountainous land; Low Thaless, to the west toward Safi, was where the famous vines grew, in the heart of the nation. There were only three roads fit for wheeled traffic going up into the high country and Mirries controlled the northernmost, with its great fort built by the kings of Thaless. It was High Thaless that was in revolt; Cahilar, meeting resistance that he never expected in Drimmanë, had been forced to retreat to the edge of the lowlands, from where it was easy passage all the way to Safi. The rebels had surrounded him there, and he could go neither forward nor back, but they had no means of reducing the fortress, with its wells and enormous storerooms, unless it were by lengthy siege and starvation; and every day they waited saw more of their forces slipping away back to their homes and needful occupations. In a little while they would not even have been able to maintain the blockade; but then the flags of the allied army appeared on the southeastern skyline. Within a day the entire valley was choked with their camps. Aleizon Ailix Ayndra sent heralds to call for a parley, but no one inside the fortress would respond. She set the archers of S'Thurrulass to snipe at any of the besieged who showed themselves, and retired to consult with her officers and allies.

'As soon as we have this place it will be a straight road to Safi. We shall be there before year's end even!'

'I have had letters from my agents in Caoni,' said Ylureen. 'They have heard that everyone in Safi expects a siege, and your brother has forbidden anyone to go outside of the city for more than one stretch of daylight. All the merchants are laying up stocks against the crisis, and the price of corn is three times what it was a month ago. Sulakon wishes even to prevent merchant ships leaving the city, for fear that they will never return, or that we will shortly blockade him with our fleet and they will be apprehended by it.' She reached out to offer a fuming smokestick to Aleizon Ailix Ayndra, who asked, 'And how did they learn this, in Caoni, then?'

'From the few Safic ships which have braved the Regent's displeasure in search of profit.'

'You mean that none of Pilith's ships have put into Safi, even with the price of corn shooting up faster than the new wheat in the fields?' Ayndra dragged hard and exhaled a long blue plume of smoke.

'How could they?' said Ylureen. 'We are enemies; for sure your brother recognises no truce of trade.'

Ayndra looked at her with slitted eyes. She put her hand on the alabaster jar next to the chabe stove. 'Is the oil warm yet?'

'Shall I rub you with it?'

'Do you wish to?'

'Do you wish me to?'

'Indeed, I would be enchanted an you rubbed me with it.'

'Very well then. Only let me smoke this first. God bless, this is very fine smoke, Ylureen.'

'New come from South Lysmal, from Caoni with the letters. I will send you half a pound of it.' Ylureen signed to Hahhni, who laid a straw pallet on the floor by the stove and spread clean towels over it. Ylureen took off her gown and removed the linen band which supported her breasts. Underneath she wore a long, full shift of the finest semi-transparent linen, closed down the middle by gold clasps, which she unfastened before lying down. Hahhni slid a cushion underneath her head and returned to her endless task of rolling up smokesticks. Aleizon Ailix Ayndra rolled her shirt sleeves above her elbows and poured the warm sweet oil into the palm of her hand. She began to rub it in slow circles over Ylureen's body.

'Do you recall those machines which Sandar used against us at Purrllum? I managed to salvage one of them. I was thinking just this morning, what if we were to bring that up before the gates?'

'You did not see those machines in action. Their rate of fire is inferior to that of your catapults, and one of them misfired and was riven in half and all the men tending it died. I do not think they are of much use.'

'No, but they are rather impressive.'

'Now, the idea that S'Thiraidi had, of mixing powderfire with nails and potshards; there was a fine idea.'

'You think so?'

Ylureen opened her eyes, hearing a tone of surprise. 'Sometimes you puzzle me,' Ayndra said. 'You condemn us barbarians because we are always fighting, and have such a taste for war; but when you devise weapons, you conceive articles of a barbarity our swords and pikes could never achieve.'

'What do you mean, barbarity?'

'I met some of the Purrllese who had been wounded by those boxes with nails in.'

'The whole notion of throwing boxes with catapults was your idea in original, was it not?'

'Yes. But I never put nails in them,' Ayndra said; her hands continued their rhythmic motion. 'I want a quick end to this siege.'

'Why do they not capitulate? Surely they see already that there is no hope for them.'

'They see no hope an they capitulate. I am sure they believe that they will all be murdered, just as Hasmon's people in Drimmanë were. I never realised that the people

69

were held in such fear; I suppose I have never lived in a settled country, I know only cities and ports and crude barbarians. Daior-deor was telling me a passel of stories of uprisings. He says that the panic in Safi is at least as much due to them as it is to fear of us and our army – you see, an lords fight, they kill one another and in the end one is victorious and they leave the people much as they were; but an these rebels enter a city, who knows what they will do? And then, as if that were not enough, you have you and I and all our notorious court of sorceresses waiting to drink their blood. Their only hope is that Sulakon send an army to relieve them.'

'And will he?'

Aleizon Ailix Ayndra burst out laughing for reply. 'We may expect to meet him in the field, perhaps, when we are in Safi-the-land; but not before. I suspect that he could not presently field an army that would not desert as soon as it travelled thirty miles outside the city. Have not your ships going to Safi told you so?'

Ylureen said nothing, as though the massage had sent her into a stupor.

'I confess it was very clever of you to hire Lysmalish crews, so that only the captains and the helmsmen came from S'Thurrulass, and they staying on board all the time that the ship was in harbour; and Golaron's portmaster was happy to accept gifts to allow Pilith ships to sail under Lysmalish colours. I do not think Golaron knew of it either.'

'And will you tell him?'

'O, of course not! They would all think it utter treachery, to trade with our worst enemy, indeed to sell him supplies which will better able him to withstand our siege.' She giggled. 'It would be more proper to blockade him now, so that they would be half starved by the time we came there – indeed, I would protest at your treachery, an I were not impressed more by your cleverness.' A faint smile formed on Ylureen's sleeping face. 'I mean– !' said Aleizon Ailix Ayndra, 'to come up on one side part of a great army, whose formation you have materially assisted, whose presence creates panic and speculation – and then, on the other side, to trade under false colours in every kind of specu-

70

lative good and reap colossal profits!' She laughed uproariously.

Ylureen opened her eyes again. 'Are you angry?'

'No! I am not angry. Will you provide ships to take off refugees when we are at the gates? Perhaps you should give a ship a Safic flag and offer it to take Sulakon away!'

'Besides, we have been selling corn, which the people need to eat, so they do not suffer; and we never planned to starve them—'

'Corn at treble and quadruple its common price, which will starve the poor as effectively as any blockade could. Ylureen, do not pretend to be philanthropic when you are only pursuing your own advantage.'

'I could say the same to you!'

'Ah, but it is only politicking, when I pretend to that; when have I ever attempted to convince you that I was philanthropic? Hahhni, have you any more of that excellent smoke?' She sucked greedily on it when it came, squatting on her haunches.

Ylureen lifted herself up on one elbow and reached out to stroke her cheek. 'You look like a little frog.'

Aleizon Ailix Ayndra snorted; but she caught hold of Ylureen's hand and held it. 'We shall have to send the fleet in sooner or later,' she said. 'But I will make sure that all your ships have time to escape.'

The army councils met in the open air because there was no tent big enough to hold them all: Aleizon Ailix Ayndra in the middle on her black horse, the other lords and the high officers mounted beside her, the rebel leaders on horseback, and a great indiscriminate mass of people on foot. Getaleen appeared as the military representative of S'Thurrulass, with S'Thiraidi at her back; as the mood of the gathering grew more elevated so they withdrew to the back of the group of dignitaries, and when the rebels started to charge round and round in a circle cheering and cracking whips they pushed their way out of the crowd and were gone. Ayndra gave up trying to shout above the uproar and beckoned to Golaron to bring his horse up beside her; she leant over and yelled in his ear. 'Come with me now, to the walls. You heard what I said about a safe-conduct? Let us

71

go and cry it to Cahilar now, ourselves. After that it will have to be the general assault – is your herald here?'

It was half an hour before she had fielded all those who would make demands on her, found Haldin and the rest of her entourage, unfurled a couple of green banners and they could make their way up to the wall. They approached slowly until they came within the shot of a short Safic bow, and Golaron's trumpeters blew the Grand Army fanfare. Cothir his herald inflated his iron lungs. 'Cahilar, lord of Safi! The lords of Lysmal and Haramin beg your audience! Come forth and speak to us in peace!' They all held up their right hands to show that they carried no weapons, and he repeated the call three or four times. A red flag with Sulakon's gold emblem of the sacred flame appeared on the battlements and came towards them. The whoops of the rioters could be heard still. Half a dozen men armed like Silver Shields poked their heads over the wall and a heavy-featured man in an ornate silver collar stepped into the embrasure. 'What do you want of me?'

Aleizon Ailix Ayndra urged Tarap closer to the wall. 'Cahilar! We come to announce that we shall shortly begin the assault on your fortress. We do not wish to slaughter innocent people in the attack; we offer a safe-conduct to all the women, the children, and those who cannot and will not fight. An you open the gates and let them go out, we will receive them and let them go without molestation to whatever destination they choose. They may bring what goods they can carry, but an we find any of them with weapons they will be killed as though they were one of your army. Will you accept this offer?'

Cahilar sneered. 'And what guarantees do you offer, that we let our families go out into the arms of yonder horde of animals?' He gestured contemptuously in the direction of the rebel assembly.

'We offer our word as lords of Safi,' rumbled Golaron.

'You admit, then, that you have caused the people to rise up against their masters and threaten the ruin of the whole country?'

'We have not caused them to rise up!' Ayndra shouted. 'By the abuse and unwisdom of your Lord Regent's governors were they driven into revolt! Every day they cry for

72

your blood. We offer you this promise now so that the sack of Mirries is not turned into a bloody massacre. I cannot promise for the safety of you and your men, even were you to lay down your arms, but I can promise that they will not harm those who have never harmed them – unless they enter the fortress in full fury of battle.'

'The way is still open for you to capitulate,' Golaron said.

'Capitulate? To an old man and a whore at the head of a mob of barbarians?'

Ayndra looked up at him and raised her arm to indicate the camp behind her. 'A mob it may be; yet it is the wind that will blow your house down.'

Cahilar laughed. 'Is it the wind? Then it is you who will reap the whirlwind.'

She gave her lopsided smile and said clearly, 'It was the rebels that brought me here, not I who ordered them; who is reaped and who the reaper, we shall see. But I am not the reaper of those who take no part in the quarrel. I can answer for my own people, but there are many who have come here freely and are under no order at all. I cannot exclude them from the fight, nor can I restrain their actions. I can hold off the assault until first light next morning. If you decide to open the gates, have your trumpeters give the lights-out – you know it? As they did in the Grand Army.'

'I know it,' said Cahilar.

She saluted him with her raised hand and turned to leave. Cahilar leant forward. 'Golaron! Are you of the witch's party now? I knew that bed-presser Polem had run to her, but . . .'

'An you are wise, brother, you will open the gates. The gods' blessing go with you and with all of us. Good day.' Golaron touched his horse's side with his spurs and it sprang after Tarap. The people who had gathered around Cahilar set up a hum of talk, while he, as if oblivious, watched the lords of Lysmal and Haramin ride away.

The gates of the fortress opened at midnight to let out more than four hundred people, most of them terrified by the flaring torches and the noise and smell of the Haraminharn cavalry flanking them on either side, and obsessively concerned for the safety of the chattels they carried. At the edge

73

of the camp a detachment of women of S'Thurrulass waited, and, separating the women from the men, took them to Ylureen's great tent where it appeared that the dance had been hurriedly ended. The men had to camp round braziers in the middle of the Haraminharn encampment. Even the smallest boy-children had been left with them, except for those that were still nursing. They wailed throughout the night, until with the dawn the noise of the assault took over. Their guards changed watch, but either they did not understand Safic or they had no desire to talk; bands of armed men on foot or horseback rushed through the camp and strange thunders came from the direction of the fortress, carried in rags of bitter smoke on the wind. Later in the day some women in northern-style headclothes came with steaming tubs of barley porridge and strips of dried meat; a few parties of smoke-blackened, bloodstained fighters limped past, but the guards brought wicker screens to keep the wind off and shut off the prisoners' view. As night fell, distant, riotous music and the beating of drums replaced the strange thunders, and they knew that Lord Cahilar's garrison had not held out. They prepared to spend a second night in the open.

In the morning, a small man with flaming red hair came to them while porridge was being doled out and instructed them to give the clerks following him the names of their female relatives or companions, did they wish to be reunited with them, and then to pack up their baggage and make ready to walk through the rebel camp to the place where they would be released. He returned an hour later on a horse at the head of a detachment of phalanxmen with half-pikes and ordered them to take up the children and march.

The main body of the army was encamped a little way down the valley from Mirries, astraddle the road to Safi and largely out of sight of the fortress. As one walked back towards it, so the number of tents and pavilions decreased and the number of rough bivouacs, straw huts, hutments of branches and rags and windshields made out of hurdles grew. The leaderless rebel army, which had been dissolving, had been bloated by the numerous hangers-on of my lord of Haramin and her companions, and in the few days since they had been settled outside Mirries, malcontents, vagrants, landless peasants and wanderers of every stripe had flocked to its innumerable banners: they came with their bare feet and homespun clothes to stare at the grand-fathers and beardless youths, consumptives and clubfoots and coward remnants of the burgesses of Drimmanë and High Thaless, in such a way that they clutched their few valuables inside their shirts and feared for the moment when the armed escort abandoned them. Then they came in sight of where the fortress used to be, and saw their womenfolk gathered under its blasted walls. A little way up the valley, ranks of funeral pyres were burning, figures running through the smoke and priestly chants resonating from the narrow hillsides. Mirries, which forty hours ago had stood so fine with the close-fitting ashlars of its walls, the hammered iron faces of its gates, the gilded spires of its keep, was a shell. People were still bearing shrouded bodies out between the ruptured shreds of the gates.

One of the old men asked the red-haired officer, 'What are we to do, sir?'

'Will you put us out on the road as we are?'

'We will give you free passage out of our camp,' said Daior-deor. 'We cannot promise you more.'

'But where are we to go? We have lost our homes already.'

'Are they all dead, them that were in the fort?'

'Sir, have mercy on us. We cannot wander the roads as we are. How will we live?'

'You'll live by begging and thieving,' said one of the pikemen, 'same as you did before.'

'Sir, sir, let us come with you, we will serve you however you ask. Only do not cast us out on the roads!'

'I have no authority to take you as servants,' said Daior-deor. 'An you choose to follow our camp, or join with the rebel army, we will not stop you.'

'Go into the market!'

'Find a merchant there, sell yourself as a slave.'

'Free passage to the mines!'

The children were wailing again, milling about in the crowd. Daior-deor ordered the pikemen to marshal the group towards the road into High Thaless. Some of them cried after him, holding out their arms. 'Where are you going? Where are you going?'

'To Safi! To Safi! To Safi we come!' The pikemen made a chant out of it. A good few of the women were missing. 'Where are they? Did they take them?'

'The foreign women, who put us in their tent, they asked for servants.'

'Are they going to Safi?'

'I know not, they were all foreign.'

'But they were good to us.'

'Lacha is there. Let us wait around a little while and go to her. Mayhap the foreign women will take us too.'

'But where will they go? Mayhap they take us to any barbarian land.'

'Why do you care? Where else have we to go?'

The file-leader of the pikemen asked Daior-deor if it were true that the S'Thurrulans had taken on refugees as servants. 'They call it servants,' said Daior-deor, 'But in our tongue we would call them slaves.'

'It was a bloodbath,' said Ylureen.

'I did what I could,' said Aleizon Ailix Ayndra. 'In its way it was a triumph, to overrun a famous fortress with more than two thousand men in it, in the space of a single day.'

'And a triumph also, that you slew them all?'

Ayndra crossed one leg negligently over the other. 'This is war.' She took out a knife and began to trim her nails with it.

'How many did you put an end to yourself?'

'Ylureen. You know I am a murderess. Is it not too late to provoke me with it now? Were they cousins of yours, that you are so incensed?' She tore off a stubborn fragment of nail with her teeth.

'There are clean killings and unclean ones.'

'Look. Most of these "unclean killings" were due to many people who have come to this war to seek revenge. In this there is much brutality, it sickens me: but one does not come to war to be fastidious. And it was a fortress of soldiers that they sacked, not a city full of people.'

'Then what will they do when we come to Safi?'

76

Ayndra frowned. 'I will cross that bridge when I come to it.'

Ylureen knelt down by her chair and put one hand on her knee. 'Aleizon. Will you take these rebels with you when we march?'

Ayndra widened her blue gaze. 'I do not see how I can prevent them, an they will come.'

'I do not think it is wise, what you have done.'

'You mean, to welcome those who have taken up arms against their masters?'

'You have never held land—'

'What do you mean? I have held Haramin—'

'No, no, I do not mean government. Let me speak. I mean that you have never been lord of an estate, you do not know how it stands between the lord and the peasant. An the lord is not there, I tell you, they will not work, they will feed themselves and no more, the markets of the cities will empty. I have heard what they say about your lord Sulakon in Drimmanë, and I understand why they should throw him off. But now you must put Lord Polem back in Drimmanë, and tell everyone to go back to their lands and plant whatever they can, if they have not missed the season of planting altogether. You must not let them march with you into Safi spreading revolt throughout the countryside, else, I tell you, you will have nothing left to govern when you at last capture it. You are releasing forces you do not understand.'

Aleizon Ailix Ayndra looked at her for a while. 'I must take Safi,' she said. 'In a month this whole matter will be decided. I think I can ride the whirlwind until then.'

'I do not doubt it,' said Ylureen. 'It is the time which will follow that concerns me. Polem wants to see the restitution of his estates in Safi; how will he get it an his tenants are every one in arms?'

'The peasantry in Safi are not in revolt,' Ayndra said.

'Not yet,' said Ylureen.

'Ylureen, they sing as they march; have you not heard them? Will you say that they should give up all that for a handful of ashes and return to tilling the soil?'

'What will they find in Safi, beyond a handful of ordure from the city streets? What can you offer them? They are

77

country people, Aleizon, the soil is their life; why do you entice them with false hopes of the city?'

'Who have I enticed with false hopes?' exclaimed Ayndra. 'I promise nothing beyond liberty.'

'That is the false hope,' said Ylureen.

Aleizon Ailix Ayndra raised her eyebrows. She patted Ylureen's hand and lifted it from her thigh as she got up to go. 'You will be here late in the evening?'

'Of course.' The large mirror stood in a wooden stand near the entrance of the tent. Ayndra paused in front of her reflection, tossed her mop of hair over to one side and ran her hands through it; she laughed with pleasure at the gallant image that confronted her, and pranced out of doors.

Sumakas' slavewoman opened the massive door that separated the House of Women from the rest of the palace; she made a sour face when she saw the armed men outside, and blocked the opening with her body. Sulakon asked his escort to go and wait in the courtyard. 'I have come to speak to Lady Setha,' he said. 'Will you permit me to enter?'

The main door gave on an antechamber, lit by glazed skylights and furnished with several couches, chairs and tables; curtained doors in each wall led to the inner rooms. Sulakon did not sit down, but stood in the sunlight pouring down from the roof, holding his helmet under his arm. The slavewoman went behind the curtain without speaking to him. It was a good few moments before another curtain parted and Setha came in, the gilded heels of her sandals clicking on the marble floor. She held her rose-coloured veil across her face until she was next to him, then let it fall as she curtsied. 'My lord husband,' she said musically.

Sulakon took her hand and lifted her to her feet. 'Lady.' He put his helmet down on a little round table and gently embraced her, careful not to crush her against his mailed chest. She propped her hands over his heart and gave him a sad smile. 'You are going now.'

'I must.'

'I not want you to.' She reached up and caressed his rough chin. 'What will happen? I fear!'

'You must not fear.'

'Let another go and command the army. We need you here!'

'Setha, I am the Regent; who should command the army if not I? I will think of you, I will come back. You must stay here and look after Parakison.'

'But the rebels are thousands, they will kill you. Parakison a big boy, he does not need me. Stay with us!'

'I must go. It is my duty.'

Setha ducked her head against him and began to whimper. Sulakon was distressed; he stroked her hair. 'Lady, you must not weep!' Setha looked up, and he bent to kiss her. She opened her mouth and stretched her arms up round his neck. Neither responded to the approaching footsteps till they stopped. Ailissa was standing by the door, a faint sardonic smile on her face. Sulakon immediately adopted his rigid lordly pose. Setha pulled her veil over her face and looked away.

'She is not really weeping,' Ailissa said. 'She only whines; she dare not let tears come, they would spoil her eyepaint.'

Sulakon patted Setha's shoulder and released her. He offered his hand to Ailissa. 'Lady, I have come to say farewell to you before I lead our army out against the rebels!'

Ailissa looked him up and down, took his hand, curtsied and rose again. Her smile spread wider and wider. 'I hope that whatever is best for our Empire befalls us,' she said, and swept out again.

Sulakon turned back to Setha, who exclaimed, 'She is insolent, you should put her away!'

Sulakon took her hand and stroked it between his callused palms. 'You know that I do not visit her any longer. But she has borne me six children, and she has never given me cause to divorce her. It is her jealousy that renders her spiteful. You must not let it touch you.'

'She is all the time with Lady Sumakas, they plot against me and against you also. Why do you not send them both away?'

'Lady, I would an I could. But they have many friends, and they are the mother and sister of Lord Ailixond. There would be an uprising in the city were I to send them away.' Several peremptory raps sounded on the door; the slavewoman had whisked out to open it before Sulakon could. Takarem stood in the doorway, armed just like his father; but whereas Sulakon's face showed the ravages of almost half a century, his son was radiant with the strength of his twenty-one years. 'Father, we are all waiting. Captain Tezin says it is time.'

'I will come directly. Have you spoken to your mother?'

'Yes, I came here to breakfast, and she helped me put my mail on.'

'Very well. My lady, I pray you, do not weep. An you will go to the temple, the High Priest will aid you in prayers and sacrifices for our safety. Until I return.' He bent to kiss her briefly on both cheeks and strode out. Takarem lingered to give her a dirty look and followed his father.

'Deploy into line of battle,' Sulakon said. 'You know the order. Make sure that the phalanx occupy the valley floor and do not flinch, no matter what they see coming. I am going up on the hill so that I can see what they are doing as they advance, but you may call me down at any time.'

The defile of Shili lay a little more than forty miles east of the city, where the broad coastal plain began to climb into rolling hills; the road into north Thaless ran through a narrow valley, seeking always the smoothest route for wagons, before it reached the town of Shili itself. In past centuries this point had often marked the frontier between Safi and Thaless, and several kings had fought battles there. Sulakon had marched his troops there in a day and a half, and then camped across the road while they rested, practised drills and waited for the rebels to come up. When news of the fate of Mirries reached him, he had instituted a requirement of registration for every man between eighteen and fifty in the city; a number now considerably swelled by people flocking inside the walls as the revolt spread towards them. Strict controls had been placed on the sale of corn, flour and bread, in an attempt to curb speculation, and armed guards regulated sales from every bakery in the city; only those who could produce a registration paper for themselves, their father, husband or son, could purchase the stipulated ration. From the beginning of Eighth Month, warships with flags of Suthine and Haramin flying beside the waves of Safi had begun to cruise the coastal waters, driving away or capturing all the merchantmen save a few brave vessels with Lysmalish flags who managed to slip through in the hours of darkness; as soon as they tied up at the quays they were besieged by people wanting food, and had often sold half their cargo off by the bowlful to women and unregistered people before the Port Comptroller's agents reached them with orders to buy up the whole cargo at the official price. The hysteria in the city mounted daily; when Sulakon called for volunteers to go out and face the rebels, he found no shortage of them; and if he had, the threat of withdrawal of rations for the families of those who would not fight was enough to drive many men into the militias. The only thing they lacked was training.

The remnants of the garrisons of Thaless, Sulakon's own standing army and Grand Army veterans recalled for this special service made up four battalions of phalanx; ranked in files ten deep, they were enough to block the flat bottom of the valley where the road ran. Militia companies interspersed with trained infantrymen stood on the wings, reaching round so that the line of battle was a crescent with its extremities reaching up the hillsides. The ground was too rough for cavalry to take up its usual position on the wings; instead they were scattered among scouting parties, outliers ready to harass the advancing enemy, messengers and guards of the camp. The rest of the militia formed a reserve behind the main army, where it was hoped that they would give confidence to the regulars without actually entering the battle, until the rebels had been routed and even the most inept enthusiasts could be sent in pursuit of them. From the bottom of the valley it was impossible to see more than half a mile or so ahead, and the reserve could see nothing beyond the uplifted pikes and banners of their own army. It was almost midday already, and the sun blazed on the polished helmets and the blades of the sarissas. As Sulakon's party climbed the grassy hillside, the vista opened up beyond the confining hills. The first thing they saw of the enemy was the colossal grey-gold dust cloud raised by its tramping feet. 'Shumar! Are they still advancing in column of march?'

'How many of them are there?'

'Can you see where the witch is?'

'In that cluster of banners, that must be her. She rides a black horse.'

'They are spreading out as they come on,' said Sulakon. 'They cannot deploy their full line here in any case; they cannot bring up more than four battalions of phalanx in the valley, even had they so many.'

'I think they have at least so many,' said Ellakon. His horse kept fidgeting, catching its rider's nerves; Sulakon ordered him to go down and review the phalanx. He turned to Takarem and started pointing out various bodies distinguishable in the approaching mass of the enemy, explaining what he thought their intentions were and how he intended to respond to them; Takarem listened with anxious concentration. 'See, they are pausing now to put their sarissas together . . . now they are forming files . . . look, they have horse archers from the Land-beyond-the-Mountains . . . do you see our officers going among the files? They are handing out wine, for the heat, and to give courage for the assault . . .'

'They outnumber us, do they not?' said Takarem.

'They do, and we have known so for a month and more. But remember that they are a passel of barbarians, of twenty nations, and their commanders disunited under the witch. You see how I have chosen the ground so that they cannot make good use of their strength. And recall that our men cannot see what you can.'

'But should we not tell them?'

'What matters now is to preserve their morale. Afterwards they will be the more joyful to discover that they have defeated a force of twice their number and more. Until then, it is better that they know only what they see.'

'Are we to stay up here all the time, then?' Takarem slid back his helmet to mop his sweating forehead; with his hair off his face his resemblance to Ailixond was very marked. 'I wish to do something,' he said, 'you have seen a hundred battles, but I, I cannot sit here and watch—'

'You wish to go and join the outriders? Then go; I will leave it to you to choose which unit you attach yourself to. You may give orders an you see a need for them, but do not contradict the orders of the officers, however contrary your wishes. An you are not seen to respect them, they will lose authority with the men.'

'Thank you, Father.'

'The gods bless and protect you, Takarem.' Sulakon watched his son gallop away, his blue silk parade cloak flying in the warm wind; then he turned his face back to the battlefield. The enemy phalanx had finished ordering their files and were advancing with remarkable regularity, so that the neat blocks moved as one man; drumbeats and shrilling horns accompanied them, a wild music that must be audible down there in the valley. He beckoned to a message-rider. 'Go down and tell the trumpeters to sound the call to arms.'

The valley made a sharp bend before it debouched into the plain of Shili, and though it sloped down from the crest where the Regent's forces were stationed, they could not see any further than the flanks of those last hills; they began to hear the drums long before the first of the forest of sarissas came into view. A narrow gap opened between the two midmost battalions, and a rider on a black horse, followed by two standard bearers with a black flag and a blue and white, shot through it and curvetted back and forth in front of the advancing mass, waving a sword high above her head and shrieking some inflammatory address. Then she gathered speed and came galloping toward Sulakon's line, pulling up a short bowshot away. 'Men of Safi!' she howled. 'Lay down your arms! We bring the rightful government!' She gestured at the waves of Safi fluttering above her head. 'Lay down your arms!' There was a rumble and a rustle in the files, but no one spoke aloud; a disturbance boiled on the right wing, and a rider in a green cloak burst out of it, sword in hand. He rode straight for her; she headed her horse to meet him, and their blades clashed; one spun away like a flying fish above water, and then the witch was spurring her horse furiously for the safety of her own line, which let her pass, closed up and continued to advance. Ellakon dismounted to pick up her sword and rode back to his own side, which cheered mightily; until they were drowned out by a thunderstorm of drumming from the enemy, who began to advance at a pace so fast it was almost a trot, sarissas lowering into the attack position. Trumpets cried on the Regent's side, and his phalanx began to move.

In another few moments the drumming was buried in the clash and grate of the sarissas, the chants of the file leaders, the groans and cries of the combatants. The heavy-armed infantry who flanked the witch's phalanx threw themselves at the militia either side; horse-archers on hairy ponies came tearing up from behind, spreading out over the hillsides that were too rough for the Safic cavalry, swinging round Sulakon's left to spray them with arrows, racing between the phalanx and the reserves and back round to rejoin their own. The drummers ranked at the back of the enemy phalanx were beating themselves into a frenzy, and the two masses of sarissas were completely entangled; Sulakon ordered his messengers to bring up the cavalry from the camp to protect the reserves, who had clearly been thrown into disorder by the passage of the barbarian archers, and himself headed downhill to enter more closely into the fight. He could hear more horns and trumpets as he descended but he believed that it must come out of the hell of dust and screams where the two armies were engaged; the rest of the rebel army was backing up behind their phalanx, unable to bring their force to bear but making it impossible for their men to retreat, even though the Safic phalanx, with the assistance of the slope, was pressing them hard, trying to distress them to the point where they could start to swing the pikes side-to-side and scythe them like the corn. He was behind his own left wing when there were cries of, 'Here they come again!' and another horde of mounted tribesmen came rushing at them. 'After them!' he roared, drew his sword and rammed his spurs into the side of his charger. He hit the first ponyman with such force that he actually knocked him right over; his stallion leapt over the struggling pony and he used his sword on the next. The rest of the Safic cavalry were joining in, while the barbarians turned round, rode in circles, tried to evade them, headed round the back of the reserves to shower them with arrows at the same time as they escaped. When he had time to look he saw that some of the militia had abandoned their places and were running away toward the camp. 'Deserters! Drive them back!'

'My lord! My lord!'

'What is it?'

'Look up there, my lord! Look! They're everywhere!'

They were indeed everywhere, on both sides of the valley, streaming over the skyline, waving all kinds of sticks and farm-tools and weapons, beating on their shields and howling as they came; not a one of them in armour, hardly any with so much as a leather cap, in all kinds of frieze rags and peasant garb, but hundreds and hundreds and thousands of them and noisy as a chorus of devils. Sulakon took in the situation at a glance. 'Reserves! Close up with the phalanx! Durrio! Order the left and right battalions to move back, to form a square – prepare to retreat in good order–'

The rebels were running down the hill now; the militia were gawping at them, some had already dropped their weapons and were holding up their hands, others clustered round their officers crying out for help and advice or had joined their fellows in flight. Sulakon dashed round to the rear. 'Get back! Get back! We must close up with the phalanx, it is our only hope – get back, I say!'

He started beating at deserters with the flat of his sword; some of them clung on to his legs. 'My lord! Save us!'

'Close up with the phalanx, I say – we must form a square– ' And then the rebels were on them, and everything collapsed into chaos. He thought he saw women among them, or was it just the flapping gowns that they wore? Some of the phalanx had tried to disengage, and move backwards, but retreat was a difficult manoeuvre, and if the rear of the battalions was not protected it could not turn into other than a rout; the militia had not been able to form a solid block between the phalanx and the oncoming rebels; he saw a shrieking ruffian stab a phalanxman in the back, then heard a chant and thought for a moment that they had made it after all, but no, it was the enemy who were swinging their pikes now. 'Trumpeter!'

'My lord?'

'Sound the call to save yourselves. Sound it till you have no breath left, and follow me.'

'Lady Sumakas' orders, my lord. No one has gone in or out since we had the news from Shili. You know that the House of Women has its own well, my lord, and who knows what stocks of food Lady Sumakas has laid up in there? She has all the keys and has locked up every door, the windows too, she has locks on all of them. None of us have been able to enter. My wife is in there, my lord, and both our daughters, but I have not been able to speak to them.'

'What? This time her arrogance has passed all limits! I will not be kept from my own family! We shall break the doors down an she will not open up.'

'But it is for fear of the enemy, sir — she invited all the women to take shelter in there—'

'The time for taking shelter is passed. No doubt she wishes to wait in there until the witch has entered the town and then they will all emerge to welcome her. Well, I will not tolerate it! I am still Regent in this city and I demand entrance.' He strode down the corridor that led to the women's rooms; his steward and the rest of his entourage scuttled after. They piled up in front of the great door. 'Give me that.' Sulakon snatched the steward's rod of office and beat upon the door. 'Open up! Open for the Lord Regent!' he cried, in the voice he used to carry above the sound of battle. 'Open up, or I break down the door!'

There were sounds, a rattle of keys, and the door creaked open; the withered face of one of Sumakas' oldest slaves appeared in the crack. When she saw who it was, she nipped through and closed the door again behind her. 'My lord?'

'Summon Lady Setha, Lady Ailissa and Master Parakison here. Tell them that the rebels have overrun Thaless Gate and will shortly be raging throughout the city. I have given leave to all loyal troops to save themselves as best they can. A boat awaits us in the harbour. Let them waste no time packing, but come directly, and we shall leave. And my daughters too, let Ailissa bring them. But waste no time! — and let me enter!' He tried to get his foot in the door as the slavewoman went to go back inside, but a dozen other female hands clutched at it, pushed his foot out of the way and slammed the door to again. He heard a high-pitched chatter within, folded his arms and stood waiting. Behind him the steward coughed and the soldiers escorting them shifted from foot to foot, mail ringing gently.

Parakison was with Ailissa's daughter Lisanë in the dayroom with the green-tiled pool; they were bent over, puffing at the sails of a couple of nutshell boats in an attempt to race them across the water. 'Cheat! You blew mine out of the way.'

'I did not so.'

'Yes you did! Start again now.' Parakison grabbed both vessels.

'Wa! I was winning. Put them back.'

'No, now we have to start again.'

'Parakison! Parakison!' Setha came dashing through the archway and seized Parakison's wrist. She was red-faced and panting; she had not run so far or so fast since she became a woman fifteen years ago. 'Come with me! We leave now.'

Parakison resisted her tug. 'Leave where?'

'Leave the city. The rebels are here! We must escape!'

'Where are we going?'

'Away! Come now! Uncle Sulakon is waiting!'

'Are we going with him?'

'Yes! Yes!' Setha was towing him across the room by main force.

He raised his voice. 'Why? I don't want to go!'

'You must go! We all go! You, Lisanë, run to your mother! The rebels are here, they kill us all.'

Lisanë ran out of the room. Parakison cried, 'No! I shan't go! I hate Uncle Suli, I hate him! I shan't go!'

'You will go!'

'No!' They struggled furiously. Parakison threshed from side to side and screamed. Setha got his head trapped under her arm and dragged him toward the archway. He twisted round so that he got a mouthful of breast and bit her savagely through her gown. She screamed, and he kicked her ankles. 'I hate you all, I hate you! I'm the King here! I'll stay here and be King of the rebels!'

'The rebels will kill you and put your head on a pole!'

'I'll put Uncle Suli's head on a pole!' He caught hold of her arm and sank his teeth into it as if it were a leg of chicken; Setha howled; he kicked her ankles so that she stumbled, he was out of her grip and fled.

Sulakon waited for a while, then beat on the door again. Voices inside called, 'Wait! Wait!'

'Ailissa!' he shouted.

The door swung open and there was his senior wife. 'What do you want?' she exclaimed.

He caught hold of her hand. 'Ailissa, we must fly. There is no time to waste. A boat awaits us in the harbour– '

'What? You wish to leave?'

'Ailissa, we are all leaving – where are the children? And Setha, and Parakison– '

Ailissa folded her arms and tilted her head back. 'You may be leaving,' she said in her haughtiest voice.

'Lady! The rebels are overrunning the city– '

Ailissa interrupted him, laughing. He stopped short. 'Indeed they are!' she exclaimed. 'For the first time in two hundred years the enemy is at the very gates of the city, yea, and inside them! And you wish me to accompany you in your defeat? I should say not! I shall stay here, faithful to the memory of my brother, and take whatever comes. I am not going to abandon Safi like a rat! You may take that foreign woman an you wish, but you will not take me. I was born in Safi and I shall die in Safi!' She shook off his pleading hands and moved backwards.

Sulakon was pale with fury. 'Lady, you are my wife. I order you to obey me! I shall give you an hourtenth to collect your jewels, and then we leave. Where are the children?'

'The children will stay with me,' said Ailissa.

'They will not!' Sulakon shouted, just as Setha burst through one of the curtains and threw herself into his arms. She was genuinely weeping now. '. . . gone! Can' fin'm! Gone!'

'What is it? Where is Parakison?'

'Gone! He bit me an' ran'way!' She pulled up her sleeve and displayed a bleeding halfmoon of toothmarks. 'I know not where he is! I cannot fin'm!' Ailissa looked at her with sheer contempt. Histri and Sistri came into the antechamber, each with a blanket-wrapped bundle tied on their backs, like poor women going to market. Sulakon gently detached Setha from his side and let them take her. 'Ailissa,' said Sulakon. 'I order you to go and find Parakison, and our children, bring them here, and then we shall leave.'

'No,' said Ailissa insolently.

'I order you!'

88

'I will not take your orders!'

'You will obey me!' Sulakon struck her across the side of her head. She staggered back against the wall and gave an animal shriek.

'Bastard! Son of a whore! You dare to strike me!' She raised her voice and cried 'MOTHER!' The curtain over the west door was snatched back and Sumakas, flanked by two hefty kitchen slaves carrying enormous meat cleavers, pounced into the room.

'My lord! My lord!' Sulakon looked over his shoulder and saw a battlestained message runner leaning on the doorpost. 'My lord. The rebels have overrun the Gate of Horn. They are as far as . . . Yellow Temple Square . . . the mob are, out in Great Market . . .'

'Sistri, Histri,' said the Lord Regent. 'Take your mistress down to the harbour. Do not delay for anything. Reserak, escort them to the ship. Ailissa, this is your last chance. Will you come with me?' The kitchen slaves were advancing on his entourage, who had already moved back on the men's side of the door. Sumakas had her arm round Ailissa's shoulders. His wife of twenty-three years looked once at him and spat on the floor. The door slammed between them, and he heard its several bolts ram home.

'Go to the Street of the Vintners and tell them, an they value their lives, they should roll every barrel they have down to Great Market and distribute drink among the crowd. Then as soon as done, Selanor, send your messengers round the walls crying out to all that there is a festival of victory in Great Market with gifts for all and they should go there directly. Ylureen is going to send people with firewater. Let them bring old wine and new, barley beer, any drink which they have. I am going to enter the palace.'

'But you will have a drunken riot in Great Market,' Selanor said.

'Better a drunken riot in Great Market than looting and riots throughout the city. Once everyone is in Great Market we can throw a cordon round it and impose some order.'

'I shall lead troops for that also, then, after I have procured the drink.'

'Do so, Selanor, do so. Where is Daior-deor? Daior-deor! Let us go!'

'When will you come back?' cried Selanor.

'An hour, two hours!'

'What are you doing?' But she was already out of earshot.

Tarap's iron warshoes rang and sparked on the cobbles of the Street of Dreams; they thundered down it to the Fountain of Joy, saw a few people scattered and running in the King's Road, turned left into a side-road and dashed through a warren of tenements into a street lined by workshops, all barred up and shuttered. When it became clear that Sulakon's forces had lost the fight, and it remained only to take control of the city, Aleizon Ailix Ayndra said that she was going to look for Lady Sumakas, whom she believed closeted in the House of Women; nor would it be any use attacking the doors of the palace with a ram, or staging an escalade to get at her, for the House of Women was like a fortress within a fortress. Instead she proposed to make a clandestine entrance, draw the lady's notice, and get her to surrender the palace to them and order her friends in the city to come out in support of the rebels. When her officers objected that Sulakon would surely be making a last stand in the palace itself, she said that that was why she was going to make a clandestine entrance, and asked Daior-deor to come with her; all she needed was one man to protect her back. They hurried through backstreets so as to come up close to the palace without its guards, presumed concentrated on the side giving onto Great Market, taking notice of them. 'Firumin has told me the best way to enter, he knows every side of the palace. All I worry for is that someone will steal the horses.'

'Surely they will not steal your horse,' said Daior-deor.

'At a time like this people will steal anything. In especial anything which seems good to escape on. Look, this is the place. Where can we tie them up out of sight?'

She bent over as if she were playing leapfrog and Daior-deor stood on her back to get up on top of the wall; they had sneaked round to the back section of the palace where the slaves were quartered, and where there was one short section of wall low enough that they could climb over it to

90

meet their lovers. In moments they were down on the inside. 'That was easy!' said Daior-deor.

'It is the servants' secret, the one place where one can climb into the palace. Let us march through here as though we were something to do with Sulakon. Lord! It looks all deserted. Very likely they are all locked in the cellars.' She rapidly led them out of the rows of single-room dwellings into a section clearly intended for people of the better sort, through double doors which, if barred, could have held off a company, but had been left to swing open. Within there was every sign that the inhabitants had left in a hurry: articles of clothing dropped on the floor, doors and shutters gaping, chests standing open with their contents rifled, niches that had held ornaments empty or with their treasure lying smashed on the tiles. Aleizon Ailix Ayndra led them one way until they came out in a courtyard full of scarlet flowers; she swore, and hustled Daior-deor back again. 'God's teeth! I can never find my way in this place. Let us go down here. But where have all the people gone?'

Daior-deor was distracted by the magnificence of the surroundings, the endless variety of marbles, the carved capitals of the columns, the painted and coffered ceilings. Ayndra scuttled along muttering, 'God-cursed rabbit warren!' They entered a colonnade whose inner wall had been frescoed with the waves of Safi and scenes of maidens carrying garlands of flowers; at the far end was an enormous iron-studded door. 'Here we are! There is only one door to the House of Women.' She drew her sword, which was still smeared with the lifeblood of those she had despatched earlier in the day, and knocked with its reversed hilt. 'Sumakas Queen of Safi! Sùmakas! Aleizon Ailix Ayndra calls you! Sumakas!' Daior-deor likewise drew his sword and went a little way back down the corridor, checking all its entrances. He heard a grating of bolts behind him, but did not desist from his search; then a flicker of motion high up caught his eye. Rafters painted white with a blue wave zigzagging along each went between the columns and the wall; there was a space above them. 'Who are you up there? Come down!'

Two small hands and a face framed by black hair appeared in one of the gaps. A childish voice said, 'Are you rebels?'

As the door swung open, Ayndra took her sword in her right hand and a long knife in her left; she placed her feet ready to jump. At first she could see no one inside; then three or four women in slaves' dress, with meat cleavers. 'Friend!' she called. 'Where is Lady Sumakas?' They did not answer; there were sounds of a scuffle behind them, a cry of 'I will so!' — and then a figure in a white tunic, sword in hand, black hair flopping over its face, thrust between them. Her jaw dropped and she forgot to put her weapons on guard. The apparition thrust its sword at her and she saw its blue eyes staring. 'Out!' it shrieked.

'Aah!' she said. 'Ailissa! Ailissa, put up your sword, it is I!'

'We are honest people,' said Daior-deor. 'Come down, and I will not hurt you.'

The child poked its head through the gap. 'O look! There's my Aunt 'lissa.'

Daior-deor knew better than to succumb to such a stratagem. 'Come down.'

'O all right then.' The head disappeared; dust and debris cascaded through the gap, followed by a pair of grimy boots, thin legs in breeches white with plaster, and the rest of their owner. Parakison landed on the floor and bounced up, grinning white in a dirty face. He held up his hand to Daior-deor, who looked grim.

'What are you doing here?'

'Ailissa! What are you doing with that sword? You near gave me an apoplexy, I – I thought you were Ailixond come again.'

Parakison poked his bent wrist at Daior-deor. 'Come on.'

'What?'

'Do you not know anything? You're supposed to kiss my hand!'

'Pardon?' said Daior-deor.

Parakison jabbed his hand forward. 'You have to kiss my hand! I'm the King!'

'I am defending my patrimony,' said Ailissa.

'Where is Sulakon?'

'Sulakon has fled with the foreign woman. I have left him. I am sick of marriage, I am going to act for myself. Have you taken the city?'

'I think so,' said Aleizon Ailix Ayndra. She leant back against the wall, sheathed her weapons and started to unbuckle her helmet. 'You mean that there is no defence here any more? Sulakon has run away?'

Daior-deor bent down and planted a reluctant kiss on the grubby wrist. Parakison smiled charmingly and took hold of his hand as if they were going for a walk together. 'Now come and see Aunt 'lissa. Aunt 'lissa! Look, I'm to be King of the rebels. Here is one, he kisses my hand already . . . why have you got my Dada's clothes on?' He looked Aleizon Ailix Ayndra up and down. 'Are you another rebel?'

Aleizon Ailix Ayndra held up her hand. She said 'No! I am the government now!' and burst out laughing. She pulled off her helmet and whooped like a fairground rider. The kitchen slaves marched out into the corridor, opening the door wide, and a wrinkled, aquiline woman in a deep blue gown glided towards them. 'Sumakas!' Ayndra yanked off a glove and offered her sweaty hand; Sumakas took it, sank into a graceful curtsey and kissed her fingers.

'My daughter!' She rose and embraced her, they kissed each other several times. Sumakas gestured at Daior-deor. 'Are you here already? Are your troops in the palace?'

'No, only the two of us, they are mostly on the walls still – we believed Sulakon still here, I aimed to enter secretly and ask you for the keys – what have you there?'

Sumakas was undoing something at her waist; she lifted up a massive double ring with dozens of keys on it, and dropped it into Ayndra's hand. Ayndra's face lit up; she fumbled through it till she lighted upon a couple of gigantic iron keys, and held them up. 'Come then!' said Sumakas. 'Let us go to the yard and show ourselves to Great Market. Ailissa, will you come with us – Parakison!'

'Gramma,' said Parakison. 'They wanted me to go with Uncle Suli, but I would not.'

'So you hid yourself! My peach!' She rustled forward and kissed his blackened cheek. 'Let us all go straightway to Great Market. Parakison, I thought they had taken you away somewhere! Where *were* you?'

'In a secret place!' The child caught Daior-deor's eye and gave him a large wink.

'Blessed angel!' Sumakas exclaimed. She spun round and

93

started firing orders at the crowd of women who had gathered behind them. Ailissa was scrutinising Daior-deor; she must have been taken in by his height, for she said, 'Are you one of Lord Polem's bastard sons? We heard that you were travelling with Lord Aleizon Ailix Ayndra.'

'Lady,' said Daior-deor. He looked at her tunic and breeches, of a distinctly old-fashioned cut and straining over her bosom, the belt all crooked, the sword she clearly knew not how to hold, and for heaven's sake! gilded flat sandals on her feet and the ankle laces trailing; however, she took his silence for consent and went on. 'Is your father with you? I have not had the pleasure of his company for many a year, I should be glad to see him again. You know he was a best friend of my brother.'

'Lady, my name is Captain Daior-deor, Thaless born, at present captain in the army of my lord of Haramin. To the best of my knowledge I am no kin to Lord Polem what so ever.'

'Your pardon,' Ailissa said, as if she had merely jogged his arm in passing.

Her mother turned round. 'Ailissa, do put up that sword; you will hurt someone with it.'

'It's my Dada's sword!' said Parakison. 'Let me carry it.'

'It is too big for you,' said Ailissa.

'Carry it on your shoulder, like this.' Ayndra showed her what to do. 'There is no need to wave it now; you look dashing, Ailissa, I am impressed.' To Daior-deor's amusement, the oddly clad lady herself began to blush.

Parakison cried, 'I want the sword! Gimme it.'

'Hush, Parakison,' said Sumakas. 'Let us go.' She took Ayndra's arm, careless of its coat of blood and dust. 'Bring Parakison, Ailissa. To Great Market!' Her kitchener bodyguard fell in to either side; Parakison, however, was recalcitrant, and Ailissa, encumbered with the sword, had only one hand to deal with him. 'Help me!' she snapped at Daior-deor, who took hold of the boy.

'We are going to Great Market to see the rebels,' he said. 'They will all be there dancing and drinking, and we shall go up on the walls for them to cheer us. Will you not come?' As he spoke, he and Ailissa towed Parakison after his grandmother. He consented to come without fighting.

As they raced through deserted corridors, he looked up at Daior-deor. 'How old are you?'

'Twenty-seven.'

'O. You're old! I thought you were a boy.'

'No, merely stubby-legged,' said Daior-deor.

Ayndra looked over her shoulder and made congratulatory gestures. They were all laughing. 'I have told my people, as soon as I appear above Great Market, they will know that all is settled and will give out the word that you are our new Regent,' said Sumakas to Ayndra.

'You may find that there are more people than merely yours in Great Market now,' Ayndra replied.

'But then they will be yours, will they not?'

'It is not quite that simple . . . you know that we came here in hot pursuit of Sulakon . . . and besides, are you sure that everyone has deserted the palace?'

'You saw no one as you came here, did you? And besides, there are only two of you; I thought that you had seen that it was all safe.'

'Is there a way we may approach the palace yard without that anyone who is there sees us?' Sumakas looked at Ayndra as she spoke, and recognised the gravity in her expression. 'Of course. Follow me.' They whisked off down a side corridor and stopped at a door which Sumakas borrowed the keys back to unlock, up a flight of stairs, and emerged onto a flat roof surrounded by other walls and roofs. One had a section of reinforced tiles with ridges at intervals built into them, enabling one to climb the ridge.

Parakison had been caught up in the excitement of the moment and forgot to fret; he broke loose from Ailissa and ran up behind Aleizon Ailix Ayndra. 'Where are we going now?'

'We are going to spy on the palace yard. Come over the roof quickly, and do exactly as I say.'

'What is all the noise? Are the people cheering us already?'

'I think the people are beginning to riot, Parakison.' The tiles were hot from the sun; crossing the ridge they had a brief view of the open market; there were a large number of people milling about in it. A repetitive thunder came from the direction of the main gates.

'Is that your people beating on the gate?' Sumakas asked as they bent down behind the parapet.

'I am not sure whose they might be.' The parapet was crowned with an ornamental coping of glazed tiles, bearing a succession of romping animals leaping along their crests. Aleizon Ailix Ayndra peered between the legs of a cat and whistled softly. Parakison stood up beside her. 'Let me see!'

Sumakas pulled him down. 'Parri! We are hiding, do you understand? I will tell you when it is time to show yourself.'

There were perhaps thirty horses in the yard, and twice as many armed men, with a few dozen more in servants' or slaves' livery, carrying gardening tools, broomsticks and kitchen knives. The horses ranged from two or three fine chargers to broken-down hacks that might pull a rag-and-bone cart; the best of them already had two riders up, and more were trying to mount, arguing with those already astride. There was a good deal of argument going on, but the racket from beyond the wall made it hard to hear any words; the gates were quaking under the assault from without. 'God save us,' said Ayndra, 'the fools are going to open the gates and make a run for it.'

'What?'

'The ones on horseback think that they can save themselves. Do the gates open inward or outward?'

'Inward,' said Ailissa.

Ayndra was jamming her helmet back on her head. 'Lady, you must go back to the House of Women as fast as you can, and do not open the doors for anything, not until – not until you hear battle trumpets sounding the victory, do you understand? Go now!'

'I want to see the riot,' Parakison complained.

'As soon as they open the gates there will be riot all over the palace. Daior-deor, let us go; we must get our horses and go back to the Gate of Horn, bring the Haraminharn cavalry–'

'Have you not ordered that all looters will be slain?' Sumakas interjected.

'Lady, I have so ordered my own people, but there are a great many rebels with us over whom I have no jurisdiction, and all the militia who deserted from Sulakon, and all the street people of the city, truly I know not whom. Ailissa, get over the roof, do not stand to look! – I will come back at the head of a regiment, and I promise that I will drive the looters out of the palace, but beyond that I cannot promise.'

Sumakas was staring at her. 'What have you brought upon us?' she said.

'Do you not know? I thought that you knew everything.' Ayndra handed Sumakas over the ridge and they slid down the far side. In a few moments they were back in the corridor.

'This way.' Sumakas took the lead; she was very sprightly for a woman of her years. 'Now, we go this way, you go that.'

'That way?'

'Yes, into the next courtyard and through the arched passage, and you will be in the slaves' quarters – you see, I know by which place you must have entered. Ailissa, Parri, go along!'

'And if you have occasion to use that sword, swing it like this, do not stab, you cannot stab with a long sword,' Ayndra added. Ailissa delivered an inept salute and headed off in the company of the slaves; Parakison stayed, hanging onto his grandmother's hand.

'I ask you again, what have you brought upon us?' Sumakas said.

'Lady, I do not know what I have brought. But I tell you, everything will be different. Run now!' She brushed Sumakas' withered cheek with her lips, and set off running.

Selanor had set up temporary headquarters for the allied army in the towers of Thaless Gate; the scantily furnished rooms were like a boiling pot with people coming and going and shouting in six tongues. When Aleizon Ailix Ayndra rushed in crying his name he all but threw himself into her arms, if she had not been waving them so enthusiastically. 'Selanor! Sulakon has fled – his garrison have opened the palace gates, the mob will be all over it in half an hour. Have we all the gates now? Then I want them all garrisoned by men and officers who do not know the city, while you and I and those of us who do will go down to the palace. Who have we here? Anko! Will you take the Gate of Ivory? – go there directly. Aq'ren! I want you to take the first Haraminharn foot down to the castle at the south end of the wall, by the sea. Haldin, go to Ylureen and tell her that Sulakon has escaped in a boat and I want that the fleet should stop him . . .' She stood there firing off orders as a wet dog sprays water, shouting out the names of prominent rebels and demanding that they be brought to her and running about the gate like a wild bird in a bedroom while she waited for them to come, and Selanor collected city-born Safeen downstairs. Of the dozen rebels she named, only four could be found, and they terrified at being manhandled into a tower full of armed men; they wrung their hands and lamented that they could do nothing about their people, now they had got into the city, but Ayndra silenced them, put them each at the side of the troop leader of a troop of Haraminharn cavalry, and dismissed them to range through the streets and apply whatever measures were necessary to contain the riot. She left orders that any other leading rebels were to be drawn similarly into police work, and that all looters were to be clearly challenged to give up their evil work and go to Great Market, which if after a fair chance they did not do, they were to be killed, or tied up to be sold into slavery. She stuck her head out of a narrow window giving on the gate-court. 'Selanor! Are you ready? — Selanor!' she shrilled. Selanor was drinking from an up-ended leather flask, which he tried to conceal in a guilty fashion as soon as he heard her voice. 'Son of a snake!' she shrieked, and went tearing down the stairs. Selanor had hidden the bottle and was ready by Tarap's side, so that he could catch her foot and catapult her onto horseback without she even paused. 'Draw your swords! To the palace!'

'Sir, I seek my lord of Haramin, with word from Lady Ylureen. You know where she is gone?'

'She is not here, lady, she went back to the palace. Have you sought for her there?'

'Sir, open the gate to me; I seek my lord of Haramin.'

'Lady, she has gone down to the harbour. Have you sought for her there?'

'Where shall I find her in the harbour?'

'An you take that street there and turn left at the big

crossroads, you will come to the portmaster's office; very likely she is there.'

By the time the messenger found her way to the office she was in a foul mood. 'Thy mother's skirt! Why cannot these witless savages put names to their streets? How does anyone find their way among these slums?' She addressed the man who confronted her in Safic. 'You are portmaster?'

'Lady, the portmaster has gone down to the quay. Shall I escort you to him?'

'I want no portmaster. Where is my lord of Haramin?'

'You mean Lord Aleizon Ailix Ayndra?'

'Foolfathered, of course I do! Where is she?'

The fool's child looked askance at her and consulted with his colleagues; they agreed that Lord Ayndra was where the grain ships were unloading. They did not offer to escort the messenger there. 'You cannot miss it,' they said. She gave them a curt bow and flounced out. They proved, however, to be quite correct when they said that she could not miss it; the ranks of torches, the porters bent double under sacks, the lines of men with swords and half-pikes guarding them, the draught oxen snorting, the cracks of whips and the cries of the loaders. There were three grain ships tied up and each had two gangplanks up to its open holds. At the far end of the quay there was a great crowd of people, pullulating round some sort of auctioneers' dais as the yellow corn was poured into upheld buckets and more guards protected those who carried it away. She caught sight of a blonde head gleaming under the flares on the dais, and thrust through the marching porters towards it.

My lord of Haramin was attending to a queue of men in the robes of Safic merchants and did not take kindly to interruption. 'What is it?' she snapped in S'Thurrulan.

'My lord, Lady Ylureen reminds you that this night is the dance of the first full moon, and begs that you will attend and dance with us.'

'Dance? What does she think this is, the damned Summer Festival? You mean you will dance this night?'

'Yes, my lord,' the messenger said, placatory.

'Gods' teeth!' Ayndra swore in Safic. 'Did you come here on your own? I take it she sent you from the camp. It is hardly safe for women to walk the streets yet.'

'But my lord, last night the city was ours already. We will dance all night, my lord, Lady Ylureen says that you may come any time before dawn an you will. Or afterwards. But it is the first full moon, my lord, she prays that you will come.'

'Let me send someone to go back with you.'

'My lord, I am quite safe.' The woman whipped a long knife out of her broad sash, to the consternation of the merchants who were regarding her with interest, since she was clearly several months with child. 'My lord, Lady Ylureen says that she has not seen you for two days now; you will be sure to come? We all like to see you dance.'

'I have not slept properly for two days either,' said Aleizon Ailix Ayndra. 'And I must see that these cargoes are distributed, or stored in safety. When it is done, I will come; tell her that.' She offered her hand to the pregnant woman, who kissed it and left; Ayndra spoke briefly to one of her guards, who followed, catching up with the woman beside one of the carts; they could be seen to argue a little, the woman shrugged, and they set off together.

There had not been much left in the public rooms of the palace by the time the rioters surged in from Great Market, and the soldiers of my lord of Haramin had caught up with them before they had got very far into the private rooms, the storerooms and cellars. They had still had time to set fire to the tapestried walls of the Hall of Stars, and add to the blaze with furniture smashed up in their anger at failing to find either the hated Lord Regent and his lackeys, or gold and treasures. The fire had reached the cedar beams of the roof, destroyed the famous ceiling, and left the hall standing a blackened shell; many of the noblemen's apartments had suffered similar outrage, although the House of Women had survived intact, designed as it was to exclude all outsiders. Until basic repairs had been completed, the nobles of the allied army preferred to reside in their pavilions outside the walls, with Ylureen's great tent the largest of them all. The midsummer nights were warm, and its heavy outer walls were brailed, letting the light shine through the silk inner tent (which could not be rolled up, lest profane eyes witness the ceremonies within); it was only an hour or so to dawn, but the drums were still throbbing, audible even from within the walls. Aleizon Ailix Ayndra rode Tarap round to the horse-lines, dismissed her escort and went up to the tent on foot. The night-watch, waiting now for the early-day, were slovenly in their guard, and she easily crept up to a place where she could cut a little slit in the silk and watch unobserved.

The great tent occupied an oval space, its long axis aligned from the sun's path, with the door to the south. Ayndra was spying from the west end, where the watchers sat or dozed on the ground among scattered cushions; at the east end there was a crowd of low and high beds arranged for seating. On the north side were the drummers, beating on everything from a pair of gigantic kettle-drums to small tambours and slender double-headed drums shaped like an hourglass. Little stoves for brewing chabe, with women clustered around them, were placed at either end. The open, canvas-covered dance floor was presently occupied by a couple of dozen women dancing in a circle, clapping their hands and stamping to the beat; their hair was dressed in multiple plaits weighted and decorated with bright beads and coins, which swung and glittered under the suspended lamps. Ayndra parted the cloth a little with her fingers and peered beyond the lifted arms and flying hair to the beds where the noblewomen sat, and Ylureen on the largest of them all, reclining on a heap of cushions as rich and colourful as a field of wild flowers. S'Thiraidi's pale green hair showed by her shoulder; she appeared to be sleeping. Ylureen snapped her fingers; in a few moments Hahhni was bowing in front of her, a steaming cup of chabe in hand. Ylureen sat sipping it as the dancers completed their figures, and went chattering from the floor, while those who were still awake watching made some desultory applause. S'Thiraidi sat up suddenly and joined in the clapping; Ylureen laughed, shifted to the edge of the bed and got ponderously to her feet. She disappeared behind the curtain at the easternmost point of the tent. While she was gone, Getaleen appeared at S'Thiraidi's side; they chatted for a while, and Getaleen went to speak to the drummers, who were waiting till Ylureen returned to begin another dance, though the players of small drums went on tapping out a soft rhythm like a heartbeat all the time. Aleizon Ailix Ayndra pulled out the kerchief she wore to protect her neck from the rough frieze of her gambeson and unrolled a smokestick from its folds; she walked round to the avenue of flares that lit the way to the door, making the S'Thurrulan salute at the guards, who did not recognise her in the poor light, lit it in one of them and returned to her spy-place. She saw Ylureen reappear and climb back into her seat, with Hahhni fussing about her until she was comfortably settled. She scanned the sleepy gathering and beckoned to Esas'thi, but S'Thiraidi leant over and they had a brief discussion; Ylureen argued for a while and then gave in. S'Thiraidi signed to Getaleen, and the kettle-drums started to thunder. Getaleen bounded onto the dance floor, crossed her hands, snapped them apart and a long knife was suddenly glittering in each. 'What!' exclaimed Ayndra, so loudly that several heads turned inside the tent; she ducked back out of the light, and saw her spyhole widen suddenly, then the black outline of a hand thrust through it and disappear again. Handclapping was added to the noise of the drums, then loud whoops. She shuffled toward the tent, watching the shadows shift and blur on the silk; she paused, then drew her sword and charged straight at it, ripping a great tear in the wall – there was a chorus of screams as the blade appeared – and she leapt through it and onto the dance floor. Getaleen had spun round to face the cries. 'Ha!' she said, tossed up one knife and caught it, and began to juggle the two of them in time with the kettle-drums, which had not missed a stroke. Ayndra saluted Ylureen with her sword and drove it upright into the floor. She reached into her sleeves and pulled out her throwing knives. Facing Getaleen, she began to stamp in time with the rhythm.

S'Thiraidi started to stand up, but Ylureen seized her wrist in a grip like iron and forced her to stay seated. 'Watch,' she said. 'You asked me for this.'

'But she – she cut a hole in the wall – and look at her! She is dressed like a *man*– '

'Do not distract them,' said Ylureen in a voice like the polish on steel.

S'Thiraidi subsided, but knelt up with her eyes glued to the dancers. All those who still woke were likewise transfixed, and the new beat had brought many of the sleepers out of their blankets, but they were all silent now. Aleizon Ailix Ayndra and Getaleen were dancing as though each reflected the other in a mirror, but a magic mirror, that could turn a flowing tunic and long trousers into a stained frieze gambeson, military boots and studded breeches; the only change of clothes my lord of Haramin had made for two days was to take off her mailshirt, polished gorget and helmet. The empty scabbard of her sword danced at her side and her greasy hair flew. She was dancing Getaleen out of the ring, backing her up to the door. Getaleen's painted mouth was set like a wire. Ayndra tossed her head and cried, 'Faster!' The head drummer cast a glance at Y!ureen, and immediately obeyed. Getaleen's mouth widened; she whirled the knife in her right hand, and tossed it at Ayndra, who caught it like a juggler, and threw her other blade at Getaleen. They started to circle the floor, the four knives dancing between them in time to their feet; they were staring at each other, wrapped up in concentration. Ayndra suddenly stamped her right foot twice and tossed the knife she held in that hand at Getaleen's right instead of her left; they began to juggle in a cross pattern instead of a square, moving closer and closer to the east end. Ayndra shouted, 'Another!'

For a moment no one responded; then Ylureen pushed Hahhni, who jerked the knife she carried from her belt and threw it at them. It missed Getaleen's cheek by inches, and Ayndra caught it out of the air without a break in her movements. Getaleen looked desperate now. S'Thiraidi pulled Ylureen's sleeve. 'Lady! I beg you—'

'Silence!' The two dancers were standing right in front of the moon-seat, still stamping but on the spot now, all their attention on the five knives flying between them. 'Another?' said Aleizon Ailix Ayndra. Getaleen managed to flash her eyes at S'Thiraidi, who drew her knife and advanced towards them; she held it out at arm's length until Getaleen could snatch it, then dashed out of range. Ayndra's mouth curved up in a smile; she started to throw the knives high, so that they spun end over end, and pranced from foot to foot as she threw. Getaleen's eyes tried to follow the flashing steel, snatched at one of her own long blades and cried out;

she tried to grab the next one with her other hand, missed it and fell over in a clatter of falling weapons, clasping her left hand with her right. Blood dripped from it onto the floor. Aleizon Ailix Ayndra caught the knife she had just thrown and halted; the drummers stopped; there was a brief instant of silence in which one could hear Getaleen whimpering, before the drums started again with a different beat and S'Thiraidi jumped up to succour her line sister. Ayndra picked up Hahhni's knife and offered it back to its owner, who bowed to her and kissed the blade. She sheathed her own, went back and pulled the sword out of the floor; balanced it in her hand, then threw it up in the air so that it turned a somersault among the hanging lamps, caught it by the hilt and stuck it back in the scabbard. The watchers beat their palms on the ground. She saluted them and strolled up to the great bed, where Ylureen sat still, fingers interlaced on her domed belly. 'The old dog still knows its tricks,' she said cheerfully. 'Next time shall I dance with two swords?'

For answer, Ylureen took her hands and pressed them against her: the child inside was kicking up a storm. Ayndra sat down beside her and put one arm round her shoulders. They looked very closely into each other's eyes. 'You were spectacular,' said Ylureen, 'but not very wise.'

'What do you have for breakfast?' said Aleizon Ailix Ayndra.

'You are too much dedicated to this, what is it you say? This *manly honour*.' Ylureen used Safic words. She looked Ayndra over, from the bloodstains on her boots to the cleaner stripe where her helmet had covered her forehead; the war-dress reeked of the thick femininity of her sweat, unmasked by any perfume. 'You are not really a man, you know; nor would I want you to be.'

'The knife dance is a women's dance.'

'But not as you dance it.'

'Getaleen understood the way I danced it.'

'And now you have made her your enemy. Are you hungered?'

'Ylureen, I starve! I have not had a good meal, nor lain down in a bed, since I left yours the night before the battle at Shili.' She peered up at the smokeflaps, raised to let the vapours of the lamps pass out. 'It must be almost dawn,' she said, flopping among the cushions with an enormous yawn.

'I shall scrub you before I let you between my sheets! Have you a bathhouse in this palace of yours, that I have not yet seen?'

'I know the women have one . . . there is one for men too, but I think it has no water in it presently . . .'

'What do we care about the men's one? Let me send for my chair, and we will go together and bathe.'

'Very well; only let me eat first.'

'The servants are bringing it now.' Esas'thi offered a plate of rolls still warm from the oven; Ayndra seized two and stuffed them into her mouth. 'You are more greedy than a beggar,' said Ylureen.

'I am hungrier than a beggar,' said she, spraying crumbs. Ylureen patted her, smiling, and told Hahhni to call the bearers. The outer walls of the tent were being let down against the dawn wind, and numerous servitors in Pilith livery brought hot bread and chabe to the audience, who were preparing to go about their duties or to lie down and sleep. Ayndra, when she had reached temporary satiation, lounged and scrutinised the servants; it was plain that some of them were not very sure of their duties, indeed did not even speak S'Thurrulan beyond the most basic of commands, and were employed mainly to carry burdens for the better trained. They talked to each other in Thaless dialect. Hahhni came bustling in with Ylureen's shawl, and they went outside, where the four men who carried Ylureen's chair were waiting at some distance from the tent. The sun had just peered over the hills of Thaless, painting the patched walls of the city pale gold and fawn. Ylureen sat down, and Hahhni tucked a blanket over her knees; Ayndra ran off, saying that she went to get her horse and would follow shortly. When she caught up with the bearers, who went along at a smooth lope, they were almost at the gate of the city. The early-day watch had just opened the gate, and the women who sold milk were tethering their cows just inside it, ready to fill the buckets and jugs held out to them. Ayndra waved to them all, but they were more interested in the sight of Ylureen in her inlaid carrying-chair. She directed the bearers to go down the Street of Dreams. 'You will be disappointed in the palace, Ylureen; it was never a match for the palace in Suthine, even before people set fire to half of it.'

'No matter,' said Ylureen, gazing about her; it was the first time she had ever set foot in Safi. 'This is far more pleasant than making a state entry,' she said, looking at the women carrying jugs to the public fountains, the bakers' boys running with trays of fresh bread, the street-sellers on the corners offering spiced wine and fried dough-cakes fresh from the boiling-fat. 'How peaceful it is! You said that it was all in riot.'

'Can you not see the marks on the houses? Look, there was a barricade there, and it was set fire to; see the smoke up the walls either side.' Ayndra stopped to purchase some dough-cakes and came back with her chin all smeared with grease, wiping her fingers in Tarap's mane. They took the King's Road into Great Market. 'Now you see,' she said; the whole square had turned into a vast bivouac, thrusting the stalls of the vendors to its edges; people had even thrown up lean-tos against the palace wall. As they passed in among the shacks, they were besieged by children crying out for alms, and then older people with all manner of requests. Ayndra touched as many hands as she could and told them to be patient only a few days and there would be an answer; nevertheless, a noisy and surging crowd had gathered round them by the time they reached the battered red gates, and when they opened, there was a fence of soldiers inside, thrusting sarissas in the face of the crowd to make sure they did not enter. The doors closed on a chorus of pleas and wails. Aleizon Ailix Ayndra shook her head as she dismounted. 'A bad business.' She spotted a palace slavewoman and told her to run ahead and tell Lady Sumakas that they were coming to take a bath. 'Will you walk now, Ylureen, or will you be carried to the water?'

'To be sure, I should rather be carried.'

'I think you should walk, Ylureen; it will be better for you. You have got prodigious fat since you took to going about in that chair; one would think you carried twins.'

'Take me as far as the steps, and I shall walk from there.' She took Ayndra's arm, and they walked through the main door of the palace, which was opened for them as they approached. 'You are right,' said Ylureen, 'it is not much more than our house in Pilith Acha. What are you going to do about all those people in the square? I take it that they are mostly runaway peasants. You should order them back to the land.'

'I am thinking now about what I shall do with them,' said Ayndra.

'We have seen already that every child among them is a beggar; no doubt they are all thieves and pickpockets too.'

'Indeed. They remind me of the child that I was, always in the street.'

'Then you will know how important it is to be rid of them!'

Ayndra said nothing to that; she let Ylureen comment negatively upon the buildings and decoration, until they reached the House of Women and knocked on the door. 'Will Lady Sumakas be up at such an hour?' Ylureen asked.

'She sleeps little, and always rises early; she says that it is how she has time to inform herself of so many things.'

They followed a pair of slaves into the dayroom of the queen's apartments, and Sumakas herself, her hair still unbound and wearing a loose robe without petticoats, came gliding to meet them. 'My lord, my lady Ylureen! What an unexpected pleasure! Lady, pray take a seat, do not stand any longer. Will you have a drink, something to eat?'

'We would like a hot bath more than anything,' said Aleizon Ailix Ayndra.

'Of course; the furnaces are already hot, I have set the slaves to filling it. My lord, I have not seen you since we parted under such inauspicious circumstances. Let me thank you for saving our city!'

'I did not make so good a job of saving it; certainly not of saving the palace.' Ayndra sat down; fatigue showed plainly now in her face.

'The Hall of Stars? It is nothing; it was high time in any case that it was decorated in a new style. Huna, bring that stool so that the lady can put her feet up on it. Introduce us, my lord.'

'I think you know who each other is already,' said Ayndra, upon which Sumakas gave her a sharp glance, and she stood up. 'Ylureen, this is Lady Sumakas, Dowager

Queen of Safi and mother of the great Ailixond. My lady, this is Lady Ylureen, future line mother of Pilith and a power in the land of S'Thurrulass. May you have great joy of your friendship. O yes, and let me mention that Lady Ylureen speaks our Safic tongue, an you did not know so already.' She propped her feet up on a couch and lay down with a sigh.

Sumakas pulled up a chair next to Ylureen and took her hand. 'A pleasure to meet you at last! For years I have been hearing of you. Is this your first visit to our city of Safi? A pity that you find it in such reduced circumstances. When my son ruled here we were a flourishing nation, but under my wittol son-in-law we have become a nation of beggars. I pray that with you and my lord Ayndra we shall soon restore us to our former glory.'

'I hope our alliance prosper, surely,' said Ylureen. 'You are the mother of Lord Ailixond? I met him when our King and Queen send me on embassy to him in our land; he was a true nobleman, and I knew he must have an even nobler mother.'

Sumakas fluttered with pleasure. 'He was my only son,' she said, 'and my only sadness is that he was taken from me before I had a chance to see him again. But of course I have my grandson still, that is Parakison that they call the Little King – but will you have some of these cakes? And a drink; it is only flavoured with wine, I do not like to drink so early in the day.'

'I thank you. Your health, noble lady.'

'Your health, likewise – and your child's! I must ask you, lady, have you not suffered a great deal, leading an army in your condition?'

'I do not lead army, that is what my lord Aleizon Ailix Ayndra do; she a very great leader, I could never do what she do.'

'Thank you, Ylureen,' said the couch.

'And beside,' said Ylureen, 'this is my six child. I am very used, I have no sickness, I am very well. You say you have one son only?'

'And my daughter Ailissa.'

'Ah! a daughter. Thass good. The daughter is the comfort; I hope this my child a girl. I have already three girl and two boy.'

'And they are with you?'

'No, they are with family, with my sisters. Perhaps they come visit an I stay.'

'How old are they?'

The two women discussed children, childbearing, rearing and upbringing until a slave came to say that the bath was ready; they had to shake Aleizon Ailix Ayndra to wake her up. She tottered after them into the steam-filled bathroom, dropped her stinking clothes in a heap on the floor, and was lying in the water before Ylureen had even taken her shift off. At Ylureen's urging, she rubbed herself with a sponge, and submitted to having some clay rubbed through her hair and rinsed out again by one of the bath-attendants, before she crawled back into the hot pool. An hourtenth later they had to fish her out unconscious. They wrapped her in white towels, laid her on the tile bench at the side of the cold-water room and combed out her wet hair in a halo round her sleeping face. 'How many scars she has!' said Sumakas. 'As man as a man . . . and this.' She held the Royal Ring, still on its long chain, in her palm.

'Your Ailixond give it to her when he die,' said Ylureen.

'Yes, I know.' Sumakas turned the jewel back and forth, looking into it as if it were a diviner's crystal. 'He meant it for Parakison.'

Ylureen gave her a sly look, which she did not notice; she said, 'What is the stone on it? Is it a diamond?'

'It is a diamond. The King who founded our city, our ancestor Ailixond first, found it on the sea shore. We keep it uncut, you see, just as he found it. And she has kept it ever since . . . does she ever wear it on her finger?'

'No, never, she keep it hidden. Most people I think they do'know she even have it.'

'Quite right.' Sumakas tucked the jewel out of sight again.

'I think she sleep a very long time now,' said Ylureen. 'Perhaps you are have a bed in your room? She haven' put 'er tent up even.'

'Of course. Is there anything I may do for your noble self the while?'

'O yes. I need a room to meet with all my people, you

understand, I have many business and today I must begin with it. You can lend me a room perhaps?'

'Why, lady, you shall have a whole apartment. Although, an you wish to receive the public, it will have to be in the lords' rooms.'

'You don't have the people in here to see you?'

Sumakas looked aghast. 'Why, no! Only ladies visit me here, and my servants, of course. We may lack any proper men these days, but this is still a decent house.'

'O, I am sorry; I do not well understand your custom. You see, I know only my lord Ayndra in Haramin, and the camp of war.'

'Of course, nothing is done decently in such conditions. But we live properly here.'

'You talk to the women only?'

Sumakas nodded.

'Thass good,' said Ylureen. 'Much better to talk to the women.'

'I can show you to an apartment this very day, an you will; no doubt your servants will wish to decorate it for you. Let us dress first, and my maids will escort us – but may I ask you a favour in return? I should like to meet with your companion, the Lady S'Thiraidi. Perhaps you could ask her to come to see me here when she has time.'

'Whenever please you, lady. I am sure she will be delighted.'

'When I woke up, I had not the least idea where I was! – I leapt out of bed like a lover who sees the husband coming through the door, I was in the next room before I recalled. And then I saw that she had dressed me in a long white nightgown, opening down the front with ruffles either side – ay! It was an hour before I could even get my proper clothes sent to me. And then I went out, and what should I find but Ylureen already installed, and in Sulakon's office yet! – that is, the rooms Sulakon used to use to conduct his business in. Shumar, I well recall standing in there just after Ailixond's funeral, and he telling me I should give back the Royal Ring. And what do I find now but Ylureen sitting there with a queue of petitioners waiting to see her that stretched halfway round the court outside, all asking for licences to trade in this and that, and she giving them out. I told her that none of them could be ratified before the Council of Lords, and after that we would have to set all the taxes over again, for I am going to throw out Sulakon's system entire, but she said that all that was very well, she was only arranging which of her people should be allowed to trade from their side, and she would also give out licences to our merchants an they wished to sell goods to Suthine. And then she gave me this to keep me sweet.' Aleizon Ailix Ayndra reached inside her tunic and took out a bundle of fifty smokesticks tied round with a red and black ribbon. 'Do send for a lamp,' she said.

Daior-deor got up and called to one of the soldiers dicing in the guard-room to fetch a lit lamp from the kitchen. 'I take it we will not attend this Council of Lords,' he said.

'You mean you and the rest of the officers? Well, I should like you to be there, certainly, and Selanor; after all, Ylureen and the rest will certainly be there, and they not lords of Safi either. Of course the lords will have to vote for me to be Regent, but I do not think any of them will object. It is not as if there were very many of them left anyway, what with all the ones I have done away with, and no king to make any new ones.' She sat down on the windowsill and began counting on her fingers, then got distracted staring out at the view. 'What a fine situation you have here.'

'Selanor asked me if I wanted this or Thaless Gate, and I chose this one.' They were in the gate-captain's room in the western tower of the Gate of Ivory, where one could look out to the forest of masts in the harbour and the shifting plains of the sea beyond. 'I think it better that you are not on Thaless Gate,' said Ayndra, 'after all, you might have all your relatives coming in from there to beg favours of you, and then I would have to dismiss you for corruption.'

'What? Never!' Daior-deor answered a knock at the door, and brought the oil-lamp to her. He said, as she bent to hold the smokestick in its flame, 'Did you ever find out where Lord Sulakon escaped to?'

'They left on some fishing smack, piloted by the Lord Admiral Parhannon; I must say, I always thought that Parhannon had more sense. We think that they have run away north of here, perhaps to wherever it is that Meraptar is hiding. But Parhannon is a very skilful pilot, and they managed somehow to slip through the blockade and evade our pursuit. Not that our allies' blockade was all that it might have been in any case. You must have thought it a little surprising that five grainships all loaded to the gunwales were tied up here before all the warships had even come in off station.'

'I thought that they must have been waiting outside for the blockade to lift,' said Daior-deor.

'Ay, but a very short distance outside, for they are slow as turtles, tubs like those; and an they were so close, why did the fleet not apprehend them?'

'They were Lysmalish ships, friendly to us. I presumed that they paid the captains to leave them alone, knowing that as soon as they put into harbour they could sell every grain of corn they carried.'

'I suppose that is the truth,' said Ayndra, grinning. 'Have some of this.'

'Thank you, my lord.'

'Ah! I see that you have learnt to smoke them properly, at last.'

He laughed. 'So my education in vice progresses.'

'At least you have not acquired the vice of drinking firewater for breakfast, like some I could name.'

'You mean Selanor.'

'I cannot recall the last time I spoke to him and could not smell the vapours of it on his breath.'

'That may be, my lord, but it does not seem to cloud his judgement. And I cannot remember the last time I saw him drunk, that is drunken and riotous. Indeed, you might as well condemn me for drunkenness; I recall more than a few times you have come upon me disgracefully out of my senses.'

'But only at festivals, and after dark at that.' She looked out of the window again. 'Look, do you see that building there, with the short tower on it? That is where Sulakon had me imprisoned after my trial, before I escaped and came to Kemmyss looking for you. God's teeth! One can even see Great Market from here, or the corner of it at least. And you receive the sea breezes! Why, I shall come and visit you here all the time.'

'You would always be welcome, my lord. Would you like this?'

'Thank you.' She smoked the remainder of it slowly, gazing out of the window. The sky was blue and clear; the lowering sun deepened the terracotta and rose of the tiled roofs and slanted past her to make a deep yellow rectangle on the white plaster of the far wall, marbled like water with the coiling smoke. Where it caught in the edges of her hair it turned its fading straw to brilliant gold. Daior-deor had never seen her look so happy. 'When is this Council of Lords to meet?' he said.

'On the third; there is no one who has to come from far away, except those who will not come anyway, like Sulakon and Meraptar. We shall meet in the morning, and then have a council of the army in the afternoon. I would like you to help me prepare things for that. You realise that I no longer need such a large field army.'

'It is always a difficulty, what to do with soldiers when there are no longer wars for them to fight.'

'I very much doubt that we shall go for long without a war of one kind or another. Certainly I shall wish to maintain a good-sized standing army, if only to garrison the provinces. But at least half of those following our flags at present will have to abandon the sword. Between now and the Council I want to select those of our officers and men who are best trained and cleverest, and offer them permanent posts; the rest to be dismissed.'

'But what will you do with them then? You must know what troubles have been caused in these last years by troops of paid-off mercenaries and the like going about ravaging the countryside in preference to finding useful work.'

'The provincial levies, I will offer to pay their passage home. And then there are more than a few estates in Safi-the-land whose owners have died or abandoned them; I propose to declare them property of the state, and then to divide them into parcels to be given out to those who have rendered me good service. And after that there is a good deal of building work to be done in Safi, and I have no end of plans for roads and bridges; trade and communication is the way to unify the Empire. The only problem is where to find the good hard coin to pay for them all. Ay! Perhaps I will ask Ylureen to lend me some of her vast profits.'

'Without interest,' said Daior-deor.

Aleizon Ailix Ayndra burst out laughing. 'Ylureen would not lend her own mother money without she charged interest on it! What excellent stuff this is! Let us have some more.'

'But Lady Ylureen has made all these profits as a result of the concessions you have given her, has she not? Surely she will share her profits with you.'

Shaking her head, 'Trade is trade,' said Aleizon Ailix Ayndra.

Arpalond's son dismounted first, and ran to hold his father's horse; Arpalond got down slowly, and shuffled towards the group who had come to greet him. When he got within a short distance of them he became more sure, straightened up and offered his hand to Aleizon Ailix Ayndra. She kissed him on both cheeks, and released him into the arms of Ditarris and the rest of his family, who had come into the city when the rebel army approached, leaving the father and the heir to defend the property. 'Not that I can defend very much these days,' said Arpalond, 'I can hardly see someone six feet off in bright sunlight.'

'But you were our commander,' said his son; turning to the rest of them, he said, 'He is too modest. When we saw how many of them there were, he told us to mount up and ride out, and he went at the head of us all; and then we met a great crowd of them at the entrance to the demesne, and went alone and unarmed into the middle of them and talked to them until they let us pass through without a blow.'

'And left them in possession of my lands,' Arpalond said. 'And not even my lands, but yours, Polem – Ditarris must have told you that we were living on your estate of Samala these last two years?'

'What?' exclaimed Polem. 'The rebels have taken Samala? Samala!'

'When did they arrive there?' asked Aleizon Ailix Ayndra.

'They started to arrive months ago,' said the son.

'What?' she said.

Arpalond went on. 'Samala is a very large estate – Polem will tell you – and we do not visit all parts of it often. People began to settle in the outlands after the trouble in Drimmanë began, and by the time we heard that your army, my lord, was near, there were more than we could have dislodged, unless we armed all our tenants and set them to fight them; and I have never driven my people to war on my behalf. Then a sixday ago a great horde of vagabonds arrived, waving halfpikes and headed by some ruffians dressed in gear that looked stolen from a battlefield – at least, if what my eyes here say is true,' he jerked his thumb at his son, who smiled. 'I told them that they could camp on my land and continue their journey when they were rested. But they were not content to move on until they had taken what they could, and we did not have enough men-at-arms to defend the house. So we left as Antinar has told you. Sometimes I thank the gods that I am half blind; I find that I can show courage far more easily to an enemy I cannot see.' He laughed. Polem was not cheered. 'And these rascals are in Samala?'

'They must have come away after the battle at Shili,' Ayndra said. 'Did they say whose side they had been on?'

'Both sides, or any, I am sure,' said Arpalond. 'They were that kind of vagrant which attaches to any passing troop, with loyalty that lasts no longer than their last full belly. Polem, do not distress yourself! We may have lost this year's harvest, perhaps, but they cannot destroy the land. They will drive off the stock, eat the fruit off the trees, glut themselves on the autumn produce and forget to salt it away; in Sixth Month we will find them already starving, and drive them out with the flats of our blades.' He took Polem's sleeve. 'Lead me into the palace; it is hard for me to see the steps.'

Aleizon Ailix Ayndra gave Ditarris her arm. 'I did not know that his blindness had progressed so far,' she said in a lowered voice. 'When he came to see me in Stabor, he seemed to see as clearly as ever.'

Ditarris shook her head. 'You know he has never had strong eyes. He learnt as a child to find his way as one who walks in a mist, and when his sight began to fail, he went on for a long time before even I noticed it. He needs all his books and letters read to him, unless the scribe write them out in a special large hand, and then he is bent over it like this.' She held an invisible sheet of paper in front of her nose, and went on shaking her head. Ayndra squeezed her arm. Ditarris sighed. 'It is a blessing that it has come slowly; we will all have learnt to live with it when he goes blind. I think often of that poor lord you were imprisoned with in the grass plains, the one they blinded with hot irons.'

'Lord Thaskeldar,' Ayndra said reflectively. 'He died two years later, I recall . . . but were you not worried, then, to leave him to face these marauders?'

'I am his wife,' Ditarris said calmly. Ayndra looked at her as if she expected more reason than that, but forebore to demand it; in any case, Firumin appeared to greet them and invite the visitors into a room where they could wash before they went to the meal which he would have served to them. Ayndra went to talk to Polem, who was wringing his hands over the fate of Samala, which he said had been in his family for six generations and only lately leased to Arpalond; he talked of taking a couple of regiments to drive out the rebels.

'They are not rebels,' said Ayndra.

'Of course they are rebels! What is it but rebellion, to drive a lord off his property?'

'We do not know who they are. Let us hold our judgement. Neither Arpalond nor Antinar have had time to talk in full. And he was right when he said that with patience you will have Samala back without bloodshed.'

'The Council of Lords will discuss it. What a terrible thing! First Drimmanë, and now this.'

'Are you sure you do not want to go back to Drimmanë?'

'I wish to be secured of my patrimony in Safi! I shall have to send armed guards to protect the rest of my lands.'

'So long as you pay their wages,' said Ayndra. 'But there will be all those soldiers idle,' Polem said.

'Why, then you will be able to take on hordes of them at very low wages, will you not?' She was relieved when Firumin announced that supper was served. Not until the meal was finished, and Firumin ready to show the guests to their quarters, did she have a chance to speak to Arpalond in private as he sent his son on ahead.

116

'I did not tell you the whole truth in the yard,' he said without preamble. 'They had fought on your side at Shili, although most of their gear had been seized from Sulakon's troops. They shouted your name, and some of them alleged that you had announced that no lords any longer owned land and that it would be given to any who lived on it and tilled it.'

Ayndra struck her forehead with her open palm. 'Gods' teeth! I have never announced any such thing.' Arpalond's cloudy eyes remained fixed on her, unflinching. 'I have said from time to time that the lands of lords dead or absent will be given to others; Sandar's estates, for example,' she said. 'Certainly I have never said that lords should not own land.'

'You do not own any land, do you?'

She laughed. 'I own almost nothing beyond my horses and accoutrements!'

Arpalond thought for a while before he answered. 'I suppose that since Sandar's heirs are dead, they cannot contest your confiscation; and Meraptar is holed up in Gingito and, I am told, increasingly infirm.'

'Maishis! How do you know these things? Who told you that Sandar's heirs were dead? And where is Gingito?'

'Do you recall a place called Shinalt?'

'I remember it well.'

'It is a day's ride or so north of Shinalt. There is a castle there. I spoke to a wool merchant who had been through those hills last summer, and he said that he had seen Meraptar there, but he looked very aged and walked with a stick. As for Sandar's heirs, why, they died in the sack of Purrllum, did they not, along with their father?'

'Sandar died there. But we never saw hide nor hair of his wife, nor his family; it seemed that they had escaped. And a well-organised escape it must have been, to go all unseen and so quickly.'

'No doubt Sandar planned it in advance; he was always a man to prepare for all eventualities.'

'Not quite all,' said Aleizon Ailix Ayndra.

Arpalond looked at her. He said, 'Cahilar died in the assault on Mirries; that at least is true?'

'It is true. He had fifteen wounds and all on the front of

117

his body. I saw them when they were laying him out for burning.'

'And yet you still want a Council of Lords to ratify your succession to the Regency,' said Arpalond.

'What?' she said. 'You think I should seize power by main force? Shall I cut off Parakison's head into the bargain?'

'An you are going to fly in every interest of the noble born, very likely it were better an you did so.' Ayndra made a noise of outrage. Arpalond put his hand on her shoulder. 'Soft! I never meant that you would do it.'

'Is this what you will say at the Council?' she said, looking at his hand and back to his face again. He smiled sadly. 'They know me for a purblind fool already; they will think it no surprise when I vote for the woman who has lost me half my land.'

'But it was rented land.'

'It was twice the size of all the parcels I inherited put together. I take it that Casik and Golaron are here? I should like to go and talk with them before the Council begins. Is it still the day which you cited?'

'The third of Second Month, at sixth hour of morning. The day after next, that is.'

'That is very well. Shall I come to you next day's evening, then, and tell you what has been said?'

'Most willingly! You can come and speak to Ylureen as well.'

'But after I have spoken with you.'

'Why, of course. Let me walk with you to your room.'

They found Polem already there, being regaled with stories of pillage and rapine by Antinar and the half-dozen men-at-arms who had come from Samala with them. He turned to wave his arms at them as they entered. 'Have you heard! What horror! My lord Ayndra, we must act, else we will lose everything!'

'Have you heard that your other lands are endangered?' she responded drily.

'They soon will be! And Antinar was just saying, what about that great camp they have made in Great Market? What are they going to do? Will they not go out into the country soon and overrun everything? I am going to go and guard my property!'

'Polem, do not distress yourself; you must wait until the Council of Lords has met. Then after that we will have a council of the army, and these things can be discussed. These vagrants have possession of your land already, after all, it is not a question of rushing to hold off an attack.'

Polem snorted in a way which showed that he was not convinced. Firumin hurried forward to offer him some more wine. Aleizon Ailix Ayndra politely excused herself.

Lord Domar levered himself to his feet with the help of a cane and his nephew, Lord Haligon. 'This is a Council of Lords,' he declared in a wavering voice. 'What do all these people here?' His pointing finger jiggled along the row of chairs against the wall, where Sumakas sat with Ailissa, Ylureen, S'Thiraidi, Derezhaid, Faracaln and Siriane. Golaron occupied the head of the lords' table; Aleizon Ailix Ayndra sat halfway down on his right side, with the S'Thurrulans at her back. It was she who spoke now.

'These visitors are our noble allies of S'Thurrulass. They have been invited to attend our Council as a mark of honour. Of course they do not expect to vote. My lady Sumakas and Lady Ailissa have come to accompany Paraki-son. As his guardians in the absence of his mother and stepfather, such is their duty.'

'I request that they be asked to leave,' said Domar. 'It was never the custom to observe the Council of Lords, and they not even Safeen at that.'

'I favour the presence of our allies,' said Golaron. 'What view does the rest of the Council take?' He scanned the ring of faces. When the last full Council was summoned to find Ailixond's successor, with the proxies there had been fifty-four electors. Now there were barely forty, and a good few of those were like Antinar and Takarem, youths who had come of age since the King's death and so had not received their bracelets; they were allowed to attend, so that they should learn statecraft, but they could not vote. Antinar sat next to his father; Takarem sat at the far end of the table, glowering in a manner reminiscent of his own absent genitor. In the confusion after Sulakon's line broke at Shili, he had escaped with a small party of horsemen and they had ranged over the countryside for days before they found their way back to Safi, only to discover it already in rebel hands and the Lord Regent fled. Ailissa had argued with him for days until she managed to quell his desire to take a fishing smack up the coast to look for his father, and convinced him that his better duty was to stay in the city with her. He had come to the Council in the company of Ellakon and a number of other younger lords, all veterans of Sulakon's wars against some of the men they now shared a council table with, and all armed and angry. Lord Rinahar spoke for them. 'We oppose it. What right do they have?'

'Let the foreigners go.'

'Let them all go!' said Haligon, with a glance at Sumakas.

Lord Garadon coughed. 'What matter? This is not a Council of Lords anyway. How many of us are missing? Even of those who are not dead or absent – where is Lord Polem? Why is he not here?'

'Lord Polem rode out of the city this dawn, at the head of a troop of mercenaries, to go to the defence of his estate at Samala,' said Ayndra. 'He sent his regrets to the Council that he could not attend, but he considered the preservation of his property of greater importance than the affairs of the state.'

This caused a buzz of chatter, and many glances at Arpalond, who appeared blind to it all. 'No doubt my lord Ayndra desired him to stay,' said Ellakon.

'I pleaded with him, to lend his voice to our debate before he departed,' she said, 'but he would have none of it. My lord Arpalond, he said, could speak for him.'

'And what about this matter of Samala?' wheezed Domar. 'There is no order in the land! We all stand endangered! What is to be done? You say that Samala has been invaded?'

Golaron rapped on the table. 'My lords! It is to deal with the question of order that we have gathered here. More than six years ago we elected Lord Sulakon Regent of Safi. No one will deny that he has forfeited his right to the post, since he fled the city and has not presented himself to this Council. Therefore, we have gathered to choose his successor. We all agree that Master Parakison should continue as the heir to the kingdom, to be crowned when he comes of age.'

Parakison, seated between Sumakas and Ailissa, stretched his head up when he heard his name. There was a murmur of assent. 'I call upon Parakison to speak,' said Golaron.

Heads swivelled; Sumakas patted Parakison on the back, and he got up, strutted towards the table and began to recite. 'My lords, my ladies. I have not spoken before you, and I know that my youth lacks authority, but I pray that you will listen to my words. This my Empire, which you hold in honourable trust for me, has been tormented by years of civil strife, only lately brought to an end by one who has united the provinces under one banner and carried that banner into Safi itself. My uncle, who governed here, has laid down his office and with it the years of dismal austerity which he imposed upon the city. My lord Aleizon Ailix Ayndra is the only one among us with the power and authority to take it up. Nor will she bring austerity and suffering, but a new era of peace and prosperity. Therefore I say that you should elect her Regent. It was for this that my father gave her his ring.' He turned to Aleizon Ailix Ayndra and said, 'Show them the ring.'

Absolutely deadpan, as though it was a crowned king who addressed her, she pulled it out of her shirt and let it swing on its chain in front of them. Parakison pointed to it and said, 'This is a token of my father's trust in her. I think you should trust her too. Thank you.' He made a sharp bow and dashed back to his chair, looking up at Sumakas with great expectant eyes. She looked at him with a restrained but adoring smile, and put her finger to her lips. Parakison nodded excitedly and grasped the edges of his seat, squirming back and forth; then he saw how many people were gawping at him, and poked his chin up in pride. Aleizon Ailix Ayndra, still impassive, let the ring fall back inside her shirt.

'Let us vote upon the proposal, that my lord Aleizon Ailix Ayndra be Lord Regent of Safi,' said Golaron. 'I take it that there are no other candidates?'

Domar rapped his cane on the floor. 'What, what is this? This woman, this, this – training a child to speak – she is a fugitive from justice! I tried her! Myself! She had her head shaved– '

Ayndra was looking at him, opaque blue eyes in a face like stone. In a calm voice she said, 'The old justice is no more. Many of us here have fought against Safi and in so doing have committed many crimes. Yet these are now forgotten in our search for peace. I put myself and my army, and these my allies—' She waved at Ylureen and her companions, ' —at the service of Safi and of the unity of the Empire. I only ask that you accept this service, and join me in the discard of old enmities.'

At the foot of the table Takarem stood up. 'Parakison,' he said. 'Stand up.'

Parakison looked at his grandmother for confirmation, and did so. 'Cousin, can you answer some questions for us?' Takarem asked. Parakison nodded. 'Did you write that speech for yourself?'

'I learnt it.'

'Who taught it to you?'

'Gran'ma and Lord Ayndra.'

'Do you understand its meaning?'

'Of course I do!' Parakison retorted.

'Do you yourself wish to have Lord Ayndra for Regent of Safi?'

'Why? Do you not like her?'

Several people laughed. Takarem raised his voice. 'Please answer me, Parakison: do you choose Lord Ayndra to be Regent of Safi?'

Casik interrupted. 'I object! The child may be the heir to the kingdom, but why do we concern ourselves with his opinion?' Parakison made a face at him and said loudly, 'I do so want Lord Ayndra to be Regent! And no one told me to do it. I choose her myself!'

'Master Takarem, have you done with your questions?' Golaron asked.

'I have,' said Takarem. 'Parakison, I thank you.'

'Can I sit down now?' asked Parakison.

'Let us proceed to a vote,' said Golaron.

'Let us vote by show of hands,' said Casik.

'It would be better to vote using the tablets,' said Ayndra. 'In that way, all those who dissent can show it by writing whatever name they would choose, and have it recorded.' She nodded at the foot of the table. Takarem did not return

122

it; but then, since he was not a lord, he could not vote. There were eleven dissenting voices out of thirty-four; Lord Domar gave in a blank tablet.

'I proclaim Lord Aleizon Ailix Ayndra, lord of Safi and Over-Governor of Haramin, Lord Regent of Safi.'

Arpalond got to his feet and raised one hand in salute. 'Hail!' The S'Thurrulans clapped their hands together for all they were worth and cried out in their own language. Ellakon, Takarem and the rest of the dissenters got up and walked out.

Ayndra hushed the applause, but the stone quality had left her face. The door had hardly closed behind Rinahar when it opened again to admit the Justiciar, the Treasurer and several other clerks with piles of papers. Ayndra gestured to Ylureen. 'Come and join us at the table now,' she said. While they were finding places, Sumakas came up to her with Ailissa and Parakison. Ayndra put her hands on the child's shoulders. 'You were splendid. You'll make speeches of your own to silence us all some day.'

'Can I stay for this?' Parakison asked.

'It is all very boring now. The exciting part is over; now we shall talk about money.'

Sumakas was leading him toward the door, but Ailissa lingered. 'May I stay?' she said in a low voice.

'Why, of course,' said Ayndra. She showed her to a seat next to Siriane, and gave in to Golaron's insistence that she should take over the head of the table. The Justiciar sat on one side of her, the Treasurer on the other; Hahhni leant past her to put a tiny oil-lamp on the table. She took a smokestick out of her tunic, lit it and inhaled; when she blew the smoke out it formed a perfect ring. The Council had all settled down now, ready to listen. She hooked her foot under the stretcher between the table legs and tilted her chair back. 'Very well. My lords, gentlemen. I call upon Lord Arpalond to tell us of the events in Samala. That dealt with, we shall proceed to matters of administration.'

The inner room was cool even in the suffocating heat of second hour of afternoon. The double doors of the outer room stood open on to the courtyard, admitting the radiance of the cloudless sky, but the inner chamber remained in a green gloom, refreshed by the trickling fountain in the wall opposite the door. Ylureen had her cushions laid out next to it, and invited Ailissa to lie near her. As they finished eating their own lunches and clearing up after those of others, the other women of the household came in to share the cool throughout the hottest hours. Some lay down to doze on the cushioned benches round the walls of the inner room; more brought books or pieces of handwork and sat outside where the light was better. The maidservants helped their mistresses, or rested while they read or sewed. Hahhni sat fanning Ylureen, who lay back on the cushions with her eyes closed. 'I visit this house on a day as hot as this,' she murmured in Safic. 'When I come into this room I know I buy it.'

'You were very wise; I know no room in the palace as pleasant as this in this weather.'

'Indeed,' said Ylureen with a sigh. 'I will show you the rest of the house when it a cooler.' She plucked the fine silk of her gown away from her belly and fanned it to and fro above her thighs. 'I find it a very trial, iss so hot.'

'I am sure you must; it is always a difficult time. Why do you not sleep for now?'

'I try to do so.' Ylureen spoke to Hahhni, who handed her the fan with which to cool herself the while and went to fetch the waterpipe. Ailissa refused the first offers of the mouthpiece, but when she had lain for a while with nothing to listen to but the sound of the fountain and muffled whispers in an incomprehensible language, she yielded to Hahhni's blandishments. When they had finished with the pipe, the slave lit a stick of incense and started to waft its vapours over Ylureen's sleeping form. The slice of court-yard showing beyond the open doors shone brighter than the sunlit snows of a northern winter; she closed her eyes against the glare. When she opened them again it was golden, and the people in the outer room had gone.

Ylureen was sitting in a wide chair, still fanning herself while Hahhni laced her sandals. Ailissa sat up and put her hands to her hair; another serving-woman in a red tunic was instantly at her side offering a mirror. They understood her needs so well that she was tidied, shod and delivered to Ylureen who stood waiting in the doorway without a word being said by anyone. Ylureen linked an arm through hers. 'Come now: you will see all our houses. The others first, and we will come back to this one.'

They were more warehouses than houses proper, running either side of a narrow alley and surrounding the cramped square at its blind end, with small, older dwellings in the interstices. Builders were everywhere, as well as hordes of S'Thurrulans, and Safic families hanging out washing and cobbling shoes on the balconies of the old tenements. 'Are all these your property?' Ailissa asked.

'Pilith buy the land. They living here stay, we rent them. See, here we make our shop. Will you see the cellars?'

'Of course. I should love to see everything.'

Ylureen looked Ailissa in the eye and smiled warmly. 'This way.'

They made frequent halts, so that Ylureen could sit down on the folding chair which Hahhni carried and rest her legs, while she discoursed to Ailissa on the condition of each building and the uses she intended to put it to. Ailissa was saucer-eyed with the strain on her memory. Sumakas had promised to wait up for her till the small hours, if need be, so as to hear it all from her while the details were freshly recalled; but so many details! It was blue dusk when they came back to the real house, secluded behind its owner's place of business like the mansions of many merchant princes in the city. Ylureen seated herself with relief in the seat of honour in the main room on the first floor; when a Safin had owned the house it had been the room where the patron received his male clients and friends. Servants brought them fruit syrups which had been cooled in deep wells and a dozen different kinds of sweetmeats and delicacies. As they were lighting the hanging lamps, there was a rattle of spurs on the stone staircase and Aleizon Ailix Ayndra came running in. She pulled off her hat and bent over to kiss Ylureen, who caressed her neck. 'Still the size of a house,' she said.

'I have said to you, it will be another ten days; we have not even held the last dance yet.'

Ailissa was sitting up, looking inquisitive. Ayndra turned to greet her. 'Lady, welcome; I think you have not come here before?'

'It is my first visit. Lady Ylureen has shown me all round the district.'

'Has she? Very good.' Ayndra sat down next to Ailissa, took a cheese pie and bit into it. Spraying shards of puff pastry, she said, 'I must speak to you concerning Takarem, Ailissa; but not just now; first I must send Parakison home.'

'Parakison?'

'Here he comes now.'

The Little King entered the room with Derezhaid at his side; while the latter was paying his respects to Ylureen, his charge exclaimed, 'Aunt 'lissa!' and scrambled up on the silk seat beside her.

'Where have you been?' she asked; all three newcomers were covered in dust and smelt of horse sweat. 'Derrijai took me to where they practise archery, and then we went to the drill ground and met Lord Ayndra, and then we saw the New Companions practising, and do you know, Aunt' lissa, I rode with them, I got up on a big horse, Lord Golaron was there and he let me borrow his one, his name was Yelto, and at the end we even went at full gallop and I was never scared . . . have you been in this house before?'

'No, I never have; have you?'

'O, yes, Lord Ayndra often brings me here. I have to go home now for Gran'ma to cut my hair. Will you come home?'

'I shall come home later. Have you someone to escort you?'

'Derrijai will take me.' He poked at the assorted titbits on the tray before them, selected one, put it in his mouth and made an inarticulate noise of disgust as he spat it out on the floor.

'Parakison!' said Ailissa.

'Urh!' said the Little King.

'I think you had better go home,' said Ailissa.

'I shall go home. Hor'ble food! Urh! Urh!' His childish cries echoed between Derezhaid's soft bass as they went down to their horses. Aleizon Ailix Ayndra picked up a napkin and wiped her mouth before tossing it down in the ruins of a plateful of cheese pies. She lifted her head to make sure that only Ylureen's personal servants remained in the room before she spoke, and that not loudly. 'Ailissa, we

126

think that we know where Sulakon is. Takarem is not at all happy here. Were we to tell you where the place is, and find him armed companions for the journey, and you proposed to him that he leave, would he be willing to go?'

'What?' said Ailissa, her voice rising. 'Sulakon?'

Ayndra made hushing motions with her hand. 'It is all very secret. You understand that it would help no one were it to become generally known.'

'But you . . . what are you going to do?'

'You think it odd that I should encourage Takarem to go and join my enemy? Ailissa, I shall not sweeten my mouth for you. Takarem is no fool, but his youth makes him rash, and his flamboyance draws followers. I cannot tolerate him here for more than a few months more – he has been spreading open sedition against me already. I could, of course, dismiss him to some provincial garrison, but with that salt in his wound I would very likely find the province in rebellion against me in a year's time. Whereas, an I send him – though of course he must never think that I send him – to look for his father, with followers of my own choosing . . .' She spread her hands like a carpet-seller soliciting a purchase. 'And does he not want to go and join his father?'

'My lord, I want that he should stay here with me,' Ailissa said.

'Ah! I say you are say that,' said Ylureen. Ayndra gave her a filthy look, which she affected not to see.

'Nevertheless, something will have to be done,' she said. 'Takarem is like a burning-glass for the fire of the young lords. I should not like to have to send any of them away to the back hills with orders that someone stick a knife in their back in the middle of some tribal skirmish. An he goes away to look for Sulakon, I shall not have to send any at all.' She looked calmly at Ailissa, who drew herself up.

'You ask me to suggest this to him.'

'You are 'is mother,' said Ylureen.

'And until now I have besought him every day to stay here with us and to be peaceable and favour your party,' said Ailissa. 'Shall I now tell him to go?'

'You did not know before where his father was,' said Ayndra. 'Having this news brought through to you by a faithful servitor, you have suffered a change of heart, and recommend him to go to the place where his true loyalty lies. Yes?'

'I do not know where his father is,' Ailissa said. 'My lord, these are family matters. My son is . . . that is, my son is a grown man, and besides, since his father left, he is the head of the family in Safi.'

'You need not answer presently,' Ayndra said.

'And what, should I go to him now and tell him what you have told me?'

'It is always your right to speak to anyone you wish to,' Ayndra replied. She turned aside to receive a steaming cup of chabe from Hahhni and passed another to Ailissa. Ylureen asked her if she liked music, and when she said yes, snapped her fingers and a flattanharpist began to play. Ylureen beckoned to Ailissa to come and sit by her side, and began to ask her questions about her dress, her hairdressing, her younger children; the slave brought the waterpipe round again. Aleizon Ailix Ayndra wandered round the room, trying to blow smoke-rings and mostly failing. Ylureen got up to relieve herself as the Regent had revolved to face Ailissa again. She knelt down at her feet and offered her the smokestick. Ailissa took it, but did not smoke it. She leant forward and asked, 'Where is Sulakon? Where is he?'

'In a place called Gingito,' said Aleizon Ailix Ayndra. 'Setha is there with him, but Parhannon is not. Meraptar is there. I can give you four caravan guards who know how to travel there, and there are four or six more among the palace guards who will as it were volunteer should Takarem ask them — I will give you their names . . .' She went on talking, the gaze of her dilated eyes never shifting. 'Tell him to wait until Ylureen's time comes, it will not be long now; then he may trust that I shall be with her, and he can leave unseen.'

'Unseen?' said Ailissa. Ayndra grinned and patted her knee as she stood up.

Ylureen came back in, walking slowly and yawning. 'I think I go to rest now,' she said. 'You will go back to the palace, lady?'

'We shall go together,' Ayndra said. Ylureen frowned; Ayndra shrugged. 'I have to work this night,' she said, 'next morning I am going out to Lakkanar's lands. It is not far to go; an I leave at first light, I should be back by sunset. I will come here directly my business is finished. Is that well?'

'Let me see you to the door.' Ylureen called out in her own tongue, and a servant brought Ailissa's mantle. She followed the Regent and the Ambassador down the stairs. The slaves with Ailissa's carrying chair were waiting beside Tarap in the courtyard at the back of the house, liveried servants bowing either side of them. Ylureen kissed Ailissa on both cheeks. 'Lady, when my time comes I send for you, to come to the birth – you come? I welcome you.'

'Lady, of course I shall come; I thank you again for your kindness.'

'Iss a pleasure, my lady. This house is yours; at any time you come.' She turned to Aleizon Ailix Ayndra and took both her hands; they looked into each other's eyes. Ylureen ruffled her loose hair and pulled to her in a brief embrace; they kissed, and Ayndra broke away to leap up on the back of the black horse.

When Ailissa glanced back through the closing gates, the courtyard was empty except for servants. 'My lord Regent,' she said. 'Surely we should not go home together.'

'We met in the street, and you asked if I would see you through the vagabonds in Great Market. What could be more innocent? I know that these your bearers are silent men.' She favoured them with one of her smiles that went no further than her mouth; they muttered assent, and moved into a smooth lope to keep up with the pace of the warhorse.

The Lord Regent's party returned to the city through the Gate of Ivory; she insisted that they wait in the gate-court while she went to get a drink of water. In fact she went directly to the gate-captain's room. 'Daior-deor? Do not bother to stand up; I cannot stay: only listen to this.' She made sure the door was shut and no one in the passage outside. 'The gate-guard called Larat is going to accept a bribe, for the night when Ylureen gives birth, to let some people out of the city after dark. No people of Ylureen's, I might add.'

'Going to take a bribe? What should I do, dismiss him now?'

'No, merely let him accept it and do what he has been paid to do.'

Daior-deor looked at her, but she was giving nothing away. 'You can watch him do it, an you do it discreetly,' she said with a smile.

'But what an his friends report him to me?'

'Send him to Magarrla for two years, for unlawful benefit of kin. The man who will give him the bribe is his cousin. Merely send me the papers and I will sign them. An the other guards do not tell you of it, you know nothing, except arrest him an he takes bribes which I have not told you about beforehand. Good day, Daior, I will see you shortly.' The door slammed, sending a gust of wind to riffle the sheets of the pay-list on Daior-deor's desk. He put the inkwell on top of them to keep them still and picked up an uncut quill and the penknife. Then the door opened again. This time she was laughing. 'Come and tell me directly it happens; I shall be at Ylureen's house.'

He saluted her without speaking, she returned it and whisked out again.

The thunderclouds piled slowly during the day, while the air in the city grew thicker and thicker. Ylureen's waters had broken an hour before dawn; she laboured through the heat of the day in the room with the fountain, while her people gathered with the storm, the men in the warehouse and the front rooms of the house, the women in the interior courtyard and the rooms around it. In the middle of the day it was too hot to dance, but the chatter of little drums and high sweet voices drifted into the outer parts of the house. It was a slow travail; more than a hundred people were in the house waiting when the first rolls of thunder tumbled over the roofs, and the downpour began, an hour after the sun had disappeared in the louring murk. Within moments the streets were deserted and the pelting rain had transformed late summer into wintery desolation; the public rooms of Ylureen's house were crammed with people reeking from wet woollens and demanding smokes and drinks from the servants, who were labouring in droves in the kitchens to prepare the feast that would be generally distributed as soon as the child gave its first cry. Daior-deor had to hammer on the front door with the hilt of his sword before someone came to open it. To his surprise it was a Thaless woman, who addressed him in accented Safic; he asked her in dialect if he could speak to the Lord Regent.

'She is with my lady, sir. Will you go upstairs? The gentlemen are all received there.'

'I must speak to my lord; I have a message which she asked me to bring to her.' The woman told him that he could not go in and see her, that no men were allowed in, that he should go upstairs; he insisted. Eventually she agreed to go into the women's part and see if my lord would come out, while Daior-deor agreed to go upstairs. He pushed his way through damp backs and an uproar of male voices; it was worse than a guardroom at the change of watch. The seat of honour was occupied by the youth Sabraid, with Derezhaid and Faracaln and other notables around him. Everyone had a shot glass in hand, and menservants struggled through the crowd refilling them after every toast. There was not a woman in sight. It was just like a wedding party at home. He turned suddenly as a hand touched his shoulder. 'Good day! Good day, captain, good night, whatever it may be – have you come to join the celebration? Delighted to see you!'

'Good day, Selanor, and I should be delighted to join it. But I have orders to see the Governor. Yet she seems hidden in some part of the house, and the woman would not let me go – I wait for her presently – '

'What do you say? Heaven's blood, I cannot hear my own voice in here. I must go outside, beside. Will you come with me?' He headed out of the door, clearly under some pressure, downstairs to an alleyway leading back towards the kitchen quarters. Rainwater was pouring from the gutterspouts into a drain along the floor. As Selanor was gratefully adding his offering to the stream, a woman came hurrying from the kitchens, holding a square of canvas over her head. Seeing Selanor, she dashed up to him and seized him from behind. He almost fell over in surprise; she grabbed his arm and dragged him into the dry while he tried to make himself decent. She was talking to him in S'Thurrulan. He looked at Daior-deor, bent over and whispered in the woman's ear. Her face lit up with excitement and she giggled as she replied. Selanor beckoned to Daior-deor. 'She will find my lord for us, an we come away with her and wait where she leave us.' The woman pulled Daior-deor's hood up over his head and made Selanor assume her canvas shawl; the two of them set off chuckling like adolescents. The woman left them to wait in a windowless mop-closet which echoed with the beat of drums and music on the other side of one wall. Selanor lolled against it with a beatific grin on his face, arms folded under his mantle.

'I do not think we make very convincing women,' Daior-deor said.

Selanor gave a happily drunken shrug. 'A pity she did not leave a bottle for us,' he said.

Daior-deor overturned a bucket and sat down on it. 'By all means go and fetch one,' he said. 'I must wait.'

'O no,' said Selanor. 'I too must wait!' He laughed. The music and voices mingled with the sound of the rain, until a shrill whistle sounded from the dark passage. Selanor, emerging, was instantly whisked away by his friend; Daior-deor was confronted by the glimmer of a white shirt in the darkness and a dense vapour of sweat, sweetsmoke and medicinal herbs. 'Have they gone?' said a familiar voice.

'Yes, I saw them leave. It was just after the gates had closed and the rain started; with the thunder one did not hear the noise of the hinges.'

'Bless you!' The red eye of a burning smokestick swung at him, and he took it. Ayndra tossed her hair back. 'God save me, it is like an iron foundry in there.'

'And like a back scullery here,' said Daior-deor. 'My lord, can we not go into the light?'

'We should not be talking to each other at all. I am Ylureen's head-helper, I cannot stay more than a moment. And you should be at the men's gathering, an you are here at all – ay! But what was that? Daior, excuse me!'

'I would like to–' he began; but she had gone, and left him the smokestick. He crept along the corridor to the door which she had left swinging open in a patch of lamplight. The women were shouting in unison, some phrase repeated over and over; they were all crowded over the far side of the courtyard, round the double doors of a brightly lit room, as though they were all trying to cram themselves into it. A dozen of them were beating drums in a frenzy under the colonnade, and the rest clapped their hands above their heads. One burst free of the press and fell on the ground, threshing about like a landed fish; half a dozen others tried to restrain her, but they all went on shouting their chant and stamping their feet in time with the drums. Others began leaping up and down like devil-possessed in a temple. Then there was an enormous scream from within and pandemonium broke loose. Women erupted all over the courtyard as if possessed by frenzy, ignoring the rain, jumping and dancing and kissing one another and rolling on the ground; there was boiling in the doorway and Aleizon Ailix Ayndra appeared, holding a live red bundle above her head. For an instant it looked as if it were a deformed monster, then it resolved into an infant, still smeared with the blood of birth, howling and kicking half out of a red cloth. She was holding it in such a way that its enlarged vulva was clearly displayed. Ayndra had her mouth wide open and was screaming as loudly as the rest; her shirt was stuck to her breasts with sweat and there was a big patch of blood down the front of it. A forest of hands closed round her, reaching out to touch the child, and she disappeared inside the room again. Women rushed in all directions, like woodlice when a stone is overturned, toward every doorway. Daior-deor turned and fled.

When he saw Selanor again it was two days later, outside Aleizon Ailix Ayndra's office, in the courtyard with the red flowers, now reduced to seed-pods and a few last rags of colour. He told him what he had seen after they parted. Selanor whistled. 'You were a wise man to run away. They would have killed you an they caught you.'

'What?'

'O yes; it is a very sacred thing that you saw. Will you have some of these?'

'What are they?'

'You chew them to sweeten the breath. To quell the odour . . . but perhaps you do not need them. I have to go and speak to my lord, you see.'

'And I too,' said Daior-deor.

Selanor shook his head sadly. 'You do not need them,' he said, and rapped on the door.

133

Aleizon Ailix Ayndra herself opened it. She let Selanor step inside, but put her nose close to his mouth as he entered. Her eyebrows rose but she said nothing. 'Come in, captain,' she said to Daior-deor.

A circle of chairs stood in the middle of the large room; Polem, Arpalond, Sumakas and Diamoon were already seated. Daior-deor bowed and greeted them. 'My lord,' he said to Polem, 'I congratulate you on your successes in Samala.'

'Rather I should thank you, sir; you know I had all officers from your troop of mercenaries, and your friend Chamarin in charge; without them I should have done nothing, they advised me in everything.'

'And this time you were content to do no more than take their advice,' Ayndra said. She picked up a tray of cups and bottles from her desk and carried it to the middle of the circle.

'I have learnt to take advice now,' Polem said. 'Diamoon has trained me to it.'

'I am glad to hear it.' She pulled the cork from one bottle and poured herself a cup of some steaming infusion. 'Help yourself. First of all let me remind you that all we say here remains within this circle. Now what we have to discuss this day is the conduct of our faithful allies.'

'Lady Ylureen and her people,' said Sumakas.

'Lady Ylureen and her people. And may I ask you all to speak honestly, without any regard for my feelings? The love I bear Ylureen does not blind me to her many offences. To begin with, there is the matter of the numbers of Thalessi and Safeen she has taken on as servants of her line and others.'

'And why should she not have servants?' Selanor said. 'They are well treated, I can vouch for it. Some have even pleaded to become her servants. Did she not give homes to all those refugees of Mirries who would accept it?'

'The trouble is that they are not servants so much as slaves,' said Arpalon.

'Nor are they slaves as we hold slaves,' Ayndra said. 'The line holds them, and they cannot be sold to any other line without they give their permission to the sale. They will not generally accept a man unless they take his wife or his sister

134

or daughter first.' She sipped her drink. 'The trouble is that Ellakon has discovered that our allies have purchased subjects of the Empire as slaves. I think he would not care had they stayed with Thalessi, but since we entered the city they have sought many people to assist them with their building work, and a good few of the Safeen among the rebels have joined them. As Selanor says, they are well treated.'

Polem asked, 'What will become of them when Lady Ylureen returns home?'

'They will stay here, I imagine, in the Yard of Suthine.'

'Is that what they call it? It covers very much more than a yard.'

'Excuse me,' said Polem, 'but I have been away – how did they come by it? You gave it to them?'

'They bought it,' said Aleizon Ailix Ayndra. 'And paid for it in gold sols. The former owners were delighted to accept. I had nothing to do with it. The administrations of property titles is no duty of mine, God be praised.'

'But trade treaties are,' said Sumakas.

Ayndra made a graceful gesture in her direction. 'Lady, perhaps you would tell us the word of the merchants.'

'I will indeed. It is not two months since you entered the city, my lord, but already they complain that the S'Thurrulans have brought in a multitude of merchandises of their country and allow no one else to take part in the trade, not even to buy them from their ships, unless it be in small quantities. I suggest that when you do compose your trade treaty, you forbid this monopoly. After all, they are here in Safi at our pleasure. This is widespread intelligence. It is not so widespread that, when your fleet was blockading the city and we had to ration the corn, certain ships entered under the Lysmalish flag to supply grain at the exceptional prices of the day; but they were not Lysmalish ships.'

'Does it matter whose ships they were?' said Ayndra. 'They brought bread to the people when there was none; what else is there to say?' She gave Sumakas a very hard look. 'You will not have expected them to offer it as a charity.'

'Whose ships were they?' said Polem. An idea crossed his face and he broke into a smile. 'They were not yours, were they?'

'I suppose there is no point in keeping my lips sealed here,' said Ayndra. 'They belonged to Ylureen, though she put Lysmalish crews in them.'

Arpalond's cloudy gaze caught hers. 'So,' he said, in a voice of soft admiration. 'While your army approached the city and threw its markets into panic, so your ally was smuggling corn past the blockade.'

'And as far as the Council of Lords is concerned, I knew nothing of any of it.'

'Why, of course.' He felt among the bottles on the tray; she pointed one out to him, and he started to pour out the wine. 'Was it part of your alliance with Lady Ylureen?'

'The terms of my alliance with Lady Ylureen are vague. At the outset I was promised many things by the King and Queen in Suthine, and did not receive more than the half of them. Since then we have proceeded by verbal agreement, no more, with the intention of forming a treaty when we were in Safi. Now we are in Safi; I cannot delay the treaty any longer. Ylureen will be lying-in for another sixday; then I can expect her to come to me with a list of proposed concessions as long as your arm. That is why I have called you here, to find out what knowledge and what opinion people have of our allies, and to arm myself against excessive demands.'

'The war is over, my lord; surely you can avoid any concessions at all,' said Diamoon.

Ayndra shook her head. 'One war may be over,' she said. She got up and went to light a smokestick in the tiny lamp on the table. 'And I need money.'

'You always need money!' said Polem. Sumakas sat with her hands in her lap, eyeing the Lord Regent like a heron watching a river for fish. 'What terms do you propose for the treaty?' she asked.

'I have not proposed any terms at all, as yet,' Ayndra said peacefully. She tipped her head back and exhaled. 'Look at her! A smoke ring!' When Sumakas looked round, she gave her a delightfully ingenuous smile. 'Let us talk about terms, as long as you like. Then I shall go and make the treaty up on my own.'

Aleizon Ailix Ayndra declined the palace guards' offer of an escort through the dark streets. She went through the backstreets to the stable entrance of Ylureen's house; even from there one could hear the music and voices. She likewise declined the porter's offer of a couple of attendants to escort her to the Lady; she drifted like a black crow through the lamplit porticoes, past the dance in the court-yard, to the front room where the banquet had been served and Ylureen had spent the day receiving congratulations, while the nurse sat behind her with the child, ready to hand it to its mother whenever it cried for food. It was almost last hour of evening, and most of the people she passed were too far gone in pleasure to notice who she was. She was just taking her hat off at the top of the stairs when someone called to her in Safic. Ailissa came rustling up to her, all dressed up as if she had been at a long-robe dinner. 'My lord! We have all been asking after you.'

'I received three lots of despatches this day; I have not even read them all yet, but I thought I had better leave them before it was too late.' She stood knocking dust off her hat, a slight frown marking her forehead.

Ailissa took her hand and said in a lowered voice, 'You have not yet had any news from . . .'

'From Takarem? It is only eight days, I think they have not even reached the Chiaral yet. And then there has to be someone to take the message back, without Sulakon knows it; it will be a halfmonth or more, before we know. Be assured I shall send for you the instant we do. Have you been here all the day?'

'Lady Ylureen invited me for the special banquet, for the women, before the public congratulations. I made sure that you would be there – I mean, my lord, for your namesake– ' At that, the frown turned into a grimace. Ailissa paused. 'I thought it charming, that she should call her after you – do you not like it?'

Ayndra gave a lopsided smile. 'I thought I was the only one in the world with my name,' she said. 'Shall we go in?'

'Where are your people? Surely we should wait for them.'

'What people?'

'Why, your entourage.'

Ayndra blinked at Ailissa. Finally she said, 'I cannot get into this habit of having people to follow me everywhere. Do you suppose I should try to acquire it?'

'You are the Lord Regent,' Ailissa said.

'Let us go in,' said Ayndra. 'I shall be the Lord Regent as soon as I have passed through that door.'

Ylureen greeted her effusively when she approached the seat of honour; she did the Lord Regent the honour of getting to her feet, taking her arm and leading her round the room to introduce her to rows of S'Thurrulans, cousins and cousins' husbands, all of them merchants of one kind or another. They bowed and kissed her hand and she spoke most graciously to them. 'I am delighted to receive you in our city of Safi . . . of course I welcome every one of our sisters of Pilith . . . we of Safi love to see this proof of the friendship and trust which has grown up between our nations . . .'

'Love to see the colour of our money, you mean,' muttered Getaleen, who was attending S'Thiraidi in Ylureen's train. S'Thiraidi kicked her. Ylureen suddenly turned on them, but it was not their words but the short-breathed wa-wa-wa from the seats which had drawn her attention. They all followed her back and made an eager circle round her seat while she settled herself on the cushions and undid the front of her gown. The nurse handed her the infant, two tiny hands and a little crumpled face in a water-lily of lace and soft white wool, and bent forward with a napkin to mop the milk leaking from Ylureen's left breast while the child fastened on the right. The onlookers made a chorus of delight. 'Lady, you are a true mother! Beloved older sister, the goddess has blessed you . . . may we all be so blessed with abundance . . . lady, you bring blessing upon us all . . .'

Ailissa had turned aside with her handkerchief held up to her face. She whispered to Aleizon Ailix Ayndra, 'Can they find no wet-nurses here?'

'They never use wet-nurses, unless the mother have no milk at all; and then she tries to find a line sister with milk, before she pays a nurse.' Ayndra flicked her eyebrows. 'Come now; you must have seen this happen fifteen times already.'

Ailissa took one glance, and saw that the child was being put on the other breast; she immediately turned away again. 'In front of so many,' she hissed. 'And what do they say?'

'They say that Ylureen blesses all of us by the abundance of her milk ... sweet heaven!' Two other women with nursing infants had been allowed to go to the front of the crowd, and were now offering them to Ylureen, while the nurse took small Aleizon to burp her on her shoulder.

Ailissa had all but turned green. 'Are these her ... her ...'

'Line sisters,' said Aleizon Ailix Ayndra. 'Shumar, I had no idea that Ylureen's prestige had progressed so far.' Ylureen, who was presently feeding a baby perhaps five months old, turned her head to smile at them and beckoned with her free hand. Aleizon Ailix Ayndra patted Ailissa's shoulder and went to take up her place by Ylureen's side. 'Soon you will be line mother to all of us,' she said.

Ylureen handed the baby to a man with a crimped beard and leaned back to let Hahhni dry her, tuck some absorbent cloths in her bodice and fasten it again. 'Call Lady Ailissa to join us,' she said, 'I think she is lonely here for not speaking our tongue.'

'She is also confused; Safic ladies do not always suckle their own children, and then only in secret.'

'But how can they feed them, an they must do it in secret all the time?'

'They lead their whole lives in secret, as you know. And only a poor woman would suckle another's child.'

'But these are my younger sisters, bringing their daughters to me. They would never give them to someone not of our blood.'

'All Safic children are their fathers' daughters; I suppose that is why they let them drink the milk of any mother.'

'But you must have suckled your own daughter.'

Ayndra raised her voice. 'Ailissa! Come and sit with us now,' she called in Safic, and to Ylureen, 'Does any food remain from the banquet? I have eaten no more than a bread roll since noon.'

'It has been sent to the kitchens, for the servants and the poor.'

'Have some of it sent back again, then; or I shall go to the kitchens to look for it.' Ylureen made some hand signals to Hahhni, who nodded and left, while she showed Ailissa the cushion next to her, and called the nurse back with the baby, who was now happy with repletion. She unwrapped the blankets the better to show her to Ailissa, and started asking her advice about the best kind of water for bathing babies in, whether it should be spring water or rain water or boiled water with herbs of what kind ... while Hahhni came back with a plateful of delicacies and Aleizon Ailix Ayndra speared and gobbled them. After midnight the guests started to leave for their quarters elsewhere in the yard of Suthine, and Ailissa, considerably mollified by Ylureen's deference, departed for the palace.

'No doubt to speak to her mother,' said Ayndra, when she had gone out of the door.

'Her mother is a very fine woman; but greedy for power.'

'I know it; for that reason I am including her in some of my private councils. I do not wish to fall into the same bind as the two former Regents in Safi, when they ruled one half of the city and Sumakas ruled the other and ever the twain plotted against each other.' She dragged thoughtfully on her smokestick. 'But she must have been plotting from those rooms in the palace for forty years.'

'Old habits die hard?'

'I gather that she has been meeting with S'Thiraidi.'

'S'Thiraidi would not dare move against me here.' Ylureen stood up and wrapped her shawl round her shoulders. 'I go to my bed now.' She did not ask Ayndra to follow her; the Lord Regent remained seated until she had finished her smoke, ground it out under her heel and went along the gallery to Ylureen's own room. The Ambassador was taking off her paint; she smiled in the mirror when she saw Ayndra come in, and beckoned to her. 'Will you take my hair down for me?'

'Of course.' The gold pins clinked one by one on to the tray enamelled in a pattern of trumpet-flowers; Ylureen closed her eyes. Aleizon Ailix Ayndra picked up an ivory comb and began to draw it gently through the hennaed tresses. 'Where does the child sleep?'

'Small Aleizon? My dressing-room has been made a bedroom for her and the nurse; we have put a curtain in place of the door, so that I can hear them.'

'And they can hear us,' said Ayndra in an aggrieved voice.

'The nurse is the daughter of my woman Esas'thi. Think

you I would put my daughter in the hands of any woman whom I could not trust with my life?'

'But it is not my life.'

'Of course it is your life! My lord, I have given her your *name*. How can you say it is not your life?' The comb dragged so harshly at her hair that she opened her eyes.

'I never asked you for it,' said Aleizon Ailix Ayndra.

'But I thought to make you happy,' said Ylureen, 'because your child is dead—' The comb fell to the floor; Aleizon Ailix Ayndra put her hands over her face. Ylureen leapt up and put her arms round her. 'Is that why—? I never understood! Why, if you had said — this last month I have hardly seen you, why, it is twenty-four days and more since you stayed—'

'Whenever I came,' said Ayndra with difficulty, 'it seemed that you were sleeping.'

'One needs a good deal of rest, in the last month. You must remember.'

'I used to have to scrub the floors.' The narrow shoulders under the stiff padded embroidery shook three or four times, then consciously relaxed, and the harsh breathing was replaced by deep regular sighs.

'How thin you have grown!' said Ylureen. 'I recall when I met you at Merultine, I thought, how you had filled out at last, how pretty you looked, but now—'

'Do not remind me of it.' Ayndra lifted her head and reached up to stroke Ylureen's neck, her lips parted. Ylureen began to kiss her, very slowly, running her hands up and down the corduroy of her ribs until she could feel that the tense muscles had relaxed. Then she suddenly scooped one arm under Ayndra's arms, one under her buttocks, bent her knees and she had lifted her up and carried her the five paces to the bed. The Lord Regent had hardly had time to yelp in astonishment before she was sprawling on the counterpane with Ylureen leaning over her on all fours. 'Ylureen! I never thought you were so strong.'

'One does not have to run around in mail swinging a sword to be strong.' Ylureen deftly unlaced one boot, then the other, and tossed them into a corner. 'And you are smaller than I.' She unbuckled Ayndra's belt and threw it after the boots, then started on the ankle-fastenings of her breeches. Aleizon Ailix Ayndra started to laugh. 'Did your Ailixond do this to you?' Ylureen said.

'No, never!' Ylureen's hands were fumbling with her waistband now. She bent her legs back and pulled up onto her knees, started on the other woman's bodice. 'Let us race for it then!'

Meraptar's painful ascent of the staircase could be heard long before he entered the solar, a series of thumps and wheezes, the scrape of the iron foot of his staff on the stone, the salutations and ill-tempered apologies he exchanged with those who tried to ascend or descend past him. He greeted them unnecessarily as he pushed the door open and shuffled into the room. Setha put her embroidery down and got up to assist him to his customary place in the inglenook. 'Why, thank you, my dear . . . thank you . . . it is a sad day, when I need a young beauty like you to help me to my seat, eh, it's I should be helping you, eh?' He gave a senile cackle which turned into a cough. When she had gone back to the women's seats by the window, he addressed Sulakon in a voice made penetrating by deafness. 'It is the curse of age, my lord, when you cannot even sit by the fire, for you have no longer sat down than ye have to get up, and that takes ye so long ye have no more than regained your seat before you have to get up again. As god's my help, I ne'er believed I would come to this, eh, withering away in a draughty hunting lodge while a whore's bastard rules in Safi, eh? Ay, 's a sad time we live in, a sad time. In my grandfather's time we all lived like this in Safi, eh, cowering over a fire and waiting for the neighbours to come and steal the sheep. Eh, I remember how we used to go hunting wolves, in Safi-the-land even, in the winter they came down, I remember old Lord Parakison, that was before he even got his bracelets, eh, an old she-wolf, he spitted her right through the chest . . .' The audience had long since learnt to ignore his repetitive discourse, and the ladies pretended not to hear when Meraptar forgot that there was no separate room for them here. Sulakon continued his game of draughts with their host's crippled uncle, whose deformed leg had condemned him to a life by the fireside. Meraptar held forth until his kidneys began to trouble him again. The act of standing up and going to the door reminded him of what he had heard when he last stepped outside. 'They say there's some riders coming from Safi,' he declared. As usual, no one listened. 'They were in Shinalt the day before last, asking for the road to Gingito. Ten of them, they said. They had the name of one of them . . . what name was it? Damn me if I can remember a name. From Safi, they said. Merchants, I should think. Past the time of year for the shearing, though. A poor country here for merchanting. Did they have packhorses with them? Pack ponies, that is what ye need, in a roadless country like this . . .' His voice receded into the stairwell.

Setha got up to close the door after him; she stood by it and caught Sulakon's eye. 'Riders from Safi? It is the witch come to look for us!'

Sulakon, appearing not to listen, made another move; the cripple replied; Sulakon reached forward and swept up half a dozen of his opponent's men in one go. The cripple spread his hands, laughing; Sulakon nodded to him and stood up. He said to Setha, 'Lady, stay in here, where you can bar the door an you need to. I will send Lord Meraptar up for you to take care of him, and go out to see to these riders. More than likely they are merchants, as he said.' He took down his sword, which was hanging with other weapons above the fire, and went out. Setha joined Sistri and Histri with the three women of the noble family of Gingito at the single three-lighted window, overlooking the muddy courtyard of the fortress. They chattered together in a pidgin of Safic and the local dialect; Meraptar, when he had crawled once more up the stairs, found no one to help him to his seat and had to deliver his monologue unattended.

Tiris, the lord of Gingito, was standing in the courtyard with several of his cousins and his son-in-law, looking at a pair of hunting dogs. He displayed little interest in the concerns of his guest until the latter suggested that the witch of Haramin might have sent out her men to look for him. Tiris proposed that Sulakon should take his family and hide in a shepherd's croft until the danger had passed – he promised to say nothing an they took all their horses and gear out of his castle. Sulakon replied that the enemy were only ten, and that he would be willing to lead a party to accost them on the road before they reached the castle; the witch had none but a few peasants and coward mercenaries in her service, they would not be able to put up a fight against the brave men of Gingito. This captured the fancy of several of the youths who had been playing with the dogs, and within half-an-hour they were riding out of the gate in the full splendour of boiled leather jackets and heirloom helmets. Tiris closed the gate behind them and went upstairs to make sure that his wife had the key with which to lock herself in if strangers arrived.

They found them at the place where the road from Shinalt descended for a stretch along a boulder-strewn river bed; they had dismounted to lead their horses, which were not the surefooted mountain breed, among the sliding stones. Sulakon told his followers to tether their horses behind the crest and observe the newcomers from some place of concealment on the skyline. He himself lay down in the wet grass to watch. The leaders of the party looked like any other caravaneers, but just behind them came a figure in a raincloak thrown back to reveal a dark tunic, leading a strikingly familiar bay horse; but the animal came between him and his object, so he had watched until the invaders were almost free of the stones, before he got a clear view. Then he slithered backwards, got to his feet and ran to where his pony was tied. Tiris's son-in-law came after him, but he told him to wait. 'I will go down alone; I think I know them. An you see me draw my sword, come to my aid straightaway, but do not show yourselves unless I tell you.' He kicked the pony away. The caravan spotted him as soon as he came over the hill, and drove on to get on to open ground, while those at the head jumped into the saddle and reached for weapons. He reined in a good bowshot away and raised his hand. 'Takarem!' he cried, and then found the full force of his lungs. 'Takarem!'

When they reached Gingito the news had got there ahead of them; everyone in the hamlet had gathered in the castle yard, even the lady of Gingito and her daughters. A pale sun glittered on the puddles in the trampled mud and glamorised Takarem's laughter as he tossed his long hair out of his face and bowed to the welcomers, Sulakon at his back

144

looking lighthearted as he had not done since he assumed the Regency. Meraptar emerged from the tower as Takarem was lavishing his court gallantries on the provincial ladies and Sulakon, in a fit of unaccustomed loquacity, was telling Tiris how he had lost sight of his son during the battle of Shili and believed him dead ever since. The old lord tottered up to Takarem and interrupted him by pulling at his sleeve. 'Good day, my boy,' he said. 'Your father told us that the witch had slain you. Where have you been?'

'We have escaped from Safi, sir, you know that Lord A—that the witch is Regent there now?'

'You should call me *my lord*, boy, I am not one of your officers. Do you not know me? Ay, you youths you grew up away from the city, you know nothing of the nobility, ay, we have not even a king to make lords now. I am Lord Meraptar, boy, I was Regent in Safi when your grandfather was King. Is your grandmother in Safi still?'

'My lady Sumakas? Why, of course; and my mother, and my sisters and brothers. At first I was minded to stay with them, my lord, and oppose the witch in all her doings, but then my mother found out that Father was here and told me that I should escape.'

'Your mother, eh? Has she softened her heart toward your father, eh? A bad business. Old Lord Parakison should never have married a woman from a merchant family: bad blood, all of them. Deceit, it runs in the blood, all merchants, all liars. No offence to you, boy, your father is a true nobleman, you are your father's son, I can see that, eh? Found your way to this benighted stronghold, eh?'

'Master Eko guided us, he has been here before.'

'Master Eko, eh? Escaped from the witch's city, did you? Did not see you in her magic mirrors, did she, send her familiars after you?'

'No one in the city says she is a witch,' Takarem said. 'But she has taken over the Regency, and filled the city with vagabonds, and given land to her followers, that were rebels.'

'Take me to see Master Eko,' Meraptar said querulously. He insisted on being introduced to each one of Takarem's escort, and asking them about the journey; he was still maundering at them when Sulakon came to take him back indoors, where Takarem could pay his respects to Lady Setha and eat the meal she had directed her slaves to prepare. Takarem greeted her coldly and applied himself to the food with enthusiasm; Setha made a silent curtsey and sat next to Meraptar, cutting up his food into small pieces so that he could mumble over them with his few remaining teeth. He complained, as he did at every meal, of the pains of old age, and repeatedly complimented Setha on her kindness to him. 'As a daughter to me you are, lady. Lost my own daughter, I have, my dear Gallaria, killed by the witch, eh, the witch and Lady Sumakas . . .' The others conversed without regard to him; Takarem related his adventures in high style. Meraptar declared that he had to go outside again and asked Sulakon to accompany him. Takarem, describing how he had escaped from a party of rebels on the way back to Safi after Shili, did not notice them leave. Sulakon patiently attended Meraptar's slow progress, as far as the squalid alley against the outer wall that served as urinal, and would have left him there for the sake of modesty, but Meraptar held on to him. After looking around several times, he stretched up to Sulakon's ear. 'A word in secret, my lord. Could not say where they were listening, but that man, Kereno is his name, the man who came with your son, he is Lady Sumakas' man. I had reason to deal with him in the past. I was in judgement, I remember, what year was it, four hundred and sixty, or was it four hundred and sixty-two, the year of the drought, now what was the charge, affray was it, disorderly conduct, public affray was it, we had six of 'em on trial, I was the judge, old Patto was the prosecutor I recall . . .'

Sulakon listened until the old man had run out of memories. 'Are you sure?'

'Sure?' Meraptar banged his stick on the wall and pointed a trembling finger at his head. 'Sure, my lord? I may be a dithering old fool, no teeth, no legs, yes, but I assure you, I remember what I have done, and I remember, that man was in Sumakas' service, and she, she never lets go of her own. O no. Like her father. A miser. All of them misers. No, he is Lady Sumakas' man.'

Sulakon's fugitive joy had disappeared. 'Do you suppose

146

that my son has been sent here by that woman, by her and the Witch of Haramin, that he may betray us all?'

'I do not say. You must talk to your boy, my lord, no doubt you will know when he speaks the truth. I will say no more. Not with Lady Sumakas' man here. Who knows how many more of them she may have in her pocket? Let me give you my advice, and then you had better go and talk to your boy: put them to sleep in the stable, and that Kereno, put a cloth over his face in the night. No marks, you see. It was an evil spirit came in the night, ye see. Very likely the witch herself sent it. Go now, my lord, else you'll see me caught short.' He cackled as he turned his back. Sulakon thanked him and went back to the solar.

The next morning, Kereno did not come with his companions to look for breakfast in the kitchen; Eko went back to look for him, found him still sleeping, and when he tried to shake him, found that he was past all waking. That night, after dark, one of the caravaneers disappeared, and they did not realise that his horse had gone until too late. But Sulakon was convinced that Takarem's surprised innocence was unfeigned, and none of the rest of the party tried to flee. They all joined the Gingitey in the great autumn round-up that brought the sheep down from the high pastures, and settled in for a winter in the hills.

'I think that we have been a little too clever for ourselves this time,' said Sumakas. She rubbed her hands up and down her upper arms as she walked; rain pattered on the alabaster sheets of the skylights.

'You need not say *we* merely to be charitable,' said Aleizon Ailix Ayndra, rocking her chair back and forth. 'At least we know where they are for the time being.'

'Kereno was one of my best people. He used to work for me even before my husband died. I could trust him with anything.'

'You should have sent someone less familiar.'

'That old goat Meraptar! God send that another winter in those hills does for him.'

'Very likely it will; it seems that he has fallen off considerably in the last twenty months. And beside, Takarem in Gingito with no more than a bunch of shepherds to follow him is far less of a danger than Takarem in Safi with bitter-hearted nobles all around him.'

'Takarem is my oldest grandson,' Sumakas said plaintively.

Ayndra gave her a look of exasperation. 'An you were going to plead family sentiment, you should have done so two months ago,' she said, offhand.

Parakison, who was pretending to play with a mosaic puzzle in the bay window, pricked up his ears at the change in tone. He heard Sumakas say, 'It is too cold; I shall go and ask for a brazier,' and the click of her high heels going towards the common rooms. He put down the tile he held and went up behind Aleizon Ailix Ayndra. 'My lord,' he said. She tipped her chair even further back and peered round at him with a bright eye. He said, 'Will my Mamma come back?' She did not answer immediately, so he said, 'You sent Cousin Takarem to find Uncle Suli. Did he find my Mamma too?'

'I think so. It was only a soldier that told us, and he never saw her – you know your Mamma does not like to go out. He never went into the castle where she was. Cousin Takarem wanted to go, and it was Aunt 'lissa told him. He never knew that I sent him. I think your Mamma will not come back unless Lord Sulakon does, and he will not come back to Safi while I am here.'

'Lord Suli hates you.'

'Yes, he does.' She set the chair upright again and looked properly at him. 'Do you want that your mother comes back?'

Parakison ducked his head. 'I hate Uncle Suli,' he said, scuffing one foot on the floor. 'He told the teacher to beat me with a stick if I forgot my lesson. When I had Mamma's teacher she never let him beat me.' He gave a noisy sniff. 'I want Mamma to come back.'

'Yes,' said Aleizon Ailix Ayndra. She took Parakison's hand. He came closer, but still kept the back of the chair between them. They looked at each other. Parakison wiped his nose with his fist. 'Have a handkerchief.' She pulled one out of her sleeve and gave it to him. Parakison went into a pose of sullen patience, until he realised that she was not going to wipe his nose for him. The act of snorting noisily into the linen, examining the results and crumpling them up in a ball seemed to cheer him up. He offered it back to her. 'Keep it with you. You can have it.'

'Thank you, my lord,' he said, well trained in politeness, and stuffed the bundle in his sleeve in imitation of her. He looked up at the roof. 'Look, it is not raining. Can we go out?'

'I have to go shortly and see the man who is in charge of building in the city. Do you want to go out riding? I am sure Haldin would take you.'

'Let me come with you.'

'It will be very boring, Parakison; even I find it rather boring, and half my life is taken up with such matters, which renders them more interesting to me.'

'Granma says that when I am eighteen I shall have to do all the things which you do. Are they all boring?'

'Not quite all of them,' she said, smiling.

'Let me come with you.'

'You will have to sit quietly while I talk to this man for hours.'

'Let me come,' he said again, giving her his coquettish smile.

The doors opened to admit two slaves carrying a brazier full of hot coals, followed by Sumakas and her friend Mistress Cadinsha, whose husband was that year head of the Pawnbrokers' Guild. Ayndra got up to salute them, they exchanged numerous pleasantries, and she got ready to leave; Sumakas, engrossed in what promised to be a series of fascinating revelations, hardly spared the time to kiss Parakison's cheek before he left. She said to Ayndra, 'Have you not thought about sending a party of traders, as it were, to Gingito?'

'We shall have to wait for the spring, lady; after the sheep-shearing is the only time when traders go to Gingito. I must go.' They kissed, and Sumakas closed the door behind her. Followed by Parakison, she went first of all to her office to get something to smoke before she went to the stables.

Parakison watched her lighting the smokestick with great interest. 'What is that for?' he said.

She laughed. 'To improve my state of mind.'

He digested this in silence on the way to the stables.

149

While the grooms were fetching the horses, he asked, 'Can I have some of it?'

'Do you want some?'

'I want to see what it is like.'

'It will make you cough.'

'Let me try.' He was putting on his seductive act again. 'Now I know where your father learnt it,' she said. 'Paraki-son, everyone will think me entirely degenerate an I let you have some of this. Besides, it will make you cough; I used to cough my head off in the beginning. Some day soon we will go to Lady Ylureen's house, and she will make a drink with it in, and you can have it there, where none of our servants will see us. Is that well?' She took an intense drag and dropped the butt on the ground. 'There, finished. Let us go.'

'Tell me, then, whom she does confide in,' S'Thiraidi said.

'I think she confides in no one very much, unless it be my lady,' Derezhaid responded. 'She expects her retinue to take orders, not to come to her with advice.'

'I think you are mistaken,' said Getaleen. 'What about that mercenary captain that sits in Ivory Gate? She goes from Ylureen's to breakfast with him, day after day.'

S'Thiraidi adopted a more magisterial pose. 'The problem which confronts us,' she said, 'is that Ylureen, having procured the royal appointment, negotiates in secret with my lord of Haramin, and allots all privileges exclus-ively to Suthine and line Pilith. You and we are children of different sisters, but we share an interest in restricting the fullness of Pilith. Our first step must be to gain a voice in the barbarian's councils.'

'We were better to pursue the factions among the barba-rians,' opined Getaleen. 'They do not all love my lord of Haramin, not at all. Were she to lose power, Ylureen would be empty and dry.'

'And we would have exchanged a lesser evil for a greater. Whatever the woman failings of my lord, at least she favours our way of life. The most of the barbarians have no more understanding than animals. You have told me so yourself, a hundred times.' S'Thiraidi turned back to Der-ezhaid, who had been waiting to speak. He leant forward.

'So you want to know which of her retinue has a dry palm? You should have said so earlier.'

'You are very slow to understand!'

'Lady, intrigue is not my natural medium; I am all at sea in these waters.' Derezhaid cast his eyes down in deprecation. 'You know that the barbarians think it a crime to dip their fingers in the honey.'

'There are far more things one can offer them than payments for services, as you should know,' S'Thiraidi said drily. 'What do you think of this mercenary? You all know what I think of him!' They laughed.

'I think you would have better fortune with her Captain Selanor.' Derezhaid grinned. 'It was a sad day for that gentleman when he was invited to drink with Lord Faracaln.'

'You are misguided,' Getaleen said angrily. 'An you did send one of your maids to lick him till he told, what could he do then? She would never ask his advice on trade in any case. Better that you suborn the trade guilds – can you not induce Lady Sumakas to hand them over to you? She seems to find you sweeter than honey.'

'Jealous!' chuckled Derezhaid.

'Sot,' Getaleen said contemptuously. He made a face. 'You have adopted my lord of Haramin's manner, if you will have none of her party.'

'It would cost far more than we have,' said S'Thiraidi. 'And we already have several guilds inclined to us. They are aggrieved that they cannot trade with Suthine themselves. Now we know that the King and Queen will never let foreign ships into Suthine harbour, but there are other ports than Suthine, and many guilds in Safi. The only pity is that their law does not allow the barbarians to make contracts with us without their lord gives them consent – is that not what you said?'

'The law forbids it; the witch Diamoon said that when my lord was imprisoned that was one of the charges.'

'You mean that my lord had done as she liked, and thrown the law out of the window, as is her wont,' said Getaleen.

'Merely because she did it in the past, does not mean that she will allow her subjects to do it presently,' S'Thiraidi said.

Derezhaid added, 'After all, had she not had our aid, she would never have taken the Regency.'

'Regency!' said Getaleen. 'That poor child that they call their King, so cosseted that he howls at a blister.'

S'Thiraidi tapped on the table. 'Sister, friend; we have not come here to exchange gossip. I say, what we need is a voice in the Lord Regent's councils. Now whom do you know whom we might borrow a tongue from?'

'The law is about *treaties*,' said Derezhaid. 'They are not the same as contracts.' He used the Safic word for the first, his own tongue for the second.

S'Thiraidi asked, 'What is the difference, then?'

'They make a *treaty* between two nations.'

'So, an I make a contract with Master Canto, we have made a treaty.'

'No, because you are only two people.'

'But we are of two nations.'

'No,' said Derezhaid.

Getaleen got up and left before he could continue with the explanation. 'Older sister, I am going to see Missio; call me an you ever find a thing you can decide on.' The latch rattled after her.

S'Thiraidi clapped her hands for chabe and settled among the cushions. 'Tell me of these treaties then; you understand the barbarians far better than do I,' she said with benevolent sarcasm.

'Lord Polem is the one,' said Derezhaid.

'Your pardon?'

'He is forever praising the banquets my lady offers him. You have three cooks with you, and beside, any of your younger sisters could cook well enough for him. Could you not offer him a cook, and her attendants of course, as a gift? Lord Polem hears my lord's councils, and the kitchen servants come to hear everything in a house, do they not?'

'Mother of men,' S'Thiraidi said, 'and I believed Siriane was the wise one.'

'Watch out for the steps here,' said Aleizon Ailix Ayndra. She offered her hand to Arpalond, but he declined.

'I know these corridors well enough.' He began to descend cautiously.

Ayndra, hearing a thunder of feet behind them, turned to look. 'You should have a stick like a blind beggar – Lisanë!'

The girl came tearing round the corner, her short gown tucked up at the waist, and cannoned into Arpalond. She bounced off him, gasped, 'My lord!' and dashed on. Arpalond, who had not seen her coming, toppled backward, just in time to meet the flying feet of the rest of the posse. Parakison appeared last of all. The other children shrieked when they saw the Little King and ran on without any concern for their victim, who was sprawled on his back on the stairs.

'Parakison!' said Ayndra.

The Little King managed to fit in a bow with a sort of skating step, exclaim, 'My lord, I'm the fisherman!' and disappeared on the trail of his quarry. Ayndra helped Arpalond to get to his feet.

'I shall have to listen more carefully,' he said.

'I shall tell them to play in the courtyards, not the corridors.'

'Let them play while they can; Parakison most of all. I can endure that a few small children tread on me.'

'Let us go and sit in the portico.'

'I spoke with Parakison only yesterday.'

'What did he say to you?'

'He said that you were going to bring his mother back in the spring.'

'He did? It was his own invention, then,' said Aleizon Ailix Ayndra. 'I said to him that his mother would not come back till Sulakon did, and that not while I was here. Did he say that I would go away in the spring?'

'He said that he would rather have you to be Regent than Uncle Suli.'

'Well, some compliment at least.' Grass sprouted between the decorative paving of the courtyard, and the fountain in the middle had long since run dry. She spread out her cloak on one of the stone benches and they sat down.

'I suppose we will have to open these rooms in a few years,' she said. 'They have been standing empty for so long that they are falling apart; there is nothing inside but dust and spiders.'

'It is more than twenty years now, since we had a king in Safi,' said Arpalond. He gazed round the courtyard, blinking as if memory would restore his vision.

'At least no one will disturb us for a while.' She stretched out her legs to appreciate the pallid sunshine, and looked up at the sky to determine the hour. 'Not until fourth hour have I to see the Treasury report; then Polem has invited me to dine with him, and I said I would go and see Ylureen, but she will not mind an it's midnight when I come.'

'You will see Polem? Perhaps you could ask him for me, if he will permit Mistress Diamoon to help me in the archives, should she have time to do so.'

'Ask Polem? I will ask Mistress Diamoon directly. But what do you want in the archives?'

'I am told that she is very skilful at finding old texts. It is all in any order, and there are several documents I should like to find for my history; but my readers cannot place them, though they have searched for months.'

'Your history?' she said in surprise.

'Yes, the Acts of Lord Ailixond; you cannot have forgotten that I promised to write his history.'

'Have you written much of it?'

'I have not written a word of it presently. I have been gathering tales for years, to add to all the tales I gathered when I was in the Grand Army. The day that I find myself utterly pitch-black blind, why, then I shall begin to write – or rather my clerks will write; I shall see the past rising up in the darkness, and speak what I see.'

'Will you put me in it, then?'

'Why, how could I leave you out of it?'

She fidgeted on the bench and waved her hand.

'Do you not wish to be in a history book? Surely you do.'

'I should rather be in a romance!' She laughed. 'Ailixond said he thought that they would scrub me out of them.'

'Of romances?'

'No, of history books!'

'You shall not be scrubbed out of mine,' he said. She only laughed. He tipped his face up to the winter sun. 'Rinahar has been talking about Takarem, saying what a courageous act it was to go and look for his father; he speculates of doing likewise.'

'Does he know where Sulakon is?'

'"Somewhere north of the Chiaral."' Arpalond mimicked Rinahar's gruff diction, to her amusement. 'They are often in the Street of Dreams,' he said. 'Shall I ask Antinar to keep an eye on them?'

'If he would.'

'I am sure it would prove congenial duty, if it were required to frequent the Street of Dreams at all times.' He paused. 'Since Polem returned to Safi, of course, we have returned Samala to him, and gone back to Chingadi; only to find that the bailiff mustered half the young men to join the rebellion, and most of them still here in Safi, inviting their families to come join them every month. And while he was away, the tenants that remained emptied the storehouses. Last year we had no harvest at all. Only now are we preparing for planting.'

'An you want a stipend for him, you have only to ask,' Ayndra said.

'I fear that my honour as a noble lord prevents any such request,' he said.

'What, do you not want money then?'

'I did not say that, my lord.'

'Out with it!'

'No, no, no!'

'Ay! When have I ever feared to ask for money?'

'But my lord, your mother was a common woman!'

Laughing uproariously, she made to push him off the bench; Arpalond hit her on the head with his stick. She sat there rubbing her head. 'Of course I will give you some money. How much will you need?'

The thick sky had not quite reached the point of rain, but the wind was chasing white horses over the bay, and every time one slammed against the mole the gale threw a coat of spray over the Lord Regent and her attendants. She held on to her hat with one hand and kept her cloak bundled together at the throat with the other, while she shrieked in the teeth of the wind at the engineers; they were all huddled together like sheep in a snowstorm. 'My lord, we have to dredge it first, and then dump plenty of gravel, and could we build a coffer-dam – but in these conditions– '

'I freeze,' Parakison complained. He pulled at Aleizon Ailix Ayndra's cloak. She threw a fold of it round him and brought him in under her arm, letting go of her hat; the wind immediately seized it and sent it bowling over the soaked stones. Parakison slipped free and ran after it; fortunately it fetched up against a heap of builders' sand, and he caught it before it went over into the sea. She beat it a few times and jammed it back on her head. 'Let us go to the portmaster's office and look at the plans. One cannot talk here.' Parakison, back inside her cloak, shivered theatrically and grinned up at her.

In the porthouse the lamps had been lit to supplement the light filtered through ones of stretched gut on the inner shutters, and a couple of braziers added to the fug. A large map of the harbour was painted on one wall, with the names of vessels chalked against the berths they occupied. The head engineer unrolled several other plans on the table, and they all clustered round them again. Parakison looked at the map for a while, reading out the names, then went and stood peering over the shoulders of the clerks in the adjoining room. When he was satisfied that every single one of them was working on something boring, he went back and poked his head between two of the engineers.

'The weather has been so poor this last month, that we can only work two days in six; and beside, it would not matter an we could, since the ships have to come up from Lysmal with the stone.'

'But the *Southern Star* put in yesterday,' said Ayndra.

'I know, my lord, they are unloading now, despite the heavy sea.'

'This is nowhere near a storm,' Ayndra said impatiently.

'But it is not easy to sway stone blocks up out of the hold in any but a calm sea, my lord. I swear that we have been working every day that we may.'

'I hope that you have. We are going to begin on the road to Haramin as soon as Seventh Month begins, and it is Sixth Month already; I thought that you had progressed further than this.'

'We cannot help the weather, my lord.'

'How many more cargoes are you waiting for?'

Parakison pulled his head out again and tucked his

thumbs in his belt. A carved figurehead of a woman holding lighting bolts was fixed between the wall and ceiling above the portmaster's own desk; some kind of small animal peered over the goddess's shoulder. Parakison climbed up on the unoccupied chair and put one foot on the desk; he stretched up to touch the carving. A cloud of old dust puffed off it, and he sneezed. Aleizon Ailix Ayndra looked up. 'Parakison, what do you there?'

'My lord, I am just— ah!' An inkwell shot off the desk and landed in a black splash on the floor.

'Parakison,' said Ayndra, 'either attend to what we say, or be silent, or go outdoors; do not wander around destroying the furnishings.'

'Yes, my lord,' Parakison said sulkily. They went on poring over their maps and disputing the quantity of shaped blocks they needed. He lifted the latch and quietly slipped outside.

There was almost no one on the quayside; piles of wood and brick stood unattended, draped with tarpaulins. He passed between them to a place where the quay was slippery with fishscales and brine; porters were carrying baskets of fish from the boats tied up at a floating jetty, and several dozen women, huddled in dirty shawls, were gutting fish in an open-sided warehouse. Fish-blood trickled between the cobbles and the smell was overpowering. Parakison sunk his head in his deep blue cloak and hurried on, ignoring the cries of the women. A little further down a big ship was tied up, facing a tall warehouse with a massive iron beam protruding from its walls over the dock; a lacework of cables went along the arm and into the hold of the ship. As he watched, a block of stone longer than a man rose up out of the ship, was hauled in till it was over the quayside, and lowered on to a wooden sledge waiting there. Six men took hold of leather ropes attached to the sledge and hauled it into another building, while others pushed a new sledge into place. Parakison edged up to the door of the warehouse and looked inside; the ceiling went up enormously high, higher than the Hall of Stars. A group of men in the coarse hooded tunics of harbour slaves stood around flexing their arms and conversing in gruff voices. As he watched, a man in a green cloak cracked a whip at them, and they took hold of ropes and began to heave in time to the shouts of one of them. The man with the whip looked around and caught sight of Parakison. 'Boy! What do you here? Out!' He cracked his whip again. Parakison ducked out of sight. The ropes above his head were vibrating with the strain; the cradle holding another stone rose, inch by inch, out of the ship's hold. Somebody on the ship was shouting; the men with the sledge were waiting to put it into position. Parakison walked forward to get a better look. At first they did not see him, their attention fixed on the stone. The ship rose suddenly on a high swell and the side of the hold caught the stone as it rose; it swung dangerously, and started to tilt out of the cradle. The sledge handlers were ready to run out of danger; as they looked around one caught sight of Parakison.

'Hola, what is that boy doing there? Boy!'

Parakison put his hands on his hips. 'I am not a boy,' he said. 'Do you not know me? I am the King of Safi!'

'I care not an you are the King of the Demons, boy, get out of there! Can you not see that stone? Boy!'

'Do you not tell me what to do,' Parakison said. He took another step forward and looked up just in time to see the stone tilt over so far that it broke free of the cradle and came falling end first for him. He lifted up his hands.

The door of the portmaster's office rattled under the force of the blows. 'Sir! Sir! Sir!' One of the engineers went to open it. A fishwife was shivering on the steps. 'Sir! 's the portmaster here?'

'He is gone out. Can you not come back later?'

'Sir, there's an accident, sir, someone dead.'

'Who is dead?'

'A boy, sir, the stone fell on him.'

'What boy? It is no concern of ours.'

'Sir, let me see the portmaster then.'

Aleizon Ailix Ayndra stepped past him. 'The portmaster is not here. May I assist you, mistress?'

'Yes, sir, there is a dead boy, sir, on the stonemason's quay. A stone fell on him, sir, and crushed him, he is all dead and bleeding—'

'One of the stonemasons? Or a loader?'

'No, sir, a good boy, not a beggar-boy nor a slave neither.'

158

'A–' Ayndra's face changed. 'What sort of clothes was he wearing?' she said in a faint voice.

'Fine clothes, sir – my lady–'

'A dark blue cloak . . . and a light blue tunic, with gold, gold cloak brooches?'

'Yes, er, my–' Ayndra did not wait to hear any more, but pushed past the woman and ran down the steps.

'That was the Lord Regent you spoke to!' said the engineer to the fishwife, who started to bow like a hen eating barley, over and over again. The head engineer picked up the Lord Regent's hat. 'Follow me!' He gave the frightened woman a push. 'Take us to this stone!'

In fact one could find it without any help, by the size of the crowd that had already gathered. Ayndra shouted, 'Make way! Make way!' and drove between the backs of the porters and women with gutting knives still in hand. 'Let me through!' The men clustered right by the stone did not move, so she grabbed one of them by the neck of his tunic. 'Let me through!' He turned round in fury, then saw who it was and drew back; a sort of charmed circle opened round her like a mouth. She dropped to her knees on the cobbles. The block had fallen across Parakison's body, crushing his left leg, his chest and hips; his upper body, right arm and part of his right leg were intact. He lay on his back, one hand thrown up beside his head, his mouth and eyes wide open to the soft grey rain. She put her hand, fingers spread, on his throat for a moment, and then picked up the free hand and felt the wrist. She felt it three times more than she needed to. Then she stood up. 'Crowbars!' she shouted. 'Lift this damned block and get it out of the way!' She turned her back on it and said, 'Who was in charge of this? Who was directing the haulers?'

'Sir, it was, it was I . . . that is, who I . . . who we . . .' It was the man whom she had hauled up by the collar. She merely looked at him until his voice petered out.

'You know what you have done,' she said.

'My lord!' He fell on all fours and scrabbled for her foot. She ignored him. 'Where are those motherless crowbars? Get to work!'

'My lord, what is it? My lord . . .' It was the head engineer. 'Is the Little King . . .'

159

She pointed. He followed her hand, gawped in horror and put her hat over his face. She snatched it out of his hand. 'Go directly to the palace,' she said in a voice like a saw on slate. 'Tell Master Firumin to come here straightway with linen and a stretcher. Straightway, you understand, to hell with whatever duties he may have. Go!'

The chief stonemason was pawing her foot and repeating, 'An accident, my lord, we never saw, sir, we told him, twice, my lord, we never . . .'

She kicked his hands away. 'Be silent! Help us clear up this mess. Then you can come with me to the palace and tell Lady Sumakas how it happened. Get up! And you, what are you standing there for? Go and fetch the damned portmaster. What are you at with those crowbars? Put your backs into it. HEAVE!'

A couple of guards in the parade uniform of the Silver Shields stood either side of the hall doors; they stood to attention when they saw Daior-deor. 'At ease,' he said, and gently pushed the door. It swung open easily; they had been oiling the hinges. The coffin stood on a table, draped with Safic flags, and surrounded by standing lamps. At the far end of the room, under the wall with Serannin's portrait of the Outer Council, stood a row of chairs. Aleizon Ailix Ayndra was sitting on the middle one, head bent so that all one could see was the shine of her hair. His spurs rattled on the polished tiles, but she did not look up till he had passed the catafalque. He bowed, without removing his hat.

'I heard the news, my lord. I came to sit with you.'

'I thank you,' she said, indicating one of the chairs.

He sat down. 'You are not keeping the wake alone?'

'My lady Sumakas was here. She wept and screamed an hour and a half together. That was after she . . . I made the man who was in charge of the unloading tell her himself how it happened. I made Ailissa take her away. I have not asked anyone else to come.' She delivered the sentences like broken logs, as if she lost herself after each one and had to make an effort to come back again. Her hands, in her lap, repetitively flattened the brim of her hat. 'The coffin is closed,' she said. 'In the morning they will open it up and open the doors for the people to come in. It has to lie here six days. The embalmers said they . . . there is too much damage for their work, so we must begin the lying-in-state directly, and hope that . . . at least it is winter still.' She tipped her head to one side. 'In that time we have to hold the Council of Lords, for the . . . election.'

'Yes,' said Daior-deor.

She looked at him, once, then away into space again, and bent forward with one elbow on her knee and her forehead propped on her hand. She said, 'I never wanted it to be like this—' The pause stretched out in the late night silence. Daior-deor reached out and took her left hand. The dry slender fingers closed hard on his own. He sat listening to the hiss of the lamps mingling with the sound of his own blood like the sea. Outside the door one of the guards coughed, and the sound echoed in the corridor. Her grip loosened, and she sat up, with a watery smile. 'I thank you again.'

'It is nothing, my lord.'

She shook her head. 'You are a great help to me.'

'You are tired; you should go and rest. I can sit here. You should go to my lady Ylureen.'

'No,' she said unhappily. 'Ylureen thinks me a fool to be distressed.'

'What? How can—'

'A fool to be as distressed as I am. For, after all, it is only — the child of my . . . lover in another woman . . . he ran and caught my hat when it was taken away by the wind, before it could fall into the sea. And then an hour later he was dead. And now I think I shall be elected King of Safi.' She wrapped one arm round her body and put the other hand over her eyes.

'An I had a vote, I would give it to you.'

'I know you would.' She bounded out of her chair like a spring uncoiling and went to light a smokestick in the lamps. They passed it back and forth in silence; Daior-deor sat still, while she went up and down, twitching at her hair, taking her hat on and off, turning it round in her hands, pleating her handkerchief into a fan.

There was a loud clang from the doors and they swung open; Lord Polem came striding in. He went straight up to Aleizon Ailix Ayndra, put his arms round her and kissed her

161

on both cheeks. 'What are you doing here, my lord? You cannot keep a wake with two of you. Here comes Arpalond, look, and Antinar, and Golaron will come as soon as we have him out of bed, and Firumin is bringing us food and drink, you cannot have a wake without food and drink.' He stopped as he caught sight of the portrait on the wall. 'Maishis! I did not know that that was here. Sweet heaven! Do we not all look young! Look, there am I, with plenty of hair still and no belly. Bless me, no wonder that I was so popular with women in those days. These days no one would have me who was not paid to. How long ago was it?'

'Seven years,' said Aleizon Ailix Ayndra, 'or a little more, not so much as eight years.'

'Gods! It feels as if it were twenty. How greatly have I fallen off in such a short time! It has not helped that Lady S'Thiraidi has gifted me one of her cooks; you know I cannot resist the things that they prepare.' He looked at Daior-deor. 'Welcome, captain, welcome; you are good to join us. Now you know that it is not good to speak of death at a wake. Diamoon is coming too; she is just collecting some special sweets from our new cook. My lord, you should let our allies prepare your coronation banquet; it would be remembered for years.'

'Hush! You tempt fate,' responded Ayndra.

'I do no more than say what we all expect.' He drew her to him again and pointed at Ailixond in the portrait. 'You know that it was what he wanted. This has been a tragic accident, no one is other than sorrowed by it, but it was a clean end, and we must let the dead bury the dead; we must live for the new day. Your day.' He looked into her eyes. Unwilling as she was, she could not help but warm a little. He patted her shoulder and let her go. She took out another smokestick, went to light it, and stood gazing at the picture. The smoke rose in sweet blue coils around her head.

'There are so many people I should wish to see at the banquet,' she said. 'I should not want it held for a month at least. Can it be put off?'

'O, of course; as long as you need. It is only the election and the funeral which must be held in time. Arpalond, have you seen this picture?'

'I have seen it in the past, but I have not seen it recently,' Arpalond said.

'There you are in it; come closer, perhaps you can see.'

Daior-deor withdrew quietly to the side of the room. Lady Ditarris came in, escorted by Takarem's next brother Damaron, and they all stood round the picture identifying its subjects and commenting on their subsequent fates, while the guards held the doors open for servants bearing a table and the food to put on it. Aleizon Ailix Ayndra was lost in their midst. He turned suddenly as someone touched his shoulder, but it was only Firumin, with the box holding his favourite dicing race-game under his arm. 'Captain,' he said, 'will you play a game or two with me? You know it is said to be good luck to gamble at a wake.'

'Good luck for you, perhaps!'

'My luck will run out, sir; no luck lasts for ever.' Firumin rattled the dice cup under his nose.

'O, very well,' said Daior-deor.

Firumin ordered the servants to bring them the best Thaless wine while they were playing; as a result he was inclined to sentimental effusions over Lord Ailixond and Parakison both, and did not bet with his usual acuity. In spite of the late hour, several lords appeared, bowed to Lord Ayndra, expressed condolences and prayed for a private audience with her next day, before accepting some wine, engaging in a half-hour's chat with the rest of her party, and leaving. Ditarris nodded off in her chair and Antinar took her home. When it reached the dead time far after midnight but not yet near dawn, Aleizon Ailix Ayndra slipped out and came back with a flattanharp. She sat down at the head of the coffin, with her back to it, facing the picture, and began to play. When she desired a rest, Arpalond took it from her, but the rest were content to listen to the melodies weeping from the strings, while the clerestory windows slowly turned from black to midnight blue to grey. She was still playing when Daior-deor had to leave, because the day-guards would be coming on watch and he had to unlock the gate. A yawning Firumin directed the servants to clear away the debris of the night and bring in the newly-made mourning-frames and ready the hall for the public lying-in-

163

state. When they began to skirt carefully round Polem
Arpalond, and Golaron, as they pushed mops and brushes
over the floor, they knew that it was time to go. Aleizor
Ailix Ayndra nodded to them, but she seemed lost in a
musical fantasia whose chimes pursued them till they were
out of earshot. She finished just as the cleaning slaves were
carrying their buckets out. She slung the instrument by its
carrying-strap over her shoulder and walked up to the
picture. In the middle of the group, the painted Ailixond
gazed away over her head. She stood looking at him until
one of the priestly acolytes who had come to watch over the
body approached her.

'My lord, we are about to open the doors. Will you stay
here?'

'What? O, no. I shall be gone in a moment.'

He bowed and retired. She looked up again.

'It would be a coward's act to retreat from it now,' she
said, and walked out.

'It is better that it has been held off until now. It is not as it
was in 467, when we had been scattered over the Empire for
more than a decade. All the lords who have any interest in
the result at all have been here for months, and we have had
the past five days to talk to one another. There is nothing to
be had out in public debate that has not been so thoroughly
chewed over in private that everyone has formed unchange-
able opinions on it. Have you the crown box? I heard that
you had it.'

Sumakas did not move from her chair. 'What of Lord
Parhannon?'

'Parhannon has returned to Safi because he wishes to
support the side which promotes order. He told me that he
had seen the entire Empire at peace for half a year, and a
truer peace than any he had witnessed since Ailixond died,
and for this reason he decided to cease skulking in pirate
coves and come home. He did not tell me whom he intended
to vote for, but I think we may infer, may we not? Lady, the
Council begins in a quarter-hour; will you let me have the
crown?'

'It is not a coronation that you are going to,' Sumakas
returned.

Aleizon Ailix Ayndra flicked her hand through the air. 'Ay! All you wish is to come to the Council as it closes, crown in hand, and present it to whomever has been chosen. As if the election had to be ratified by the other powers in the city, yes?' Sumakas looked at her without speaking. The Lord Regent smiled at her. 'The lords, and only the lords, finally elect the King,' she said.

'It would look ill were you to carry it there in your hand,' Sumakas said. 'I give you my word that I will send it with an escort to the Council, so that it is there when you begin the debate. Had you not better go there presently yourself?' She gave Ayndra an equally insincere smile.

The Lord Regent chuckled. 'Very well, my lady. Wish for me as you sit here.' She offered her hand to be kissed, and swept out.

Arpalond was sitting on the stone bench opposite the doors of the Council, his blind-cane by his side; he must have heard her coming, for he rose and bowed. She gave him her hand. 'My lord!' he said. 'Where is your bow?'

'What? O, yes.' She performed the courtesy, laughing. 'I have been too long in places where I am the only lord.'

'You must remember that you are one among equals.'

'I understand; I thank you.'

'I sacrificed in your name last night, and the priest read it as Great Elevation and Caution Required. I know you do not take any account of omens, but . . .'

'Are they all here already?'

'All but a few. Will you go in now?'

She nodded, her eyes already turned to the door. He let her go, and shuffled in afterward. They were all silent round the long table. The voting tablets lay blank in front of them. He found his seat and let his dim gaze wander round the table. 'My lords. Are we all present?'

There was a cough and a scrape of chair-legs; the voice which spoke was Ellakon. 'My lord Rinahar has asked me to say that he will not attend. He knows of the Council but refuses to countenance it. My lords.' He sat down again; three or four others spoke similarly, naming altogether seven lords.

'What are we to do?' said Polem. 'Let us send for them to come; surely they will come.'

'They will not come while . . .' Ellakon looked up and tried to speak in a more forthright manner. 'They believe that the Little King was murdered.'

'By whom?' said Aleizon Ailix Ayndra in a silky voice. Ellakon looked at her. She said, 'Do they wish to question the men and women who witnessed the accident? There were many of them. Thus they may determine how it came about. Is this a fit reason not to attend the Council?'

'An they will not come, they forswear their rights,' Haligon said.

'I think still we should send for them,' said Polem, 'to make sure.'

'Let them be counted as blank tablets.'

'Let them not be counted at all; an they do not come, how should they have a voice?'

'A blank tablet must go down as a vote against whomsoever we choose; it will be harder to gain the majority.'

'We shall need to be unanimous then,' said Haligon.

A blast of war-trumpets shattered their bickering. Aleizon Ailix Ayndra lifted her hand. 'The crown!' When the doors opened, Selanor appeared in full parade uniform, with the crown box in his hands. He advanced, dead-pan, laid the flat box with the blue waves on the table, and retreated; only just as he turned to go did he flash a sudden conspiratorial grin at Aleizon Ailix Ayndra. She got to her feet and reached inside her shirt. The great diamond of the Royal Ring fell on to the box, and she let the chain pour through her hand after it.

'Let us begin the Council,' she said.

Parhannon, who had been head-bowed and speechless since he arrived, suddenly raised his hands. 'My lords,' he said. 'Pray let me speak.' Ayndra gestured gracefully to him and he rose.

'You all know that when our present Lord Regent arrived in this city, I escaped to the north, where I carried Lord Sulakon and Lady Setha to a safe landing. When I had seen that they were safely travelled through the hills, I returned to my ship, and prepared to spend the winter among the pirates of the Girran shore. I was committed to rebellion against my lord of Haramin, whom I considered to have brought revolt and disorder upon the Empire, and I directed the pirates to attack the ships of her allies of S'Thurrulass, and to levy a tribute upon Safic merchantmen. But in the passage of the winter, and in the news which I received of Safi and of more distant provinces, I learnt that she had not brought disorder as I believed. The rebels who had followed her, an they had not gone home, lived quietly in the city, or became tenants on the estates which she had taken from our dead peers. But she did not make of these estates her patrimony, rather she held them in Treasury trust against the reappearance of their heirs. Thaless was at peace, the Needle's Eye quiet, and there was easy passage throughout the Empire as there had not been since our Lord Ailixond left us. Finally I saw the fleet of S'Thurrulass, who had come to help her in her conquest, returning in great part over the sea to Suthine, all save those who escorted the merchant ships. Then I knew that she was not a tyrant, but a just ruler, for who but a just ruler could afford to send away the ships which had brought her power? Yet I remained on the Girran shore, for my pride forbade me to return, until a twelveday ago. It was not until I set foot upon the quayside in our fair city that I learnt of the death of the Little King. I do not believe that he was murdered, for, as my lord says, I have spoken with the people in the harbour who were present. Rather it was his own pride that slew him, for he ignored the humble workmen who warned him of the danger. In this I see a message for us all. Let us unite our voices and acclaim the one whom Lord Ailixond himself wished for the Regent of his Empire, now not only Regent but King. My lord Aleizon Ailix Ayndra.' He turned to her, gave a brief formal nod, and sat down again. There was a pause.

Lord Haelis raised her voice. 'My lord, is it true what is said, that Lord Takarem was your father? And that you are in truth half-sister to Lord Sulakon?'

Ayndra looked up at the ceiling as she replied. 'There is a document, which was presented to the court when I was tried by Lord Sulakon, which presents the marriage contract between my mother and Lord Takarem. As for me, I never knew my father. My mother told me that she had married a rich man, but that he had other wives, and when he died, only a year after the wedding, they joined with their relatives to expel her and her newborn child from the house. Since that day she had to find bread for herself and the child as best she could, for they never had more to do with her. In the ordinary course of things she never spoke of him at all. It was only because she would curse her evil luck when she was drunk that I know what I have told you. She was a woman from Haramin; she said that his wives came from high-born families in Safi, and so despised her.'

'Did she say that he was a lord?'

'She was a woman who did not respect the nobility,' Ayndra said.

'Where is this document?'

'It was presented to the court. I imagine that the Justiciar could find it in his records, unless Lord Sulakon had it destroyed.'

'Blood will out,' observed Lord Domar.

'You do have blue eyes,' said Polem, 'just like Ailixond.'

'Old Lord Ailixond,' wheezed Domar. 'Ailixond Seventh. He was the one.'

Lord Garadon interrupted before the old man could begin one of his yarns on historical topics. 'What promises do you make us, for your government?'

'At least we will be able to have some lords made again,' said Haligon.

'Promises?' said Ayndra. 'I make no promises. Some of those here knew me when I was governing in Haramin, and you have heard what I have done in my wards of conquest. Now you have seen half a year of my government in Safi. I will not act differently an I wear a ring on my finger. I think you know what I will do.'

'What will you do with those vagabonds that have spent the whole winter camped up against the palace wall, so that our wives and daughters cannot go in or out without an escort? My lord,' Ellakon said.

'An escort? But they are law-abiding people. They live in shacks in Great Market because they have no other place to live. Have you not noticed that their number has grown smaller over the months, as they find better homes?'

'And with the spring more will come to join them,' said Ellakon. 'The countryside is unsettled; you have led the tenants to believe that they can leave the land and go anywhere, just as if they were free.'

'Are they not free?' said Aleizon Ailix Ayndra.

'My lord's lands have, perhaps, suffered more than others in the unrest of past years,' Arpalond said. 'My lord Polem and I can both swear that, when we returned to our estates and reformed the conditions which my lord Sulakon's tax-collectors had imposed upon them, our people settled happily and no more wish to leave. We have seen seven years of civil war in the Empire. It is not to be thought that peace and order will return overnight. We ourselves must go into the country and order our estates in person, instead of leaving them to overseers or renting them to merchants.' This last touched Ellakon in person, and he subsided.

'Open the box with the crown,' said Domar. 'Let us see the crown.' He sighed in satisfaction when Polem, at a sign from Ayndra, lifted up the solid gold circlet. 'It will be a fine thing, to have a ruling king again.'

'Then let us move to a vote,' said Golaron.

'Is it even necessary?' said Ellakon.

Golaron glared at him. 'My lord, of course it is needful. We are choosing the King!'

'Indeed? Half of us are not even present! As for you, sir, you have achieved your end of obtaining Lysmal for your son, so that you that were no more than a phalanx captain may found a dynasty—'

'My lord!' boomed Golaron. Several others told Ellakon to be silent and leave off insulting his peers.

'But what of those who are not here?' Garadon asked.

'Let us put blank tablets in the basket for them,' Arpalond said. 'Unless they have chosen proxies whom they instructed to name a candidate?' No one spoke up.

'Blank tablets,' said Aleizon Ailix Ayndra.

She herself stared at her tablet, chewing the end of the stylus, for a while; then wrote in a rapid scrawl, closed it and tossed it into the basket. The priests took it out of sight to count the results; it did not take them long.

'Without a name, seven votes. Lord Polem, two votes. Lord Sulakon, one vote. Lord Aleizon Ailix Ayndra, twenty-five votes.'

'More than two-thirds,' said Arpalond.

Polem leaned forward and picked up the ring, searching for the clasp of the chain. 'Here it is! Now put it on your finger.' He offered it on his open palm. She took it as if she did not know what to do with it. 'On your right hand. Here.' He slid it on to her finger and closed his hand over hers. She looked up at him and gave a smile that seemed to get stuck in her teeth. From the courtyard outside came a muffled ring of cheers. Ellakon got up and stalked out.

She stood up. 'My lords. I . . . aah!' She ran one hand through her hair and spread her arms like a merchant who apologises for the shortage of stock; she was laughing now. 'My lords. The funeral will be held next day in the morning. There will be a procession, but the High Priest says that since Parakison was never crowned we will not celebrate the full rite, that is, the army will not break their swords and there will be no public banquet, although I believe that Lady Sumakas has ordered a family celebration.'

'What about the coronation?' cried Salaron.

'The coronation? O, the coronation. Well, for a proper coronation, we will have to invite representatives from all the Empire, will we not? And that will take a time; a month at least, an they come here with the message-riders.' The people outside were clapping their hands in unison.

'And what about the new lords?'

'Well . . . let them present themselves to me . . . perhaps we can create them at the same time as the coronation . . .'

'You cannot create any lords until you have been crowned,' Arpalond said.

'O, is that so? Shumar, I know nothing! You will have to tell me.'

'I will, my lord, I will,' he said.

Polem had gone to look out of the door. 'Look! All your officers are there. And Lady Sumakas . . . my lady, good day – come out!' He beckoned to the new King.

'Let us all go out,' she said. 'Should we not go and stand on the wall above Great Market and announce the verdict?'

'I think it has been announced already,' Polem said. 'Let us go and ride through the whole city!'

'O yes, there was one more thing about the funeral – Lady S'Thiraidi is going to sing– '

'Come out!' The noise from without swelled as more and more people, clerks, servants, palace guards, came running to join the crowd. 'Very well,' said Ayndra. She pulled her hat well down on her head and strode out of the hall. As soon as she appeared in plain view the crowd gave a massive cheer, and Sumakas ran forward to embrace her. She snatched her right hand and ecstatically kissed the ring. Firumin was next, then Ailissa, then the Justiciar, the Treasurer, the Keeper of the Keys . . . she was swept away in a chaotic procession in the direction of the palace yard and Great Market.

Parhannon and Arpalond were left behind as they helped Lord Domar out of the hall.

'At least we have harmony at last between the Queen Dowager and the crown,' Arpalond said.

'Lady Sumakas?' Parhannon shook his head. 'That woman would send a crowd to cheer for a sea-snake an it wore the Royal Ring. It means nothing at all.'

'Your speech was very valuable; no one can suspect you of being a partisan of Haramin.'

'A winter spent in pirates' hovels on the Girran shore has led me to see sense . . . take care, my lord, step carefully . . . I only hope that others may likewise shed their illusions and come to see what harm our divisions do us.'

'Do you speak of Sulakon?'

'Sulakon will never change,' Parhannon said shortly.

'Sulakon? Do you say that Lord Sulakon will return? To be sure, it would be a fine thing,' said Domar.

'We do not know if Lord Sulakon will return. Will you go to your room and rest now?'

'No!' Domar waved his walking-stick. 'I wish to go to Great Market. Think ye I am too old to join the others? Let us go, my lords, let us go.'

When she arrived at Ylureen's the house was dark. She crossed to a side-alley and peered between two neighbouring roofs: a yellow glow poked through the shutters of Ylureen's chamber window. She led Tarap to the back gate and knocked the doorkeeper up.

Hahhni's bedding was spread, but still empty, in front of Ylureen's door. She stepped over it and went in.

Ylureen was seated at a table, writing. Letters sealed and unsealed lay all around her. Beside her, just outside the circle of light, Esas'thi's daughter sat rocking Small Aleizon. She looked up as Ayndra came in, but Ylureen did not raise her head until she was standing in front of the table. She smiled. Ayndra sat down on the edge of it. 'Why did you not come to the procession?' she said.

'Excuse me.' Ylureen dipped her pen once more, added a couple of rapid lines and dropped the sheet upon a heap of other completed missives. She said without looking up, 'Hahhni, serve my lord some chabe, and fill the long pipe.'

'What is this?' said Aleizon Ailix Ayndra. No one answered her. She got up to take the cup which Hahhni offered her and went and sat down on the seat against the wall. Hahhni bowed to her, fetched her slab and knife and sat down to her work at her feet. Ylureen went on writing. Ayndra had finished her first cup, and then a second, before she put the pen aside and pointed to the written sheets. 'Will you help me seal these up? The wax is already warm; I will drop it on, and you can stamp them.'

They worked in silence. Ayndra kept trying to catch Ylureen's eye as she rapidly folded the sheets and stamped the soft wax. Ylureen did not shift her gaze from the directions she wrote on each sealed missive or the bowl of wax over the tiny lamp. They dealt with seven letters in this way. Ayndra folded the eighth and pushed it at Ylureen, who said without looking at her, 'Lay it down on the table.'

She gave a shriek of rage and flung it down like a gauntlet. 'Ylureen, what *is* this? Am I become a slave, that you do not look me in the eye any longer? Ylureen!' Her voice rose to a scream. The baby Aleizon woke up and began to cry. Ylureen looked from one to the other, walked round the table and took Ayndra's hand. She immediately encountered the Royal Ring, and paused. Ayndra slipped out of her grip and walked backwards until the backs of her knees were against the seat. Ylureen came towards her, hand held out. She sat down and held up one hand. Ylureen halted, and sank down on to the floor.

'Our mother has been sick lately,' she said. 'She cannot order things as she did; I must write many letters. All day I write letters. But where have you been? I have not seen you since the King-child died.'

'I have had to attend to hundreds of things,' said Aleizon Ailix Ayndra. 'You know what has happened now.'

'You have got what you wanted,' said Ylureen. Behind her, the baby was refusing to be comforted. Ylureen stood up. 'Bring her over here . . . make room.' She sat down next to Ayndra and opened her bodice.

'Do you still feed her so late at night?' said the lord.

'She frets; poor lamb; I do no more than pacify her.'

'I have to go to the funeral next day morning,' said Aleizon Ailix Ayndra.

'What funeral?' Ylureen stroked the baby's head.

'Parakison's funeral, of course! Do you not hear anything of Safi?'

'I have been very busy,' Ylureen said, 'just as you have.'

'I shall go an you do not want me here.'

Ylureen turned to look at her. 'I have not said so.'

'You have not; but even a deaf-mute could not mistake it.'

The sleeping infant had let go of the breast, and Ylureen handed her back to the nurse. 'You would not forsake your tasks an I asked you to spend all day with me,' she said. 'You must grant me the same liberty.'

'It is not every day one is elected King of Safi,' said Aleizon Ailix Ayndra, as if she were swallowing something, 'and Lord of the New Empire . . . do you know, I am supposed to change my name?'

'To what? To anything you like? Great and Famous Sun, World-Mother, Sea-Mother?' Ylureen laughed. She motioned to Hahhni to light up the pipe.

'All Kings of Safi are called Ailixond and Parakison in alternate reigns.'

'Indeed? And the little one was Parakison, was he not? So . . .' Ylureen laughed again. 'Why! What a fine memorial you will be to him.'

'I am no one's memorial,' said Aleizon Ailix Ayndra. Ylureen looked at her black clothes, but she ignored her. 'They can put the other name on decrees, an they will,' she said. 'I am not going to change my name.'

'Are you truly King, then?'

173

'Look, am I not wearing this on my finger?' She held up the ring.

Ylureen took her hand and examined it. She began to smile. 'When are you to be crowned?'

'I have not yet decided; in a month, perhaps, to give time for everyone to come. Will you ask people from Suthine? You can ask anyone you like. For once I shall not carp about the expense or the number of guests!'

'Are you really to be crowned?'

'Of course I am! Do you not believe anything? I cannot believe you did not hear of it hours ago, yet here you are, acting surprised!'

'I knew that the Council was this day, and that you would likely be elected. Indeed, I have known it for some hours; but knowing it, and expecting it, is not the same as seeing it in the flesh.'

'Or being it in the flesh, either,' said Ayndra. She puffed on the tall pipe till it was giving off smoke like a geyser. Ylureen got up and walked to and fro, stretching shoulders that had been hunched over her work. She sat down in front of her mirror and began to clean the paint from her face. Ayndra got up and, unasked, began to undo her hair. Ylureen smiled gently into the mirror. 'I was sorry for the little boy's death,' she said, 'but at least it was a quick end, and merciful in that.'

'I think he saw the stone before it killed him,' Ayndra said.

'Were you with him?'

'He had been with me, but I told him to go away.' She fitted her hands round Ylureen's throat and began to caress her neck with her thumbs. Ylureen nestled her head back against her stomach and purred like a cat.

'You should come to me more often ... o, that is delicious ...'

'I must thank you again for inviting our allies to sing; that woman, the Lady S'Thiraidi, what a fine voice she has! Better than the singers in the theatre. Does she sing in her own country?'

'Not for money.' Ayndra stopped in the middle of the dayroom and took off her hat. Sumakas went on, producing

174

a small ring of keys from the folds of her black gown. She fitted one into the lock of a door on the far side of the room, half concealed in an alcove, while Ayndra unfastened her heavy cloak, shook the worst of the rain from it, and tossed it over a chair. She looked about for a place to sit, when Sumakas beckoned her from the door she had opened.

'Come in here; I have something for you.'

'What is it? I thought that that was the door of a closet.'

'This is my special room. I do not let everyone into it.' Sumakas shepherded her in and closed the door. Ayndra took a couple of steps and halted, staring around her. 'Gods' teeth,' she said, wondering. Sumakas rustled past her and knelt down to open the lock on one of the heavy chests pushed against the wall. The whole room was paved with pictures of Ailixond: charcoal drawings, chalk drawings, sketches in paint, half-finished studies, completed paintings in gilded frames. Some of them were clearly the studies which Serannin had produced shortly before his death; others showed him as an infant, as a small child, as a youth, dressed in blue, in white, in red robes, in full armour, standing in front of the Safic flag, wearing the crown, on horseback . . . Sumakas was struggling with the lock. 'I have not opened this for a while,' she said, 'It needs a little oil.' She went back into the dayroom and in a few moments returned with a small can of oil. 'A pity that it rained so much,' she said, 'but it shows the devotion of your friends who came. Otherwise it was a fine funeral. You preside with much grace and authority, my lord. A proper funeral, it was. Thank Shumar that I thought to tell the furnacemaster to store all the wood for the pyre in dry. Ah, come along now, else I shall replace you with a new lock. Ah, there we are.' Hinges creaked as she raised the heavy lid and pulled aside the sheets of muslin scattered with herbs that had been laid to protect the articles within. Ayndra was still looking all round the room in astonishment. Sumakas delved into the chest and brought forth armfuls of heavy scarlet silk, yards of it, one great bundle after another; she gathered it all up in her arms and turned to face the Lord Regent.

'This is just like a shrine,' said Aleizon Ailix Ayndra.

'I kept these for Parakison,' Sumakas said, 'but now they

belong to you.' She attracted Ayndra's attention by a toss of her head, and poured the rich fabric into her lap. She answered her surprise before she could speak it. 'Ailixond's coronation robes,' she said. The sweet lemon odour of the storage herbs, changed when the clothes were aired every few months, rose up in waves from the folds: the same herbs as Firumin used to store Ailixond's clothes with, all those years and miles away.

She buried her hands in the silk, brought it up to her face and pitched over full length on the floor; she wept like a child for the past.

At first Sumakas was too shocked to move. Then she pulled the muslin out of the chest and shuffled forward on her knees. 'Here. Here. My lord, do not cry so. My lord, here, have this . . .' She gently pulled the silk away, already blotched with big dark tears, and introduced the cheap cloth on top of it. Ayndra blew her nose into it and howled into the mess of snot and tears. Sumakas took her under the arms and pulled her up so that her head was in her lap; she stroked her hair. 'There, there. You should cry now. They told me that you never wept. It is better that you shed tears, my lord, you are not a stone. There now . . . there, there . . . have you not wept for him before now?'

'. . . both'f'm . . . everything . . .'

'Hush, now, hush. Ay! How bitterly you weep. Seven years of tears are in you, now they come on you all at once. Come into my bedchamber now; come and lie down. There is nothing you have to do until the dinner this evening, you can rest for a while. You are very tired, no wonder that you are distressed.' She sat her down on the edge of the great bed, brushed the hair back from her flushed forehead and gently kissed her.

'Is this your bed?' Ayndra said stupidly.

'This is my marriage bed, that my husband gave me when we married. Even when I did not have these rooms, yet I had this bed, I conceived and bore my children in it . . . why do you cry now? O, no, I did not mean it – you should cry; no one would denounce you for it, the gods know, you have suffered enough. Here now, lie down; I will lie down with you. Put your head on my shoulder. Hush now . . . quiet . . .'

The lords walked together at the head of the procession back from the burning ground, like a herd of crows in the rain, their heads still covered because of the wet. The commoners followed, with the women in a group in the middle of the party. Diamoon had a black raincloak on, but her scarlet gown, hem draggled with mud, showed beneath it, and she was forever pulling up her skirts to show plump legs in red stockings as she hopped over puddles. The few onlookers who had gathered to watch the cortege proceeding to the pyre had all gone indoors, and even the street-sellers had mostly shut up shop. She smiled brilliantly at Daior-deor when he came up beside her. 'Captain, good day. What miserable weather! It was a miracle that we were able to send the poor Little King up to heaven in this downpour.'

'At least he has gone where it is not raining,' said Daior-deor.

'Do you think so? Very likely it also rains in the land of the dead.'

'Do you know much of the land of the dead, mistress?'

'Because I am a witch? To be sure, we have skills to speak with the dead; but they tell us little of their lives. I think they have no concern for the living; we must force them to come to us at all.'

'But you can call up dead spirits?'

'I know how to speak to those on the other side of the curtain.'

'So you can call up the spirit of . . . of any named person . . .'

'Do you know one that you wish to engage in necromancy?'

'Mistress, I wondered . . . an I asked you to call up the spirit of Lord Ailixond, so that I could speak with him, could you do it?'

'Lord Ailixond?' Diamoon shook her head.

'Mistress, an I have trespassed, excuse me– '

'O, no, sir. May I take your arm? Thank you. Have you never consulted a necromancer before? I thought not. Let me explain a little. Necromancy is a difficult art at the best of times. The dead are unwilling, and we must constrain them to come to us, and constrain them further to speak.

177

And then, when they have come, they are not always willing to leave. Now some dead, their spirits are docile, and indeed it is possible to bind them to a particular place – for instance, an I stored my treasure in a cellar, I might bind the spirit of a slave there to protect it against robbers. To call the spirits of the new dead, or close relatives of the person who seeks the consultation, is not so hard either. But Lord Ailixond! In life Lord Ailixond was possessed of a powerful spirit, and though I met him only briefly, and you not at all, yet there are a many people here who recall him vividly, and it was in this city that he spent the first twenty-one years of his life. For all these reasons, an I did raise him, it would cost me a great deal of labour to bind him to answer my questions; and should he escape from the bond, why, I do not know what might happen then. Besides, I could not raise him alone; I should need at least two people to help me, and that is very costly indeed. Necromancy is the most costly ritual of all in any case.'

'How costly?'

'You see, there are my helpers, and then a multitude of herbs and compounds, and then I need a piece of Lord Ailixond's hair, or his intimate clothing, or, even better, a little phial of his ashes – but how is that to be procured?'

'His tomb lies in the kings' mausoleum; his ashes are laid within it.'

'But the tomb is sealed.'

'The tomb itself is not sealed; the ashes are put into it in a sealed jar, and the slab with the effigy is laid on top, no more. One of the priests was explaining it to me.'

'I see,' said Diamoon reflectively. She looked Daior-deor in the eye. 'May I ask, sir, what it is that you wish to ask Lord Ailixond, should I raise him?'

'Raise him for me, and you will find out,' said Daior-deor.

'It will cost you ten gold sols.'

Daior-deor only blinked once. 'I will pay it.'

'And you will have to steal the ashes out of his tomb.'

'Come with me, and I will do it.'

'When do you wish for it?'

'They are building the new tomb presently; we should do it while there are still tools and stone dust strewn around in the mausoleum, so that we can better cover our tracks.'

'Indeed,' said Diamoon. 'This is what I will do: I will cast the omens to find out which is the most favourable day in the next month, and inform you of it. I will find all the other requisites. Then we will go and obtain the ashes, and raise the spirit – an we can raise him at all, which I do not promise – that same night; once the tomb has been opened, there is no time to waste. Is that well?'

'It is very well,' said Daior-deor.

The moon had just risen over the Tower of the Heavens. Its light filled the round courtyard but did not penetrate into the porticoes where stood the tombs of the Kings. They had not dared bring a light for fear that someone might notice it. Diamoon carried the crowbar, Daior-deor a hammer and chisel and a small leather bag. They worked without speaking. Diamoon introduced the flattened end of the bar under the marble slab and pressed down. Daior-deor got a purchase on the edge as it lifted and together they pushed it aside. It gave a grating shriek as the unpolished base of the slab slid over the vault, revealing the dim form of the tall jar with the ashes. Daior-deor immediately applied the chisel to its seal. Fragments of wax and clay scattered into the vault. He could see nothing inside when he finally levered the stopper out. Diamoon tapped his shoulder and pushed an item into his hand: a spoon. As he lowered it into the jar it knocked against something metallic within; the urn seemed to be full of twisted scrap metal. 'Where are the ashes?'

'Down!' Diamoon pushed his arm. He sunk his arm into the urn and cursed under his breath as some sharp edge seared across his hand; his fingers sank into something powdery. He tried to spoon it up, but the spoon got tangled in the scrap. He dropped it, reached down, grabbed a fistful, pulled his hand out and dropped it into the bag. Diamoon grabbed it from him, felt how much there was, nodded and pushed him again. They scrambled to get the stopper back in place, heaved the slab back over the vault and ran.

Diamoon's apartment was the last one in the section of guest rooms, on the opposite side of the palace from the House of Women. It had two windows looking out on a small courtyard with a dovecote in it, but all their shutters had been stuffed with rags. The room itself had been thoroughly carpeted with mats, blankets, cushions and quilts, and all the furnishings put in the bedchamber behind, except for a large charcoal brazier which stood in the middle. The two attendants opened the door to them. One was very short, much smaller than Daior-deor, and the other appeared a rather bulky woman, but they were both so swathed in veiling that he could not guess at their identity. Diamoon had said that it was better for him not to know. They had a little stove in the corner on which a pot was boiling; its vapours added to the smell of the four incense lamps that were the only source of light apart from the sanguinary glow of the coals. They hastened to block up the cracks round the door with more rags while Diamoon took up her place. The small woman sat down and began to tap out a rhythm on a set of hand-drums. The other carried the pot forward and set it in front of Diamoon, who poured some of the ashes into it and gave her the rest in the bag. The woman sat down behind her and handed her a series of potions and substances which she stirred into the pot or threw on the fire; some of them smelt extraordinarily like sweetsmoke when they burnt. The smokes started to form a thick pall under the ceiling. The cut on Daior-deor's hand throbbed in time to the drumming.

'Did you fast as I told you to?'

'I did.'

'Drink this.' Diamoon filled two bowls with the liquid from the pot and gave one to Daior-deor. She saw him hesitate when he smelt it and made a peremptory gesture. 'Drink it!' She drained hers in one, rested her hands on the knees of her crossed legs and began to rock back and forth. The woman threw more herbs on the brazier.

'Daior-deor,' said Diamoon. 'In a very little while I shall go to look for the spirit. When I come back with him, I will not be able to speak to you. You must ask him the questions which you have. You must be . . . firm in your purpose . . . and fear . . . nothing . . .' The woman gave her another bowl full of the potion, then another. The insistent drumming seemed to fill the stuffy room. Diamoon's arms started to tremble and she rolled her head back and forth on her shoulders; she rose in one liquid movement to her feet and danced, stamping in time to the drums, her head thrown back and her arms hanging loose. The other woman took up a second set of drums and joined the pattern. 'I see colours – like little snakes– ' Daior-deor began, but the big woman hissed at him and he fell silent. The tremors in Diamoon's body grew every moment stronger, shaking her from head to foot; sweat gleamed on her forehead and her mouth hung slack. Incoherent words emerged from her throat. She put her hands up to her head. 'I command you! I command you! Ai-ai-ailixond! I command you!' She screamed 'RIDE!' and fell to her knees, writhing. Daior-deor started to get up, but the big woman immediately seized him and held him down until he was still, except for the hot trembling in his limbs. Diamoon threshed to and fro like a landed fish, her mouth working, uttering a mishmash of groans and animal cries; she staggered to her feet and took a couple of steps forward, until she was right over the brazier. The woman tossed a heap of powder and herbs on to it, which burst in a gush of red flames and smoke. Diamoon gave a couple of inarticulate cries, wreathed in the coloured smoke, experienced a colossal spasm, and said in a clear, melodious tenor voice, 'What do you here? Why have you brought me to you? What do you want?' Diamoon was holding her hands out over the brazier; when she spoke in her own voice it was choked and gasping.

'Lord Ailixond, Lord Ailixond, by the power which is in me I conjure you to – answer these questions– '

'Questions!' said the alien voice. 'Will you waste my time with your questions? I shall not stay, for I have promises to keep, and – ah! – miles to go before I sleep– '

Diamoon's tremors began again. 'The rod!' she exclaimed. The big woman snatched a red lacquered rod from the bundle of magic things and pushed it at her. She gripped it in both hands and held it over the fire. 'Speak! Answer!'

'I know you,' said the voice in her mouth. Its cool tones took on a shade of interest. 'How hot your . . . blood is . . . I do not know *you*.' Daior-deor knew that it meant him. He stood up. The potion was whirling in his head like a firestorm. The voice said, 'What is your name?'

181

'Daior-deor, captain in my lord's army.'

'What is your nation?'

'Thaless is my nation.'

'You do not know me.'

'You are Lord Ailixond of Safi,' said Daior-deor.

Diamoon was wrestling with the forces which racked her body; the rod kept trying to twist round, she endeavoured to keep it horizontal in front of her. She shrieked, 'Speak!'

'I was Lord Ailixond of Safi,' said the voice, laughter tainting its aristocratic intonation. 'What do you want, Captain Daior-deor, Thaless mercenary? What do you want of me?'

'I want you to leave go of my lord Aleizon Ailix Ayndra!'

'Aaah!' Diamoon shuddered.

'Ailix!' cried the voice. 'Ailix.' It thrilled with emotion. 'Leave her? Ailix, the fever in my bones? My Aleizon Ailix Ayndra?'

'She is not your Aleizon Ailix Ayndra! They all speak of you as though you were still with them. You are dead, I have seen your ashes in the tomb. She needs, she needs – more than a dead man. Leave her!'

'I wait for her,' said the voice. 'I wait for all of them. They will all be with me in the end. Come now, Ailix. Come to me!'

'If she will be with you,' Daior-deor cried through the confusion of lights, 'then can you not leave her to me now? I am nothing, I do not want her for ever – only a little time – however short a time – but let her go! Leave her! Please!' Diamoon was bending over backward like a Lysmalish rope dancer. The door rattled; someone was trying to force it. The voice said, 'What do you know she needs? And how do you think that she belongs to me?'

'She loved you!'

'O Ailix,' said the voice. 'Ailix belongs to no one, captain, and she will never ask you for it, but, captain – be gentle with her – Ailix!'

Diamoon screamed 'NO!' and went into convulsions. The rod sprang out of her hands and clattered against the wall; she fell over on the ground and slammed against the brazier. It toppled over as the door flew open. The whole room seemed to explode, as though a wind tore through it;

182

hot coals poured over the mats and blankets on the floor, and in the middle of it the voice spoke in giant disembodied syllables:

'*When the time comes, I'll be there.*'

'Gods' teeth!' Aleizon Ailix Ayndra was standing in the doorway, staring into midair as if she had just witnessed an epiphany. The big woman was scrambling to get hold of Diamoon and ram a cloth into her mouth to stop her choking, shrieking about fire; the small woman tossed her drums aside and leapt up with a blanket to jump about among the coals, beating at the flames that had already broken out and kicking the burning lumps outside onto the stone floor. Ayndra dropped her cloak over her hands to muffle them and set the brazier upright, and they all three ran after the remnants of the fire while the big woman tended Diamoon. It was some time before all the smouldering fragments had been sought out and doused. With the principal lamps alight, the room looked half-derelict.

'What have you been doing?' said Aleizon Ailix Ayndra. She knelt down beside Diamoon, who was lying on her back, eyes closed, shifting and mumbling as though she were in a dream-laden sleep. She peeled back one of her eyelids and let it drop again. 'Ha! Daior-deor, come a little closer. Let me see your eyes. Ha. Did she give you much of it?'

'I think not,' said Daior-deor.

'Indeed, otherwise you would not be sitting calmly as you are now. And I only came looking for something to smoke! Did you know what it was that she was conjuring?'

'A dead spirit, my lord,' said the big woman.

'But it has left her now.'

'It was riding her, my lord, but when you entered it flew.'

'And tried to set the palace on fire at the same time. And your hand, Daior, is it burnt?' She took his hand in hers and turned it over, whistled softly when she saw the cut. 'This is not a burn. How did you get it?'

'On a – on an old piece of metal.' Her touch was like hot lead in his veins.

'You did not put any blood in the– ' she indicated the brazier ' –did you?'

'O, no,' he said.

'It looks unclean. Will you come with me? Sumakas has a slave doctor, he has a wonderfully gentle hand on a wound. He will not mind an we wake him. Is Diamoon well now?'

'As well as can be. I will stay here with her, my lord, there is no need to worry.'

'Thank you, mistress.' She turned to the small woman, and, smiling, said something in S'Thurrulan. The small woman knelt, put her forehead on the floor, and, as she rose, slipped a packet from her robes and offered it to Ayndra, who accepted and dismissed her with a few more foreign phrases. 'Come then, Daior. Mistress, please say to Diamoon, that I am sorry an I inadvertently caused her harm—'

'My lord, you did not, not at all.'

'—and I hope she is well soon; let her send to me, or come, as soon as she may, and we shall talk then. I thank you.' She offered her ring to the woman, who kissed it through her veil, and opened the door to leave.

In the corridor outside she said, 'Now you see why they make laws against necromancy.'

'I hope you are not going to arrest me for it.'

'Arrest you? Of course not. I shall have all the laws against sorcery repealed. Burn their law-books!' She laughed. 'I hope Diamoon was well paid for her services.'

'Very well paid,' said Daior-deor. The tiled floor lurched under his feet and he stumbled against the wall. Cold sweat drenched his shirt.

Aleizon Ailix Ayndra took hold of him. 'Ay! Do not worry, it will have passed off soon. Put your arm round my shoulder, here. Are you going to be sick? Good. For gods' sake cry out an you are. Come and lie down . . . I'll bring the doctor to you . . .'

'Again you are helping me,' he said, 'I am always sick when you . . .'

'It matters nothing. That Diamoon is a witch.'

'What? . . . I thought you did not believe.' She lowered him on to a couch under a coffered ceiling. Its ornament filled with hallucinatory life.

'What did I say that I believed? She is a witch, that is all I said. Look, I will leave some water for you, and there is a

184

pot. I shall return shortly.' A door slammed. The ceiling rippled in sympathy. He closed his eyes.

'S'Thiraidi has been damnably clever, Arpalond; I know it was only the guild masters that came to congratulate me, but when they revealed the true nature of their visit, why, I could see her stamp all over it. And they were all planning to trade with the west coast of S'Thurrulass, while Ylureen is an easterner. She knows that I cannot refuse licences to so many of the rich men of this city without I risk my neck, therefore I will grant them and then I will have to face Ylureen. While S'Thiraidi receives that which she wished in peace and innocence.'

'Why should Lady Ylureen be angry?' Arpalond asked.

'Because she wishes that her family shall have the monopoly on trade between Suthine and Safi, that is why. And then she can give out licences to trade in Safi to all her friends in Suthine. No profits without you kiss Ylureen. Thus S'Thiraidi pits me against Ylureen in search of her own ends. God curse them all for double-dealers!'

'Have you granted the licences?'

'I will grant them. I shall go and tell Ylureen before they are issued. I shall do that next day. Damn!' She exhaled a long plume of smoke.

Arpalond shrugged. 'How are the preparations for the coronation going ahead?' he asked.

Chatting, they heard nothing until the door was flung open and Antinar burst in. He skidded to a halt, gasping. 'My lord! We have them! Rinahar! We overheard it all. They are going to run away on the night of the coronation when no one will notice them!'

'The night of the vigil or the night of the banquet?' Ayndra asked, as though he had offered a choice of honey-cake or fruit pasty.

'My lord?' said Antinar.

'The first night I have to keep vigil in the temple with the sacred flame. Then all the lords come, and I am crowned, and they take me all round the city, and then we return for the banquet, and then I create you and all the rest of the new lords. They must be going to leave on the night of the banquet, no?'

185

'I suppose it must be,' said Antinar awkwardly, the wind taken out of his sails.

'They said that no one would notice them? Then it must be during the banquet, when we are all too drunk to see.'

'But they do not want to go to the coronation at all. They said—'

'Tell me what they said; you can repeat as many treasonable remarks as you like, so long as you do no more than repeat them.' She got up to fetch a chair for him. 'Surely all those who are to be created with you will stay.'

'Taranon and Hadar were there. Rinahar was trying to convince them that they should not let you create them lords, because – he said – you had murdered Parakison. He said that you ordered your stonemasons to entice him on to the quayside with the pretext of showing him their work, and then dropped the stone to crush him. He wants that they should all run away to, what is it, Gingi or some such place—'

'Gingito. To go to Gingito where Lord Sulakon is.'

'Yes, where Takarem went to. But there's more than that, my lord, he said that Ellakon was with them and would encourage the other lords to take away their support from you.'

'Ay! I think I shall have to arrest Rinahar, or at least put him under guard. Perhaps I shall pay someone to pretend to assassinate him in the street.'

'Pretend to assassinate him?' said Antinar blankly.

'Yes, for then I can give him a guard for his own safety.'

'But why do you not assassinate him straightway?' he asked.

She shook her head with a smile. 'Did they name anyone else – Casik, perhaps?' To Arpalond she said, 'He has been at me again to make him Governor of Purrllum. I have never seen him so loving in my life!'

'Perhaps you should give it to him,' said Arpalond.

'Perhaps I should send a war party up to Gingito and take them all prisoner. Now I am King I should not tolerate any sort of rebellion.'

'Should a Lord Regent tolerate it, then?' said Arpalond.

'The Lord Regent can blame it on the other lords.' She laughed. 'Antinar, go on, tell me more of what you heard. How did you find out all this?'

'I heard them speaking my name, and followed. They said, shall we ask him to join us? and Rinahar said No, he will go babble it all straightway to the witch. And all the time I was standing directly behind them with a hat pulled down over my eyes!'

The state receptions for the coronation began five days before the ceremony, when the flagship of line Pilith entered the harbour, escorted by four other vessels, bearing Lord Gishiin, Ylureen's husband, and two lords of the royal lineage sent as honour-envoys by the King and Queen. Lady Sumakas and Ailissa led a party of noble women to view the occasion. They ignored the royal envoys except in so far as etiquette demanded, but they were fascinated by Ylureen's partner, his substantial figure, his receding blue hair and crimped and shaped blue beard, his long coat with gold clasps all down the front of it and his high-heeled boots which made him the same height as his wife. 'Look! She has brought the child to show him. What will he say?'

'He has taken it in his arms . . . but what is she doing?'

'Will she give suck in front of all these people?'

'What? You do not mean that she feeds it herself?'

'Look at that! Like a peasant in a country cart!'

'Really, I cannot look. How can she?'

'No, no, look now, here comes Lord Ayndra. What will he say to her?'

'He knows her of old,' said Sumakas, who contemplated all unmoved.

'Indeed!' exclaimed the lady who had been unable to look. 'He kisses her as if she were his sister.'

'Peace, my ladies,' said Sumakas. 'They are coming to greet us now.' She arranged her veil and went to do the honours. Gishiin was courteous to all, but had not a word of Safic. Lord Ayndra conveyed his invitation to them all to attend a banquet next day, when he had rested from the journey. Ylureen for once said very little; she stood there, tucking her breasts back inside her bodice as if she were putting two pet animals to bed, and gazing at Gishiin in a shameless fashion. He, meanwhile, was being extra-ordinarily pleasant to Aleizon Ailix Ayndra. All three of them set off at the head of the procession to the Yard of

187

Suthine. The ladies regretted that they had to return to the palace, and looked forward with excitement to next night's banquet.

Gishiin confined his speech to reports of his voyage, greetings and congratulations until he had held every hand offered to him and excused himself with the need of a true bath after so much time washing in sea water. Instead of the bathroom, however, he went straight to Ylureen's chamber. In less than an hourtenth she had joined him. He held out his arms. 'Ylureen! When are you going to leave all this and come home to us?'

'My husband,' said Ylureen. She ruffled his hair and started to undo the clasps on his coat. 'You know that I miss you.'

'You never seem to lack for company,' said Gishiin.

'But none of them can take your place for me; you know that.'

'I have a letter for you from our mother, Ylureen. She writes that you must come home soon. She is old, she needs her eldest daughter by her side. How much longer will you stay in this foreign nation?' He caught Ylureen's hand as it dived down the curve of his stomach and made her look him in the eyes. 'She pines for the sight of her new grand-daughter.'

'She will see her! Do you not see how honoured we are here, Gishiin? Would they have sent two – two! – men of the royal family to any of our festivals before?' She got her hands free; it was true that Gishiin was not trying very hard to restrain them.

He said faintly, 'That is why you should come back to Suthine. How can such a great family manage without its young mother?'

'Are there problems in Suthine? That my letters do not instruct you how to deal with?'

'Many things, Ylureen . . . many things . . .'

'Then tell me about them in bed. Come now.'

'Did you ask my lord of Haramin to leave? She looked sad at the end.'

'She is very well, she is going to be King; you need have no worries for her.'

'You must make sure that you ask her to stay next night

'. . . I shall go and sleep in another part . . . ah! indeed, I shall have to – ay, Ylureen, I had forgotten how sweet you are. Come and kiss me on the mouth for a while.'

From then on they came thick and fast: two ships full of Magarrlenios with a huddle of seasick Mirkit chiefs; magisterial parties from towns in Thaless; a citizens' delegation from Purrllum, who were invited to generous hospitality by Lord Casik; Haresond at the head of a tribe of provincial nobility from Lysmal . . . Master Caiblin had written to say that he was coming by ship from Haramin, with people from as far away as the Seaward Plains, but the spring gales were at their peak and it was supposed that he must have been penned by adverse winds somewhere along the coast of Lysmal. Aleizon Ailix Ayndra had to go to Yellow Temple at dawn each day for an hour of instruction in ceremonial from the High Priest, and passed every hour of daylight meeting dignitaries of every stripe. The High Priest was the same who had shaved her head as a convicted adulteress, but neither of them cared to remember it now. At least Ailixond's robes proved to fit her with hardly an alteration, while the rest of the city was going wild with the need for robes and gowns and mantles.

The kitchen of Polem's town house was packed with unaccustomed people, half of them tenants of his who had come in for the festival; the pigs and sheep they had brought for him were all tied up in the kitchen court. Getaleen felt no need to observe her usual precautions; in the midst of such a crowd, her servant's dress was enough. She went straight to the housekeeper's room. Horen began by shouting that she was too busy, until she saw who it was, upon which she whisked her inside, put a pot of chabe on the stove and bolted the door from inside. 'Mother of men! What news I have for you! You know Diamoon Redwoman? Did you know that she conjured a dead spirit for the mercenary who lives at Ivory Gate?'

'A dead spirit? Horen, you are a credulous slave; Redwoman is a charlatan.'

'No, lady, no! This was a true dead spirit. Redwoman was brought here ten days ago, too sick to stand. They said that she had caught a fever and my lord had brought her here to tend her. It was only two days ago that I found out the truth, that the mercenary paid her to let a dead spirit possess her so that he could question it, and the spirit almost took her away with it!'

'Whose spirit was it? That coarse friend of his, no doubt; I always thought they were more than friends—'

'No!' Horen's eyes almost disappeared in the wrinkles of her smile. 'She had gone out of the palace for fear that it was loose there. She conjured up Lord Alizhan! Alizhan the Terrible!'

'Alizhan!' Getaleen began to be excited. 'What did the mercenary want with him?'

Horen rubbed her hands together. 'The mercenary,' she said luxuriously, 'is in love with my lord of Haramin.'

Getaleen burst out laughing. 'With my lord of Haramin! Why does he not challenge Lady Ylureen to a duel of *honour*?' She laughed even louder.

Horen made a face. 'Lady, do you wish to hear my news?'

'O, of course! Tell me all the story.'

Horen got up to pour the chabe before she began. They were deep in her revelations when they heard many cries from the kitchen court and a noise like a riot in the kitchen itself. Getaleen immediately drew her knife and went towards the door, but Horen threw herself across it. 'Lady, you must not be seen! Let me go out. Lady! You know we must keep our secret.' She edged round the door.

'I will wait here, then,' said Getaleen, 'but for our sisters' sake do not lock me in.'

Horen bowed to her and dashed away. She opened the door a crack and peered out. Her mouth opened in surprise. A Safic lord, one of those who hated the new King, was in the middle of the crowd, many of whom were waving sticks and knives and shouting in Safic; but the lord was supporting – of all people! – Derezhaid, who had one hand clamped to his shoulder with blood streaming over his fingers. The lord was shouting in the usual bull-like manner of such people, and Derezhaid was white as sea-foam. She opened the door wider. A deep voice bellowed, 'Silence! What is this trouble? Silence, I tell you!' Lord Polem, dressed in a vivid blue robe which gaped over the blonde-furred expanse of his chest, appeared on the stairs leading down from the first floor. The crowd gradually quieted. He asked, 'What has happened?' and the cacophony began again. Polem made a grim face, stepped down a couple of stairs and drew the long sword he was wearing at his side in one smooth movement, to swing it round and round his head in a scythe of light. The cacophony was replaced by the peace of terror. He sheathed the blade again. 'Rinahar,' he said, 'speak.'

'My lord! I was walking in the street with Lord Derez-haid, when all of a sudden some assassin leaps upon us, and Derezhaid – a hero, my lord – Derezhaid put himself in the way of the blow, it was meant for me, but Derezhaid was wounded and we gave the hue and cry, but the assassin escaped – we were chasing him down here– '

'Are you suggesting he is in my kitchen?' Polem continued to descend the stairs.

'No, no!' babbled Rinahar. 'Derezhaid, my lord – we came in to seek help – if any one had seen– ' Derezhaid was meanwhile pulling at his sleeve. A slave divined his meaning before Rinahar did and dragged up a chair for him. He collapsed into it.

Polem bent over him. 'My lord! How did this happen?'

'Wassa Safin did it,' Derezhaid said. 'In Ropemakers' Street. We were walking . . . he come from behind . . . mother! It hurt. Ay!'

'In Ropemakers' Street? Where were you going?'

'To see about– ' Rinahar began, and then stopped. 'To see about, er, my lord's business.'

'What kind of business?' said Polem. 'Do you not go to the Yard of Suthine for business?'

'We were on our way to the Yard of Suthine,' Rinahar said hastily.

'By Ropemakers' Street?'

'My lord!' wailed Derezhaid. 'I am bleeding to death. A doctor, a doctor.'

'Where is my physician?' said Polem. 'Is he here? It seems that the world and his wife is here. Can all people not busy here go out into the yard? Where is Master Anshil?' He peered round the rooms giving onto the kitchen, and stopped when he looked at the housekeeper's. 'Who is that in there? Come out, whoever you are. Mistress Horen, who is this – why! Captain Getaleen. Do you always dress as a servant on the eve of a festival?'

'Good day, my lord. My best clothes are being laundered,' said Getaleen.

'You should ask your lady to give you another suit. But what are – Rinahar!'

'My lord?'

'You cannot leave now, my lord; we must help Lord Derezhaid. And beside, did you not say that the assassin wished to kill you? Know you who they might have been?'

'A thief, a robber? I cannot tell – my lord, I have urgent duties– '

'They cannot be more urgent than this matter. An assassin in the street! I am going to send to the palace to see what can be done. You must wait here so that you can tell us all about it.'

'You cannot keep me a prisoner!' Rinahar declared, but his mien was not half so decided as his words.

'You are no prisoner,' Polem said. 'We all wish to see this matter solved. Let us stay here for now. Master Anshil! This noble lord has been wounded, as you see . . .'

Rinahar sat down at the table and tried to appear unconcerned. Getaleen began to sidle toward the door. He raised his voice. 'Where are you going?' She was made to sit down beside him. Horen was nowhere to be seen. The physician led Derezhaid away and Polem invited the other two guests to join him in some wine upstairs. He took them to a chamber lit by the last rays of the sun and excused himself to change into everyday clothes. They heard the lock rattle on the outside of the door after he had closed it. Getaleen kept her eyes on the floor.

'What did you say your name was?' asked Rinahar. She did not answer. 'What is your part in all this, eh?'

'I know nothing, my lord.' They sat in silence as the room filled with dusk. It was almost dark when the door opened to admit Polem, carrying a lamp, followed by the Redwoman with a jug and goblets. She served the wine while he sat down. 'Well, good day, Rinahar. Excuse me an I failed in respect earlier; I have to keep this my house in order. I was having my new robe fitted. Have you made all ready for the coronation yet?'

The Redwoman sat down beside Getaleen, watching her, without speaking. Polem chattered and Rinahar made sulky answers, until someone knocked and he went outside for a few moments. He only put his head in to say to Diamoon, 'I must go to the Gate of Ivory. You know what to do,' and was gone.

The Gate of Ivory was closed and barred, but no one stood in front of it or on the wall. Polem tied his horse to the great lock and went into the guardroom. When he opened the door they all stood up and tried to hide the bottles. He asked for Captain Daior-deor.

'The captain is away, my lord, I am his deputy this night.'

'O dear,' said Polem. 'You see, sir, I am looking for Lord Ayndra. They told me at the palace she had come here, and I supposed the captain . . .'

'She was here, my lord, that is, my lord was here.'

'O, splendid – then do you know where they have gone?'

'No, my lord,' said the deputy. Another man spoke up. 'I think they are in the Street of Dreams.'

'The Street of Dreams?' said Polem, surprised.

'My lord came and said . . . she said that she was going to be King after next day, and she wanted . . . she asked the captain to go down the Street of Dreams with her.'

Most of them were laughing more or less openly now. 'He wanted to go,' added a third.

'O,' said Polem. 'I see. Well, I thank you, sirs, but do not neglect the watch in your enjoyment. Where does your captain go in the Street of Dreams?'

More laughter; 'I think my lord King knows the place,' said one.

Polem turned to leave; the deputy followed him to his horse and held his foot for him, apologising for his failure of discipline. Polem did not listen. 'Where would she go to? The Street of Dreams!'

'Drink? Who is going to drink?'

'You are going to drink. I never drink.'

'What? Absolutely not! It will end with you fishing me out of the gutter again, my lord; I will not have it.'

'Do not call me that! You saw me take my bracelets off.'

'An you drink I will not call you by any honorifics, then.'

'I do not mind fishing you out of gutters, you know.'

'You may not; I mind a very great deal. Besides, I am told that you do take wine sometimes.'

'At weddings and funerals!'

'The coronation is the wedding of the King and Safic people.'

'Gods' teeth! Where shall we go, then?'

'Why do you ask? I thought that you were going to lead me on a journey through your past.'

'You wish to know about my past, do you?'

'Yes,' said Daior-deor boldly. They were sitting smoking in the end of the dusk, on the upper floor of an empty half-ruined house.

Aleizon Ailix Ayndra grinned at him and stood up. 'So long as you forget it as soon as you hear it.'

'My lips are sealed.'

'Then let us go.' She tossed the smoke-stub between the shattered shutters and they went down into the street.

The Drowned City, the Cup of Oblivion, the Demon Queen, the Mysteries of Commerce, not one had a sign over the door or an entrance above street level; all had earthen floors the better to receive spillage, home-made benches and the drink in the cheapest two-quarit pitchers. In the Demon Queen there were musicians and a woman who danced on a table. In the Mysteries of Commerce a man with a dark face like those from South Lysmal charmed a jewel-coloured snake from a basket. In the Cup of Oblivion they fell into a scuffle as they were trying to climb the steps to the door and when Daior-deor got outside he found that his purse had been sliced off his belt. Aleizon Ailix Ayndra laughed uproariously. 'Hee! I should have warned you. In these places you keep your money in your shirt.'

'Do you know any place that is not a den of thieves?'

'The Cup of Oblivion is a fine place; I have used those stairs many a time.'

'Used them?' Daior-deor looked at her, flipping the cut straps of his purse. She laughed more. 'I know where we shall go now! To the Angel and the Devil.'

It was approaching midnight and the wineshops were overflowing. The Street of Dreams seethed with sweaty men clutching coins and women in gaudy veils parading up and down in pairs. On the overhanging balconies the expensive whores sat throned amid galaxies of flowers and candles, like the images of goddesses in the temple, floating above the murk of the street. Aleizon Ailix Ayndra danced through the crowd in her age-greened tunic and wooden-soled boots, making cracks with the whores who sidled up to them, mimicking the sellers' cries, scoffing fried cakes so soaked in melted lard that they dribbled all down her front. She kissed prostitutes on the mouth and laughed when they slapped her face. She ran ahead of Daior-deor and he lost sight of her in the crowd; he halted, cursing under his breath. A woman immediately pressed herself against him. The heat of her body reached him through her flimsy garment but her breath was laden with the garlic stew on which she must have recently dined. 'This way. I have a room of my own.'

'I have no money,' said Daior-deor. She was gone as instantly as she had appeared. He pressed on. 'Do you know the sign of the Angel and the Devil?'

And it did have a sign, a proper hanging one, the Devil about to run the Angel through with a pitchfork; the Angel had its back turned and was raising one hand in the sign of blessing. It was a very insipid, sexless Angel, while the Devil looked as if he must be first cousin to a stallion. Daior-deor knocked on the door and a little tell-tale shot aside. A few moments later the door itself opened, but when he entered he was in a dark corridor and no sign of the porter. Another tiny hatch opened, showing a bright light. 'Lay your sword down.'

'I have no sword.'

The door opened and a toad-shaped man emerged. He almost blocked the passage as he ran his hands over Daior-deor and stepped backwards. 'Pass.' He was admitted into a hell of light and sound. Half a dozen women were dancing on tables and others walked stark naked through the crowd with trays of drink balanced on their heads. The room was two storeys high, with a gallery on the first floor; it looked like an inn whose courtyard had been roofed over. Double staircases at either end held a constant traffic between the two floors. The place stank of money. Daior-deor found an inconspicuous place under the gallery from where he could watch the entrance. When a hand seized him from behind he almost fell off the bench. Aleizon Ailix Ayndra shoved him bodily along it and dropped down next to him. 'Where have you been?' he said. 'I never saw you come in.'

She laughed and grabbed the neck of his shirt. Before he could do anything she had plunged her hand into her own breast, brought it out fisted and shoved it down his front. A rain of coins landed on his stomach and her hand shot out again, quicker than an eel, to seize his wrist. 'Now we have plenty of money. Let us go sit somewhere we shall be served.' As they pushed for a seat she pulled his hand across her and he felt the weight of money where her tunic sagged over her belt. 'Wine here!' she yelled. 'Best Thaless! Two!' When the naked servant brought it she ran a hand over her flawless buttocks and received another slap for her pains. She fell forward on the table laughing. Daior-deor poured himself a drink and one for her. She tossed it straight off as if it were firewater, shouting, 'Victory!'

'Who did you rob?' he said.

'Hush! Do not speak so loud.' She put her forehead close to his. 'Some fat merchant. I saw him in the street . . . I could not resist it . . . his wife is a friend of Sumakas, you see, and I saw him going into Mistress Ingele's house. Ingele's! Well, he will have to go home again an he wishes to purchase any more fourteen-year-old virgins. Ingele's!' She drained another cupful and rolled her eyes. 'Hoo! He had a bodyguard. They could not catch me!'

'So this is what you used to do in your past.'

'That was when I frequented the Drowned City. Then I began to come here to meet clients.'

'Clients who wanted a robbery?'

'I told you, speak softer!' She continued in her usual carrying voice. 'Clients who wanted a murder.'

'What?'

'I used to kill people for money,' she said happily.

The six dancers had moved three to each side and were making snaky gestures with their arms as another woman was borne up to their table. She too was naked, but painted from head to foot with an irregular pattern in russet and cream. Even her hair had been plastered to her head with it. A round basket was placed in front of her and its cover removed. She began to sing in a wordless warble and move her hands over the basket. Something started to sway up out of it. 'A snake!' said Daior-deor.

'Another damned snake-charmer? Time for a smoke.'

'No, this is different . . . look at it! How long is it? It is still coming out. Shumar! Its middle is as thick as her leg. It is the same colour as she is. I never knew there were any such serpents! How does it not bite her?'

Ayndra cast a disdainful eye at the spectacle. 'South Lysmalish serpent,' she said. 'They wrap up their prey and crush it. They have no venom.' She sniffed, but the rest of the onlookers were transfixed as the dancer let the snake loop its coils round her body and stepped back on to the litter which had borne her to the table. It started a journey round the room while she offered various clients to touch it and the others screamed with laughter at their fear, only to run themselves when it came close. Aleizon Ailix Ayndra stood up as it approached. 'Here boy!' She patted its lance-shaped head with one hand, smokestick in the other. 'Coochy-coochy-coo! Snakey!' She could hardly speak for laughing.

There was a crash from the entrance. 'There he is!' She opened her mouth, stuck out her tongue and let the snake brush it with its own.

'Get him!' The litter plunged to the ground and four or five bravos leapt over it. The doorkeepers had disarmed them but they did not look the type to rely much on additional weapons. The snake was loose on the floor, the dancer howling, people were trying to escape in every direction and Ayndra had disappeared in the mêlée. Daior-deor gulped the last of the wine and ran for the staircase at the other end of the room. He glanced at the door and saw a fat man draped in gold chains waving his arms; then he saw a blonde head on the other staircase. She reached the gallery as one of the bravos seized her arm; she pirouetted round, there was a brief flash in her other hand and the man was on his knees clutching at his stomach. She snatched up an enamelled vase full of flowers, flung it into the mass of her pursuers on the stairs, and fled.

Daior-deor met her in the middle of the gallery. 'This way!' She pulled him into a dark opening between two rooms. By the smell it was plain that it led to a privy, in the form of a wooden box tacked on to the outside of the building with holes giving on to a squalid ditch below.

'Are we going down?' he cried.

'Up!' She scrambled into the unshuttered window. For a moment her legs hung outlined against the stairs, then were replaced by her hand. Daior-deor was astonished by the power with which she swung him up and out, and they were scrambling along in a broad stone gutter between two steeply pitched roofs. 'Run like the devil!' gasped Ayndra. 'Just follow me!' Tiles shattered under her careless feet. The Street of Dreams reeled below them like a gorge filled with light. A flimsy piece of guttering shattered as they swung over it on to a tiny third-floor balcony. Ayndra smashed the shutters and charged into the room. A woman sat on the bed, a man was taking his breeches down; both screamed, but Ayndra did not even look at them as she headed for the door on the far side, into a warren of stairs and passageways and rooms opening in every angle. In a few minutes they were clearly in the private quarters, and then a kitchen, not caring whom they cannoned into along the way; out into a muddy yard, up on the midden and over the wall at its foot. They landed in a twisting unpaved alley, really no more than an open gutter fenced in by the tall houses either side. 'Are they still behind us?' she cried.

'Let us keep running!'

She bounced up, trying to see over the wall. There was certainly an unusual racket coming from the house. In the yard someone shouted, 'Where'd they go?'

She said, 'Keep running!'

'Closing up now, gentlemen. Closing up. Drink up now, it's the morning, sirs, time to go to your work. Closing up now.' The barmaid recited in a sing-song tune as she went round picking up the empty jugs and cups and swiping a damp rag across the table-tops.

'Have you any breakfast?' said Aleizon Ailix Ayndra.

'No breakfast here, sir, we close now.'

'God damn. Leave that lamp a moment, mistress ... thank you.' She puffed on a fresh smokestick as the maid extinguished the last light, and gave an evil glance at the aromatic smoke. Ayndra pulled herself upright on the table. 'Daior. Time to go.' She looped her arm round his shoulders as they crept into the greylit street and paused, swaying, wondering where to go.

The door creaked again behind them and the maid shouted, 'Runnel!' as she came out with two buckets of slops.

'Let us go to the harbour,' said Daior-deor.

'The harbour? . . . very well, very well.'

They staggered out of the way of the sheet of dirty water. A cold wind chased fragments of straw past them; the light was growing every moment. By the time they reached the quayside they had shadows that stretched in the direction of the open sea. The sea at their feet, though, was a soup of harbour refuse riding the green waves. The painful clarity of the light illuminated the fishermen's quay, where the night boats were selling their catch to fishmongers and early housewives, and picked out every broken window and peeling wall on the harbour buildings; the wind sang in the rigging and gulls screamed over the innards the boats threw away.

'It's all over now,' said Aleizon Ailix Ayndra.

'What is over?'

She had both her arms wrapped now round her ribs against the chill. 'I have to go back to the palace,' she said thinly. 'This time next day they'll be putting the crown on my head.'

'Yes,' said Daior-deor.

She said, 'I think it has all been a horrible mistake.'

'What? O no! This night was—'

'No! I never meant that.' She sat down on the edge of the quay, feet dangling over the sea. 'I never thought I would end up as King in this damned city.' Her voice broke on the last word; she clutched at Daior-deor's leg and pressed her face against the side of his thigh.

He put his hand on her head, where the yellow hair had been greased and pinned up to hide its length and colour. He said, 'It will be the same as now; it will be no different.'

'Gone too far already,' she said indistinctly. Someone behind them yelled, 'Hola!' and they sprang apart, each into a crouch, ready to run again. 'Polem!' said Aleizon Ailix Ayndra.

199

He was waving his arms as much to maintain his balance as he zigzagged over the uneven cobbles as to greet them. 'Look for you all night!'

'Good god, you are even drunker than we are.'

'You no' drunk . . . are you? Trou'le wi' look for someone in Safi, you meet so many peo'le you know.'

'I hope they gave you it for free,' Ayndra responded. 'Why were you looking for me?'

'Someon' try to kill Derezhai'. An' Rinahar. An' tha', what its, Getaleen, Getaleen was in my kitchen in *disguise*. An' then my housekeeper run away.'

'Rinahar? Who tried to kill him? Getaleen?'

'Wan'a fin' oud. You better come now.'

'Yes, we are going to the palace – what are you – aah!' A fountain of green water soused both of them as Polem plunged over the edge. Daior-deor burst into laughter. Polem's pate popped up amid the foaming scum. Ayndra waved. 'Polem! Swim ashore. Up the steps here.' She tripped down them. Polem flailed his arms and disappeared. 'Shall we throw you a rope? Where is a rope? Are all those dogs of sailors sleeping?'

'Do they not sleep on shore in port?' said Daior-deor.

Polem surged into view again, made gurgling noises and sank under the debris.

'Not a place I would choose to swim,' said Aleizon Ailix Ayndra.

Polem made one last attempt to get his head above water. 'Can' swim!' Green soup closed over him.

'Gods' teeth!' Ayndra yanked her boots off, dashed to the water's edge and dived. Polem flung his arms round her neck and they both sank. She delivered several blows to his head and half strangled him with his own collar before he understood that he should hold her gently and not struggle. She towed him to the steps; he sprawled on the weed-covered stone like a beached whale. A number of women with baskets of fish to sell had gathered at the top of the stair.

'Who is it? Is it a lord? Is he drowned?'

'Polem, I am so sorry! I never knew you could not swim. Polem? Are you well?' Polem groaned and puked up a spew of watery vomit. 'Daior-deor, help me lift him up. We must take him to the palace. Polem, can you stand?'

The women made way for them with silent greedy eyes; they broke into a foam of chatter as soon as they were a little way away.

Ayndra made them stop before she knocked on the harbour gate of the palace. 'Daior, will you go back to the gate now? I have to go and be purified and all sorts of nonsense.'

'Of course,' he said. She suddenly laid her hand along his cheek, bent forward and kissed his lips. It was like a breath of fire among the icy dribbles of harbour water; he shivered. She smiled at him, a beautiful smile, and went marching up to the gate in her rats' tails and draggled clothing, the doubly sodden Polem trailing behind. She did not look back once to see if he was still watching.

'Hotcakes, master? Hotcakes?' It was a ragged urchin with a dozen in a piece of cloth. Daior-deor gave him a coin and took two without looking. He tossed his hair out of his face, bit into a cake and set off for Ivory Gate. The urchin gawped at the gold sol he had been given, bit it a couple of times, knotted it into the corner of his undertunic and devoured the rest of his stock.

Ayndra wriggled one arm out of the bundle of linen and brocade she was wrapped in. 'Ylureen,' she said, reaching out her hand.

'Where have you been all night?' said Ylureen.

'I have been out.' Ayndra let her unwanted hand flop back on the counterpane. 'Just as the bridegroom goes out with his brothers on the eve of the wedding. I have not been to sleep all night.'

'You were sleeping just now.'

'I have to sleep sometimes.'

'Were you sleeping when you sent your men to imprison one of my citizens in your dungeons?'

'No, I told them to do that before I went to rest. What hour is it now?'

'You must give Getaleen back to me straightway.'

'Why?' Ayndra said insolently.

'Why? Why, because she is one of my people! You cannot put her in a Safic prison. And she has not even committed a crime!'

'Are you sure?'

Ylureen mewed with anger. 'Ah! What has got into you?'

'Perhaps you should ask S'Thiraidi about it.' Ayndra sat up. The covers fell from her naked shoulders. 'And you can send back that woman she gave Polem as housekeeper. Ylureen, I have had enough of Getaleen carrying out her silly plots directly under my nose. Does she think me blind? I witnessed her setting up that entire affair of the western ports which upset you so much. Now I find that someone has stabbed Derezhaid, in mistake for Rinahar – or was it in mistake for Rinahar? And when they are brought into Polem's kitchen, for the nearest safe place, there is Getaleen dressed as a slave skulking in the housekeeper's room. The housekeeper runs away, no one knows where, though I am sure an we searched S'Thiraidi's house we would find her there, and Getaleen has naught but the most feeble excuses to explain her acts. I ordered she and Rinahar both sent to Stabor till the coronation is over, in hope that they remember what they were about. I believe that Derezhaid knows more than he says, but he pretends to be prostrated with the shock of his wound. A little knife in the shoulder!'

'A little knife? It was a great sword! It was one of your lords that did it!'

'What?'

'My people have examined the wound.'

'You could not stab someone in the street with a long sword, Ylureen. Indeed it was a Safic – or so they said – but they meant to kill Rinahar. What was Derezhaid doing, in any case, walking with one of my best-known enemies?'

'Surely he may walk with anyone he likes.'

'Indeed,' said Ayndra. 'Polem would much like to have his housekeeper back.'

'She is terrified! He threatened her with a sword. She will not set foot in his house again.'

'O! So you have seen her, then.' She looked narrow-eyed at Ylureen, who said, 'An you knew all about the western ports, why did you not prevent it? And tell me?'

'Unfortunate as it may be, I feel it would be unjust were I to prevent my people walking with any they wish. And I thought it no business of mine to tell you what your people did. Did you not know that Getaleen and her friends had been meeting with Safic guildsmen for months?' She pulled the covers away and got out of bed, wrapping a length of brocade round her like a priest's robe. 'In two days my ceremonial duties will be over. Presently I have not time to question them. You are welcome to go and see them in Stabor, but I will not let them out. And I cannot believe that Polem threatened one of his favourite servants with a sword.'

'When S'Thiraidi brought Horen to me she was still shaking.'

'No doubt because S'Thiraidi had put the fear of the devil into her first.'

'Where is Polem?'

'He fell into the harbour at dawn.'

'What! Is he drowned?'

'Almost, but I was at hand. I think they have put him to bed now.'

'Quite the little hero, are you not?' said Ylureen.

Ayndra grinned. 'I do my best,' she said.

A couple of taps sounded from the door. 'My lord?'

'What is it?'

'Fifth hour is past, my lord, the High Priest has sent twice already,' said Firumin's voice.

'Send back to him that I have had one bath already this day and no dinner. I will come to the temple as soon as I have eaten.' A fresh suit of clothes was laid out on a chest. She dropped her robe and pulled the shirt over her head. The door banged. When she had her head free she saw that Ylureen had gone.

The only light in the temple came from the sacred flame in its pit before the altar. The priests had filled up its oil reserves before they retired and barred the doors from without, but the perpetual flame illuminated only a small preserve of warmth in the cavernous hall, damp with its underground setting. In the Instruction the High Priest told how it had once been the house of the idol of the underpeople, before Ailixond First cast them out, threw the idol into the sea and lit the sacred flame. In those days the temple floor had been only four steps below the ground. Now the staircase stretched down twenty steps from Yellow Temple

Square, and the vaulted ceiling had been rebuilt three or four times; but the sacred fire had never ceased to burn in its pit. Its light picked out the irregularities in the ancient floor and glinted on the shiny things that lay between it and the altar: two wide golden bracelets, a long sword out of its sheath, and the glaucous stone of a heavy ring. Aleizon Ailix Ayndra squatted on the other side of the fire, her back to the door. Neither sound nor star nor moonlight from without crept through the cyclopean walls; the flame neither rose nor diminished with the passing of time. She had her feet tucked inside the long white shirt and her head on her drawn-up knees; but when something fell down behind the altar she sat up instantly.

For a few moments there was silence. Then another rattle of falling fragments, a scrabble and grate, a troubled gasp. She leapt up, ran round the firepit and seized her sword. She held it out in front of her as she shuffled across the floor. She called, 'Who are you? Put your hands up and come into the light!'

Someone landed heavily in the out-of-sight dark. She shouted, 'Who is it?' and lifted the sword.

'My lord?' said a quavering voice.

'Who are you, damn you? Do you not know this is supposed to be a solitary vigil?'

A scruffy figure bolted round the side of the altar and skidded to all fours in front of her. 'I do, my lord, I do, I, I did not know what else to do – I am sorry– ' He was out of breath and smeared with dust and smuts.

'Antinar!' she said.

'My lord! Rinahar is trying to kill you.'

'What?' She laid down the sword and sat beside him.

He gabbled, 'I heard about it yesterday night – I mean the night before yesterday – they were going to come here! Here, in the temple! And I remember what you – what you – I tried to kill Rinahar, but he was with one of them, the man one, and in the middle of a crowd I was pushed and I stabbed him instead of Rinahar, they had their backs to me, and then – two of their women came after me, their women with long knives, because I think, that one I used to see in the White Bear, she is in charge of it and I know she sent them after me, I managed to get away and I hid in a cellar

204

but I dare not come out till it was dark and then come straight here but I fell asleep and it was too late and I had to climb in through the smokehole and I thought, I thought I would find you dead!'

'You mean Getaleen,' she said quietly.

'And the other one. Derezhaid.' He was breathing more easily now.

'Is he part of it?'

'I do not know. I think he must be. And Ellakon! They were going to hire some robbers and pay them to do it. Then they could say it was someone come to rob the temple images and they . . . they could throw you into the firepit.'

'The murderers?'

'Yes.'

'And what were they going to do with the murderers afterward? Kill them, I suppose. They could not leave them alive.'

Antinar shook his head. Relief after so much exertion had exhausted him. She said, 'You will be glad to know that Rinahar and that woman Getaleen are in Stabor. The man you wounded made them all rush to Polem's house, so that he could find a doctor. Polem acted with great wisdom; though he could not find what they were up to, he knew it was suspicious, and ordered them both held.'

'But that woman . . . was she there? I did not see her.'

'By some strange chance she was visiting Polem's kitchen when they arrived there. They gave him some S'Thurrulan servants a while ago. No doubt they served as spies, but they were not very clever, for the chief of them, when she saw Derezhaid brought in bleeding and Getaleen found, fled back to her mistress, instead of feigning utter ignorance. But who else did you say was in this plot?'

'Ellakon and . . . I only saw the two of them. I thought it was Rinahar's notion.'

'So you got a knife and made to stab him in the back in the street.'

'I thought, I could wound him and run away, and then, he would have to have guards. Then they could do nothing.'

'And you attacked him in the midst of the crowd of his followers? How brave you are!' she said with honest admiration.

'Brave? But I ran away afterwards. I never thought I could run so fast!'

'That's brave too. I know how it is when people chase you. But what are we to do now? You know we are locked in here until sunrise.'

'How long is that?'

She laughed. 'I cannot tell! Did you see the hour when you were out?'

'I could not tell. There were people about.'

'It is festival time; there are always people about at night in festivals. Do you know what time they planned to attack?'

'After midnight.'

'Third or fourth hour of morning, I should think. When most revellers have gone to sleep and the early risers are mostly sleeping still.' She picked up the sword again and laid it across her knees. 'Do you wish to sit here with me and wait for them?'

'My lord?'

She sat looking into the flames. 'This is the vigil of my coronation. Am I to run away and hide in the palace for fear that a few robbers may come? Certainly we shall hear them entering. I will help you climb out an you think it better that you go to the palace and warn them. The lords will all come here at dawn . . . it will be interesting to see which of them come.'

He looked uncertain. 'Can I . . . do you wish me to stay here?'

'I do not particularly wish you to go to the palace.'

'I'll stay here.'

'Very well. Will you lend me that jerkin you have on? This shirt is a very thin thing to sit up in all night.'

'Have my cloak!'

'No, you keep it.' She went up to the altar, felt under its embroidered cover and brought out a smokestick; she lit it in the sacred fire and sat crosslegged, exhaling slow clouds of smoke. Antinar shuffled up to her and sat by her side, watching. After a while he asked, 'What is that that you smoke?'

'Why, sweetsmoke. But you knew that already.'

'What does it do?'

206

'Have some! There you are. Care that you don't cough now . . .'

By the time an intimation of clarity appeared in the smoke-hole he had fallen asleep with his head in her lap. She let him lie until her legs began to grow stiff, then made a pad out of his jerkin and laid his head on it; she got up and trotted round and round to warm herself, then went to have a last smoke. It was nearly finished when a blast of trumpets sounded outside and the priests' key grated in the antique lock. She tossed the butt into the flames and stood up to receive the crown of Safi.

'What a little dried-up stick of a woman she is,' murmured Gishiin. He edged his chair up against Ylureen's so that he could pillow his head on her breast, and yawned. 'You have no idea how tedious it is when one cannot understand a word they say.'

'It is only oaths, and shouting, and more oaths,' said Ylureen. 'But every lord that is free and in Safi is here; even the ones that refused to come and vote her King.'

'In that case, all the shouting signifies nothing.'

Gishiin began to kiss Ylureen's neck. She continued to watch the new King. She stood in the middle of the restored Hall of Stars, where a tongue extended from the raised floor where the nobles sat with a flight of steps leading down to the common level. The new lords in their brilliant robes ringed her; when she had finished giving them their bracelets a multitude of others crowded up to the steps to kiss her hand and proffer service. Her hair, carefully crimped in a series of parallel waves, shone as bright as the gold circlet in it. The noble ladies sat either side at the back of the dais; the semicircle of table for the lords, with the throne in the middle, was still mostly empty as its occupants peacocked about on the front of the stage. Every few moments someone else proposed a toast and provoked another cheer; the unstained ceiling rang. Gishiin slipped his hand inside Ylureen's dress. She pushed him away. 'Be patient! They have not even brought the banquet yet.'

'It is not that kind of banquet I am interested in,' said Gishiin.

'You must eat the one to prepare for the other.' Ylureen

207

put his hands in his lap and stood up, shaking out the circle of her skirts as she glided into the butterfly-bright crowd of lords.

Diamoon, seeing that Gishiin was alone, drifted out of the ladies' seats and sat next to him. 'Good evening, my lord,' she said in his own speech. 'Have you enjoyed the ceremony?'

Ylureen greeted, and was greeted by, half a dozen lords as she approached the King; she remained just behind her, conversing with Lord Polem, for a good while. Polem was quite drunk already. His tailor had worked some miracle with the blue robe such that most of his paunch had disappeared; he had rings on every finger and wore a belt a handspan broad studded all over with turquoises. 'Such a fine day this has been!' he cried. 'How it reminds me of Ailixond's coronation. Twenty-two years ago! He was even then talking always of his New Empire, I used to say yes, yes Ailixond, thinking nothing of it, I thought he meant just that we would finish his father's war in Lysmal . . . I could never have imagined the truth . . .' He reminisced while Ylureen listened carefully to Lord Ayndra's conversation with Ellakon, only a few feet away.

'Ellakon,' she said, 'let me tell you a story. Do you know the story of the King without a Name?'

'Is this a fairy story? My lord,' said Ellakon.

'It is an old Safic story. It treats of the early days of the city, when Ailixond First's sons had succeeded him until the fourth generation, when Parakison Second had no sons. His three daughters were married among the lords, and he ordered that when he died the lords should elect one of the three King. They chose the husband of the youngest daughter, and he went into the temple for his vigil before the flame. But while he waited in the night, his brothers-in-law sent their servants to break through the roof and kill him. When they came next morning with the crown, they found him dead on the floor with five dead men around him. They knew from their slave-marks that his brothers-in-law had sent them. They were put to death, and after that the election was held freely among the lords, and though the dying King might express preference, it was never binding. Do you know that story? He was called the King without a

Name because he was chosen king but never came to his coronation.'

'It is an old tale,' said Ellakon.

'Perhaps not so old as all that,' returned Ayndra.

'You have come to your coronation, my lord,' he said. 'I do not know what you speak of.' He bowed to her and retired into the crowd.

Ylureen took Polem's hand. 'Most interesting,' she said, 'you must come tell me more later.' She kissed his cheek and slid past him to skirt the ring of young lords round Ayndra's twelve-foot train, pooled on the floor behind her like a lake of blood, to present herself to the King. Ayndra broke into a smile when she saw her. Ylureen went down on both knees to kiss her ring. She said clearly in Safic, 'My lord, we are all honoured to witness this day. Permit me to pledge you my loyalty and respect, now and for always.'

'Lady, I receive it with joy; may our friendship endure to our heirs.' Ayndra lifted her up and leaned forward so that they could exchange kisses. She said in S'Thurrulan, 'I thought I would not see you here.'

'How could I miss such an occasion? Of course I came! Did your vigil pass happily?'

'I thought a great deal during it.'

'And what did you think?'

'I thought that you were going to leave me, Ylureen,' Ayndra said calmly. 'But I am very glad to see you now.' She took her arm and announced in Safic, 'My lords, gentlemen, we have stood here long enough; let us sit down and dine. My lords, can you take up my train?' The new lords, swords rattling, bent down to pick it up, and stretched it out like a banner; with Ylureen on her arm and six of them following amid a much greater crowd, she wheeled round and processed up to the throne. Under the gold circlet she looked as serene as her title; she looked neither to one side nor the other.

Ylureen put her lips to her ear. 'Do you want me to leave you?'

She turned her face to her. The pale lashes blinked once over the lapiz eyes. 'No,' she said, and looked to the front again.

When they reached the throne they were separated by

rules of precedence. The seats of honour beside the King had been given on one side to the royal envoys, who had brought their own servants who could be trusted to serve them in the approved manner, approaching on their knees and never offering anything from the left side. Sumakas had accepted with delight the offer of the Queen's chair on the King's left, and insisted on Ailissa to sit next to her before any of the lords received a place. Ylureen sat next after the envoys, with Gishiin to her right; it appeared that Diamoon had been sat next to him by the preference of Polem, who followed. S'Thiraidi had to sit on the second level of the dais, with the provincial nobility. The new lords draped the King's train over the arm of the throne and retired to their seats at the furthest extension of the lords' tables, within arm's reach of the women and children and the armed guards behind the pillars. Aleizon Ailix Ayndra upturned her inverted goblet and made it ring with her eating knife; she had a place setting all in gold. 'Let the banquet begin!' As the musicians struck up and the servitors moved forward, she leant back to Firumin, who stood just behind her chair with his steward's staff in hand. 'For gods' sake bring me something to smoke before the soup gets here!'

'It is already on your table, my lord; that wooden box by the candle-lamp,' he said, without disturbing his pose; but when she looked at him he was smiling.

Once they had begun, the dishes followed one upon the other without let-up; on the open floor of the lower hall fire-eaters followed tumblers followed acrobatic dancers while people shinned up the columns to fix tight and slack ropes for an exhibition of rope-dancing. After about an hour's eating, people began to get up and stroll about on the dais, changed places, spoke to friends on the other side of the hall, encouraged the performers and accepted the homage of subordinates at the lower tables. Despite the dimensions of the hall, the activity of the crowd and the ranks upon ranks of lamps already thickened the air; lamp-smuts began to collect on the freshly painted ceiling. The wine-pourers' tunics were blotched with sweat as they ran between the tables. As the fire-eaters retired to give space for the rope-dancers, Firumin was summoned to deal with some people at the main doors, in the far screens passage. When he saw who it was, he told them to go straight through to the dais, and himself returned by the long route to see that the empty dishes were being taken away properly. When he reappeared at the back of the dais, Ayndra's table was lying on its side in a slew of golden plates, and half the lords and ladies were on their feet; she was in the middle of the dais, train stretched behind her with a great splash of wet where the golden cup lay in its folds, her arms round a bald man in a russet physician's robe. Pressing behind him were a plump woman in a Haraminharn headcloth with gold brooches, Ogo the artillery captain, and a two or three dozen others in assorted northern finery. He told the slaves to pick her table up before she turned back to sit down, and sent another to bring a folding chair, for Master Caiblin to sit between Lady Sumakas and the King. It was the best moment of the day when she called to him to fetch the Governor of Haramin a chair, and he answered that one was there for him already.

As the door closed behind Selanor, Caiblin said quietly, 'That is the third time I have seen him since the coronation, and each time he has been in drink, if not altogether drunken.'

'He has been drunk ever since we left Magarrla. From time to time he awakes sober, but makes haste to remedy that in short order.' Ayndra pulled his vacated chair closer so that she could put her feet up on it, and flicked ash over the floor.

'Do you speak to him about it?' Caiblin said.

'After we had taken the city I began to harangue him for coming drunk to my councils; and then whenever I arrived late, I would find him outside the door munching some cachous to slay the smell of firewater on his breath. So I told him not to mind it, that he could smell of drink to high heaven so long as he did not fall off his horse in duty hours, but that as soon as he did he would be sent into retirement and his deputies given all his commands.'

'It is firewater that he drinks?'

'Yes,' she said with a sigh. 'It is a terrific vice.'

'A greater vice than that?' Caiblin pointed at what she was smoking.

211

'Huh!' she said. 'This is no vice.' To prevent him grinning longer, she said, 'You have not told me of your talk with Lady Sumakas.'

'She was remarkably angered that we conversed in Haraminharn tongue when we were talking at the banquet.'

'Did you not note it at the time?'

'I suppose I did; but even now she carps at it. She says, What have you to say to each other that I cannot hear?'

'A multitude of things, as she well knows. She should be glad enough that I gave her the Queen's place in the ceremonies; she was forever going on that she had never been Queen in it before, her husband was crowned well before her day and of course Ailixond had Othanë.'

'She does not care for those things as much as you do.'

'What things?'

'Receiving public deference. The trappings of power.'

Aleizon Ailix Ayndra lifted up her hand to look at the milky diamond. 'You have it chained to your bracelet,' he said.

'It fell off once or twice before. Think an it fell down a drain! A fish might eat it, and who knows might then fish it up out of the sea?' They laughed. She got up to throw the dead smokestick out of the window. 'You still have not told me what she said. You old fox!'

'She asked if I found you much changed in the – what is it? two years? – since last we met. I said that you looked rather older–'

'A miracle an I did not! It is more than two years.'

'–but otherwise not half so much changed as I expected.'

'I thank you for that!'

'But you do look older. I said that she should make sure that you ate nourishing food.'

'Aah!' She tried to push him off his chair; they giggled like schoolchildren. 'Will you come with me to visit Rinahar in Stabor?' she asked.

'Ah! Rinahar! Now I remember the other thing she spoke of.'

'Whaat?' she cried; she kicked him in the shins. 'Now you remember!'

'O, my lord. I have not had anyone to play question-and-answer with since you left Raq'min. Will you mind an I say how much I have missed you?'

'No, why should I mind?'

He looked away. 'Now let me tell you what you want to know. Lady Andalë, that is Rinahar's mother, has twice been to see Sumakas and plead for clemency for her son. Of course, she says that she does not believe that he was ever in a plot, that it was all fabricated by foreigners and evil people, and that Sumakas should ask you to set him free straightway. Sumakas, to her credit, told Andalë that she could not influence you so directly, and that Rinahar would no doubt be put on trial. She asked Andalë to bring to her any friends of Rinahar's who could tell her how this plot had been fabricated, and meanwhile they should speak to all the lords who might be on the jury at the trial.'

'Which is to say, Sumakas offers to confect witnesses for the defence and suborn the jury so that I cannot get the death sentence, exactly as she did for me when Sulakon put me on trial.'

'Which, knowing that you knew, she will not do, surely?'

Ayndra shook her head. 'It would be very difficult to prove that she had done it. The wives, mother and daughters of the lord plead with him that he not send their cousin, or uncle or whatever, to the executioner. Can I show that this was Sumakas' doing, if he therefore refuse to give the death sentence? Lords are ever reluctant to condemn one of their number in any case. The jury is the weakest point. With the witnesses I have a better chance, an I can induce Getaleen to testify.'

'That is Captain Getaleen of the army of Suthine?'

'You remember her?'

'I do.'

'She does not like me. I have a good idea that much of this was her doing, but she has worked very cleverly. I have her in Stabor, but she will not talk, and Ylureen is at me day and night to hand her over to custody in the Yard of Suthine. But I will not let her remove her from the Empire till she has told me what she knows.'

'So Lady Andalë was not wrong when she blamed foreigners.'

'It is true that a foreigner was at the root of this plot, but for sure Rinahar was happy to listen to her. And Rinahar is not the only lord in the plot either.'

'Surely he is the principal, otherwise you would still have been murdered in the temple.'

'Surely he is the cat's paw; the others, seeing him imprisoned, have withdrawn for the time being. I want him to tell me who they were. That is why I want you to come with me. We shall both speak with him for a while, and I will tell him that Getaleen has told all – well, she promises to, since it will be the price of her freedom – and then I will leave you to speak to him about the best way to save his own skin.'

'Would you let him go free, even an he confessed?'

'It would depend what he confessed to. Shall we go?'

Rinahar's cell was one of the wide, high-ceilinged ones in the upper levels of Stabor. He was confined the twenty hours of the day, but he had several chairs, a couch and a table, a warm heap of bedding on the plank bed, and empty plates and jugs scattered around which suggested that he had not lacked for sustenance. He did not stand up when the King and her governor came in. They helped themselves to chairs.

'Good day, my lord,' she said. 'Let me introduce to you Master Caiblin, the Governor of Haramin.' Caiblin bowed to him before he sat, but Rinahar did not acknowledge him. 'I see you do not wish to waste any time in politeness,' Ayndra said. 'You know that you are accused of plotting to murder me.'

'Lies!' said Rinahar. 'You threw me in prison a day before this murder was even supposed to happen – and what murder resulted? No doubt you were frightened by the rats while you sat alone in the temple.'

'The woman who was arrested with you, Captain Getaleen. I believe you know her?' Rinahar said nothing. She continued. 'At present she is in a cell in this prison. Her people wish to remove her to Suthine. She has offered to tell me all that she knows an I commute her death sentence to banishment, and I have accepted.'

'What death sentence? You put her to the question.'

'I put no one to the question,' Ayndra said coldly. 'I will not even put you to the question.'

'I never spoke to the woman. She lies an she says I did.'

'She has not said so. She has, however, named various of the lords your friends with whom she had dealings through their servants. I know that you are not the only one in this plot. Why will you give your neck to save theirs? I have seen no sign that they are about to make a valiant assault in Stabor in order to free you.'

'So? Who are these craven friends of mine she knows?'

Ayndra laughed. 'I do not think I need to tell you who they are.'

'I do not think that you know who they are. I think this woman has told you nothing. You come here thinking to trick me, witch; I am not one of your peasant fools.' Ayndra went on watching him with her semi-precious eyes. 'I demand a trial!' he said. 'You cannot keep me penned here without trial. Even your half-brother— ' he sneered on the 'half', 'granted you trial!'

'It was the most stupid thing he ever did,' Ayndra returned.

'What will you do, then? Cut off my head?'

'Very likely,' she purred.

Rinahar was taken aback. 'What purpose is served by treason trials? Either you are a threat to me or you are my supporter. An you are my supporter, you must show it to me by betraying those who were your brothers, so that I know henceforth you have to trust me. Otherwise I'll not trust you; which means I had better cut off your head before you create worse mischief. A trial would be no more than a theatre piece to prettify one or other of these ends. Why bother?'

'Betray my brothers! Is this your notion of loyalty?'

'Either you are loyal to them, or you are loyal to me. Loyalty is indivisible. That is what it means: cleave only unto one another, leaving all others behind.'

Rinahar burst out laughing.

She got up. 'Enough of this. I am going to speak to the Comptroller. I will return shortly.' Bolts rang as the door was unlocked and locked again behind her.

'My lord,' said Caiblin. 'Your best route is to tell the honest story of what you know. This woman Getaleen is the mother of a large plot, which you have been drawn into

215

without your full knowledge. My lord the King does not jest when she says that she will execute you without trial an you do not confess.'

'Who are you?' Rinahar said sullenly.

'My name is Caiblin. I govern Haramin in my lord's absence.'

'Are you a relative of that Caiblin who used to physic Lord Ailixond?'

'The Royal Physician? I am he.'

Rinahar laughed. 'I know you! You poisoned Lord Ailixond so that he would give his ring to the witch, and then when she was not elected King you ran away with her to Haramin before your crime could be discovered.'

'Poisoned Lord Ailixond?' Caiblin was shocked.

'Of course,' said Rinahar. 'Who but yourself was best placed to do it? No wonder you are still a privy-cleaner for the witch; loyal, just as she said.'

'My lord. We do not lie when we say that we have proof that you plotted to kill the King, and that you were not the only one in the plot. In itself this is ample to condemn you, with the evidence of the S'Thurrulans.'

'Damned foreigners! They would swear black was white for the sum of three quarits.'

'Give the names of your confederates, and you will not have to take their blame.'

'No more than you took the blame for the death of Lord Ailixond?'

Caiblin stood up. 'I cannot submit to this abuse, my lord. I served Lord Ailixond faithfully to the day of his death.'

'I am a lord of Safi,' said Rinahar. 'I will swear false oaths to no one. Nor do I allow my honour to be bought with freedom, unlike physicians.'

Caiblin went to the door and knocked for the gaoler with the keys. As he was letting him out he heard Rinahar muttering, 'Damned witch! We'll have a clean King in Safi one of these days. Who can ever trust a woman?'

Aleizon Ailix Ayndra was sitting talking to the Comptroller, a nobleman from Haramin, on the bench at the head of the stairs. They looked round when they heard the door slam. She said in the northern tongue, 'I thought you would be longer.'

216

'I cannot speak with him. He accused me of poisoning Lord Ailixond.'

'What?'

'You must know, my lord, that as a man of principle I favour the rule of law, and abhor the death sentence.'

'Yes,' she said.

'But were I in your place, I would condemn him. And as Governor of your largest province, I would side with you in the act.'

'Even without a trial?'

'I would always advise you to hold a trial.'

She nodded, and addressed the Comptroller. 'Hold him without visitors, except those I send, until the midnight after next. Tell him that, unless he confesses and gives me his oath before then, he will die by the sword in the prison courtyard in the following dawn. Allow his family in only the hour before dawn. Allow in any of his friends that come then, also, noting carefully what they do.' She rose, and he bowed to kiss her ring. 'Send for me should anything happen, in the middle of the night if need be.'

'My lord.'

As they descended the staircase she said to Caiblin, 'S'Thiraidi and Siriane have been closeted with Getaleen since reveille. Ylureen promises to deliver me her testimony as soon as they have it.'

'And they do not have it yet? It must be a lengthy testimony.'

'A well-prepared testimony, no doubt. And in return they want me to tell them Derezhaid's assassin.'

'But you do not know who . . . I see.'

'Let us go back to the palace and lock ourselves in my rooms; then I will tell you the full story as I understand it.'

The King's apartments had been completely refurbished since the election, the walls freshly plastered and painted white, the shutters renewed, the rooms lined with all sorts of gilt chairs and imported nicknacks of furniture. She sat down on the floor, in a lozenge of sunlight, and lit a smokestick. 'Now. The woman Getaleen had been pursuing secret meetings with Safeen for months, and I had a person, who I shall call Chief Spy, who watched her for me. But then after a while she became clever and we were unable to watch her closely. But Rinahar, and two of the new lords, and their friends were not so clever. Thus Chief Spy heard, just before the coronation, that they intended to kill me, just like the King without a Name – you know the tale? I thought you would. They had construed other silly plots before, as when they intended to run away and join Sulakon, and these had come to naught. Chief Spy, having no time, he felt, to warn me, decided to murder Rinahar in the street. Or attempt to murder him, so that he could be put under guard for his own safety. By ill luck he stabbed Derezhaid instead. He escaped, and Derezhaid was howling for aid, and Rinahar dared not flee the scene, so they went into Polem's house. I think this was Derezhaid's doing, for S'Thiraidi had placed spies of her own among Polem's servants. It so happened that Getaleen had come to give them orders that very same evening, and when they saw Derezhaid all bleeding they gave themselves away. Chief Spy spent a day and a night hiding from Derezhaid's bodyguards before he came to me, but I had already sent Rinahar and Getaleen to Stabor. However, it is only on the testimony of my spy that I have proof of the conspiracy, though I believe that Getaleen was an advocate of it from early days and worked through her Safic friends to convince the young lords that they should slay me in Safi rather than run away to Sulakon.'

'I see,' said Caiblin. She shook her head. 'What a serpent's nest this city is!'

'You were not wise to leave them in Gingito,' he said.

'I know I was not. As soon as I was elected I sent a war party up there to demand their surrender. By next month they should be back.'

'But what will you do with Sulakon when you have him?'

'My prayer is that Sulakon will refuse to surrender, die an heroic death in the face of overwhelming odds, and return to Safi as a safe sealed jar of ashes. Yes?'

'Certainly,' said Caiblin. 'These plots are as much part of life in Safi as the summer fevers in the slums.'

'I know,' said Ayndra fervently. 'I shall cut Rinahar's head off, and the two young lords will do nothing without him; but what of Ellakon? And all the others who are after my place?' She looked up at him, but he only shrugged and spread his hands. 'I wish I could go back to Haramin,' she said.

Caiblin did not reply. He watched the slow blue arabesques of her smoke drawing dissolving cities in the air, until she stood up and began asking him about affairs in Haramin; they discussed the new highway that she was beginning to cut through Pozal t'Ill. When the door opened, unannounced, he took it for a servant, until Ylureen had rushed past and sank to her knees beside Aleizon Ailix Ayndra, like a giant inverted poppy in dull gold silk. She took both of her hands and spoke to her in the S'Thurrulan language. Ayndra's face changed dramatically; she looked suddenly like a child. He got up and backed out of the room. They did not think to look for him till he was gone.

'The royal envoys are leaving in five days' time. She can go on their second ship. No one will even notice her going. Why do you not hold off this lord's execution till that morning? Perhaps his mother may even persuade him to confess.'

'And Getaleen is taken home to justice in her own country?'

'Justice? What justice does she require? She has ruined everything with S'Thiraidi. She has ruined everything for S'Thiraidi!' Ylureen hugged her. Ayndra gave a lopsided smile. Ylureen said, 'Only send her away, and we will ask nothing about the man who stabbed Derezhaid. His family have agreed to waive the blood rights, on account of the way he deceived Siriane.'

'How did he deceive Siriane?'

'By making himself the gossip of that bitch of an Ukasheti while he was a husband of line Pilith. Two-faced little tail! I believe that he dragged them all into Polem's house because he knew that S'Thiraidi was there in the person of her servants, while I was there in the person of the landlord, so that whichever won out he could claim that he went to them.'

'I count as you, do I,' said Aleizon Ailix Ayndra.

'Because we are united.' Ylureen hugged her again.

'So? How many of my people does her confession allow me to do away with?'

'That Lord Rinahar is hung, drawn and quartered.'

'He is already. Who else?'

'There is a whole list of people they approached at one or other time and the responses they gave.'

'Aaah.' Ayndra began to look genuinely pleased. 'Of course, it shows also that Getaleen incited a vast plot which very nearly deprived me of my life, were it not for a series of happy accidents.'

'That is why she should be taken away to Suthine as fast as may be.'

'Perhaps that is not the only thing she should be.'

'She is a woman! What else can we do? Do you want Pilith and Ukasheti to be at feud for ever?'

'Pilith and Ukasheti are nothing to do with me.'

'We threatened Getaleen with making her duel with you, an she kept silent.'

'What? And then she told you everything?' Ylureen nodded. Ayndra tittered so much she bent double. Ylureen made a reproving noise. 'How vicious you are! It will come back on you in the end.'

'It has already.' Ayndra drew back and ran her hand through her hair. She said diffidently, 'You have the copy of this confession?'

'It is being copied now; it will be brought here as soon as it is done. Why do you not show me round these rooms? I have not had a proper look since the new decoration was finished.'

She was delighted with the furnishings, the table carpets, the alabaster lamps with double bowls, the fresh gilt on the coffered ceilings; she held forth fulsomely on the workmanship and the various provinces of S'Thurrulass which had originated the finest things. Ayndra shrugged. 'Sumakas and Firumin did all this between them. All I did was pay the money.'

'Your Firumin is a treasure; I could wish I had him on my staff.'

'Good old Firumin,' Ayndra said vaguely. She sat down on the edge of the big bed while Ylureen ran her hands over the carved footboard.

'This is a battered old thing. Why do you not get a new one? I will have one made for you!'

'This is the King's bed. It looks battered because it has been taken apart in pieces and carried all over the Empire.'

226

'Carried all over the Empire?' Ylureen sat down beside her and bounced up and down on the feather mattresses. 'Was this his bed?'

'It is the same bed. Other people had it before he did.'

'Then you used to . . ?'

'When we were not lying behind a bush in some desolate tract of moorland. He died in this bed.' She looked wickedly at Ylureen. 'This is the King's bed,' she said again.

'You should get a new one,' Ylureen declared.

'Why, have you had a shipment of furniture in that vessel that came in from Suthine last evening?'

'I have not. But there were things on that vessel that I must speak to you about.' She put her hand on the other woman's neck. Ayndra pushed up against her fingers. She said, 'The royal envoys are not the only people who will be leaving in five days' time.'

'They brought a letter from my sister Hiriel. Our mother is very sick. They do not think she will last another winter.'

'Next winter is a way away yet.'

'I am the oldest daughter's oldest daughter, Aleizon. I must be there before she dies. It is more than two years that I have been away. They cannot spare me any longer.'

Aleizon Ailix Ayndra sat with her head bowed, saying nothing. Ylureen parted her hair and kissed her exposed neck. She knocked her away and jumped up. 'You cannot buy me off like that again.'

'I believed that you enjoyed it.' Ylureen got up and followed her.

'I do enjoy it; there's my trouble.'

'Trouble? You do not still think it a perversion, is that it?'

'No. Only, since Gishiin came, I . . . I'm wounded in my stupid pride. And now you'll leave. And still I cannot keep my hands off you. What a disgrace!'

'This is not the end, if I must go back to Suthine. You can make a state visit to Suthine, you can come and stay with me at Pilith Acha. I'll send you sweetsmoke every month. Will you let me come and stay here in the palace until I go?'

'I think I should learn to do without it,' Ayndra said miserably.

'Why are you so hard on yourself?'

They were interrupted by a bell ringing in one of the outer

rooms. 'That must be Getaleen's papers,' Ayndra said. She took Ylureen's hand and towed her towards it. 'Let us go and read them through together.'

'His family will take the body to the burning ground at the same time as the envoys leave. That should take care of most of the crowds. Damn me if I shall send any armed guards to follow a funeral procession.'

'Are you going to send any unarmed guards? I should say, unarmoured.'

'You mean people with knives wandering around?'

Daior-deor nodded. 'No doubt there will be a few of them,' she said.

'People are saying that you have paid half the squatters in Great Market to go about the streets using clubs on anyone who slanders your name.'

'Good god! Who are these *people*? I— '

The door flew open and she immediately rose to her feet. Sumakas rustled into the room. She glanced from side to side and said to Daior-deor, 'Bring me a chair!' just as if he were a slave.

He moved one for her. 'My lady.'

She sat down and ignored him. Aleizon Ailix Ayndra resumed her seat. 'This had better not be another plea for clemency,' she said.

'It is not.' Sumakas' beringed hands plucked the folds of her veil across her throat. 'It concerns my daughter Ailissa.'

'I know that it is unprecedented for a lady to be sent as Ambassador overseas, but it was she herself who came and asked me. And in Suthine they will be delighted to receive her. As Lord Alizhan's sister she will receive even more honour than he did.'

'That is as may be. But who else did you consult?'

'The envoys of Suthine have welcomed her. And I discussed it with Ylureen of course— '

'And her family?'

'The younger children are going with her, the two elder will stay. She said that that was their choice.'

'You took her children's views before mine?'

'What?'

222

'She is a married woman. In the absence of her husband, I, as her sole living parent—'

'What nonsense is this?' said Ayndra in a scathing drawl.

Sumakas began, 'My consent is—'

'Your consent!' She slashed one hand across in front of her. 'She is as old as I am. Whose consent does she need? I am sorry if it was sudden news to you; I thought she must have planned it with you! Does she need a licence to dispose of her own person?'

'So this is how you show your thanks to me,' said Sumakas.

'I am not going to rescind the appointment, unless Ailissa asks it. Why do you not go and speak with her?'

'My only daughter! Sent over sea to a land of sluts and witches! I should have known what to expect when I accepted my son's slut as a daughter!'

Ayndra lifted to her feet. 'What did you say?'

Sumakas lifted her chin. 'Slut!'

Daior-deor had never seen so old a woman move so fast. As Ayndra snatched the lamp she was out of her chair and scooted for the door. The lamp flew through the air and smashed against the panels as it closed. Cold oil oozed down the polished wood and puddled among the alabaster fragments on the floor. Ayndra had fallen back into her seat. Daior-deor edged round her desk.

'I will go away and come back in an hour,' he said.

'Do so . . . thank you.'

He closed the door as quietly as he could and went to tell Firumin about it.

'Thank the gods that it is next morning that they all leave,' Firumin said. 'Then Rinahar shall be dead and the foreigners gone and we shall all have peace for a while.'

'I hope so,' said Daior-deor.

It was spring enough that they could dance outside, with a canopied dais at one end of the Yard for the nobility. The royal envoys, whose farewell feast this was, occupied two of the seats of honour, with the third for the King. It grew dark, but she did not come. The envoys spoke only to each other, as was their usual custom when they were not among others of royal lineage, but they made sure that Ylureen overheard them. She ordered the cooks to serve supper, while she fretted and cursed Aleizon Ailix Ayndra. Gishiin patted her arm and induced her to drink some of the hot punch he had ordered for the dancers. In her anger she drank it as greedily as if it were a mild kushi; when she returned to her seat a warm flush coloured her face and her uncovered shoulders and her manner had become unusually expansive. Gishiin smiled to himself and took up his place beside her.

Aleizon Ailix Ayndra's coming was announced by a blast of Safic trumpets outside the gate of the Yard of Suthine. A few moments later the crowd of dancers was parted by Pilith slaves and a corridor opened for the Safic party. Ailissa walked by the King's side, independently, with no one's hand on her arm. She still wore a lady's gown, but with a high collar and a very severe cut. Polem, Arpalond and the other lords followed after. They ascended the stairs to greet the envoys, who moved to either side to let Ayndra take the middle place on their seat. They greeted Ailissa and permitted the other lords to bow to them at a decent distance before they sat down. Ylureen had Arpalond led to a place between her and Siriane; she asked him what had been the delay.

'The Lady Andalë came to my lord in a fit of hysterics,' he replied. 'She decided to take her with her for a last meeting with Rinahar. She was saying that it was because she had been kept from him that he did not confess. We had to wait until they returned from Stabor.'

'And did he confess?'

Arpalond shook his head. 'His mother came back weeping that other lords had been as deep in the plot as he, for a plot that never took place, and he should not go to the sword alone.'

'Then he is still condemned to die next dawn?'

'He is, lady. If I may dare a comment, you should know that a number of people have demanded the same penalty for your captain that is a prisoner.'

'She will be taken to Suthine. Be assured that we shall there administer justice to her according to our custom.' Ylureen scanned the other diners. Diamoon had Polem by the hand and was pleading with him to dance; he indicated that the plate of food before him had a greater claim on his presence. 'My lord Polem looks to be in fine spirits.'

'I cannot tell how he looks, but I know that his feeling is better than at the last banquet; that is because he has not had to put on a corset in order to be laced into his robe.'

'A corset?'

'Surely you must have noticed at the coronation. Lord! It creaked at every step, and at every other step he sighed and puffed for the discomfort of it. This night I could hear that he was in his natural shape.' Ylureen was amused. She told the servants to bring more punch for all of them, and Arpalond told her a fund of scandalous stories about the other lords as she named them one by one to him. All the while, Ayndra remained on the high seat with the envoys and Ailissa, as if she knew no one lower down. While one course succeeded another, Ylureen paid no heed; it was only when the last plates had gone, and the servants were setting up chabe stoves and bringing out tiny cups to toast in lifewater, that she began to look around for her.

'What kind of a farewell is this?'

'She has to fulfil duties,' said Gishiin. 'You will be together later.'

'Meanwhile can she not at least do me the favour of greeting me?'

'Hush, do not molest yourself for it.'

'This is our last night together in years!'

'Peace, peace.'

Siriane, who would be the new Ambassador of Suthine in Safi, asked Derezhaid to join the dance. He declined, saying that his shoulder was still too sore. Gishiin said that he would go with her. There were at least two hundred people whirling round and round the yard in the light of the bonfires. Ylureen drained her glass and got up. Arpalond shifted. 'Peace, my lord,' she said in Safic. 'I go to see my lord of Haramin. Perhaps we dance a last time.' He heard her feet stumble as she moved away, and sat up with his ears pricked and his hand on his blind cane.

As she approached the high seat she saw that one of the envoys had agreed to dance with Ailissa, and they were making their way down the steps. His line brother sat staring into space; Ayndra was spying the dancers. She did not notice Ylureen as she sidled up and leant over the back of the seat. Ylureen blew in her ear and she jumped. 'What—'

'Come dance with me.'

'I do not wish to dance.' She sniffed suspiciously. 'Ylureen, you are not *drunk*?' The royal envoy was watching them closely. Ylureen reached over and dropped her arm round Ayndra's shoulders; she fondled her breast through her tunic. Ayndra slapped her stingingly across the face.

Ylureen was momentarily stunned. Ayndra leapt to her feet and took a step forwards. Ylureen bounded up to her, snatched her wrist as she raised it and carried on with the momentum of her superior weight and height. There was a sound of ripping fabric, several crashes, and Ayndra was lying on her back on the dais with Ylureen astraddle her chest. Her arms were raised above her head with Ylureen pinning them flat to the floor. She bucked with all the strength of her spine, but it was like trying to move a mountain. She looked up at Ylureen's foreshortened features, the roll of fat under her chin, the heavy trembling breasts. Her eyes gleamed in the flicker of the torches. She said, 'You are more bloated than I am, Ylureen; that's why you win.' Ylureen drew in breath and raised her hand, but she went on staring at her, not even closing her eyes. She let her hand fall, moved off her, shook out her torn skirts and ran down the stairs. Most of the dancers, and all the people on the dais, had stopped all to stare. She ignored them and forged on until she had found Gishiin.

Aleizon Ailix Ayndra sat up and shook her head like a puppy. She glanced behind her and saw that the envoy was still there. If he had shed his hieratic pose, it had been while she was pinned down and had missed it. The music, which had suffered a definite break, surged up again and the dancers began to move. She saw one pearl-studded hennaed coiffure moving among them and turned away.

'This is a disgraceful act of our servant, excellency,' said the smooth voice of the envoy. 'We deplore it in every way. May we enact retribution on your part?'

'What? No.' She sat down and rubbed the back of her head; the touch made her wince. 'Excellency, forgive my lapse of manners.'

226

'Excellency, it was we that lapsed. Permit me to call a healer to see to your head.'

'I thank you, excellency, but I would prefer to retire and seek my own healer's hands.'

'Of course, excellency. Let us summon your escort.' His slaves leapt to attention instantly, but she waved her hand.

'Let them take me to where my horse is. The rest of my party, the lady Ailissa and the rest, let them stay. Excuse me.'

Ylureen and Gishiin were heading an eight-couple wheel dance. Ylureen snatched a glance upward as they reeled past the dais, and saw the envoy himself leading Aleizon Ailix Ayndra to the stairs at the back. She applied her attention to the dance.

The sunlight flickered across the harbour in silver sheets pleated by the wind and the scattered clouds, snapping the banners and bunting around the decorated gangplanks of the envoys' ships and flaring the cloaks of the guards who stood to rigid attention with full-length sarissas raised. Two processions were supposed to meet on the quayside, the envoys' from the Yard of Suthine, the King's with Lady Ailissa from the palace, and a third group bringing the prisoner from Stabor. The reception was ready but so far it seemed that none of them had even opened their gates. Selanor rubbed his forehead as he stepped out into the harsh spring light. 'Gods' teeth! What are they at? Bring me my flask, for gods' sake.'

The flask sat in a chased silver holder which also served as cup; they rang together like bells as he tried to fill it up without his hands shaking. Several slugs of liquor, however, stilled the tremors, and he offered the drink round among his escort. They were toasting the King when a messenger ran up to tell that the party from Stabor had arrived on the quay. 'Are they to go on board directly?'

'Put them to one side until their masters are here. Over there, behind the portmaster's house, where they will be out of sight.'

'Sir, they ask to go on board.'

'Who am I to send them on board? Let them wait.'

'Very well, sir.'

227

'Very well.' Selanor up-ended the flask and found it empty already. He cursed, and called for one of the cadets to go and fill it again. While he waited he went round to look for guards who had failed in the perfection of their parade outfits; at long last someone arrived with the news that the King had set off. In a little while they heard the trumpets, and a great hooting of horns from the direction of the Yard. The two processions appeared at opposite ends of the quay, both glittering with flags and jewels and brilliantly coloured clothes; the onlookers surged forward against the cordon of guards.

'Can you see a bump on her head? Will she take her hat off? Are they going to speak to each other?'

The envoys of Suthine were borne on carrying chairs, like Ailissa and her mother, with the other dignitaries on horseback and their escorts on foot. The chairs were set down on the platform facing the ships, the other lords dismounted and joined the envoys, and the speeches began in both tongues. Ylureen was dressed in travelling clothes, a long tunic and a coat over trousers, with her head covered by a turban and her face heavily painted. Gishiin, behind her, was rather less painted but much more haggard-looking. Sumakas wore full widow's weeds, kept drawing her black veil over her face and dabbed at her eyes with a black-bordered handkerchief. Ailissa wept openly. Aleizon Ailix Ayndra looked like stone. The envoys kissed her before they left; they descended from the platform and advanced towards the gangway of their ship. The commoners from their escort had already begun to march on board the second vessel. 'Where is the prisoner?' said Selanor. 'Send her aboard now. Go tell them first to be ready to receive her.'

Aleizon Ailix Ayndra had taken her hat off; her hair was the colour of a late summer cornfield. She exchanged a last set of kisses with the envoys (who left streaks of mouthpaint on her cheeks) and stepped back to rejoin her escort on the platform, as the prisoner's party moved out from behind the portmaster's house to cross to the second ship. She stood there in the sunlight with her back to them. No one was ready to warn her when a brief scuffle in the middle of the group gave birth to a hooded figure who sprang across the cobbles and cast itself on her; at the last moment something metallic glittered in its fist. Ayndra must have heard something then because she began to turn and the assailant buried the knife in her side rather than her back. She staggered backwards as a howl went up from the onlookers, the prisoner's escort fell on her like an avalanche, the envoys froze while the slaves told them what they could not turn round to see, Ailissa jumped down off the platform, the crowd surged forward, everyone was screaming at once, half the dignitaries cast themselves into the mêlée – Ayndra was walking backwards, crabwise, both hands pressed against her left hip, until she knocked into the whitewashed wall of the portmaster's house. She lifted her left hand from the wound. Streams of blood webbed her fingers and dripped to the ground. The black silk of her tunic was sodden and hot liquid ran down her leg. Out of the chaos in front of her appeared Ylureen, her palms like two white flags. She reached behind her with her left hand and drew it down the wall in a great scarlet stroke. Ylureen's mouth was open. Her vision was beginning to cloud over. Ylureen cried, 'Aleizon!'

'Get out of here!'

The wall dug into her back but her head felt as if it was falling backwards into an abyss. Something coppery-bright appeared to her left. 'Daior-deor!' she said. 'Catch me!' and fell.

When she came round the first thing she said was, 'Where is Getaleen?'

'Dead, my lord.' Caiblin was washing something in a brass bowl beside her bed.

'Dead? Did the mob get her? Was there a riot?'

'The envoys ordered it. Lady S'Thiraidi was brought out of some dark recess and hauled up on the platform. They held Getaleen and she strangled her with a long piece of silk. Ylureen and Sumakas made speeches. It held the crowd better than a play-act.' She was lifting her head up in an attempt to see over the blanket barrier on her chest. He pushed her gently back onto the pillows and went on talking as he cleansed the wound. Out of the corner of his eye he saw that she had jammed a fold of blanket between

229

her teeth to keep from screaming. 'While they went on they put all their people on the ships, or sent them back in groups to the Yard. Then they too took to the ships. They said that they would cruise in the vicinity of the city until they heard how it was with you, but they thought it safer to leave as planned. Sumakas told Ailissa that it was better an she did not leave with them. When we knew that you were well, then she could go to them on the ship that took the news. Until then, of course, she preferred to remain with you in your trouble. Ailissa agreed. Sumakas was very happy.' He tossed the used rag into a bowl held by his attendant.

'Am I well?' she said.

'You seem well enough presently,' he returned. 'I did not expect you to be speaking with me so soon.'

'I am not about to die because some god-cursed bitch stabs me in the back.'

'Your luck has not left you altogether. She did not puncture the bowel, although she shed a great deal of your blood. It is a deep wound.'

'Long thin blade. God bless her. Have you sewn it up yet?' He shook his head. She groaned. 'Let me sit up and have a smoke, at least, before you start on it.'

'I am obliged to say that there has been some talk of poison.'

'What? On the blade?' Her already dilated eyes seemed to grow even larger.

'Clearly it was not a rapidly fatal poison, however,' he said.

She relaxed a little. 'The smoke is in the marquetry box in that chest,' she said.

'I can give you some poppy-syrup. We are in no hurry.'

'Will it help?'

'Certainly it will help. I know you; you are ready to leap out of the bed at this moment. Do you ever smoke the tears of the poppy?'

'O! Look over there. Do you see that silver and enamel contraption? Now fetch a little box of hot coals from the kitchen – better, take it there and fill it with them.'

'I thought you might have one of those,' he said, 'among all your trinkets from Suthine. Let me help you to sit up – no! Do not move. An you strain it at all it will break out bleeding again. It took us half an hour to staunch it.' They lifted her, one on each side and one to put the pillows behind her; the grace with which she submitted was a sign of her weakness. He let her smoke the tears till her eyes were a solid field of blue, though he could already feel the heat of the fever rising in her blood; despite her dreaminess, when he had done she asked that Ailissa be let in to talk to her. He knew, from the press of people in the antechambers, that she would be the first of many.

'What are you doing here?'

Daior-deor jerked out of a doze and looked around for the person who spoke.

'Is this the time?'

He could see no one in the bedchamber, until he looked at the bed. Aleizon Ailix Ayndra was sitting up, eyes open, looking into the darkness of the windowless wall. The lamp beside her bed and a second light on the table where Daior-deor kept his vigil were two yellow bubbles in an ocean of gloom. Since Firumin had left them, she had lain sprawled in the big bed, sometimes quiet, other times tossing and uttering disjointed phrases, throwing off the covers till her teeth chattered with the fever and he got up to cover her again. There was a covered pitcher by her lamp; he was supposed to give her to drink an she woke up, but until now she had been deep in the forest of delirium. She spoke again.

'You look older.' There was a pause, and she laughed. 'I thought they remained the same for ever. Or that they were all aged twenty-one.' She went on gazing into the dark, as if someone stood there who was replying to her speech. 'Of course I look older,' she said, 'I've been fighting hard ever since you left me. In a few years I shall be forty! I'll be an old woman in a little while.' The bitterness of her words was belied by the brilliance of her smile. She got on all fours and crawled across the bed. The unknown interlocutor said something that made her laugh. She put her hand on her stomach, where the ample linen of the nightshirt covered the livid purple and seeping pus of the wound. 'I am not going to die of this one . . . am I? . . . why should I not laugh?' She knelt on the edge of the bed and extended her

231

hand towards the darkness. Daior-deor saw a white gleam
in the tapestries on the wall, as if a slice of moonlight had
got between the shutters; but they were all closed up and it
was past moonset. Aleizon Ailix Ayndra was facing away
from him now. 'Sometimes I think it was a foul thing you
did to me,' she said. 'An you'd said nothing . . .' Her
companion answered her at length; she shook her head and
made gestures with her hands. She said, 'Because then I
would have thought, well, what was it but a dream anyway?
And I would have gone on and forgotten in a while.' Her
voice chimed in the madrugal silence. 'The time before, we
were so happy. And what else is there, except to be happy
for a time?' The lamps hissed in the pause. She reached her
hand out again. 'Come into the light, where I can see you.'
The temperature in the room had been falling toward dawn,
until Daior-deor was chilled in his hooded tunic; she had
nothing but the fine linen of her nightshirt, but the short
hairs were not even standing up on her bare arms. 'O Ailix!'
she said. The white gleam shifted over the hangings, and
entered her bubble of light, slowly, like the great kelp plants
moving in the sea, and in the material light it became the
smooth front of a white woollen tunic, crisp linen at the
collar, a long fall of hair that shone as black and heavy as
obsidian, and a straight profile that Daior-deor had seen on
fifty thousand coins. The apparition looked down, sweeping its cheeks with doe-like eyelashes; a pink tongue
emerged between its soft lips and it opened its mouth as it
approached Aleizon Ailix Ayndra. She leant forward,
turning her head, offering her mouth. It opened its eyes and
looked directly at Daior-deor. The whites of its eyes shone
like snow in sunshine; its gaze only touched him for a
moment but he had to stand up, just as it bent, at last, to
fasten its mouth on hers, not seeing that his foot was caught
in the table carpet. He stepped forward and the carpet was
tugged after him. The lamp fell off the table and smashed,
hot oil spilled over the tiles and burst into flames. Daior-
deor cried out and seized the carpet. He threw it over the
flames but the oil – the lamp had been filled to the brim less
than an hour ago – was already alight over half the floor. He
ran to the door and cried, 'Fire!' The three slaves sleeping
on pallets in the antechamber leapt up; one ran in with a

bucket of water and threw it over the fire – spreading the oil over an even wider expanse, so that it started to lick at the hangings. Daior-deor sprayed a clutch of ornaments over the floor as he seized another carpet to beat them with. The slaves were shouting, 'Fire! Fire!' and he could hear feet running outside. In a few moments the bedchamber was full of people with buckets of sand and water and firebrooms and smothering blankets. Before long the last of the flames were dead and Firumin, in a long gown and a nightcap, was berating the servitors as they cleared up the mess. Aleizon Ailix Ayndra was sweeping up sand with a broom and complaining about the fool who thought to put out an oil fire with water, as wide awake and cheerful as if she had never been sick.

Caiblin charged through the door, took the broom from her hands and made her sit down on the bed. 'What happened? Who was with you? You could have been killed!'

'It was my fault,' said Daior-deor, before anyone else could speak.

'How was it your fault?' she said. 'You raised the alarm; did you not save me?'

'I knocked the lamp over,' he said.

'How so?'

'I think I fell asleep – and woke up with a start – I think I was dreaming.'

'It is the fault of those silly tables, not you at all,' she said. Were you not with me last night as well?'

'And the night before that,' he said unwillingly.

'What! I cannot remember, only all sorts of strange dreams. It is too much; you should rest.'

Caiblin meanwhile was taking her pulse at wrist and throat, while the slaves remade the bed. 'I think your fever has broken,' he said. 'But you must rest a while more.'

'Daior, you have cured me with the shock; it must have been a god sent the dream that made you break it.'

'Perhaps,' he said.

'What were you dreaming of?'

'It has all gone from me now.'

They sat and talked while the slaves finished clearing, and Caiblin gave her a tonic to drink; after which she very soon became groggy and was put to bed. Caiblin told Daior-deor to do the same. He went instead to Polem's house and asked for Diamoon.

She was sitting in front of a glass mirror while another of Polem's woman friends tried various ornaments in her hair. He said without preamble, 'Did you ever close the tomb up afterwards?'

'Why, what is the matter?'

'I think it should be sealed, an it is not already,' he said. 'I sat up with the King the last three nights, in the palace.'

'Do you mean that you felt it too? Felt his presence there?'

'Whose presence?' said the other woman.

'Pretend you are not here, Amalaya, else I shall have to send you out. We talk of a spirit which I unwisely raised. Captain, I am sorry that I ever embarked upon the project. An I had more wisdom in my craft, I would have refused you.'

'Had I more wisdom, I would never have asked for it,' Daior-deor said.

'You know that I will not stay in the palace any longer. I would not even go there in darkness unless I must. How did you sit there all night, alone? You are a hero!'

'O, come now,' said Daior-deor. 'Will you then send me to seal it up alone?'

Diamoon turned round and looked at him for a while. 'Of course not,' she said. 'I should have done it months ago. Do not concern yourself; I will do all, and leave you to sleep in peace this night.'

Chamarin, captain of my lord's expedition, greets Aleizon Ailix Ayndra. Most Serene Lord and King of Safi and Lord of the New Empire. My lord, I have bad news. We hurried to Gingito but when we came there we discovered that those we sought had left more than a month ago. Two months ago some others came to join them, the lord of Gingito said that it was the old man's grandson, who asked them to go away with him. But the old man Lord Meraptar was too sick to move then and a little while later he died. They showed me where his pyre was but his ashes were put in a jar and his grandson carried it away. Master Gallallo says that it must have been Lord Sandar's son who escaped us at Purrllum who came. He came out of the east with twenty men and they went away into the east afterward. The lady of Gingito said that Lady Setha was got with child this winter and very sick and they made a horse litter to carry her away. Lord Sulakon wanted her to stay in Gingito until her time had come but she would not for fear that we would come and slaughter her. Lord Sandar's son said that he had a place in the mountains east of the Pozal where they could stay and make plots against you, my lord. The people in Gingito said they did not know what was the place. Some said it was called Shirri Chula but they had never been east of Pozal and knew nothing of it. Lord Takarem and Lord Sulakon and all departed going there. We are here in Gingito awaiting your orders, my lord, whether we should follow them or return to Safi. With respect to your questions about the loyalty of the province, the people here are two-faced but they fear your power and for this reason they gave horses to Lord Sulakon so that he could go and leave them in peace, they wanted nothing of his wars. They offer sheep's wool to pay their taxes. They say that the people from the north have been stealing their flocks and they pray that you send some men to drive them away. Saving your permission, my lord, while this letter travels to you we have set out with the men of Gingito to raid some castles of bandits. We asked along the way where are bandits and we know that these we assault are indeed robbers and not merely enemies of Gingito. We shall return here to await your next order. We pray that you are all well and blessed by fortune in Safi. Given the sixth day of Ninth Month in Gingito in the hand of Master Gallallo.

Early summer sunlight filled the King's courtyard and glittered in the restored fountain. A huge cage of singing birds had been hung up under the portico, where Aleizon Ailix Ayndra was lying on a blanket spread out to absorb the sun. A couple of treasury clerks sat crosslegged between the bundles of records which surrounded her, but when Firumin approached she made a sign to them and they bowed and retired. She smiled at him with her eyes creased up against the sun, and invited him to sit down. 'Firumin.

235

You recall that when we first arrived here I gave you a key to the Treasury, and told you to take out any monies you required, no matter what they were, so long as you noted them all in the book I gave you.'

'Of course, my lord, and I have done so. I hope I have not been too extravagant?'

'You have never been extravagant, and I understand that a king's household in a great city must be more costly than a mere provincial governor's. Nevertheless, Firumin, I wish you would write down everything in the book, as I asked you to.'

'My lord?'

She tapped the papers in front of her. 'I find that the recorded outgoings from the Treasury do not match the quantity of money which has gone from it. So I must conclude that someone has made a false record— '

'My lord! What! Do you propose that I, that I – do you accuse me of falsehood— '

'Firumin, I said nothing of falsehood. All I said was that you should write it all down, otherwise— '

'My lord, I have written everything down! Not so much as a tallow dip is bought for the household without it is tallied. I have served this house twenty-five years and more, and I have never stolen so much as a napkin! And now you say I am a liar. Well, my lord, if that is how— '

She reached forward and took his hand. 'Forgive me. I never meant to accuse you, nor do I doubt your honesty.'

'But you say that I do not keep the records!'

'Let me explain. The Treasurer has been summing the accounts over the past tenmonth. We find that some quantity of money, as I said, has gone out but is not in the records. I believe that all the clerks are honest, and beside, they are never allowed to work in there alone. Only the Treasurer and his two deputies, myself, and you have keys, and I know that I gave you licence to help yourself. I believe you an you say that you have taken nothing you were not entitled to. But do you know, then, who the thief may be?'

'You know, my lord, that I was born in the city,' he said.

'Yes?'

'My father was a silversmith, but he was very fond of drink, and my mother was his second wife. He had five children already, and she gave him six more. I was the third of her sons, and they needed money for a dowry for my half-sister. You know, my lord, that poor families must sometimes sell their children to the rich when they lack money to keep them?' She nodded. He said, 'Lady Sumakas' father bought me, to bring up as a house servant. He gave me to Lady Sumakas when she married, and she brought me to the palace. I was with my lord, my lord Ailixond, from when he was a little child. I asked my lady if I could be his steward when the time came for him to have a household of his own. She gave me more than that, on the day of his wedding to Lady Othanë she gave me my freedom, and burnt all the slave papers for me. They never put a slave mark on me, you see, they liked their slave servants to appear the same as free people. I do not know if there is anyone beyond her old slaves who even remembers now that I used to be among them.'

'This is most interesting, Firumin, but I cannot see immediately how it answers my question.'

'You see, my lord, I have been with Lady Sumakas since I was six years old.' She still looked puzzled. He said, 'I am explaining to you why I cannot tell you who it was took the money.'

'Aah!' She slapped her hands together. 'Gods' teeth! I might have known.'

'Please, my lord, I know I am a coward, but an you speak to her, please do not—'

'Shumar, I do not wish to confront her any more than you do; most certainly I shall not mention your name. Has this been going on for a long time?'

'When Lord Meraptar was Regent in Safi he had a treasurer whose wife was a cousin of Lady Sumakas. She borrowed his keys.'

'And the Treasury has had the same keys ever since?'

'After that, I believe that all the treasurers in Safi were relatives of the first man, or his wife, until you brought your Treasurer from Haramin.'

'Gods in heaven! I shall change all the locks in the Treasury this very day. Who is the locksmith in the palace?'

'I know the man, my lord, Lady Sumakas chose him. You know that she had keys to every door there is in the palace.'

'I recall how she gave me them when I arrived here. I suppose I should have known she would keep copies. Do you know any locksmiths in the city?'

'Why, of course, my lord. Shall I go and find one for you now?'

'Tell him to bring all his tools and materials, and bring him to me here. I shall be waiting.'

'He will be here directly, my lord.'

'A thousand thanks, Firumin. Could you tell those clerks to come back in as you leave?'

'They have fallen behind again. Wait among those rocks. I shall be back shortly.' Takarem kicked his horse back on to the winding path that scratched an uncertain route between the pine trees clinging to the slope. When he came in sight of the river he saw what he had expected. The horse-litter, like a giant stretcher with a canopy and curtains, was being dismantled while the grooms led its two beasts across the river. A little way ahead of them his father and young Meraptar were plodding through the torrent with their arms entwined to form a chair for the bulbous figure of his stepmother. Her twin maids waded behind with the rest of the things from the litter on their backs, skirts kilted up above their bony knees. He cursed and turned his mount back up the hill.

'Up! What manner of watch is this?'

Takarem rolled over slowly and squinted up at his father. 'I had fallen asleep through boredom at yet another delay,' he said.

'You should be keeping a watch while we make these crossings. In this country one cannot travel fast.'

'One could travel a good deal faster an one left one's burdens to bear their brats in some hovel along the way,' he said insolently, then winced as Sulakon's whip snapped across the back of his hand. He reached for his sword. 'Lay that down,' said Sulakon. 'Let me remind you that I am your father and Lady Setha is your mother. An you use such words of her again I will beat you black and blue.'

'Do you think I am a child? How dare you beat me!'

'Child or man, you are my son. It is your duty to respect your parents. Now let us mount and go. We must find a safe

238

dwelling before nightfall; your mother cannot spend another night in the open.' He strode away.

Takarem stood glowering while Meraptar came up to him leading both their horses. 'We all chafe at the delay,' he said, 'do not let it molest you.'

'Go share your platitudes with that slut; she has more time for them than I.' Takarem leapt astride his horse and raked its sides with his spurs. The rest of the party did not see him again till they were camped in a settlement of charcoal burners, the nearest to a village that could be found in these hills. Sistri and Histri took Setha to a group of huts at the far end of the circle where the charcoal burners' wild-looking women were gathered, avoiding the newcomers. The men shared their supper of acorn-flour porage. When they had eaten, one of the twins came up to Sulakon leading an old woman, who spoke excitedly and gestured with her hands to indicate a full belly and two things in conflict.

'The two children fight in the womb,' said the slave. 'Better we stay here till they come out. It be very bad to go on. This woman knows.'

'Tell her that we will carry her in a litter,' said Sulakon. 'We cannot stay here.'

The old woman, when she understood him, gave vent to a storm of protest. The slave, Sistri or Histri, stood blank-faced through it all and said finally, 'The children fight, we go on, she dies. That's what she say.'

'This is an ignorant old woman,' Sulakon said; but she had already departed in a huff. The slave made a sardonic curtsey and retired. Sulakon asked Meraptar how many days more it was to the place he had spoken of.

'Perhaps six, perhaps ten. I have not been in this place before; it is hard to find the paths in this forest.'

'Are you sure that you can find it?'

'O yes,' said Meraptar. 'In a sixday we will be there, without trouble. Is my lady worse?'

'It is the witch who has done this,' Sulakon said, 'who has sent all this swelling and sickness upon her. She has put a curse upon our family.'

'The witch slew my father,' Meraptar said, 'and gave our land to her rebels.'

'The witch desires to build a road through this forest,' Takarem said, 'in order to relieve its barbarism; I for one would favour her.' When his father and Meraptar looked at him, he got up and walked away.

Two days later, the distant snow peaks of the mountains began to appear above the ranks of trees; like dream castles they never seemed to come any closer. Setha was too sick even to walk from whatever bivouac they found for her to the litter; her head swathed in a grey veil, she let herself be carried from one to the other like a gross sack of mountain homespun. On the third day one of the twins came up to Sulakon and told him that Setha was suffering and needed to be still. He replied that they had to go on, that she could lie in the litter. The slave retired and emerged a few moments later with a cloth folded into an oblong. She pushed it under Sulakon's face so that he could not help but see the bloodstains on it. 'You know what is this? My lord!'

He turned his face away in disgust. 'Do not show me the thing. I accept your argument. We will find a place.'

Three tumbledown stone circles beside a stream, shepherds' huts which had long lost their shepherds, was the best they could discover. They laid Setha down inside the least decrepit and hastened to convert the litter into a roof for it. Sulakon went up and down outside, twisting his hands; he heard Setha's voice calling him, and pushed past the blanket that stood in for a door. In the dark Setha's pale face looked disembodied, her eyes merging into the purple blotches that surrounded them. Under the heaped grey blankets they had stripped her down to her shift. She extended one white arm to Sulakon; its pathetic slenderness belied the exaggerated fertility of her body. She said nothing. Behind him the twins were wittering in their own language. Setha's hand pulled on Sulakon's callused fingers and her body convulsed under the blankets. The twins chittered and one pulled at Sulakon's tunic, but however often they asked him to leave, Setha would not let go of him. Eventually they pushed him to sit at the head of the bed, hand in hand with her, while they got about the business.

Takarem had excellent luck hunting; this empty country abounded with game. In the end they could not carry all the meat back with them, but cut the best haunches of venison for a roast feast that night. They were delighted to see that the men who had remained round the huts had already collected a good quantity of firewood, and began to ready their bonfire. Meraptar came up and asked what they did. 'Cooking? Sir! This is for the pyre!'

'The pyre?' Takarem dropped the branch he held and dashed into the covered hut. Inside it was so dark that he had his hands on the corpse before he knew what he did; he recoiled. There was a movement further in. He crawled backwards and lifted up the blanket to admit the evening light. The room stank of blood. 'Where is my father?' he said.

The hunched figure at the end of the pallet lifted its head. Sulakon's lined face was furrowed deeper with grief; the low light glittered on his tears, like crystal beads in the engraved lines under his eyes. He said, 'Your mother is dead. And your new brothers with her.'

Takarem, speechless, made the sign of blessing.

Sulakon said, 'Now you will help me raise an army. The witch is going to pay.'

'My lady! How delightful to see you.' Sumakas embraced Oborenë and they kissed.

'The pleasure is mine, my lady. What a fine day! Let us go and sit in the fountain court.'

A striped silk awning covered the small court so that no sunshine should touch the ladies; slaves served them with sweetmeats and fruit drinks which had been cooled in deep wells. Oborenë kicked off her high-heeled shoes and relaxed with a sigh on the cushions. Sumakas made sure that the sweets were within easy reach, complimented her on her gown and the arrangements of her hair, and asked, 'Is Haligon well?'

'Haligon? O, you will never guess! We have had an offer for our Tissamë.'

'O indeed? Is the suitor well known to you?'

'He is well known to all of us! Can you guess who it is?'

'One of the young lords, is it?'

'No! It is Polem!'

'Pardon?' Sumakas put down the sweetmeat which she had been about to bite.

'He sent his cousin Baramon with the spear and the sword and the sheepskin and everything, just like in the old books! Haligon wanted to accept straight away. But I said that Tissamë was very young and we must consider it carefully.'

'You could hardly hope for a better offer than Polem,' Sumakas said. 'She will be his first wife; there is no doubt but that her sons will inherit all his lands.'

'But he has so many children already! And all those concubines.'

'What husband does not? Only a poor man lacks concubines.'

'Yes, but to live with them so openly! And all those children.'

'They are all bastards; they cannot inherit his property,' pronounced Sumakas. Oborenë frowned. 'What can have possessed him to consider marriage after all these years?' Sumakas signed to a waiting woman to refill Oborenë's cup.

'He told Haligon that he had thought all his estates lost to him in the civil war, but now that he had regained them he felt the need of heirs to whom he could give his father's title.'

'What better could you ask for, then? Few lords of Safi are as rich as he. My husband himself had not half Polem's wealth.'

'But he is an old man,' said Oborenë. 'And Tissamë is just fifteen, and so fresh and pretty, for her to turn into a brood mare for an old man!'

'I would seize the chance. She can bear him two or three children, and in ten years he will have died of an apoplexy brought on by overeating. Then she will be a widow in charge of the greatest estates in Safi-the-land. What more could any woman desire? You must counsel her against silly dreams of young men. Property is the cornerstone of a marriage.'

'But what an he decides to share the land among his bastards?'

'They are bastards,' said Sumakas. 'They may inherit moveable goods, but not the land, nor the lordship.'

'Perhaps you could ask the King to make sure, if he is to marry Tissamë.'

'The King!' Sumakas laughed. 'She would favour the rights of the bastards.'

'Pardon?'

'Being the mother of one – if not one herself; I was never sure of that document she fetched up with Lord Takarem's name on it.'

'The mother of a bastard? Why, I heard tell that Lord Polem's son Haldin – you know, the one with a beard– '

'O no. Her bastard died of neglect, thus freeing her to pursue a life of ill-fame, having dried up her womb with the diseases of her profession.' Oborenë was so goggle-eyed she was forgetting to munch her favourite sweets. 'She was a whore for two years in a house on the Street of Dreams, before she left it to walk the streets on her own account,' Sumakas said. 'For a while she went to study the arts of the sluts in S'Thurrulass, and then returned to bewitch my son with her filth. Did you not see her with the Lady Ylureen? I think there is no one among her captains whom she has not enticed by the same method.'

'Mother Maishis!' said Oborenë.

Sumakas smiled. 'She is an enemy of marriage in every decent form,' she said. 'You have seen how she sent my poor Ailissa, after Sulakon left her, away to that whorehouse of Suthine. What sink of iniquity is there, if one of the noblest women in the land gives suck to her bastard in the public view! And then there is the matter of my dowry.'

'Your dowry?'

'As a widow, my dowry is provided to me for my own support, and since my husband was the King, I receive it in the form of payments from the Treasury. I have drawn it tranquilly for almost twenty-five years, ever since my husband's unfortunate death – until she took the seat of power in this city. Now she deprives me of my own dowry, and offers me instead a paltry stipend! A stipend, as if I were a vulgar clerk! She has even changed all the locks on the Treasury, and put her own clerks in there. Half of them do not even speak Safic, and I can get nothing from them unless I first kiss her toe. Is it not villainous?'

'It is unbelievable,' said Oborenë. 'I had heard tales about her, but I had no idea that they were true. I shall not ask her anything about this marriage!'

'Do not,' said Sumakas. 'Instead demand of Polem that he sign a marriage contract in which he awards all his lands to Tissamë's heirs and excludes his bastards. I will recommend to you a lawyer who will draw it up in accordance with all the laws.'

'How generous your advice is, my lady! I do not know what I would do without you.'

'There is no need to thank me; just do as I say.'

'Most certainly. Do you have more of these excellent comfits?'

'Gods' teeth! Is there any order in this at all?' Aleizon Ailix Ayndra pulled the lid off an antique book-box and sneezed in the cloud of dust that tumbled off it.

'I think in each bin are supposed to be papers of the same kind; the right side of each alcove is for the Treasury, the left for the Justiciary. Marriage contracts are on the left side. But people have taken them out and put them back with no care for the order.' Diamoon bent over one of the closed bins and dabbed at its name-plate with her handkerchief. Ayndra shook a colony of silverfish out of her book-box and made noises of disgust. Diamoon shuffled slowly along the line of alcoves, quiet, and looking unusually shrunken.

'Is this the place where you found that paper you brought to me in prison?'

'Yes, my lord.'

'However did you find it?'

'By witchcraft, how else would I find it?'

Ayndra laughed. Diamoon shook her head and continued her patient search. 'Ah! Here it says Marriages. An it's not in this . . .'

'It will take us long enough to find out what is in this!' Diamoon had opened the door of a thing like a gigantic dovecote, and every pigeonhole overflowing with sealed and ribboned, mildewed and frayed documents.

'Let me look at it for a while,' said Diamoon. She put one arm round her waist and leant her forehead on her hand. 'You said the marriage contract of Lord Parakison and Lady Sumakas.'

'Either that, or the whatever they have for their dowries; truly I know nothing of dowries. The marriage contract will do for a start . . . do you know, this is a book of plays . . . Diamoon?'

'Diamoon snuffled in her handkerchief, shoulders hunched. Ayndra put her book down and joined her in the alcove. 'Diamoon?'

Diamoon gave a couple of convulsive sobs, and struck twice at the dovecot, quick as a snake; two wadded documents sailed through the air and burst in a cloud of dust and shattered brittle seals on the stone floor. Ayndra scrambled to pick them up and Diamoon started crying. 'Ah!' said Ayndra. 'The waves of Safi . . . and what is this? "I, Dalar, Lord of Safi, do hereby announce my intention to take to wife, with all due rite, law and ceremony, Letitia, daughter of Candarond . . ." Diamoon, what is the matter? Are you hurt?' She sat down on the cold floor beside her. 'Dalar was Polem's father, was he not? But this other is Parakison Sixth, and Ailixond's father was Parakison Seventh . . . Diamoon?' She put her hand on her knee. Diamoon clasped her hand over it and spoke through her crumpled handkerchief.

'He asked me to draft it! He says he cannot put words into writing properly, and he would rather trust it to me than to a clerk. For that he wanted . . . his father's . . .' She sobbed. Ayndra stroked her arm. 'She is only fifteen!' Diamoon wailed. 'I went to the house, but they would not even open the door to me, they said, Begone, you foreign slut!'

'But Diamoon, you could have married him yourself years ago.'

'I cannot! I already have a husband. Besides, we do not marry outside the guild, it is forbidden.'

'The guild?'

'The Fire Witches.'

'Polem came to tell me about it two days ago. I asked him why he could not will his estates to Parro and Haldin and the rest, an that worried him, but he babbled about his patrimony and an heir with his father's name and he could never give a bastard his father's name, and I said what does it matter about your father's name, how can you marry a young girl like that, younger than your own sons? And we ended up in a quarrel. Diamoon, do not weep so! You

245

always said that you were going to leave him. And then I went to see the girl. Diamoon, she's a child, all she knows is that Polem is famous and wealthy and an ideal match. They had her there like a doll with old men all around her. I asked to speak to her alone, but it was all yes my lord, no my lord, curtsey and bob, I might as well have been another old man for all the difference it made to her.'

'It is all because of these damned estates! When we were in Drimmanë and had nothing he never talked about these things.'

'This city is poison. You can come away with me. In a little while I shall leave.'

'My lord?'

'I am going back to Haramin.' Ayndra stood up and began taking papers from the dovecote and reading the names on their spotted wrappers. 'I am sick unto death of all these purulent nobles and their gossip and their intrigues. Did I tell you that Sumakas intends to bring a lawsuit against me for the recovery of her dowry? I found that she had spent twenty years stealing from the Treasury whenever she desired gold, and prevented it; since then she claims that I have deprived her of her dowry which was provided to her for her widow's maintenance.'

'Take her to the court for theft!'

'I cannot; I have not a single witness who will stand up and swear against her. God knows if any of the papers on it are here. Marriage contracts specify the dowry, do they not?'

'Lady Sumakas has been telling foul tales about you, my lord; rumours are all over the place, and I swear she has something to do with it.'

'O indeed? What sorts of tale?'

'You will not be offended an I speak frankly, my lord? Well then, she says that you used to be in a house on the Street of Dreams, and you had a bastard child which died of neglect, and you learnt all sorts of arts of seduction which you practised on Lord Ailixond and others in order to get your way with them.'

'The last part is a pack of lies,' Ayndra said calmly, but her mouth drew down. 'The rest is, as they say, almost true. It was a long time ago; I wonder who she found who recalled it. But then after Sandar told me that he knew, I knew it could not be any great secret. I did have a bastard child, and for two years I was a whore on the Street of Dreams. When the child died I left the life and the devil and all his legions would not return me to it. These damned respectable women!' She went on taking out documents one after the other. 'It was a fine job you did when you found Lord Takarem's marriage lines in this den of dust and spiders.'

'You do believe that I found it, my lord?'

'I used to be sceptical, as you know; but Ailixond says that he remembers a great scandal among the ladies concerning Lord Takarem's new wife, "neither a virgin nor a widow" and not even Safic born. It must have been when he was four or five, because the next thing he recalls is his first day in the palace school and Sulakon in a mourning tunic with his hair cut short. So perhaps it is all true after all.' She smiled at Diamoon with a flash of her bright blue eyes.

Diamoon reached out and clasped her ankle. 'You will take me with you?'

'Of course I will! Only can you help me now to find this thing?'

'I think it's not here, my lord, unless she has put a hiding spell on it.'

'O come now! Sumakas is no witch.'

'She is not, but she has most of the sorceresses in Safi to help her at one time or another. I cannot see it here at all. Will she not have taken it away already?'

'Very likely; but I must comfort my mind by searching.'

Diamoon got up and joined her in the task. 'Perhaps you should leave before the case comes to court,' she said.

'Perhaps I will! The only trouble is that I must find a governor for the city before I leave . . . eh! What an I offered Sumakas herself to be Governor? Ay! She would make an ant's nest for whomsoever else I left here. Sumakas Governor! I shall have to think about it.'

'There is no law which says that the King has to stay always in Safi. Do you know that this is the anniversary of our victory of Shili? A year is long enough in one place. I must

247

go to the stables now and fetch Tarap; will you walk with me?'

Arpalond asked, 'Why do you not have him brought round to the palace yard?'

'Last day he threw a groom who was doing just that, and ran amok in Great Market; he even knocked down two stalls. Henceforward only I shall take him out.'

'That is an ill-tempered horse.'

'I know; but we have grown used to each other.' They crossed the courtyard and took the passage which led towards the slaves' quarters.

'By all means go and survey the new road,' said Arpalond, 'but you cannot afford to abandon Safi for long.'

'Surely that depends who I leave in my place here.'

'Exactly,' he said.

She laughed. 'How would you like to be Regent in Safi?'

'I? My lord!' Arpalond almost dropped his blind-cane. 'How could I – my eyes– '

'Forgive me! I never meant it. No, I have an idea to offer the Regency to Sumakas.'

Redoubled surprise stopped him in his tracks. 'Sumakas?'

'It is what she has always wanted. An I leave anyone else here at all, she will make mischief.'

'There is no doubt about that,' he said.

'Quite. So what am I to do? Even were I to banish her to the country, it would not stop her intrigues. What may I do that will compel her to my standard? Why, give her the government.'

'Have you offered it to her?'

'It will all be revealed when I am ready to leave. I will not give it her while I am here, else she will be poaching all my functions quicker than fry an egg. I think she has a little inkling of my intent; she has not served me the writs which I was expecting.'

'So you will give Sumakas the long sword and depart? Sweet heaven! You are always the cat among we pigeons.'

'Pigeons indeed!' She gave a peal of unforced laughter.

'You have grown very sanguine since you recovered from your illness,' he said.

She spread her hands, then realised he could not well discern the gesture. 'Let happen what happens. I shall do as

I like; and what I like is to leave Safi. Gods' teeth! We cannot go on governing this realm as though we were still a petty coastal principality. Is the King to spend a lifetime in Safi intriguing about councils and noble marriages while the provincial governors line their own pockets and carve up hereditary domains?'

'But your governors have not so far threatened this, save for Golaron, and you condoned his son's inheritance of Lysmal.'

'And Golaron, an I find no one else, will take my chair in Safi for the time being. He has achieved his final ambition, which renders him trustworthy at last. Shumar! What a rare commodity.'

'Trustworthiness?'

'Yes.'

By the smells and sounds he told that they were in the stables now. 'You are going to the Yard of Suthine,' he said.

'I am; Siriane has asked me to a banquet to commemorate our victory.'

'It was your victory; why do you not have a feast in the palace?'

'O no! Better I celebrate it with them. I shall declare that it was the culmination of our alliance, so fruitful in trade and profit, and so on and so forth; but should I gather the Safeen and make them rejoice for being overrun by a pack of wild rebels?'

'You could celebrate the peace which will last for a thousand years.'

'A thousand years! You wish to call a thunderbolt down on my head!'

He heard the black horse's iron shoes on the cobbles of the yard. 'Forgive me for harping on one string,' he said, 'but I repeat that you jeopardise your position an you establish yourself outside Safi; and I do not think that giving Sumakas the Regency will hold her back in her mischief.'

'Do you not? Power breeds responsibility, surely; she will have to put down riots as well as start them, and so should start many fewer. Do you not see how restrained and upright I have become since I attained high dignity?'

'Restrained? You are restrained as the Timerill bore is

249

restrained by its banks; thus it is smaller than a tidal wave, yet those it drowns are just as dead.'

'We shall talk more on these topics, Arpalond; I thank you for your words.' He felt her mouth warm on his cheeks, and then the clatter of the warhorse as it reared away.

When she came back it was three hours past midnight and the palace was asleep. She collected Siriane's gift from her escort and dismissed them; she walked carrying it through the dark corridors, a black-hatted shadow crossing the long reflections of guttering flambeaux in the marble floors. The sleepy guards at the door to the King's apartment saluted her as she passed them. The antechambers were all dark but a nightlamp glimmered in her bedroom. She pulled a smokestick out of her tunic, lit it in the lamp, and went round the room with one of them in each hand to light a couple of standard lamps. She sat down on the bed, smoking, and undid the silk wrappings of the parcel with her free hand, tossed its contents across the pillows: a S'Thurrulan loose bedgown, embroidered with flames rising from the hem and the cuffs of the winged sleeves. It was nearly a copy of the one Ylureen had. She got up again, opened a chest, took out a glass mirror the size of her palm, and pulled her hat off. Her hair burst out in a bleached corona. She considered her reflection. 'What do you think? I was complaining that it looked as though someone had dipped their hands in ash and run their fingers through it, and Siriane said, why do you not colour it then? You would say that! I think it looks like white gold.' She put the mirror down and stripped off her clothes, casting them in a heap on the chest; she walked naked to the bed and wrapped herself in the embroidered gown. 'This is in truth a gift from Ylureen,' she said. 'She ordered it in the winter, to be given to me this day. It has taken half a year to embroider it.' She tucked her feet up on the bed, lit another smokestick, and settled down like a cat in front of a fire. 'Arpalond thinks I should not go to Haramin,' she said, 'what's your mind on it?' and remained transfixed by the voice she heard in silence.

There was no one about in the common room of the House of Women. She crossed it swiftly, unlocked the door of

Sumakas' apartment, and shut it soundlessly behind her. Sunlight poured through the translucent roof panels and the still air was redolent of rose perfume. She walked round the dayroom looking at the Suthine ornaments that had lately appeared there; glanced into some of the other rooms; finally went into the bedroom and lit a smokestick in the perpetual lamp burning in front of the little shrine in the corner. She lay down on the couch to smoke it, dropping ash into one of the porcelain bowls. The thick walls quelled all sound from without, so that she heard nothing of their approach till the key rattled in the lock. She tossed the stub into the bowl and folded her arms behind her head.

'O my lady! Half our girls are in mourning for it. They all want to go and watch the wedding procession so that they can deplore the bride.'

'The bride is a beautiful girl,' said Sumakas. She came into view, followed by a small woman with a breast like a pouter pigeon who titupped on heels like towers, who said, 'But lady, why such haste? Surely they do not have to marry, yet they are feeding every gossip in town!'

'They wish the King to attend the ceremony,' Sumakas purred.

They both laughed. The high-heeled woman tipped her head back, revealing a terrific collection of precious necklaces on her plump throat; in doing so she caught sight of the figure on the couch. She gave a start so violent that all her jewellery shook. 'My lady!'

'My lord,' said Aleizon Ailix Ayndra.

Sumakas swung round and gave a squeal of outrage. 'How—'

Ayndra reached inside her tunic, brought out a great ring of keys which she whirled like a dancer her tambourine and stowed it away again. Sumakas started to say, 'My lord, I protest at this, this intrusion—'

Ayndra swung her feet to the floor. 'Please be seated,' she said, 'I have matters of state to discuss with you.' She gave a nasty look to the bejewelled woman, whose paint might conceal her pallor but could not hide her trembling. 'Well, well, well,' she said. 'You must have your own house by now, if your trappings are any guide.'

The other woman said nothing. 'Mistress,' said Sumakas,

'perhaps you could wait in the common room. I will send my slaves to attend to you.'

The woman curtsied hastily and hurried out. Ayndra smiled so as to show all her teeth. 'Please be seated,' she said again. 'I see that Old Mother taught all her girls well: Mari has a house in Purrllum, Teli must be on the Street of Dreams, whereas I– ' She laughed. 'The largest house of the lot!'

'My lord,' said Sumakas. 'I must request you not to taint the air of my rooms with that drug smoke.'

'And I must ask you to tell your friends that, an they do not cease to spread tales, the Counter of Taxes will arrive at the house demanding to examine all their accounts over the past ten years. But I have not come to exchange spite with you, Sumakas, rather I wish to make you a proposal. You know that I am going to visit the new road and the northern provinces, and must leave a Regent in Safi.'

'Of course.'

'And who is better suited to the post than you?'

Sumakas opened her mouth but no sound came out.

'You can secure peace among the common people in the city; you have friends in every noble family; you have many years' experience of state. An you accept the Governor's seal, I will present it ceremonially on the morning of my departure; of course we shall visit the Treasury and the Justiciary and all the other departments of state for you to prepare them before that.'

'Ah,' said Sumakas.

'I know that only twelve days remain before I leave, but you know the city so well I hardly imagine that you will need teaching. Lord Golaron has promised me that he will advise you faithfully on military matters, but God send that such will not be needed. Lady, you have said nothing; am I to take it that you will not accept?'

'My lord, you have quite shaken me,' said Sumakas. 'And there has never been a woman Regent in Safi.'

'Never? What am I, then, a hermaphrodite sea-monster? My Treasurer and Justiciar will stay, with all their staff; I shall take you to meet them, unless you would rather they came here.'

'I shall have to receive all these men?'

'How else will you govern? No one will suspect a lady of your age and reputation. It would please me an you could indicate your will now, lady, for an you refuse I shall have to follow my secondary plans.'

Sumakas put one hand on her breast. 'You will make me Regent in Safi?'

'Have I not said so? Lord! Are your wits addled?'

Sumakas shook her head and looked up with an articeless gaze. 'I thought that you hated me!'

'O *no*,' said Aleizon Ailix Ayndra. 'Merely you make me angry when you thwart my will; and I do not like it that you dig up my forgotten past. I know I spent two years as a cheap whore, and two years in the nether hell it was; why remember suffering? But I do not hate you, no. How should I hate you? O, do not look at me like that; it reminds me of Ailixond. Please tell me, will you accept?'

'Yes,' said Sumakas.

'Good,' said Aleizon Ailix Ayndra. She took her hand. 'I am with the Justiciar this afternoon; come with me now and he will greet you. That Teli woman can wait; she will be here for ever. Send her home for now.' She picked Sumakas up out of her chair.

Sumakas said, 'What have you done to your hair? Was it your illness?'

'No, it was a bottle out of Suthine. Come now, we have work to do.'

Diamoon intercepted Aleizon Ailix Ayndra in the dark screens passage behind the dais, between the empty wine jars and the chamber pots. She clutched at her hands. 'My lord! You are not going to sing?'

'I am to sing the next verse, Diamoon, let me go in.'

'Why?' cried Diamoon.

'Because he asked me to and, gods' teeth, we are friends, you're my friend too, it would have been petty to refuse nevertheless, thank god Arpalond is going to sing for the bride's going to bed, he fancies himself as a blind harpist nowadays—'

Diamoon broke away and fled into the servants' passage. Ayndra shrugged and went back into the hall to regain her seat. Her head passed like a comet behind the backs of the noble guests' chairs, then the black of her robe with silver sleeves appeared on the right hand of the bridegroom, who was all in vivid scarlet the same as his bride. Ellakon struck a final discord and put the flattanharp down with a sigh of relief. The musicmaster picked it up and carried it round to the King, who took about four notes to tune it and then stood up to play. She played the wedding song tune through once and then she began to sing, high-pitched and electric. Daior-deor sat up in his seat. Selanor sighed and then burst out laughing; but the hubbub in the hall, which had almost drowned the amateur renditions of most of Polem's friends, was dying down as her voice soared, and the last two lines were heard in perfect clarity. She sat down again; some people forgot themselves enough to applaud, and they saw her laughing as she passed the instrument to Arpalond, who sat on the left of the bride.

'Ay yi yi!' said Selanor in a blurred voice. 'An I were a sentimental man I would weep. Sure and away I would.'

'Why should you weep?' said Daior-deor. 'This must be a happy occasion. I never heard her sing like that before . . . I think I've never heard her sing ever.'

'Ay yi yi!' said Selanor again. He asked for more wine, drank off half of it, and topped up the rest with firewater from his flask.

He offered Daior-deor a slug, but the latter said he would drink wine while it lasted. 'There's no wine that's not vinegar by the time it reaches Haramin.'

'You are joining this jaunt to Haramin, then.'

'Of course – are you not going?'

'I,' said Selanor carefully, 'am to leave my flask behind, and lead a clean life on the road. Yes.' He drained his goblet and thumped it on the table. 'Wine here!'

'Look, the bride's party is getting ready to leave,' said Daior-deor.

'Then let us leave too. Let us go; I know a place. Come. I will pay for you.'

'I meant to stay till the bridegroom's procession.'

'Because my lord has promised to stay until then,' said Selanor, 'yes.' He looked at Daior-deor. 'You make yourself miserable.'

Daior-deor said nothing. Selanor managed to secure an

entire jug from the wine server. The bride, gold glittering inside a trailing mist of red gauze, was being shepherded from her chair by her mother, various female relatives of Polem's, and the rest of the ladies present, as they prepared to escort her to Polem's house and make the bed ready for him. Aleizon Ailix Ayndra got up to say farewell to her. Selanor deliberately interposed his hand between Daior-deor and the sightline which led to her face. He said thickly, 'She'll not sing again for you. Know it.'

'What?' said Daior-deor.

Selanor took his sleeve in one hand and the wine jug in the other. 'Ladies are leaving. Follow the ladies. Yes. Come!'

The palace yard was aswarm with bearers, carrying chairs, torch carriers, maidens with wreaths of flowers and an entire choir of young priests. They wove through the back of the crowd while Tissamë was escorted to her chair and raised shoulder-high above the crowd and the priests sang a specially-composed wedding hymn. Outside the open gates guards with halfpikes held back a mass of onlookers, and Great Market was roaring with life as far as the Street of Dreams. Many of the people in the street were known to them as soldiers, no doubt running through the bonus they had been given in advance of the march north so that they could, as was customary, start the journey without a quarit to their names. Some of them cheered when they observed their officers. Selanor took no notice; he careered through the crowd, using Daior-deor as a crutch, until they came to a door in a side-street. Daior-deor knew what it was before he looked up and saw the devil still about to pitchfork the angel. 'I cannot go in here,' he said.

Selanor up-ended the wine jug, but it was dry; he tossed it at the far wall, where it shattered. He put both hands on Daior-deor's shoulders, and concentrated hard. 'No doubt of it that I am a drunkard, and some doubt that I'm not a fool. But I know something, and I know that my lord is one woman in an army of men. We are brothers. She's our sister. Captain, you cannot marry your sister, no, nor make her your concubine. The King who marries his sister brings the land under a curse. There are a myriad of women in the world. Here–ʼ he gestured at the doorway, ' –are fine women. Come with me and forget all this. I tell you, you eat your heart out.' He swayed, and his eyes slid out of focus. 'I know,' he said significantly.

'I cannot go in there,' said Daior-deor. 'The owners believe me a thief.'

'Nonsense! Owner's a friend of mine. I speak to him. Come now.'

'But I do not like these places,' said Daior-deor.

'What? That's your foolishness speaking. You need a night with a good woman you've paid for, then you'll see what the foolishness is. Come in now.' He hammered on the door.

In a few moments they had passed through the dark lobby and the huge hall and were in a capacious closed room occupied by several richly clad men and many more women in gowns of gauze thinner than Tissamë's veil. The oldest of the men shook Selanor's hand and the women gathered round to welcome them; a carafe of firewater and several jars of wine appeared without need of asking; they were shown to couches, two flautists began to play and various women danced. Others of them took a man by the hand and drew him through a curtained doorway at one end; other men appeared through the entrance door, some of them wearing lord's robes with the swords still strapped at their sides. Selanor introduced Daior-deor to a woman named Peranna, who sat down without touching him and asked him pleasant questions about his military feats; he did not notice that some other females were whispering and pointing at him. Selanor polished off the firewater, made some incoherent speeches to the woman who acted as his pillow, and fell into an open-mouthed sleep. Peranna asked Daior-deor if he wished to wash his hands. He said yes, and followed her through the curtain to turn aside into a squalid alcove whose odour made its purpose obvious even in the dark. When he had finished she poured water over his hands and suggested they go upstairs. He declined, and turned back towards the curtain. At that point they fell on him. Before he had time to reach the knife inside his shirt he was face down on the soaked floor with four or five heavy bodies atop him and voices yelling, 'The thief! The thief! Where's the other! Make him tell! Take him to Stabor!

The room where they dragged him was lined with pipe-rolls and had lists of names chalked on its walls, with sums of money beside them. The man who had shaken Selanor's hand was there. 'Where is your yellowheaded friend? Eh? What did you do with the money? Thought you'd come and spend it, did you? We remember who's done what in our house, master. You can masquerade as the King's captain anywhere else, but we'd know you here, be you never so clever. Now tell us where your friend is, that stabbed one of my men in the guts and broke the pates of three more.'

'I masquerade as nothing,' said Daior-deor. 'I— ' One of the men who held him hit him across the face. 'Answer the question!'

'How many more have you robbed since the coronation, eh?'

'I am no thief!'

'Throw him against the wall,' said the owner. While they did so, he opened one of the cupboards and took out a slavemaster's whip. 'D'you know what this is?'

'Of course I do,' said Daior-deor indistinctly; his mouth was full of blood and it felt as though several teeth were loose in it. 'You are mistaken. I am the King's captain and I have committed no crime.'

'We saw your coppernob in here with that robber on the night of the coronation. When our client asked us to apprehend him, you ran away. Why d'you run away if you'd committed no crime, eh? Now you come back dressed up and perfumed like a little lord on a spree, even lying to Captain Selanor to let you in here. Your lies are finished now. Now answer me.'

'I know nothing of it,' said Daior-deor.

'Bastinado,' said one of his captors.

'Throw him in Stabor for a sixday or two,' said another. 'Then bail him out, and he'll sing like a linnet in the springtime.'

The owner flexed the whipstock between his hands. 'Bastinado for a beginning,' he said.

The shouts and banging promised an unacceptably riotous crowd of revellers, and the doorkeeper opened his telltale with caution; when he saw that the horsemen wore lords' dress and the men who surrounded them were mailed and armed, he slammed it shut and ran to get the owner, who told everyone to be ready in case of a raid and went to open the street door himself. 'My lords, what is your pleasure? It is late at night, and we are preparing for bed; but should you wish a little music in the night, why then, I am sure we could rouse ourselves—'

'We are not looking for pleasure,' said one of the riders in a youthful arrogant voice. 'My lord the King has come here in search of her Captain Daior-deor.'

'My lord?'

The middle rider pushed forward and said drily, 'I gather that my Captain Selanor was here, and Daior-deor with him.'

'Captain Selanor has left, my lord.' The owner bowed.

'I am well aware of that, sir, since it was he who told me that they had been here. He thought that Daior-deor had left also, while he slept; but we have reason to believe that this is not so. An he left, where did he go? And, an he did not leave, where is he?'

'My lord, why, we had a man here who masqueraded as Captain Daior-deor, but the true captain—'

'So you have him,' she said.

'We have the impostor, my lord.'

'Indeed? Then show me this man who impersonates my most trusted officer.'

'My lord, he is within, that is, of course we have punished him—'

She dismounted and strode past him to push the door open. 'Show me.' She walked in as though she already knew the way; the owner puffed after her. She said, 'Haldin, bring six men after me; the rest of you, please wait. We shall not be long.'

The clients in the hall fell silent when they saw the armed men; the mother ran up behind the owner and whined, 'Is it a raid?'

'It is my lord the King,' he said. There was a general huff of amazement and people began bowing or sinking to their knees. Aleizon Ailix Ayndra acknowledged them with a wave. Some of the women leaning over the balustrade were examining her profile as she passed. The owner hastened to unlock the door of the broom-cupboard and the mother reached in with a lamp. The prisoner groaned and tried to move away from the light. Aleizon Ailix Ayndra cried, 'Daior-deor! What have they done to you?' and scattered mops to right and left to kneel down by his side. 'Where is the light? God in heaven! You must come home. Can you walk?'

'My feet.' He showed her one lacerated sole.

Behind them the owner was babbling, 'An honest mistake – we did not know – my lord, we will pay, whatever you ask, the fine–'

She ignored him, said to Daior-deor, 'Can you crawl?'

Despite the cuts and bruises distorting his face, he was smiling; two of his front teeth were missing. 'I can crawl.'

'Crawl out here and we'll take you home. Haldin! Bring Annatto and we'll carry the captain, he cannot walk.' As they emerged into the light the owner's darting eyes were fixed on her face. Haldin and Annatto lifted Daior-deor between them and headed for the door. The owner followed at Ayndra's side, still pleading.

A woman ran up to the mother, hissed in her ear, 'It is the other one! I saw him kissing the snake! The very same!'

The owner heard them and ventured to ask, 'My lord, that is, have you ever, this establishment – of course we welcome–'

Ayndra turned and flashed her eyes at him. 'You think that you might have seen me here before?'

'My lord.'

'As you saw the captain, no doubt.'

'An honest mistake, my lord – his unusual colouring, we were misled–'

'No doubt. Your honesty does not exempt you from the charge of wrongful arrest and assault upon a citizen.' He replied by making a gesture of supplication. 'I think that a fine will settle the matter,' she said. 'I will send one of my men under the royal seal to collect it later this day.' She strode outside, and he heard her say, 'Let me get up, and then you come up behind me. Put your arms round my waist and forget what you've heard about this horse.'

Boots and iron shoes marched away. He closed the street door with a sigh and returned to the hall, which was once more in uproar. 'Thieves! Both of them! The King! In disguise! Thieves . . .'

'They've marked you presently, but none of it will last for long, beyond the teeth.' Ayndra dipped her rag in the bowl of hot water and made a few more dabs at Daior-deor's forehead.

'What have they done to my teeth?' he said. 'My mouth feels like a tomb after the grave-robbers have been in it.'

'Will you have a look? I'll bring you a mirror.' She disappeared into her bedroom as Firumin came in with a bundle of quilts which he began to make up into a bed; she returned with the small glass mirror and a fuming smoke stick. Daior-deor exclaimed with dismay at his reflection.

'The bruises will go,' said Aleizon Ailix Ayndra.

'Ay, but my teeth are gone for ever – I am twenty years older in a day and a night!' He winced as he probed the sites where his left incisor and canine had been.

'It's my damned teeth they should have knocked out. Did you never even say to them that you knew the thief and could tell of him?'

'What benefit in it? Had I said I know the man, it is my lord the King disguised as a vagabond and robbing her subjects in the street, they would have beaten me twice for a liar and an insolent one. Better I had stayed at the wedding.'

'Better you had; had you stayed till after the bride groom's procession, why, then you would have seen me dance with Antinar on the high table.'

'What? Is this true?' he said to Firumin.

'O, very true, sir.' Firumin was grinning as he put a pillow in a case.

'In front of the table?'

'On the table!' She handed him the smokestick. 'You should have gold teeth put in; I'll give you the metal for them.'

'Gold teeth? The true robbers will all believe then that I have fifty gold sols in my shirt and I shall be assaulted wherever I go.'

'You will merely have to keep your mouth shut in the street.'

'Do I not always?' He swayed as he offered her the smoke and ended by leaning on her shoulder.

260

'Ah! Stay there,' she said, 'now I'll put the end of this in your mouth and you just breathe in, no cough.' She popped the glowing end of it between her lips and leaned forward. Firumin shook his head as he tucked in the sheets. They reeled apart in a cloud of smoke, wheezing and laughing. 'Can you do one for me now?' she asked; but Daior-deor was laughing too much. She laughed too. 'This is Siriane's gift to me, this smoke; she wishes to show that she can surpass Ylureen in every respect!'

They went on talking, but before long he was ready to sleep. She went into her own chamber, but did not lie down; she pulled back the tapestry on the windowless wall, and unlocked the heavy door revealed behind it. She took a lamp with her and let the curtain fall to hide her route. When she unlocked the second door in the dark passage she stood at the foot of the Tower of the Heavens. The staircase which spiralled up the inside of the wall rose above her into the dark; her single flame did not approach its upper reaches. She looked up into it for a while, and then passed on, toward the mausoleum. The lamplight bobbed over the crude effigies of the ancient Kings, the stiff bearded men of the previous century, the smooth marbles of Ailixond Seventh and old Lord Parakison. It came to rest on the circular inlay at the foot of Ailixond's tomb, metal land in a lapiz sea, Safi-the-city a diamond in the gold that marked the extent of his domains on the day that he was crowned, the other cities of the Empire beryls in the silver of his domains on the day of his death. The gold gleamed, but the silver was tarnished already. The light moved up to the carved feet of the effigy, along the regular folds of the robe, till it reached the quiet features of the face. She sat down on the edge of the marble lid and ran her fingers over the cold stone of cheek and brow. She was sitting with her hand on the forehead of the stone Ailixond, static in reverie, when she twitched suddenly and jumped, as if someone unseen had touched her shoulder; but before she had stood up she relaxed and sat down again, laughing silently. 'You should not surprise me like that. I suppose I might have expected to find you here.'

'. . . . . . .'

'But you stay in the palace, do you not? I have not seen you in Great Market even.'

'. . . . .'

'You know that I shall go away from Safi soon.'

'. . . . .'

At that she laughed aloud and clapped her hands. 'Will you, truly? Anywhere I go?'

'. . . . .'

She tipped her head back and reached out. 'Come closer and hold my hand.'

'. . . . . .'

Her hand fell back to her side. 'But you can come for a walk with me?'

'. . . . . .'

She got up, holding the lamp, then paused to listen. 'I shall need it . . . are you sure? Very well, then.' She put it down beside the tomb; then bent over with a grin, and lit a smokestick in it before she left it, to walk without hesitation into the dark.

Ayndra utterly forbade any farewells with flowers or choirs of children, but she allowed the building of a stand over Thaless Gate for those who would watch the cavalcade leave. The lords came, divided between those who clustered round Sumakas to comment on the parade, and those who stood further back and talked among themselves as though they cared not what forces were leaving the city.

'She has changed all the gate captains? How fortunate!'

'Half the gate crews are naught but Lysmalish scum these days.'

'But she has left half her Safic footmen here.'

'She never had many in any case; her army are all barbarians. Look at these that pass now. Pony men!'

'And besides, who has she left to command them?'

'The old witch's magic is stronger than hers!' They laughed.

Sumakas leaned back in her chair and spoke to the Silver Shield captain who stood at her side. 'Pray ask Lord Ellakon to come up here to me a moment; he is such a great warrior, I wish him to explain to me the armaments of these men.'

'My lady.' The man saluted and approached Ellakon, who consented with a bad grace. Casik smirked behind his hand.

One of Ailissa's children shouted, 'Here she comes now!' There was a general stampede of the young to the city side of the stand; Polem patted Tissamë's bottom and set her down to run after her age-mates. They joined the people in the street in cheering as the King's party approached, black and blue-and-white banners flaunting in the wind. Aleizon Ailix Ayndra took her hat off and waved to them as she passed underneath the arch. The Mirkit horsemen who went before were a good way down the road now. As they emerged from shadow into light she said to her escort, 'Are you ready?' They nodded, shortening their reins; she flourished her hat once more, and let it drop. A terrific report burst from all sides of the gate; the crowd screamed, Sumakas leapt out of her seat, half the lords drew their swords and four clusters of rockets trailing red and black smoke arched up into the flawless sky. The banner men and the rest of the escort had shot up the road, but Aleizon Ailix Ayndra was still there, clinging to the furiously curvetting Tarap who danced round and round in circles; she got him still enough to take one hand from the reins, drew her sword, looked up as she raised it and tossed it upward. It turned its full length in the air and she caught it again, sheathed it with one shove and stabbed Tarap with her spurs. He took off like a blast of powderfire. She was still laughing when she caught up with her escort.

Golaron, Lord of Safi and Over-governor of the Province of Lysmal, greets Ailixond Ninth of that name, Most Serene Lord and King of Safi, Lord of the New Empire. With great urgency, my lord. Lady Sumakas has convened her first Council. She is inviting all the lords to this to give her counsel. Lord Casik came and again presented his demand for the governorship of Purrllum and the Needle's Eye; he mocking her when it proved she knew not presently who governed there, and Ellakon and others I list in the enclosure favouring him. My lady of course refused and he left in high dudgeon. This day morning, two days later, we found him gone. I have despatched at the same time as this letter a fast ship to Caoni, to warn my lord and son Haresond, and then to go on past the Timerill to Cambar and send by land to Purrllum. We have several of Casik's slaves and will find from them what they know but no doubt he has gone to Purrllum, or will go there, but by what route we do not know. Also my lord be pleased to send me a paper to take an army or a detachment into the field, for I intended to go directly with horsemen for Casik but my lady Sumakas said that his flight was not so grave that it justified me taking the garrison out of the city. You will however believe me when I say that I am assured that he will go to his former territory of Cambar with purpose of a rebellion in Purrllum. My lady has at least been willing to provide monies for a clandestine watch on those lords who demonstrated their failing loyalty at the council. The enclosure tells of them. Awaiting your answer by return of post, given in my own hand this twelfth day of First Month, in the four hundred and seventy-fifth year of the city.

Aleizon Ailix Ayndra greets Golaron. I will spare you my lamentations upon your news and proceed briefly to the point. I enclose signed and sealed an authority for you to take an army into the field should it prove necessary, but Casik has not run away with an army, so why should you take an army after him? Better that you send out parties of horsemen by all highways and byways to look for him with the aim of bringing him back. Neither should you assume that he has gone to Purrllum, or will go there, although you should indeed tell Haresond to patrol his marches. We have not entered the New Road yet but we hear already that some warriors have attacked the road crews with arrows from a distance and once raided a camp. Very likely they are no more than the tribes of the forest who do not wish for a road, but you will recall what I told you, that Sulakon, Takarem and the young Meraptar were said to have gone east into the mountains this spring. Do not neglect the roads to Drimmanë and beyond. Send immediately to Pelto in Drimmanë to keep watch and ask Polem to help you in this. Indeed it would benefit me to have Polem here, for despite his protestations of inconsequence his name is held in some respect in the lands east of here. You could perhaps propose to him that it is time he rose from the marriage bed and took up his duties. As for Sumakas, I am writing to her under a separate cover. In the matter of Casik's slaves, it is always

264

*best to put slaves to question slaves an you wish honest
answers, and Sumakas has some of her old slaves who are as
skilled at questioning without resort to machines as any I
have met. I write to her instructing her to put them at your
service, to make known to you all the intelligences she
receives by that or any other road, and to consent to your
decisions in matters of military conduct. I think, however,
she is wise to wish to retain a large garrison in the city, for
we never know what unexpected evils may come upon us.
She knows little about provincial government, but in
matters of the mood of Safi she is rarely wrong. I wish you
good fortune, good counsel, and write rapidly to me in any
event. Given in my own hand this fifteenth day of First
Month in the four hundred and seventy-fifth year of the city.*

The track of the new road was visible half a day away, a
great red-brown scar carved through the dark ranks of the
forest, appearing and disappearing across the ascending
ranks of hills. Heavy wagons lumbered up its gradients,
carrying loads of gravel shovelled out of the river beds and
sand dug from the hillsides, to be dumped in the raw ruts of
the foundations and tamped down by lines of women
workers. Other gangs climbed through the pines, searching
out straight-trunked trees to be felled and rolled or dragged
to where they build bridges and shored up the outer edges of
the road as it crawled up the side of a steep slope. The
surveyors moved days ahead of the labourers, marking out
the easiest routes; after them Amurret the old miner
directed the actual cutting of the road bed, and the wagons
followed as far as the surface was made up to deposit the
materials to advance its next stage. Polem's party was
content to proceed at a leisurely pace; he spent most of his
time sitting in the open front of Tissamë's carriage, along
with his daughters, Lia, Tikkidi and Little Thio; a whole
horde of attendants and servitors trundled along behind
with carts and pack-mules. From time to time they went out
riding, he on a quiet hack and Tissamë on the gentle pony he
had bought for her; until they reached the end of the made
road, and took to horseback entirely, leaving the servants to
struggle with the task of transferring the baggage to animal
back. They picked their way down valleys resounding with

the plink-plink of hammers and axes, between lines of men and women with baskets of earth on their backs, past dust-covered labourers who leant on their spades and called out in barbarous tongues. By the time they reached the top of the ridge there was nothing deserving of the name of road under their feet, only a carpet of pine needles and sand; they paused in the resinous breeze, and looked at rank upon rank of hills marching out of sight into the milky distance. The King's camp was in the valley below them, where the trees opened out into a sparse green lawn either side of a brook of iron-tainted water: a scatter of multicoloured tents and grazing horses, with a cluster of banners outside a tent no bigger and duller coloured than the rest to show who lived in it.

The kitchen tents were pitched furthest upstream of all, to get the clean water; there was a sheltered hollow behind the windbreaks where the cooks rested from their labours. At present they were busy with the evening meal, and Firumin and Daior-deor were enjoying the late sunshine undisturbed. Firumin had only to clap his hands, and someone served them from his store of red Thaless. Daior-deor, who had been on nightwatch and only lately risen, lay on the grass yawning. He covered his cup when Firumin tried to refill it. 'I thank you; I cannot drink so much just out of bed, I shall end up like Selanor.'

'Selanor has not touched a drop of strong drink since we left the city.'

'Indeed. I have noted his foul temper because of it.'

'It is a great sacrifice which he makes for my lord's sake,' said Firumin.

'I think it will not last,' Daior-deor replied. He stretched out on his back and looked up at the mares' tails streaking the pale blue sky, measuring the position of the sun. 'I must go and look for Pasdaran,' he said without moving.

'Before you go, sir, might I ask you something?'

'Why not?' Daior-deor tipped his face toward Firumin, who shuffled his stool closer and bent forward.

'You remember, sir, what you said, about that night you slept in the antechamber: you said you heard my lord talking to someone in the night, and wondered who it might be.'

'And you said that it was most likely Lady Sumakas, an they had replied so quietly.'

'I know I did. But it has happened again since then.'

'That Lady Sumakas came to visit my lord?'

'No. That my lord has been talking in the night. And not only in the night, either. Talking when nobody else is there.'

Daior-deor shrugged. 'Very likely she talks to herself.'

'No, it is like you said: a conversation, but one cannot hear the other person. And there is something else, sir, an you'd not mind my asking: did not you and Mistress Diamoon a few months ago make a conjuration?' Daior-deor said nothing, and he went on in a whisper, 'A necromantic conjuration?'

Daior-deor's eyes narrowed. 'I did ask Mistress Diamoon to do such a thing, yes, but as for what followed – she is a very accomplished performer, no doubt; more I cannot say.'

'But it is true that she tried to summon the spirit of, of a person my lord and I both knew very well?'

Daior-deor began to say, 'Do you mean L– ' but Firumin hushed him.

'Do not say the name! It is bad luck to mention one of their names.'

'Surely, master, that is pure superstition.' Daior-deor began to get up.

Firumin shook his head and said in a nervous whisper, 'Not at all. She talks to him.'

'Firumin, this cannot be. I know what you speak of, and I confess that I feared it in the past, after the conjuration, but I asked Mistress Diamoon to go up and seal the tomb that we– '

Firumin's mouth gaped open. 'You took ashes from the tomb?' he said in horror.

'Well, to be sure; Mistress Diamoon asked for them. There was all sorts of metal in the tomb, I never expected it to be so cluttered; I cut my hand– '

He fell silent when he saw how sick Firumin looked. 'This is evil magic!' said the steward.

'Sir, I know it; I only entered upon it because I was ignorant of sorcery. But Mistress Diamoon swore to me that she had sealed up the tomb. Have you asked my lord if she has seen the spirit since?'

'No, sir, I have not, and you know as well as I do what she would say an I did.' He raised his voice and said in an acid drawl, 'Firumin, you superstitious peasant! Have you been listening to tales of ghosts in the darkness again?'

'True enough,' said Daior-deor, laughing. More seriously he said, 'You should ask Mistress Diamoon; perhaps she can make an exorcism without my lord's knowledge. She swears that the spirit is safely away, as I said.'

'I hope she speaks the truth,' said Firumin. 'One moment, sir.' He took a light hold of Daior-deor's sleeve and picked a strand of grass out of his hair, then knelt down to flick dust off the skirts of his tunic.

'I only go to see about the night guards!' said Daior-deor.

'Of course; but we must all do honour to our household.'

Daior-deor went on shaking his head as he walked down to the stream, crossed the log laid across it and headed for the horse-lines. One of the cadets ran up to him as he approached. 'Sir! Lord Polem is coming, he'll be on top of the hill soon. Shall we go to meet him, sir?'

'God's dog! I believed he had stayed at the end of the carriage road.'

'No, sir. They left the carriages there and came on on horseback. The ladies too.'

'Then we must certainly go to meet him. Tell the trumpeter to sound for it.'

As the blue dusk filled the hollow, red and green and yellow lights sprang up among the swinging branches of the firs: glass hanging lamps had been scattered around the camp like giant fireflies, and some of the people coming back from their labours were singing as they approached. Little Thio and Tissamë wanted to run around and look at the decorations, but Polem was reluctant to let them go alone, and beside, the king had not yet appeared. 'Here she comes now,' said Firumin. He pointed into the gloom, in the direction of a faint chorus of male voices, interspersed with whoops and laughter; as he spoke a single female voice began to sing a descant, a phosphorescent scribble in the dark sea of men's voices. On the skyline the outline of a troop of horsemen appeared against the frieze of treetrunks and orange sunset sky, and headed down into the camp as other women took up the song. In a few moments they emerged in the bright circle of flares in front of the King's tent.

'Father, can we go now?' whined Thio.

'Hush, hush,' said Polem, and in a loud voice, 'My lord!' He strode forward, offering his hand.

Aleizon Ailix Ayndra tucked both hers behind her back. 'Do not kiss my hand, it is too filthy,' she said. Mud streaked the front and back of her tunic and her legs were caked with sand.

'Let me kiss you at least,' said Polem. She gave him her sideways look, but put her face forward, and he carefully kissed her cheeks without touching any other part.

'Father— ' said Thio.

'Hush!'

'What do you want?' said Aleizon Ailix Ayndra.

Tissamë also tried to quiet her two-years-younger step-daughter, but Thio said, 'Father, why do we wait so long? Let us go and look round.'

'I think it is not safe,' said Polem. 'The King is here, Thio, come and greet her.'

'O, let them go,' said Ayndra, 'an they stay within the camp, no one will molest them at all; they can run where they wish.' She accepted both their curtsies, and they ran off under the trees, stepmother and daughter together, while Polem looked fondly after them. Tissamë wore no veil and both had the short dresses of maidens, with tanned and freckled faces that would have horrified Oborenë. 'I thought you would have left the young lady in the House of Women,' Ayndra said.

'O no! She asked to come with me, how could I say no? Her father and mother were making her stay in the house all the time and wear a long gown and a veil, but Maishis knows, she is too young for all that, I cannot keep her to it – are you sure it is safe here, with all these soldiers?'

'O entirely. They know I'd have them flayed alive did they molest any woman against her will. You have brought all your baggage up here with you?'

'We left it at the end of the road, where the wagons

could go no further. I think the slaves will put it on horses.'

'You left the guards there as well?'

'Guards? We have no guards.'

'Hoo! You are very trusting. Have you not heard the news?'

'We are peaceful travellers, and beside, have you not driven away all the robbers? Since you became King there are no robbers anywhere, everyone says so.'

Ayndra laughed. 'No robbers except under the royal banner, is that not what they truly say? No, we lost two wagons only a sixday ago, that were coming up from Thaless with food and weapons; one broke an axle, and another stayed with it while the rest went on to make camp. They found them the next morning empty and all the wagoneers dead. It's not the first such assault we have suffered either.'

'What! Had you not better call the girls—'

'O no, nothing in our camp here. There are guards scattered for miles around and riders sweeping the forest. It is only the outlying camps, the surveyors and the supply train that has suffered.'

'Shumar! Know you who they are that raid you?'

'Whichever leader of the hill tribes I speak with, they say it is the people in the next valley, who are thieves and murderers to a man. We have killed a twothree raiders and they were always hillmen; when I was here a few years ago I asked them then about this road, and they did not all favour it. You ought not to travel on the open road without guards.'

'We came here safely, we saw nothing at all.'

'You are fortunate; still I think you should not leave your goods down there. But do you not wish to bathe and change your clothes?'

'Can we bathe?'

'You can do anything here; no comfort of civilisation is denied to us.' She tossed her bleached hair back, laughing; she looked five years younger than she had at the time of her coronation. 'Come, let me show you to the bathing place. I will send Haldin down to put a guard on your wagons.'

'I have no clothes to change into till they bring them up, and besides, may I ask you – is Diamoon here with you?'

'She's not here at this moment.'

'But she is . . ?'

'Polem, she does not wish to see you, she asked me to tell you so.'

Polem's face crumpled pathetically. 'I only wish to speak to her, no more than that – I mean, I would be happy if – why will she not see me?'

'Because you are married now,' said Ayndra, folding her arms over her sandy tunic.

'But I miss talking to her,' Polem said, 'I want her to advise me.'

Come and sit down while you await your things, and you can talk to me at least.' Between her tent and the stream a collection of stout logs had been set out as crude seats. 'Tell me all about the happenings in Safi. Is Governor Sumakas a success?'

By the time Haldin reached the roadhead the twilight was almost at an end, and the crews had all carried their tools away to the guarded camps where they slept; there was no one on the road at all. Rather than search in the dark, he led his troop up the valley till he found some people round a campfire. The lord's party had tried to camp on the road itself, they said, till one of the engineers ordered them out of the way, upon which they got their dancers up and had driven away southward to look for a place where they could make a proper camp; it had taken them a while because they had already begun to take one of the carts apart. They intended to take them all apart, they said, put the goods on packhorses and cache the vehicles in some hut or grotto till they had use for them again. No, they did not know quite where they might have gone: down the road somewhere, they'd seen them going over the hill. They were a noisy mob; there'd not be much difficulty in finding them. Haldin cursed and asked them for a half-dozen of torches to light his search.

'When I reached here it was already too late. There was nothing I could have done,' said Haldin. 'Thanks be to god you took my sisters with you.'

'But you said that you heard them at it and for that you

271

came up here,' Polem complained. 'Yet you let them all escape!'

'Father, our people were dying! What else could I do but stay with them? There could have been fifty more hidden in the trees around for all I knew.'

Ayndra thrust her hand with a chopping motion between the two snarling faces. 'Harsh words never mended a broken jar,' she said cheerfully. 'They have taken two women away with them. Do you know an they've taken the money? You did have your money in one of these?'

'Money!' exclaimed Polem, raising his hands. He seemed ready to deliver some tirade; Ayndra looped her arms round one of his and brought it down. She started to lead him back among the wagons. 'We shall have to make up some stretchers to take the worst hurt back with us to our camp; no one must stay out here after this. We'll take what we can and leave the rest for now, so we must collect your clothes, and the valuables . . .'

Haldin scowled at their retreating backs; he went and sat down on a fallen tree. He observed the King saying a few words to Daior-deor, after which the mercenary started directing the soldiers of Haldin's troop in taking the carts apart to make stretchers. When Haldin appeared behind and, looking down on him, said, 'Permit me to order that,' he merely smiled with a flash of his new teeth, said, 'Of course,' with a brief salute, and disappeared from the scene. Haldin got on with the job.

Polem now vented his guilt on Aleizon Ailix Ayndra. 'Why did you not write that I should have guards? You never even wrote to me at all, sending Golaron to tell me, indeed.'

'I believed that you would think to bring them of your own accord. What merchant travels without guards in these days?'

'I am not a merchant,' said Polem.

'Quite,' she replied. He was put at a loss by this, and said no more; she saw some of her people coming out of the trees, and ran off to talk to them. She jumped up and down and waved her hat for him to come over. When he had strolled up, they were gathered round a ragged man with blue tattoos on his cheekbones and his hands roped together. 'Look!' she cried. 'They have left one of their number behind after all. A charcoal-burner from the eastern forest. For a sprained ankle he could not get away, we found him under a bush. It is time we put an end to these raids. We shall take him with us and he can show us where they came from. Will you stay here, Polem, and command the road camps? Selanor shall help you with the guards . . .'

'When do you mean to go?' he asked.

'Next day!' she replied.

They started singing again as they marched away from the stripped vehicles, a string of torches wavering under the dark branches while she led her men in some Haraminharn folk chorus. Even some of the ones carrying the wounded on tail-boards and tilt stretchers sang. The tattooed man stumbled along at the tail of her horse, his captors jerking his tether whenever his bandaged ankle held him up. He looked up as Polem urged his horse on to the head of the party and watched him pass with unafraid liquid eyes.

'My lord!' he called.

'Yes?'

He did not speak till he was right up beside her. 'You mean that you will leave me in charge of all this?'

'What, are you not willing?'

'I have not been here two days even!'

'You will be the senior lord here when I leave. All you need do is see that Selanor has nothing to drink and everyone else will go about their business.'

'But then why must you leave me here at all?'

'By all means come, but you will have to leave Tissamë behind.'

'Leave her? For gods' sake, I could not do that.'

'Well then,' she said, grinning. 'You'll stay here and protect her. Ailixond said you'd turn out trustworthy now you are a married man.'

'Shumar! One would think marriage had turned me into a monkey. I am the same man I ever was.'

She laughed immoderately and said, 'You will take the command, then?'

'Certainly,' he said.

'Excellent!' she cried, and burst into song again.

273

'Sweeter, sweeter, sweeter than new honey
Nimble, nimble as a humble bee
Wicked, wicked as a wasp in autumn
Devil take you far away from me!'

'What has got into you? I never heard you sing so much!'
'Ailixond likes it when I sing,' she replied.
'Liked it,' he said.
'Yes.'

In the end they did not leave the next day, but the dawn following, on account of the number of people who had to be introduced to Lord Polem and their work explained to him, while those chosen for the expedition ran about collecting hardtack and frieze cloaks.

'It is our last chance to hammer these raiders in this season. We are well into Second Month already, and by Fourth Month we shall have gone into winter quarters. We shall march up into Haramin and send the heavy wagons back south. There is a party coming out from Haramin, they should arrive any day now, there's a Captain Sassafrange in command of them. They have been marking out the path of the road from that side and labouring on the northern section, that's south from Gaba . . .'

'What is Gaba?'

'The last town of Haramin on the way to Pozal. Now, there's the matter of the sand pits. Make sure that no one camps out at them overnight . . .'

Polem managed to secure a break in his instruction at the supper hour and went in search of Haldin. He found him in the quartermaster's tent. 'Good day, father,' he said.

'Haldin.' Polem embraced him and kissed him in spite of his beard. 'You are not packing to leave?'

'Of course I am. I command my lord's bodyguard, did you not know? Of course I shall leave.'

'But Haldin. I want you to stay here and help me keep your mother and sisters safe.'

'She is not my mother.' Haldin went on stuffing hardtack into a leather bag.

'Haldin!'

'Father.' Haldin put the bag down and faced up to him.

'What do you want of me? Last day you left our people alone and then berated me for going to their rescue. Now you tell me I should not pursue the killers after all. In Drimmanë you were forever passing over me in favour of that wittol Parro, who does nothing but laze about and get more bastards to the family name, so I went to seek my fortune – well thought that was too, since you've determined that you must get some legitimate brats in order not to give us, your faithful children, any share in the patrimony! I am a poor bastard, I must work for my bread. Do not ask me to abandon my labours for some foolery of sentiment. I follow my lord the King.' He gathered the bag's mouth together with a snap. 'Good day, my lord.' Polem was left staring after him. The only comfort was that Firumin stayed behind.

'A dinner in the style of S'Thurrulass? Well, my lord, our supplies here are not very rich, but I will do what I can. Perhaps if you could wait a day or two, and eat Safic food the while?'

They picked up the cold trail without difficulty, though the prisoner gave little aid; he would only speak in his own dialect, and whenever he was asked a difficult question he claimed he could not understand the words. Thus he made out that he knew nothing at all of any other raids, nor who commanded them, nor why; but he did lead them to a clearing whose rings of blackened stones still had heaps of ashes in them and a couple of saddlebags with Polem's emblem on them lay slashed and rifled on the ground. The raiders had made no effort to conceal the direction they took on leaving; one might almost think that drovers had passed by, the track of hoofprints was so dense. They pursued it eastwards into the forest. After a day or so it became slighter, and it seemed that the quarry had scattered into smaller parties; Aleizon Ailix Ayndra dictated the route that they should follow, apparently plucking certainty out of the air. Two days later they saw carrion birds circling a distant hilltop, and when they reached it they knew she had not been wrong. She had been dead less than twenty hours and beaten savagely before she died; her skirts were bundled up around her waist and flies congregated between her exposed thighs. Aleizon Ailix Ayndra covered her mouth with a handkerchief. 'Let us halt to collect firewood and burn her . . . you are sure this is one of the two who went missing?'

'I know her by her bracelet, my lord.'

'Do you wish to take it off? If she has any . . . relatives . . .' She turned away. They searched for a place where a blaze would not set the whole hillside afire, and began to heap up old pine branches. 'Are you sure we should not dig a grave?' said Daior-deor. 'They will see the smoke for miles.'

'Let them think it is charcoal-burners. Graves are for malefactors, not their victims.'

'Very well, my lord.'

'I'll come back when I see it lit.'

From the hilltop one could see the distant snowpeaks, a token of how far east they had come, but down in the valley by the side of the stream she could have been in any quiet section of the immense crumpled wilderness, where neither axes nor animals grazed and late summer filtered through the dusty trees. The stream began to cut a tiny gorge for itself; she hobbled Tarap and went on on foot, until it emerged in a waterfall between two rocks and broadened out into a pond; and there she saw him on the other side of it.

He was dressed like a hillman in short wide breeches and jacket of unbleached wool, and the ruffled linen shirt under them was grimy and frayed; he scooped up water in his hands as his horse drank greedily beside him. Its coat had lost the shine acquired from daily care by patient grooms, but no amount of mud could have made it look like anything other than a Safic charger. He looked at his reflection in the beer-coloured water, ran wet hands a couple of times through his long black hair and flicked it back off his face as he stood up. Then he saw her. She waved. His eyes grew large with astonishment and he reached for a sword which was not at his side. She laughed. 'There it is on the rock behind you,' she said. 'I never thought I'd find you like this! Why, you look years younger than you did last night. Younger than I've ever seen you.'

The clear tenor voice rang over the water. 'What do you mean?'

'O Ailixond!' she said.

Comprehension struck Takarem like lightning. He said slowly, 'Aleizon Ailix Ayndra.'

'Haha!' She sat down on a boulder and pulled her hat off, releasing an unnatural coloured mane. 'What is this, a damned recognition scene at a holy pond in a forest? I never thought you travelled on horseback, I thought you flew magically from place to place, or were conveyed by thought alone. It's a beautiful horse you have. You look beautiful yourself! It's fortunate you show yourself on the far side of the pond, indeed, else I'd find it hard not to leap upon you, no matter how ethereal you are!' She was as joyous as any drunkard at the Summer Festival. Takarem moved backwards to pick up his sword-belt, without taking his gaze from her. 'Are you going to fight?' she asked as he put it on. 'Tell me, are we about to come upon them? Will you help me murder the men who raped that poor woman? Send them to me!'

'I will,' said Takarem. He gathered up the reins and was astride his mount in one graceful leap.

She raised her hat in salute as he turned to go. 'Come to me like this again,' she said. 'Come young and beautiful!' Her laughter bubbled like a spring as he drove his spurs into the warhorse's side and drowned it with the dull thump of hooves on layered pine needles. Aleizon Ailix Ayndra shook her head and put her hat back on; she walked round the pond till she could see the hilltop, and discerned a blue-grey smudge of smoke; fortunately there was a wind up there which dissipated it as soon as it rose. She headed back to where she had left Tarap.

Takarem burst into the camp with a mad whoop; his lathered horse careered twice round the circle before he could bring it to a stop. 'Meraptar!' he yelled. 'Meraptar! Great news!' The men who had scattered out of his way regrouped, but Meraptar was not one of them. 'Where is he?'

'Gone away with her,' said one. 'We expect him back any hour.'

There was merriment; Takarem cursed. 'Son of a snake! We have the witch right in our hands and he has naught better to do than dally with a slut.' He got down from his horse and led it to a tree to tether it. 'Where is the fodder? I told you to go and collect some fodder.'

'Here it is, sir.'

'That? What do you think I have to feed, a rabbit?'

'There's not much to be had here, sir.'

'Go and bring some more. He'll have eaten that in an hourtenth. Off you go now!'

'Yes, sir,' the man said sullenly.

As he was trailing out of the camp he met Meraptar coming back in, the woman shuffling listlessly after him. She squatted beside the cold fire, matted hair swinging across her face. Meraptar swaggered into the middle of the clearing and stood there stretching with a big smile of contentment on his face. 'Takarem,' he said. 'Your turn for a different kind of ride?'

'Meraptar! I met the witch. The witch is here!'

'You what?' Meraptar stopped in mid-stretch.

'I met her! She has come right here after us. They mean to attack us, she told me so, they found the dead woman and they want our blood!'

'She told you so? You spoke to her and you did not kill her? Are you mad?'

'She was on the other side of a river – but look, over there where we left her, see? A fire! They must be burning her.'

'Why, then let us go and fall upon them straightway! That witch killed my father, I owe her one!'

'But Meraptar, the witch is mad! She thought I was Lord Ailixond. She even called to me, "Ailixond!" Her hair has gone white, I hardly knew her. Now is the time to attack their camp, she cannot have left anyone there, they have all come after us. The witch is wandering mad in the woods thinking she sees Lord Ailixond, sooner or later she will fall over a treeroot and break her neck. Let us go and tear their camp to pieces. To horse! Now!' Meraptar did not look convinced. Takarem strode over and clapped him on the shoulders. 'We'll capture her camp and lay an ambush for her. Let us not waste time fishing for minnows when we can catch a salmon.'

'What about her?' Meraptar jerked his head at the woman, who had not moved.

'That slut? I know not how you can bear to touch her, her stink turns my stomach. Do what you will with her so long as you leave her here.' He raised his voice. 'Men! To horse! We are going to ambush the witch!'

'I like it very much,' said Lia, 'every day is like a festival here.'

'Are you not scared?' asked Tikkidi.

'O no, Master Firumin says there is no danger at all.'

'You need not fear, you always have half-a-dozen men at your back in any case!' At which Lia gave a scream of mock anger, and tried to pull the comb out of Tikkidi's hair.

'Girls, girls,' said Polem. 'Have a care, or you will overturn the table.' He protected his goblet as he filled it with wine, put a little in Tissamë's cup and added a generous ration of water. 'Will you have some more wine, Lia?'

'An you do not put so much water in it, Father, I am not a child.'

'What is that noise?' cried Tissamë, pressing herself against Polem.

'Only the woodmen blowing their horns, my dove, do not fear.'

'It sounds like the horns Lady Ylureen's people played,' declared Thio.

'It must be our visitors from Haramin,' Polem said. He listened. 'I think you speak truly, Thio, they must have some of our allies with them – and what has that man got on his face?'

He stood up and went to greet Selanor and the fellow who accompanied him. The metallic glitter between his cheeks turned out to be a false nose, held on by leather straps but itself indisputably golden, or at least heavily gilt. 'My lord, may I present Captain Sassafrange?' said Selanor. 'Lord Polem, who commands in my lord the King's absence.'

'Welcome, welcome! Come and sit down with us, sir, and tell us of your journey. Have you truly come all the way from Raq'min? A pity Lord Ayndra is not here to greet you. Still, will you have some wine? Captain Selanor?'

'My lord, I fear I must abstain.'

'O, I know you are not to drink on duty, but surely a drop now cannot harm.'

Sassafrange raised his cup and said in his bizarre accent, 'Lord Ayndra King of Safi! Long may she reign!' Polem's daughters stared in fascination at his nose. He gestured at Selanor. 'We are meet again after years parting! We are all drink, sir, you cannot dry. Join!' He poured half his share into an empty goblet and pushed it into Selanor's hands. Selanor looked at it, then at Polem, who had Tissamë on his lap.

Polem raised his cup. 'The new road and the New Empire! Long may they endure!' He tipped his head back and downed it in one. Selanor gave a shrug and followed suit.

Sassafrange asked, 'My lord, please, where's my lord come back?'

'The hillmen have been raiding us, she has gone to burn a few huts and chase them away. Did you have trouble with them on your way here?'

'We aren' 'ave trouble at all. Are all a frien' of Haramin in the north. All 'member my lord she come through 'ere inner pass. Very good, no? Southern people all are evil raiders, not liker north. Hail to the King!' He drank another toast.

'Do you come from Suthine, sir?' Polem asked.

'Thass so, my lord. But many years a faithful servant of my lord in Haramin.'

'I thought I heard horns of S'Thurrulass when you approached. Do you have a cook with you? Or musicians?'

'Music, my lord? I play music for you. Dance too, as you will.'

'O!' cried Lia. 'Can we have dancing this night?'

Polem said, 'It may be the captain is tired from his journey,' but Sassafrange was bowing to Lia and offering his services already. 'Music! Dance! Drink, smoke – a present I bring you!'

'What is it? What is it?'

'Moments, lady, I bring.'

It came in the form of a cask, a porcelain carafe, and six thumb-sized porcelain cups. The cask was set up on a tree stump, and Sassafrange filled the carafe from it. As soon as the tap had been fitted, the vapour was unmistakable. 'Wess Shore lifewater,' said Sassafrange. 'The bess in the world! The King!' This time Selanor did not hesitate at all in drinking the toast, and proposed another right after it. 'My lord, serve yourself generous,' said Sassafrange. 'This present my lord don' like any way, are bring another for her. You, my lord, finish it and we all have music and dance. A little half-hour are see to all of it – hail to the King!' He excused himself to go and arrange the music.

'Lia,' said Polem, 'really I do not think you should drink that stuff; it is very strong. Has it not burnt your throat already?'

Lia shook her head through her coughs and said nothing.

'How . . . man'ese barrels you brough' wiz you? No, don' hol' your fingers up, I can' damn well see to coun' them.'

'I brang three,' said Sassafrange. 'Here's two. Nother to come, no worry.'

'I am not . . . worried,' Selanor said thickly. 'My only worry, my lord come back an' fin' me.'

'Wish my lord are come now! Years I don' see her.'

'No, no. Not now.' Selanor lifted his bloodshot eyes. 'She kill me an she see me now. I swear it. You don' know.'

'Ah, she say, you a drunken fool, beastly, lie down now, iss no matter what she say. Drink up!'

'No.' Selanor leant forward in a miasma of liquor fumes. 'Iss when tha' Getaleen tried to kill her – you hear about that? Yes, well. I was commanding her bodyguard, and I . . . it wasn' even midday, not as if I were drunk. But I didn' . . . I should've put her on the ship.' He swayed dangerously. 'Haven' ha' drop of fire in, I don' know. Two months.' He tried to refill both their cups, but his hand was so unsteady he knocked one of them over.

Sassafrange took the carafe from him. 'You ress now I think.'

'Ress?'

'Ress, lie down ress, sir, y'are drunk too much.'

'Drunk?' Selanor put both hands on the table and enunciated carefully, 'I am not drunk.'

He was too sozzled to notice the look Sassafrange gave

him. 'Esscuse,' said the mercenary, and slipped the bottle under his cloak as he got up to leave.

'Ay!' cried Selanor. 'Bring it back!'

Sassafrange pretended not to hear. Selanor heaved himself upright, Sassafrange tried to pass swiftly out of the tent, but he ran into Polem in the doorway. The lord was waving his arms and crying, 'Lia! Lia! Where are you? Captain, sir, have you seen my daughter?'

Selanor caught up with Sassafrange and snatched at the bulge under his cloak. 'Gi'it back!' Sassafrange jabbed him with his elbow. He roared with rage and flung himself on the mercenary, who clubbed him over the head with the bottle. It shattered and Selanor fell to the floor. Blood began to stream down his face mingled with firewater.

'Sir!' cried Polem.

'Very sorry, very sorry, my lord – where's my lord come, my lord Ayndra?'

'Gods know where she is! What have you done? Is he dead?'

''E's drunk, my lord, 'e fight me, I am trying leave. Look, e's sidup already.' Selanor had raised himself on one elbow and put a hand up to his head. He groaned when he saw the crimson staining his fingers and fell back to the floor. 'You 'ave trouble, my lord?' Sassafrange enquired politely.

'My daughter, my daughter is lost!'

'You look in the dancers?'

'I cannot see her anywhere. Lia!' he called frantically.

'Come my lord, we are look in the dancers. We find her no doubt. Come now.' They left Selanor on the floor.

'Here you are, my lord. The milk is fresh, I saw them milk the cow myself. Would you like some bread? I am afraid it is yesterday's baking.'

'Thank you, Firumin. Perhaps you have a potion for a headache? It would benefit me more than food at present.'

'I will see what I can do, my lord. Will you be going to inspect the bridge this day? Captain Daiket asked me to ask you.'

'Perhaps later. I will sit here for now and drink your excellent posset – o, and Firumin, you have not seen Lia anywhere?'

'The moment I see her, my lord, I will send her to you. Most likely she is still sleeping.' Firumin withdrew before he could be treated to any more lamentation. The slaves had brought the three casks to the kitchen tent; one was still half full. 'Pour it all away and chop them up for firewood. Devil's juice that it is! I hope they have no more bottles of it with them . . . what is it? You can have no more breakfast, it is too late; get about your duty.'

'Master, could you tell me who is in charge of the patrols this morning?'

'Most certainly not.'

'But sir, we do not know if we are to go north or south— '

'You can go to the devil for all the concern of mine it is! Go ask Captain Selanor.'

'He's sick, sir. If you could— '

'Someone is blowing a trumpet over there, it must be they that you want. Go!' Firumin flourished his hand at the man, who turned away in a huff. 'Gods' teeth!' the steward exclaimed. 'Has no one any respect these days? Put it under the bread-oven and get the bellows to it.'

He decided to go and look at his stores. On the way up there he was accosted by Sassafrange. 'Where'ss my cask?'

'Sir, I know nothing of it.' Firumin tried to shake his arm free, but Sassafrange hung onto it. 'Tell me where slaves are put them.'

'Let me be, sir. If you still— ' The trumpets sounded again, much closer, and a wild yell rent the air. A single horseman, bent flat over his horse's neck, came tearing out of the trees to the south-east. As he came out into the open he sat up and drew a long sword but he did not slacken his pace one whit. The trumpet cries had been joined by shouts and the sound of more hooves, and then screams as the people lounging in the middle of the camp saw what was coming. They scattered to either side as the sword flashed out; several guy-ropes went flying, and the rider skimmed past the banners outside the King's tent, where Lord Polem had lately been sunning himself. He managed to snatch one of them and actually pull it away with him as he passed, his horse's flanks dark with sweat and blood from the spurs, and with reins and banner in one hand and sword in the other he was galloping out of the other side of the camp; but by then the rest of the pack had emerged from the trees. 'My lord's come!' cried Sassafrange.

'She has brought the enemy to us!' Firumin crouched on the ground. Others were fleeing through the undergrowth towards the high ground where they stood; loose horses were scattering through the camp, riders were pursuing one another with all sorts of weapons, and there was Lord Polem up on a horse, his bald head shining in the sun but not as bright as the sword he whirled. He could see the slaves cowering in the hollow behind the kitchen tent.

'Sassafrange, stand down! Do not let them see us!'

'Iss going over,' he said carelessly. 'Dead or running. Thass my lord! Her hair! How fine, beautiful.' He clapped his hand. Firumin burrowed into the debris of the forest floor.

'Sound the All Clear,' said Aleizon Ailix Ayndra, 'till you are sick of that; and then go round them up in the woods.' She looked at her bloody sword and rolled spit round in her mouth; she spat out a huge gob and sheathed it as it was, all bloody. She looked round as Polem came up behind her. She did not open her mouth. Polem said nothing either. She swung one leg over Tarap's neck and dismounted with her back to the horse. 'Bring everyone here together so that we can count them. Take up the dead and bring them here too.'

Polem's horse tossed its head and snorted while its rider desperately scanned the people creeping back into the camp. 'My daughter,' he said. 'I have lost my daughter!'

'Be patient, she will appear. I do not think they managed to take any captives this time.' Aleizon Ailix Ayndra accepted a rag from one of her scruffy companions and began to wipe her sword with it. 'Did anyone see what happened to the insolent bastard who snatched the waves of Safi?'

'Haldin was on his tail as he left the camp,' said Daiordeor. 'They went out of sight over there – who is that coming? My lord, it's Sassafrange!'

The mercenary was beckoning as he descended the hill, and men and women were coming out of the trees behind him. Others carried up three corpses and flung them to the ground. 'Is that all?' said Aleizon Ailix Ayndra.

'They were dogs, they fled as soon as they saw a drawn sword.'

'Ah,' she said, as she saw a fourth body, in a household slave's tunic.

'They must be barbarians, to kill a slave.'

'Indeed,' she said. 'Where in god's name is Selanor?' No one answered her.

'Lia!' cried Polem. He spurred his horse carelessly through the crowd. 'Lia!' His daughter stood stock still as the people around her melted away; she looked once over her shoulder, at a youth who had been by her side, but saw only his heels provoked by the sight of the horseman. 'Lia!' roared Polem. 'Lia, are you . . . where have you been all the night?' Lia looked up at him. Her cheeks flamed. Polem slashed the air with his fist. 'Mother of god! What have you done? Where is he? I'll kill him, I'll geld him like a hog, as gods are my witness. I'll– '

'Peace! Peace!' Aleizon Ailix Ayndra was hanging from his bridle. 'Your daughter is safe and well. You have not lost her. Why do you shout so?'

'Lost her? I have lost my daughter! Why she's, she's a– '

'Polem, are you not being hasty? Lia, come up and tell us that you are intact.'

Lia stood her ground. Her face was on fire. 'O, gods in heaven,' said Aleizon Ailix Ayndra. 'So you have slept the night under a bush, it is not the end of the world.'

'Not for you, perhaps!' spluttered Polem.

'What?' said Ayndra.

'It is written all over her face! You and your camp of sluts and whoremongers! My own daughter!'

Ayndra let go of the reins and walked away from him as though she had just seen plague buboes break out on his face. Lia cowered. 'And you!' shouted Polem. 'Go and cover your shame!' He turned his horse round and headed out of camp.

Ayndra took Lia by the hand; the girl was ready to howl. 'Come with me,' she said. A couple of riders came down from the high ground, and in a moment Polem was riding back where they had come with them. 'Firumin! God save me, Firumin, what has gone on here?'

Firumin glanced briefly at Sassafrange. 'My lord, perhaps we may speak of it later. Does the lady need care?'

'Take her to where Diamoon is and ask her to look after her for now. Have no worry, Lia, you can stay with Mistress Diamoon and all will turn out well. Thank you. Now Sassafrange!'

'My lord! Is it true you are the King in Safi!'

'Damn true!' She held up her ring hand. He fell to his knees and kissed her foot. She roared with laughter and gently kicked his chin up. In S'Thurrulan she said, 'I am not your King and Queen!'

Sassafrange crawled backwards and adopted a kneeling position. 'My lord!' he said piously. 'Your hair is a glory of the sun, your eyes are the living lightning, your movement is as the wind that bears the clouds across the vault of heaven– '

'Thou serpent that dips its tongue in honey! Stand on your feet and explain to me how I see not Selanor nor any of the officers in their proper place and raiders can invade my camp in broad daylight.'

'My lord, I did but arrive the night passed, and I encountered much bad order, but it was hardly my place to remedy it. Did not Lord Polem command here in your absence?'

'He did. But Selanor should have taken charge of it. Where is the devil's get?'

'My lord, the captain was exceedingly drunken the night passed, and I confess that we fell into a brawl.'

'He was what? He was drunk?'

'I think he is not used to firewater, my lord, unwittingly he harmed himself.'

'Firewater? And where in the seven hells did he procure firewater? I ordered that not so much as a flaskful should come into this camp.' She would have gone on if Daior-deor had not come up at a canter and made his horse all but sit down to stop. 'What is it?' she said. Sassafrange discreetly kissed his amulet ring.

'My lord, we have found Haldin.'

'Is he– ' She broke off.

'He's dead, my lord,' said Daior-deor. 'Lord Polem is with him already.'

She cried out once and struck her forehead with her hand. 'Can I come up behind you?'

'Of course.'

Sassafrange ran to take her foot. She looked down on him over Daior-deor's shoulder. 'You know what you have done,' she said in his own language. 'Go now and begin your reparations.' Daior-deor kicked his horse away.

Haldin lay on his back just as he had fallen. The blow had taken his head half off. He lay on top of the banner of Safi, its shaft broken and its canvas saturated with his blood. Polem knelt by his head, a handkerchief crushed to his face. The others stood some distance away, covering their heads and some praying. Aleizon Ailix Ayndra told Daior-deor to stop by them till she beckoned. Polem did not move as she approached. His right hand rested in Haldin's hair. The metallic scent of blood overrode the resin of the trees.

'Polem, let us take him up and straighten him. Close his eyes.'

'I thought you might want to look in them for the image of his killer.' He looked up at her as he said this. He saw her begin to hunch herself up, then reverse it and put on her stone face. He wiped his eyes with thumb and forefinger and flicked the tears away, got up and held up his hand to his entourage. 'Go fetch his officer's cloak to wrap him in.' He looked down his nose at the King. 'All this for the sake of your flag!' He kicked the broken banner.

'I never sent him after any flag,' she said. She squatted and took Haldin's head to move it so as to close the second mouth gaping in his neck.

'*Stop that*,' said Polem. She looked up. Her eyes widened like lamps and she breathed out softly as she rose to her feet, poised, her hands opening and one not quite touching her sword. Polem stood his ground. 'It will not do any good,' he said. She questioned him with her eyes. 'This is my son and I will burn him . . . my lord.'

'As you will. You have my condolences. My lord.' She made a curt half-bow and walked back to where Daior-deor was waiting. He took her back to her tent without her needing to ask. 'You know what there is to do,' she said as he let her down at the servants' entrance. 'See that everyone is accounted for, and set the tents up again. I will come out and show myself when I have it in me to speak to people again.' She patted his shoulder as she slid to the ground. He

287

watched her go in and urged his horse round to the parade ground. 'Gentlemen! Who is supposed to be commanding this day's patrols?'

She was sitting crosslegged on a narrow folding bed, a book unrolled in her lap; he coughed twice before he distracted her from it. 'Selanor,' she said, as peacefully as if he had come to see her for a chat before sleep. He held out the scarlet bundle in his arms and let it slide to the floor. She reached out and pulled a corner up, then let it fall. 'My lord, permit me,' he said, 'to resign every post I hold in your service.' She sat there rolling up the book and looking at the unsewn cuts gaping in the sparse hair over his crown. 'My lord, permit me to leave in the morning. I have my own horses and Andalda and Kerat will go with me, an you allow it. Captain Guldan and Captain Hourishay will take my place. Here is my officer's cloak. My lord, release me!'

'Who wounded you?'

He put his hand to his head. 'Captain Sassafrange struck me. We were drinking together and I had already lost my wits in the bottle. He thought it better to remove it. When I pursued him and attempted to snatch it back he broke it over my head. Thereafter I did a number of shameless things. Ask and you will no doubt hear of them. I recall nothing until I woke up this day morning in the pool of my own vomit with Hourishay and Daiket standing over me. They asked me who was to patrol, and I cursed them out of the tent. I had not even the strength to raise myself out of my filth when I heard fighting outside.'

'You did the wisest thing in the circumstances.'

'That may be so, but I had done so many unwise ones before it made no matter.'

'Do you truly wish to go?'

'I know what you want from me. I cannot any longer give it.'

'Captain Sassafrange owes you a debt of honour.'

'I have no honour left,' he said bleakly.

'Polem invited you to drink, Firumin told me so.'

'I had given you my oath that I would stay sober. Shumar's staff, you left the safety of our enterprise in my hand, and what have I done with it? You are kind to receive me like this, but I could not go into battle behind a man who I'd seen act as I did yesterday and this day. I cannot ask my officers to act differently. My lord, release me.' His eyes followed her like dogs as he spoke. She opened the battered travelling chest beside her pillow and took out an embroidered purse. 'No,' he said.

'Take it, man, Andalda and Kerat will need to eat. Where are you going to go? Polem is going away south as soon as he has completed the funeral, to Samala he says.'

'I'll make my own way south. To Caoni, to Kemmyss.'

'I shall be here at least until the month's end. Then the heavy wagons will go south, and I shall take what we can put on horseback to Haramin. I'm damned if I shall run away early for the sake of a few highwaymen. When the snow comes I shall be in Raq'min. I would not turn you away, Selanor. God knows I shall need someone to take the convoy down into Thaless.'

'Hourishay is a good man. My lord, I'm an old cripple. My heart is broken before I leave.'

She walked forward and laid her hand on his. 'If you ever feel it's whole again, you will know where I can be found.'

His mouth twisted. He bent to kiss her ring, and dashed out of the room. The curtains swung to and fro behind him.

'I thought you said the witch was mad,' said Meraptar.

'She is mad,' Takarem responded.

'Not so mad that she cannot follow us all the way to her camp, without we see her, and then just as we approach them at dawn, when they are all sleeping off their debauchery, she comes down on us. She is a very devil!'

'Most likely it was a devil that told her,' Takarem said, slashing at the stick he was whittling.

'And then what do you? Go galloping off to snatch a banner – which you do not manage to bring away even! – and leave the rest of us to face the witch.'

'You moved too slowly. We were all mounted and they had no guards. Had you moved faster we could have ravaged the camp.'

'And so we could have ravaged it, had you remembered that you are commanding this troop and here to order it, not to act like the hero in a romance. Merely because a mad witch calls you Lord Ailixond, do you let it go to your head?'

'So I am commanding it, and you do not command me! My lord father told us that we should harass the witch's people and leave them in fear, so that they forsook her while he raises an army in secret. What will terrify them more than that we enter their camp and even seize her banner? I know I lost it in the end, but I killed the one who came after me, and I believe it was one of Lord Polem's bastards.'

'They have put double the guard on all her camps now,' said Meraptar. 'And an you knew it was Lord Polem's bastard, did he not know you? We are supposed to appear as no more than bandits from the hills.'

'The bastard is dead now, and knows nothing.'

'But they are not all dead, and now they have guards in every part.'

'What do you mean? That we should go back?'

'I say so. Our purpose is to raise an army against the witch, not to make ourselves heroes.' His eyes creased up narrow and sly as his father's as he smiled at Takarem. Takarem gave a theatrical shrug and swaggered off towards the stream. Meraptar, still smiling, beckoned to the chief of the hillmen who accompanied them. 'The lord whose women we stole is making ready to go south,' he said. 'We Safeen cannot attack him because he knows us, and it is time for the master to return to his father. An I set you in charge to attack on your own, my man, can you do it?'

'Horsemen, my lord! Coming along by Pear Tree Bend, and armed!'

'God in heaven! Sound the trumpets, put the animals in the byres, and Parro, make sure Tissamë and the others are all inside the house, then bar up the doors. I will take the men-at-arms out. How many of them are there?'

'Not many, my lord, the fingers of two hands.'

'It is nothing, Father, must we panic?'

'Where is my leather jacket? Parro, we must drive them out, else a thousand robbers will follow after. There is no order in this land any more. My sword! Where is my long sword? And bring me my steel cap and the gorget. And the banner, we must have our banner!'

290

The banner had been made since they arrived in Samala, showing a golden sword on a purple ground; it was a response to the difficult journey they had done, but since then this was the first chance to take it out. Parro's half-brother Chirdarin carried it, and it was the first thing the raiders saw; there was a disturbance in their sparse ranks, and in a moment a second banner lifted there: a blue eagle on a white ground. 'I'll be damned!' said Polem. 'Lord Casik!' A couple more of the invaders were waving green branches. Polem told his men to put their swords up and headed towards them, holding up his empty right hand.

'Casik, my lord! I believed you had gone to Purrllum. What do you here? Are you going back to Safi?'

'Polem, my lord, I greet you; excuse this trespass on your estate, but I dared not send for you before I came.'

'It is no matter. Come back to the house, you are all welcome as guests. You should have sent a letter. We are always happy to receive guests, we have room and board for all.'

'I could not have written, my lord, for the danger of it; I come on a most secret matter. We heard that you had left the witch's camp.'

'That road is an ill-advised scheme,' Polem agreed. 'It will have naught but robbers all along it when it is done. Did you know that my poor son died in an attack on her camp? She had gone off to pursue some robbers, and left not a single guard. They seized her banner, that is the banner of Safi, and Haldin tried to rescue it.'

'I am dismayed to hear it. You have my most sincere condolences.'

'We brought his ashes back here and I am building a mausoleum. I believe she has gone away to Haramin now. I am done with her schemes, I wish only to lead a quiet life with my family.'

'That is what we all wish, my lord, but we shall have to put the witch out of the way before we can achieve it.'

'You ought not to call her a witch, she is not really one. We did elect her King after all.'

Casik said nothing to that. Polem gestured broadly, indicating the peasants' cottages, the orchards, the harvested fields and pollarded trees. Casik joined in praise of the good husbandry, and went on to pour compliments on the estate house, its lady, its rich appointments and delicious hospitality. 'Such a pity, my lady, that I can stay so short a time.'

'What?' said Polem. 'Leave next day? Surely not! You are welcome to stay a sixday, stay a month indeed, we are well supplied ...' Casik let him go on, but shook his head. When he had finished he said, 'I cast no slur upon your riches and generosity, but I cannot stay; I have urgent duties.' When Polem asked what they were, he asked if they might not have a private conference. 'I have some things I must tell you in strict confidence,' he said. When they were locked in Polem's bedchamber he began.

'You will remember that I asked the – asked my lord of Haramin to give me the governorship of Purrllum, and yet again she refused it to me. I had had doubts about her rule before that, and when I saw that quack healer whom she has to govern Haramin for her, and that gaggle of market hawkers who rule in Purrllum, not to mention all those vulgar mercenaries in her following – and then she sends Lady Ailissa as Ambassador to Suthine, and sells off half Safi to the Suthine barbarians, and then as if that were not enough, she makes Lady Sumakas Governor in Safi! I could not tolerate it longer. An we sit with our hands folded the whole Empire will soon be made prey for a pack of barbarians, witches and whores. So I left to seek out our most noble Lord Regent. You know that Lord Sulakon is not dead, though the witch would love to see him so? And Lady Ailissa, before she was drugged senseless by the barbarians, sent his eldest son to him, Takarem that should have been made a lord in the summer. They are together with Sandar's son Meraptar, who escaped the wi– the holocaust in the Needle's Eye, and now I am with them. The young lords discovered that you had chosen to retire to your estates, and I offered to risk my neck in coming to seek you out. You will understand that it is not safe for me to remain here while Sumakas governs in Safi. What I have said will, I think, convey to you what our aims are. It is your right as a noble lord to deny us all assistance, but we believe that you will understand our aims and, we hope, further them. I fear I cannot say more unless you give your word of honour that you will adhere to our cause, and extirpate all traces of Sumakas and the – the lord of Haramin in your following. What have you to say?'

'This is all very *sudden*,' said Polem. 'Let us have something to drink.' He went to the door.

'My lord!' said Casik. 'In confidence, I beg you.'

'All the servants here were born on the estate, I would trust them with my life. Some of them were killed by robbers too! O, and then there was Lia. A tragedy!' Polem sat down in the windowseat and related at length his adventures and misadventures in Pozal t'Ill, while a woman brought wine and crept out again, and Casik offered fulsome commiserations in between heaping blame upon my lord of Haramin. 'And then I heard of a party of horsemen on the estate. Maishis! I believed the robbers had entered even here. Then I saw your banner, and did not fear.' Polem laughed. 'Your cup is empty; take some more. I will serve you. This is our own last year's vintage. Do you not find it excellent?'

'Fine indeed. But I must ask you to come to the point.'

'I am not sure what is the point,' said Polem, 'unless you are asking me to join a rebellion against the King.' His brown eyes looked straight at Casik, who did not have a reply ready to that. Polem went on. 'My lord of Haramin knows that I am here, I told her so. My people are forever coming and going from the city, and Tissamë's mother intends to visit us. I can hardly go off into the hills! We all believed you had gone to Purrllum in any case. Has not Golaron gone chasing you there?'

'He may well have,' said Casik. 'Am I to understand that you do not favour our course?'

'As the father of my house I cannot go and live in a rebel camp. I must fulfil my responsibilities here.'

'We are not rebels,' said Casik, 'we are the partisans of good order and rightful government, and our cause needs more than fighters. There is much you could give us without leaving your house, an you only let our people pass safely through, allow us some forage, let your people take our messages to the city, and help us pay our mercenaries. You have said that you are in need of guards. Were you to go to Kemmyss and hire some for each of your estates, who would find it suspicious?'

Polem asked, 'Did you say that Sulakon is with you?'

'He is our commander,' said Casik, growing exasperated.

'These matters of state are difficult for my head,' said Polem. 'Perhaps, an I wrote you a letter – no, I cannot write, and you would not want such a matter in the hands of a clerk?'

'Indeed not!'

'Well, then, an I made an impression of my seal, you could take it to him, that is if you must leave next day, and he could send back to me.'

'What would he send?' exclaimed Casik.

Polem went on in his usual inconsequential manner. 'I was so surprised to see you where I had expected robbers, my lord, I can hardly put my thoughts in order yet, and, as you say, we lack the time to speak properly. I thought, an you asked Sulakon, he could write a letter perhaps, or send a secret messenger, to explain all about it. And then I could see how I could help you.' Casik's eyes were bulging. 'You have governed a province, my lord,' said Polem, 'but I am new to these matters, and need them explained as to a child.'

'What is there to explain? Either you are with us, or you are with the witch!'

'With the witch? Why, I am not going to betray you to my lord of Haramin, if that is what you mean. You are a noble lord, and I shall allow you to go in safety throughout my domains. I cannot promise more because I am lord of no more. Besides, you have not even told me where Sulakon is.'

'My lord, we are in hiding. We cannot give up our dwelling place unless to those who have given us their oath.'

'That is why I will give you a seal to take to Sulakon,' said Polem. Casik gave off a gasp like steam lifting the lid of a boiling pot. Polem rummaged in a sandalwood chest. 'Here you are! See, it has my name on one side, and my emblem on the other. Will you take it to him?'

Casik took the proffered piece of carved jade, and put it inside his tunic. He made a curt farewell and went to leave, then burst into an oath when he found the door still locked. Polem hastened to let him out and bolted the door behind him. He pulled a handkerchief out of his sleeve and flopped on the windowseat with a sigh of relief; he mopped his forehead and poured himself another cup full of wine. When he had drunk it he got up and went to look for Parro.

The constant downpours extinguished the tree-lamps as soon as they were lit; after a few days of it Firumin took them down and they were packed in straw-lined baskets to be carried on muleback. In any case there was no one left to sit beneath them; if they were not out patrolling the hillsides, they were huddled in some protected location awaiting the next raid. For the last halfmonth the tents were pitched in a horseshoe on the slope, backed up against the rocky shelf which sheltered the stores, but the enemy did not get bold enough to enter the heart of the King's establishment a second time. Early in Third Month they massacred an entire camp of surveyors to the north and a large party was surprised in the act of undermining a bridge on the road itself; that time they left three Safeen among their seven dead, picked off by Sassafrange's archers as they scattered. Sassafrange swore that one of the dead men had insulted his nose, years ago in a wineshop in Kemmyss; he even displayed a knife scar on the stiff arm which he claimed was of his own making. He had no idea what might lead such a man to be digging traps for wagons in Pozal t'Ill; perhaps he had turned highwayman and they intended to rob the vehicles delayed at the crossing. Aleizon Ailix Ayndra sent for a convoy of weapons to come up from Safi, so that everyone could be given at least a long knife or an iron-shod staff for defence on the journey home. She refused to give up the notion of sending the roadbuilders south while she took her household north where there were no more than pack-trails to travel along as yet; to those who suggested it would be safer for them all to go back to Safi, she showed a map of the Empire with the new road in prominent red, and argued that since such a route would undeniably benefit the settled lands, they should assert their right to travel along it in spite of the hostility of the unsettled peoples. 'When we come back next year, I will bring masons and architects and we shall build forts at the great river crossings. Then we shall be able to send letters between Haramin and Safi in a sixday instead of a halfmonth.' Sassafrange backed her up in all this, his gold nose glittering over her shoulder. He also gave lessons in archery with the long bow for those who desired to learn it.

'Issa nonsense,' he said to Daior-deor, 'in this time they are learn nothing; I am learn five years to shoot a man run in the trees.'

'Why do you teach them, then?'

Sassafrange laughed. 'Still they lif' up the bows, th'enemy see them, they aren' know issa nonsense, are they? An' I shoot a few them dead still. The Safin robber they all know the long bow, issa very killing weapon, since Lord Ailixond die of it.'

'Do not talk about Lord Ailixond,' said Daior-deor. 'He is dead, can you not leave him to lie buried?'

'My lord always talk about Lord Ailixond,' said Sassafrange. 'Someone tell me isser nem now.'

'In her formal titles. She never uses them.'

'Someone tell me other thing my lord an' Lord Ailixond.' Sassafrange paused. He read in Daior-deor's face that the other knew what he referred to.

'That is why I told you not to speak of him. An they hear their names, they come closer,' he said.

Sassafrange grinned. 'No wonder he're come then, they all speak him all the time.' Daior-deor shook his head. 'Why don' the Red Witch ex-or-ciser?' Sassafrange said with pride.

'Was it Firumin that told you this? It is a miserable piece of superstition. You should suppress the rumours instead of propagating them.'

'Iss many people!'

'People will believe anything. Most of all tales of spirits. Have you not heard the stories of how my lord was raised from the dead, or flew magically through the water of the Pogarrel, when Lord Lakkanar tried to drown her? We have enough fears in the camp without the officers going about saying the King is possessed of a spirit when she does no more than talk to herself,' Daior-deor said with fervour.

Sassafrange, seeing his mood, nodded and changed the subject. 'This rain go on, a hard time to go Haramin. Shall we not stay till it freeze?'

'Shumar, do not propose that to my lord! It has been hard enough to talk her into leaving by the end of Third Month.

Do you wish to march to Raq'min through a blizzard?' But he spoke in the mood of an earlier time, the time when they all sang love-songs, the time before Haldin died and Selanor disappeared overnight with no one to say where he had gone. By the thirtieth day of Third Month the road was sealed, the quarries closed and both caravans were on the march. Most of the armed men went with the southern cavalcade, by reason of its number and the slowness of the carts. It was a lean and diminished household that set out along the trail leading north. Still there was no end to the rain.

Diamoon rode in the middle of the party, under a waxed wool mantle that peaked over her head like a tent. Lia sat on a pack mule at her side and a third beast followed behind, loaded with no one to drive it; the soldiers said it was charmed and no one but the witch and her new apprentice touched it. All three harnesses had been hung with different sizes of brass bells that made a jingle constant as the rain. When they had to cross the swollen torrents Lia played upon a set of metal chimes and Diamoon sang while the soldiers who had to manhandle their chests across the stream made signs of blessing over one another. Sand, boulders, branches and whole trees bounded out of the rust-coloured spume, and the contours of valley changed overnight, but they lost no one, not even an animal, to the current or the collapsing earth of the trails. At night Diamoon always made a bivouac with its door facing the sunset and they sat up chanting to all hours inside; Aleizon Ailix Ayndra went frequently to sit with them. Sassafrange often rode beside them during the day, when he noticed a little plume of smoke issuing from the folds of Diamoon's mantle. They spoke together in S'Thurrulan, since Diamoon said she wanted to practise it. 'And why so, mistress?' asked Sassafrange.

'My fortune says that I will be voyaging east over sea in the coming year.'

'Eya! You will go to Suthine. My lord will send you as Ambassador.'

'She has an Ambassador already,' said Diamoon. She handed the smoke to Sassafrange, who drew on it badly and burst out coughing. He was irked to see the two women smirking at him.

'Perhaps you will tell my fortune.'

'I do not like to tell the fortune of you thoughtless mercenaries,' said Diamoon. 'I told the fortune of your Captain Hanno that was, and he ran onto a sword in spite of all my warnings. Then your Captain Daior-deor asked of me a conjuration much against my better judgements. My avarice betrayed me there; I shall not be induced to any more unwise acts for money.'

Sassafrange huffed. 'You could at least send away the rain, perhaps?'

'The rain keeps our enemies at home,' said Diamoon. 'In the water is our good fortune. Danger is when the cold weather comes.'

'You see danger in the winter?' he asked eagerly.

'Look,' said Diamoon, 'how much flatter is the land now. In a little while we shall be in the heathlands, and then we shall come to Gaba. Did you say you had left your wife in Gaba?'

'To Gaba she came to see it with me, but she is gone back to Raq'min now; her sister is there and we have a house in Raq'min.'

'I see! No wonder your nose is solid gold. When will you have your teeth put in gold and an emerald in the front one?'

'You will not tell me what fortune you have seen?' he said pleadingly.

'I have said I do not like to tell the fortune of you mercenaries.'

'I am not like Hanno, I will listen and obey. How do you say he died? I had not heard, I asked Daior-deor but he would hardly say. I think he misses him still; certainly he hides much sorrow in his silence.'

'As well he might,' Diamoon responded.

'Ay! Mistress, I am sunk for years in the provinces, I know nothing, I hear nothing; now I am come to court, yet no one will speak to me except to consign me to silence. It is the truth that my lord herself killed Hanno in mistake for an enemy?'

'I know not why you ask so many questions when you know the answers already,' said Diamoon, the more amused as Sassafrange grew angry. 'I will tell you truly that

I fear for us in this journey and the coming winter, and for this Lia and I sing every night and pray to the rivers, but I do not wish that you should go about scaremongering, and I will not cast fortunes upon the road. These are perilous times and many spirits are abroad. When we are within the walls of Raq'min it will be safer, but molest you me now and you endanger us all.'

'Molest you? Why, Mistress! I—'

He was interrupted by a distant sound of trumpets. Diamoon indicated in a theatrical gesture the direction from which it had come, and that he should go after it. He urged his horse on without saying farewell. She called out, 'And never worry! I have seen us safe in Raq'min!' in Haraminharn tongue, which caused his escort to snigger, and Sassafrange to grow florid in face and language. But the journey turned out safe as she had predicted, and they arrived among the green hills of Proper Haramin in a burst of autumnal radiance when they had all expected bitter frosts and the first harbingers of snow. Raq'min itself appeared like the painted cities of theatre backdrops, with the mass of White Walls gleaming above the huddled thatch of the lower city and the cream and ochre of the walls. There was an unaccustomed crowd on the road leading up to the East Gate. 'What, is it a festival?' said Aleizon Ailix Ayndra; but when they came to the crest of the last rise, they saw that people were leaving the city, not queuing to enter it, and they were all surging toward them.

'I think they have come to welcome us,' said Daior-deor.

'Either that, or they have declared the kingdom of Haramin a free nation once more, and issue to drive away the foreign tyrant!' She laughed, then flicked Tarap's reins. 'I shall go and find out!' The black horse took off like a comet.

Daior-deor shouted, 'Wait for your bodyguard!'

'Damned bodyguard!'

'Damn you!' said Daior-deor. 'Anko! Happet! Follow!'

They had to fight through jubilating crowds to reach her side; it seemed as though her prophecy might have come true, for they were all shouting in Haraminharn tongue and there was not a Safin in official garb among them. But the people hanging on to Tarap's bridle were leading him through the crush, not trying to bring down his rider, and the richly dressed Haraminharn crowded to kiss the King's hand and offer her their swords hilts first as the mass rolled back towards the gate where the banner of Safi flew. In the middle of all was a woman in a gold headcloth in a carrying chair borne by eight men, and built up so high she was clearly visible from all sides; when Daior-deor finally reached the King the two of them were proceeding side by side. The woman turned to look at him; the brooches holding her headcloth were three times as large as usual and studded with sapphires, and she wore so many precious necklaces they covered her like a breastplate. 'Daior-deor! Have you met before?' said Aleizon Ailix Ayndra.

'Do not tell me,' he said, 'it is Sassafrange's wife's sister.'

Ayndra hooted with laughter. 'No! It is the Lady Anuarl, daughter of Yourcen who was King here before Ailixond. She has come with these other lords and gentlemen to present me with the homage of the Haraminharn people. Fortunately for you, she has not a word of Safic. Allow me to present you – do you remember Haraminharn greetings?'

'Hardly a word. I have no skill at tongues.'

'Take your hat off, and I will speak for you.'

A fanfare of trumpets burst from the towers of the gate as they entered its shadow; the way was all of a sudden blocked by Safeen in the form of phalanxmen with full-length pikes, and a stocky man in an officer's cloak and a crested cavalry helmet. 'Gerrin!' yelled Aleizon Ailix Ayndra. 'Well met at last!' She hung over Tarap's neck to greet him and hung on to his hand when he kissed hers. 'What is . . . doing? I thought . . . was not let out to public occasions, eh?' she hissed, rolling her eyes at Anuarl.

'Fifteen nobles came to ask for it. Caiblin thought it would not do any harm. They believe that Haramin, incarnate in yourself, my lord, has taken the New Empire for its own, and they asked if Haramin could welcome you. Do you think we should have prevented it?' Halted, the crowd had opened a semicircle in front of the gate, and a line of maidens had begun a dance while the rest clapped and hallooed. The King's own party were marooned at the back of it all, but she could talk unheard in the clamour. 'Praise the gods that I have not any of the other lords of Safi with me, they would turn rabid at the sight. How soon may I go up to White Walls? Did my baggage arrive safely from Shgal'min?'

'More than safely, my lord, we have been piling up letters for you for a month.'

'Aah! Maybe I will stay and watch this dancing. Can you send some pikemen to let my people through? And bring me a lamp to light this with?'

The Safic welcome was in the processional way between White Gate and White Walls, with Governor Caiblin and his staff waiting to receive the King at the main doors of the palace. It took more than an hour to reach there from East Gate on account of the press of people in the streets. By the time she faced Caiblin, Aleizon Ailix Ayndra had lost all patience with formalities. 'A banquet? Gods' teeth, not another banquet. Well, an you must. Caiblin, can we not go off and talk in peace?'

In another hour she got her wish, after half the petty nobility of Pirramin and the Seaward Plains had lined up under the frescoes of Palagar to kiss her ring; not a castle in the hills, a town between Yiakarak and Great Droagon Sea but had not sent its delegation to honour the King. Finally they were able to retreat into the private apartments, to the room with casements glazed by tiny panes giving on to the garden. Anuarl had returned to her rooms tucked away on the far side of the palace and the provincial nobles had gone to look for their gold and furs for the evening. 'Home at last!' said Aleizon Ailix Ayndra. She fell limp as a rag doll into a chair. 'I never thought there would be such a reception, else I would have bathed in the river yesterday and put a silk tunic on.'

'I think everyone here is used to your lack of state,' said Caiblin. 'It does not lessen their love for you.'

'I wish I could say the same for the people of Safi. Always a passel of people there with naught better to do than criticise others' failures of dress and etiquette. Do you have such a thing as a cup of chabe and a light?'

'Of course.' He went out of the door and she heard him giving brief orders to a servant. Returning he said, 'You are going to stay with us all winter, my lord?'

301

'I hope so. If there are no excursions which call me out. Do you expect a peaceful winter?'

'It may be so; let us hope that the trouble in the west goes no further.'

'What? What trouble in the west?'

'Because of the drought in the grass plains. You must recall the report I sent you last summer?'

'I think I cannot have paid sufficient heed to it.' She propped her head in her hands.

Caiblin went on, 'It did not say much in any case, only that the pastures had shrivelled up and if it did not rain well this year after the snows had gone, then the tribes of the plains would be moving west with their herds and flocks. Gerrin went up to Pomoan while I was in Safi and fought several skirmishes with them on the edge of the cities, and we have not suffered the incursions there which we feared, but it seems now that masses of them are moving south, into the hills which lie between us and the coast, the region where Meraptar used to rule.'

'And that wittol Golaron has taken the troops I left him in Safi to guard against some purported threat in Lysmal!'

'He has done more than that, now that he has occupied Purrllum.'

Her answer to that was a shriek. 'You *have* been out of the way lately,' said Caiblin.

'Purrllum! How long has he been in Purrllum? Is Casik there? What does he think he is doing?'

'The last despatches we had from Safi said that he had been there when we passed through the Needle's Eye. That must have been at the end of Third Month. We expect more from Safi any day soon. It has been raining in the Land-beyond-the-Mountains too and everything moves slowly.'

'Deluge in the south, drought in the north, and folly on all sides save in this my faithful kingdom! Gerrin said you had a mountain of letters for me waiting.' There was a knock on the door and a woman appeared with a loaded tray. 'Yunnil!' Ayndra leapt up to kiss her, and they babbled in Haraminharn tongue. Caiblin sat down, patient, his hands in his lap. Eventually Yunnil left to return to the banquet preparations, and the King poured herself a cup of chabe.

'We have had some letters from Suthine as well,' the

physician said. 'People have been sending them here for you ever since Polem left Safi.'

'Letters from Suthine? Who has sent them?'

'From Lady Ailissa, from the King and Queen . . . a very thick one from Lady Ylureen.'

'Fetch it, fetch it!' She clapped her hands. 'O, and the ones from Purrllum, about Golaron.'

'There are no despatches from Purrllum, no official despatches, that is; it was the postmasters who told us.'

'What! He has occupied Purrllum, and not even written a god-cursed letter over it! My secretaries are all here, are they not? Ask whichever one of them who has least to do to come with the letters. Do you think he has even informed Safi?'

'I have no doubt that Safi knows, but the difficulty is for them to convey their knowledge to us. I wish that new road of yours had been built five years earlier.'

'So it might have been, had that pack of braceleted fools in the south put the good of the Empire above the pursuit of personal fortune. You must have had letters from Sumakas?'

'No merchant caravan comes from Shgal'min or Yiaka-rak without one. It would not surprise me an she began sending them through Pozal t'Ill. Even now she hardly uses the royal post.'

'I thank god for her ingenuity. It is a pity that she is not so clever at restraining the proud and incontinent as she is at sending messages through every part.' Another knock: two clerks with a satchel of letters, all sealed and sewn up in canvas. Ayndra dipped inside her tunic and flicked out the two knives. She made to toss one to Caiblin, laughed when he cried, 'Off!' and handed it to him in a civilised fashion. 'Are you ready to take a letter? Excellent.' She picked up a packet, slit it and tossed it aside. 'Ailixond Ninth of that name, Most Serene Lord and King of Safi, greets Golaron, Lord of Safi and her present military deputy in the province of the same name. I instructed you to go and search for Casik. I did not instruct you to go and occupy a city of the Empire which is already amply garrisoned and offering every proof of loyalty. I do not know what justification you have . . .' she looked at one packet and instead of slitting it, stuffed it inside her tunic and picked up another, 'for this action, unless it be some presumed threat from the former Lord of Cambar. Whatever it is, I and my chancery remain ignorant of it. I propose that you inform me straightway upon receipt of this missive what you have done, what you intend to do, and why, if you are not already returning to Safi . . . no, no. Scrub after "intend to do".' Seeing that Caiblin had finished, she reached out for the knife and broke into a smile; she put one finger to her mouth, arms crossed over her chest as if to cuddle the fat bundle in her tunic between her breasts. 'Ready? Excellent . . . what you intend to do, and how soon you will be returning to Safi. It may not have come to your attention that the tribes of the grass plains have been driven from their pastures by drought and are expected to invade the lands north of the Chiaral. An you have sound reason to remain in the south, then do so, but I shall expect you to ensure that Safi is defended whether or not you do so in person. You will of course keep me informed of all your moves and causes. Given this, what is it, fourteenth day of Fourth Month, in the city of Raq'min, in the four hundred and seventy-fifth year of the city. Thank you, Megelin. Bring it to me when it's sewn and I'll seal it. Now these I shall read later, and these I shall read now – go ahead, look at any of them, do you truly never open letters meant for other people? And this one,' she put her hand on her heart, 'I shall read in the bath . . . do you have a bath ready?'

'A bath? I am sorry, I had not thought of it. Do you wish a tub filled?'

'Please! Caiblin, forgive me, here am I sending you back and forth like an errand boy.'

'It is nothing; it is what you should do. Besides, it gratifies those who say I think myself a kingmaker, and in the end inclines them better to accept my rule.'

'Are you sure?'

'Indeed, for then they know me for the harmless lackey that I am, and can leave me to the tedious tasks of administration while they quarrel over orders of precedence and fight duels in the Morhalkor.'

'You have been permitting the resurgence of barbarian customs here, have you not?'

'They cause far less trouble than it would cost us to suppress them.'

'Indeed.' She had Sumakas' most recent letter in her hand. The packet held sheets of official paper and in their midst an unmarked leaf, which she plucked out to read. The equivalent of a tirade of curses passed cross her face. 'Ah!' she said. 'Those there are letters I may put in the archives, she says, but this is a private letter. She writes on it, burn this after you have read it, as she did on the messages she sent me in prison. Shall I read it to you?'

'Will it not break a confidence?'

'No, you must hear it. She says she has not heard from me in a month, that no one knows where I am . . . *Lord Polem came back from the forest saying it was infested with robbers and they had raided both his camp and yours. I pray that your silence is due to the remote and barbarous region into which you have gone and not a sign that you have been murdered by footpads* – she cannot have thought I was very dead, to write so! – *for I must have help from you urgently. I can summon almost no one to a council any longer. Polem is gone away to Samala and Haligon and Ellakon both gone to join him there and when I send to them I receive nothing but a piece of chatter with Polem's seal on it. He babbles of the wine harvest and the apples and I know not what all but I know there is more afoot yet I can do nothing. Then Golaron as you must know is gone to Purrllum and confecting some plot to seize the Needle's Eye for his son in Lysmal, I plead you write and deprive them both of office, the son most of all, the father to come back to Safi with his army, for the lords who still are in the city, I have only young men like Lord Antinar and his friends and when I send them to the old men they laugh in their faces and I have no pikemen to send for, Golaron having taken them. And of Casik we have no news. There is nothing but disorder and insolence among the lords here!* . . . She goes on at length. She pleads me to come back to Safi. The only thing she does not say is that she fears an invasion of ravaging horsemen from the north, for which I suppose I should be thankful.' She plucked Ylureen's letter out along with a knife, ripped it open and tipped out several bundles of smokesticks, one of which she lit. 'I think I shall take my bath now.'

She spent an inordinately long time taking it, accompanied by the witch Diamoon, Lia, a charcoal stove and a multitude of unguents and powders, while Firumin searched among the baggage which had been shipped from Safi via Shgal'min. Caiblin did not see her again until the banquet was about to start, when he received a summons to come up on the south walls of the citadel. She was sitting smoking in a sheltered angle, dressed in a scarlet ceremonial robe; her sword and belt lay on the ground beside her. He saw immediately the purpose of the unguents and powders. 'Your hair!'

'Wait until you see it under the torches.'

'Is that your coronation robe?'

'It is. I thought I should have more than one use out of it. I left the cloak and train behind. Will you have some of this?'

'Thank you, but no. Have you got the crown?'

'There is a crown here, is there not?'

'So there is. I had forgotten that.'

'Firumin will bring it as I go in.' She tucked her legs up under her on the seat.

Caiblin shivered despite his mantle. 'My lord, are you not chilled?'

She seemed not to hear the question. 'I am sorry for my exclamations earlier this day. I should have put things aside and looked at them when I was rested.'

'On the contrary, when you read me that letter – we must take action straightway–'

'No,' she said languidly. 'That letter. Ailixond says he used to receive letters like that from Sumakas every month – I know he did, indeed. She was forever accusing Meraptar of plotting to foment rebellions and conspiring together with whomsoever attracted her spite that month. I have had a falling out with Polem. I left him in command of the road camp while I went after robbers and he let it fall into a drunken riot, while the robbers doubled back and we only caught up with them just as they were entering the camp. No guards at all! And if that were not enough, his daughter Lia imitated her father's custom on such occasions, which provoked such wrath in him that he expelled her. She told him that since he had not followed good customs in getting her, he could hardly expect that she should follow them in later life. But all he could say was, "You are no daughter of mine, you whore," and would have given me the same name if he did not know to what it would provoke me. That was after Haldin was killed, the very same day. He left to take what was left of his family to Samala. I imagine he wants no more to do with politics and sends Sumakas naught but idle chatter for that reason. Do you not think so? And so he has a few guests on his estate, one of them is his own father-in-law after all; is that a conspiracy?'

'It need not be an innocent meeting either. Does Lord Polem know you have apprenticed his daughter to a witch?'

'She apprenticed herself. It is not as if they are strangers even. Diamoon was her stepmother for years in Drimmanë. Lia says she is her mother, and not that pretty child three years her junior. She plays with his other children, Caiblin, his wife. I do not know what he is thinking of.'

'It shows that he considers himself more serious than he did. You should not dismiss him out of hand, especially if you parted in bitterness.'

'Yet the mere fact of a gathering does not signify a conspiracy, and I will not be forced into fear with it.'

'That is true.'

'Is it time to go in yet?'

'It must be close. Let us go wait indoors. How can you sit here in that thin robe?'

She only laughed. As he followed her to the steps, he said, 'Ailixond says he used to receive similar letters?'

'Yes,' she said, as if nothing was amiss. 'I never paid much attention to them then.'

Caiblin nodded, and went on in silence.

'Is it raining again?'

'It is a deluge.'

'The seasons are all upside down this year,' said Caiblin as his servant took Daior-deor's dripping cloak and hat. Their owner coughed into a handkerchief.

'The damp gets into my lungs,' he said, 'I wish it would freeze.'

'Come and sit by the fire.' His sitting room had a wood fire with an actual chimney, so that the flames roared while the smoke was drawn away.

'What a fine thing!' said Daior-deor. 'The King has nothing but smoky braziers.'

'It is new made, the summer before last only. I contracted a master mason from Suthine. Our present King would think it sinful luxury to spend so much on a fireplace when after all braziers will serve.'

'They do not abolish the damp like this one.' Daior-deor's tunic steamed as he held out his arms.

Caiblin propped his elbow on the chimney-piece. 'I thank you for coming in such poor weather.'

'It is nothing. I lived in it for a halfmonth on the way here. No wonder that my lungs are full of water . . . thank you.' He accepted the mulled wine offered by Caiblin's attendant, who set up a pot of it over a box of charcoal and retired out of sight. 'What was it you wished to discuss?' His gold teeth caught the lamplight like temporary stars.

'My lord Aleizon Ailix Ayndra,' said Caiblin. Daior-deor raised his eyebrows a little and said nothing. 'I wondered,' said the physician, 'if you thought her mood had changed, let us say, over the last year or so; since you captured Safi from Lord Sulakon, say.'

'Her mood? Well, she is always subject to bad temper, as no doubt you know. I recall how around the time of her coronation . . . and then she used to have arguments with Lady Ylureen, and would be a black dog because of them. But lately she has been calmer. Even the saddest events, like Haldin's accident, do not cause her to rant any more. Or burst out in anger and throw oil-lamps across the room. She threw an oil-lamp at Lady Sumakas once. I was in the room, as god's my help, I hid behind a table. No better than a cheese in a commotion! No, I think it may be that it is easier for her since she was crowned. And, I might say, since Lady Ylureen departed.'

'You do not think she misses Lady Ylureen?'

'They were forever quarrelling. And then Ylureen's husband came. But you must know all this.'

'I do not; you must recall that I have been isolated in this province ever since my lord took the army to Shgal'min and on to Yiakarak. And then I saw her at the time of the coronation, but that was hardly usual circumstances, and then afterward she had her accident. She was hardly recovered from it before I took ship for Haramin. This last month, then, I have been with her as I have not for three years perhaps. No one is unchanged by time, no more am I, and yet I confess I find some strangeness in her which must be more than the difference between one who leaves as an aspiring rebel and one who returns crowned as the King.'

'Indeed?' said Daior-deor. 'What would you say it is?'

Caiblin described the bad news which had greeted her upon her arrival, and the few good reports which had arrived since. 'At first she was exceedingly dismayed, yet in a little while she was saying that it was nothing, that Lady Sumakas' fears were exaggerated, and that we should merely be patient and pursue our own ends.'

'And is that not the truth?'

'It is the truth that – for instance – we can do nothing about the tribes from New Hope unless they should actually invade our lands in force. But it is also true that she has damaged her position by leaving Safi. All very well to go away from the city in summer, but the King should be in Safi, not marooned in this backwater.'

'Is Haramin a backwater? To me it seems as rich and varied as Safi, Thaless and Lysmal together. We are going back to Safi next summer in any case. And I have always thought that in an Empire of this size it is sheer folly for the King to stay in one place.'

'There is more,' said Caiblin. 'She says of Sumakas' letters, "Ailixond says her letters are snow which never settle" – Ailixond *says* . . . it is not the only time I have caught her at it. Other times she will say, "Ailixond said" this or that. I do not think she knows the difference.' He paused. 'Perhaps for her there is none.'

'Lord Ailixond!' said Daior-deor. 'The gods' curse on me that I never met this paragon of royalty. It is the thing which irks me most in all my years in this household, that they can let nothing pass without harping back to Lord Ailixond. The years pass, but it makes no difference; it seems nothing is so great as in the time of Lord Ailixond.'

'But you do notice how my lord refers to him?'

'I notice it, but I confess that I try not to listen. I prefer to consider matters of the present day.'

'As well you might,' Caiblin said darkly. 'My concern is that my lord does not consider them as she ought.'

'Do you not think so? Safi is an oppressive place; I feel us all much better now that we are out of it.'

'But have you not noticed how much she talks to herself these days?'

'You are not about to tell me it is the first sign of madness?'

'No.' Caiblin sat down and poured some more wine. 'I am about to tell you that I have acted shamefully, by stopping to listen at a shutter when I heard voices inside. Or rather one voice. I kept harking to the second one, but I could hear nothing. I think there was another voice there that I could not hear.'

'Sir, you should ask Firumin about that sort of thing. He has been listening at keyholes since the age of six, he knows all there is to know about his lords' doings in private.'

'You are not going to answer my question.'

'I am a soldier. I hope I am a friend of Lord Aleizon Ailix Ayndra. More I cannot say.'

'You may be a soldier, sir, but you are not a fool; I pray you, answer me.'

'I do not know what it is you want answered. I know that there are rumours about that my lord is possessed of a spirit. I myself have now and then heard her talking to herself, just as you say, but I see her every day and she never speaks to me of spirits. I know that, as you say, our position is not perfectly secure, and we have had troubles since Captain Selanor left us, but no help will come if we, who ought to know better, go about encouraging others to believe in spirits. Sassafrange came and asked me much the same questions as you have, and I told him to abandon the matter. You are far wiser than Sassafrange; I am surprised that you pursue the affair at all.'

'If I may be so bold, the rumours also say that you yourself had more than a little to do with the advent of spirits to Safi.'

'That was a piece of arrant folly,' Daior-deor said vehemently. 'It has brought nothing but superstition in its wake. I do not know why I thought to do such a thing; certainly I shall never dabble again in necromancy.'

310

'Surely; but I wonder if you could tell me what Mistress Diamoon did, and what you witnessed.'

'Mistress Diamoon is an accomplished performer, there can be no doubt of that.'

'Do you mean to say she is a charlatan?'

'I think she is not at all a charlatan. I think my lord is a fool to abolish the laws against necromancy.' He looked into the collapsing kingdoms of fire as he spoke. 'Mistress Diamoon raised a spirit, and I spoke with it. It said to me, *I was Lord Ailixond of Safi.* But dead spirits often lie and come in false names. It cried out *Ailix! Ailix!* and then my lord came into the room and it escaped in a whirlwind. The room was set on fire and Diamoon all but died. I was sick for days afterward. God knows what kind of a devil she conjured! I paid her ten gold sols to do it, by which you can measure the extent of my folly. It would be best for all if the entire issue were forgotten. Do you not think so?'

'What else did the spirit say to you?'

'I cannot recall it now.' A log crumbled in a lava of glowing fragments. He said in a low voice, 'It said to me, *be gentle with her.*' In the still pause one could hear dishes rattling in the scullery down the corridor. 'There was another thing. It was when she was ill after Getaleen stabbed her. You recall, how she ran a fever for days.'

'Yes, I remember it well.'

'It was the night when her fever broke. I saw him.'

'You what?'

'You are the first person I have mentioned it to.' Daiordeor's face was flaming with colour, it could have been from the heat of the fire. 'For a long time I thought I had been dreaming, that I dreamt that I woke with a start and she was there talking to someone. She had been asleep, delirious, but there she was talking. I looked around for the other person. I did not see him till she called him to her, and then I saw him, he had a white tunic on and black hair, like this, he was going to kiss her. He was just about to kiss her, then he looked at me, like this.' He made owl eyes at Caiblin. 'And I stood up, without thinking about it, I know not what I meant to do but I knocked the oil-lamp over and all the oil caught fire. And when the fire was out, there she was, the fever broken. Perhaps I dreamt it all and only woke when I fell on the oil-lamp and broke it. After that I made Diamoon go and seal up his tomb, where we opened it to take some ashes. I put my hand in the urn – it was full of old metal, I cut my hand on it; I still have the scar.' He offered his hand to Caiblin. The cut had turned into an ugly purple scar.

'The lords all snap their swords and throw them into the king's pyre,' said Caiblin. 'You were lucky it did not turn gangrenous.'

Daior-deor only shook his head.

'You have not tried to discuss these matters with her.'

'Good god no!' He tossed the dregs of spices from his cup into the flames. 'If it is a spirit, then I brought it upon her. It is the very opposite of what by conjuring it I meant to do. I must have been dreaming. How could I see him? It is all trickery in any case, she makes you drink a potion and throws coloured powders in the fire.'

Caiblin got up to put some more wood on the fire. 'And that woman Diamoon is living here in White Walls,' he said.

'She wanted to take a house in the lower city. Sassafrange and I argued with her an hour and more, that if there were spirits abroad, then here she should be. My lord pays her wages, for god's sake.'

'Ah . . . so that is why I find her burning offerings up on the walls if I go up there late at night. She told me it was to teach her apprentice the chants.'

'We knew that she would purify any building she had to sleep in,' said Daior-deor. 'But she will not now admit that she has ever practised necromancy.'

'I see.' Caiblin picked up the poker and pushed the logs together in the heart of the blaze. 'Will she go to Shgal'min with you?'

'She has found an excuse to stay behind.'

'That is good news. I shall have time to speak to her while my lord is away.'

'Ha!' said Daior-deor, as though hopelessness were funny. Caiblin did not reply. His quiet, lined face looked reptilian in the firelight. 'Do you know that we've had no news from anywhere beyond Magarrla since Fifth Month began?' said the captain.

'Is that not what you are going to Shgal'min for?'

'I think we are going there for the winter festival, as we

were invited; and privately to see if it is true what the merchants' guilds claim, that Admiral Calabat lets his pirates board and seize all kinds of goods and then asserts that they were contraband and will not release them till duty has been paid. And what ship could sail to Safi at this time of year? It would be a very miracle if it were not blown onto the cliffs before it reached Magarrla.'

'No one has had news from the Needle's Eye. Avalanches, floods, landslips.'

'Forest fires?' Daior-deor said mockingly.

'Not at this season,' Caiblin replied. He looked round at the mercenary. 'Does my lord listen to your advice?'

'I thought that she listened to yours!'

'Once perhaps. But I have not been able to get any sense out of her for days and days now. I thought that you . . .' Daior-deor gazed at him without speaking, his mouth stiff in his pale face. 'Advise her to go back to Safi,' Caiblin said. 'Be damned to the Needle's Eye. Lord Sulakon took an army through the Pozal in the four hundred and seventy-first year of the city. Road or no road, it can be passed.'

'Why do you mention Lord Sulakon? Do you think . . ?' The question hung in the air.

'I know not what I think,' said Caiblin. 'I have nothing but suspicions and fear. She laughs when I try to tell her of them. I have not seen her so merry in years and I can find no reason in it. She relies upon you. Ask her to go back to Safi.'

Daior-deor nodded, but still said nothing. Caiblin's servant came in with some logs and asked if they wished for more wine. 'You are most kind,' said the captain, 'but I must go; is my cloak dry?'

At the door he said to Caiblin, 'I have heard your words. You can be sure that I will do the best I can think of.'

'Do not hesitate to call upon me for anything. I wish you a safe journey.'

'Thank you.' The rain had ended; with a clear sky it grew colder by the moment. He muffled his head in a scarf, and was quickly swallowed up by the dark.

'What in gods' name has happened here? You remember this crossing, do you not, Daior?'

'I remember that there used to be a bridge here.'

'I think there is still. Do you see that something disturbs the torrent over there? The bridge pillars, no doubt.'

'No doubt.' He watched her shout in Haraminharn tongue for their escort, who had plenty to say; they went down to the edge of the grey waters lapping in the dirty snow of the road. 'They say the trouble began last year, when the people upstream cut down so many trees for the iron-forging, but it was not so bad until the rains came this autumn and carried the bridge away. Have we brought any long cables with us?'

'How have they been crossing?'

'They have not. For twelve days now no one has been able to cross, without they go up almost as far as the Diroga.'

'Shumar! It is no wonder that there are no communications in this weather.'

'It seemed safe enough when we came this way before. We must have had the last safe crossing.' She commenced to chatter in Haraminharn again. 'An we can put a cable over the wagons will be able to cross on it. One can see from the tide-marks that the water is already lower than it has been. Where is Sassafrange? Sassafrange! Can you tie a thread to an arrow and shoot it over to the far bank?'

'But my lord, issa flood! Why don' we wai' till it go down?'

'Nonsense! We have not the time. Where are the people on the far side? May we summon them without swimming over?'

'Who are go swim in this water?' exclaimed Sassafrange when she was out of earshot. 'I hope she aren' fin' ropes er do it.'

'"Every wagon should be outfitted like a ship",' replied Daior-deor, in a reasonable parody of the King's voice. He raised one eyebrow at Sassafrange, who uttered something in his own language and rode off. Daior-deor went after the King.

The wagon creaked and groaned as they loaded it, but it ran silently down the slope and raised no more than a chuckle in the water as it rose up through the wheels and began to whisper, then trickle through, the floor. Waves slopped against the sides as they entered the current. The bloated sun could be seen sinking minute by minute behind the denuded hills, leaving an orange stain on the sheet of water the colour of steel. Purple dusk invaded the air. The men who hauled on the rope organised their gasps into a meaningless chant, as more and more water seeped into the body of the wagon and the passengers tried to huddle in the highest part, only to be ordered down into the icy bilges so as to spread out the weight. Daior-deor kept his eyes fixed on the further shore. 'There's a great party of people coming over the hill.'

'God send they do not want to cross now; it's night already.'

Aleizon Ailix Ayndra was watching the abandoned site of their last night's bivouac. Suddenly she jumped up and scrambled to the tailboard. 'Have we left someone behind? Is that . . .' Faces turned to follow her, but it was nearly dark. 'Ah!' she said, and then threw both arms in the air. 'Ailixond!' she shrieked. 'No!' The groaning rope on the upstream side gave one last wail and then burst like a harp-string. Ayndra was pirouetting on the very edge of the tailboard. 'Seize that rope! Hold it! Now pull, hand over hand!' She bounded into the middle of the crush and demonstrated what she meant. The wagon seemed to be shooting away downstream with nothing to restrain it, water flooding in at a terrifying rate. The torches of their destination were upstream of them now. 'Keep hauling, both ropes! Pull! Pull! Pull!' Suddenly the noise of the water decreased and they were swinging in towards the bank; there was a sudden bump and grind as the wheels struck the ground and then they were beached in three feet of water, with torches bobbing and shouting towards them. 'I think we shall have to wade ashore,' said Aleizon Ailix Ayndra. 'Who is first for a bath?' She bundled her cloak upon her shoulders and clambered over the side. 'Come, we shall soon be washed away from here if we do not go. Daior-deor, come after me, take my hand.' She ignored the people making witchcraft signs and continuing with their orations on all sides. Daior-deor gave his hand to the driver, and so they made a human chain through the current; before they were halfway over others had waded in to help them. The water was so cold that its touch was a numbing agony, yet as soon as they were knee-deep she let go of Daior-deor and went splashing off to attach some ropes to the wagon and haul it ashore before it was swept away. The rest of the victims hastened to hop and shiver in puddles of melting snow while a crowd gathered around them. Riders loomed out of the darkness in a chaos of torchlight.

'For love of heaven bring me some dry clothes!'

'Where is the King?'

'Did she come safe ashore?'

'What was it? The rope broke?'

'Someone cut it!'

'Here she comes now! The King, the King!'

Banners and crested helmets broke up the clutter of heads and voices. The crowd opened for her, boots in one hand, bare feet trudging in the snow; she raised the brim of her hat to the newcomers. 'Captain Gerrin! Have you brought us an honour guard?'

'I have brought you more than that, my lord. Rebels have entered the western lands. We have just received news that they have set fire to hamlets in Gaba. By now we think they have sieged the town.'

She tipped her hat further back and carelessly scratched in her glowing hair. 'Bring me my horse,' she said.

The armed men closed around her. Daior-deor found some untrodden snow and tossed his scarf down on it to stand on while he emptied his boots. He shouted for his summoner as he watched Aleizon Ailix Ayndra reappear mounted among the banners, but it was Sassafrange who appeared with his horse on a leading rein. The S'Thurrulan, after his feat of archery, had herded the draft animals half a day upstream to a place where they could swim across, while the others were occupied with the wagons. 'I tell you aren' go in those thing,' he said, as the King's cavalcade made off up the hillside towards the road. 'Wha' happen id? I see you go for all do-rown!'

'It was over so fast I scarce had time to notice. She knew it was going to happen. Did you hear her cry out? That was before the rope snapped. Do you think they will want to go on this very night for Raq'min?' He rubbed his frozen feet on the horse's sides.

316

'Why so?' said Sassafrange.

'Did you not hear what they said? There is a rebellion in Gaba.'

'Ey-ah!' Sassafrange set up a repetitive wailing. The Safic soldiers they rode among stared up at him, and some made signs against the evil eye.

'I must get on,' said Daior-deor, and kicked his horse with his bare heels.

Gerrin's men had formed a knot on the crest of the hill after the crossing. A couple of carts had already joined them, and the rest were loading and hitching up teams in the valley, a series of dark blots pullullating on the faint luminous expanse of snow. There was not a light to be seen in the sky. He turned back down the hill to look for his staff and dry boots and breeches. There was an immense hubbub of gossip and in the middle of it someone was playing a flattanharp. His summoner came tearing downhill as he was pulling his boots on. 'Sir! We are to ride for Raq'min directly.'

'I gathered as much.'

'Sir, what happened? None of us could see from the bank. Did someone cut the rope?'

'The rope broke at last under the strain. I think my lord knew from the sound of it, or from her experience, that it was about to snap; she acted so fast that we all came home safely, thanks to her.'

'It is not true, then, that . . .' Senkur looked from side to side, 'that she saw the spirit of Lord Ailixond cutting the rope?' He reached up to clutch the insignia he wore at his neck. Daior-deor remembered that the man was a follower of the religion of Yiakarak, the Deliverers. 'If Lord Ailixond was present, then he warned her of the disaster,' he said. 'That is what you should tell the rest of your people. Some snag or dead tree or the weight of the wagon snapped the rope.'

'Sir.' Senkur went on clutching his charm.

'Go and count that all our people are here and ready to march, then come back to me. And I forbid you to discuss any more of these credulous rumours. There is no spirit in the world that can cut a cable, do you hear?'

'Yes, sir.' Senkur saluted and hurried into the dark.

Daior-deor blew on his cold-clumsy fingers and began the slow task of lacing his boots. The melody of the flattanharp went on and on. 'Who can that be playing?'

'Master Hurigo found a blind harpist at the crossroads of Kurs.'

'He's in the quartermaster's wagon.'

'He's from Safi, he cannot speak the common tongue.'

'Just the same as I am, eh? I should have him to play to me.' Daior-deor stood up and stamped his feet. 'We shall need something to comfort us if we are to travel all night.'

'But you'll be riding off with the King, will you not, sir?'

'Us poor laggards need sweet music. You'll be on your way.'

'Enough of that! I shall not be leaving you until daybreak at least, else we'd all have our necks broken going at full gallop in the night. Now go and ask Master Hurigo to lend him to us for a while.'

'He'll not lend him to anyone, sir, but he says he's going to play for all of us. All through the night.'

'You do not know that they've damn well sieged the town. It's not the way of plainsmen, they prefer to burn and rob and ride on. God in heaven, I am a corpse on two legs. I am too hungry to eat even.' Aleizon Ailix Ayndra stretched her legs out with a groan. Caiblin remained with his hands folded. When he did not speak she opened one eye to look at him. 'Well, out with it, then.'

'You returned so fast we had not time to send a messenger to you. One of the garrison from Gaba reached us only this morning. He says that Lord Sulakon is at the head of the rebels. He saw the red banner with the sacred flame on it.'

'O *what*!' said the corpse, in enervated disgust. It stretched its stiff limbs again, then began to giggle, and sat up to the table where an ample supper was laid. 'Every dog has its day,' she remarked phlegmatically, and picked up the spoon. 'Caiblin, one of the quartermasters found a marvellous skilful harpist along the way. I think he is eating in the kitchen. Do you think you could ask him to come and play a while? An hour at most, before I sleep.'

'Of course, my lord.'

'And Caiblin . . .'

'Yes?'

'I do recognise the gravity of what you have said. I prefer to rest rather than to grieve over it.' She made a twisted smile.

He bowed. 'I'll fetch him for you.' The door closed softly. She looked around the room as if for someone else there, but saw no one anywhere; she shivered, and looked at the plate of food before her as if it were a pig with wings. With mechanical gestures she began to eat.

Caiblin tucked his hands in his sleeves as he hurried along the draughty corridors. There were many people about for such a late hour, but they all stepped aside and hushed their gossip when they saw him. He heard the flattanharp before he reached the kitchen. They were not even gossiping in there, let alone attending to their work; he pushed into the crowd before he was generally noticed. That was all that was needful to leave him standing before the harpist, who had paused with his hands on the string and his milky eyes raised. 'Sir?' he said pleasantly.

'My lord!' Caiblin bent down and kissed the musician's right hand. Hands all over the kitchen stopped in mid-stroke.

'Ah,' said the harpist. 'That is . . . you were Ailixond's physician, were you not? Master Caiblin!'

'My lord Arpalond! How long have you been with us? You cannot stay here. Lord Aleizon Ailix Ayndra sent me to ask you to play, but she did not tell me whom I was to fetch!'

'Perhaps you would be so kind as to lead me to her. I am as a lost child in this city.' He took some time putting his harp in a case that slung at his back, picked up a blind-cane and a little ragged bundle. 'Palo the blind harpist has all his goods. Let us go and see my lord.'

'After Sandar captured me. That was when it changed.'

Arpalond heard her before Caiblin did. He gripped the other man's sleeve so as to stop him dead and put his finger to his lips.

'Lakkanar tried to drown me, and I escaped. Then Sulakon wanted to put me to death, and he failed. That was twice I should have been dead.'

319

'Stay here,' murmured the physician. 'I will return.' Soft-soled steps whispered away down the passage. Arpalond put his hand out to the wall and swept his cane gently over the floor as he moved forward, until his hand encountered the edge of the door. Aleizon Ailix Ayndra's voice sounded clearly within.

'And then Sandar captured me. Now Lakkanar was a fool, and Sulakon an honourable man, but Sandar was none of these things, and I thought I was surely finished. You know what happened then, but afterwards – I have never been so shocked in my life! It was the day I thought I'd never see. Three times, you see. I should have died then.'

' . . . . . . '

'After that I knew that I was dead. And then it did not matter what I did. It would all go ahead anyway! It nothing matters what I do.' Her voice throbbed like the thick strings of the harp. 'All those people who rose up against their overlords in Drimmanë and Thaless. What did I do? I was a twig on the crest of a tidal wave.'

' . . . . . . '

'But I never thought it would be like this.'

' . . . . '

'O yes! I understand a multitude of things. Things I never understood before.' More footsteps in the corridor; a gust of warm air, a scent of woman overlaid by perfume. Caiblin's voice hissed, 'Now deny it! Listen!' The metallic voice within the room went on.

'Why you used to come to me in such desperation sometimes. Why you'd say to me you were so tired and yet you couldn't sleep. Why you used to . . . grip on to me so hard . . . Ylureen was forever on at me, why did you want him so much? And I said, "Ylureen, he needed me, in a way you never will" – but you do not need me now? Do you?'

' . . . . . . '

'And what were you doing at the river yesterday?'

' . . . . . '

'But I saw you walking on the water! You crossed the path of the sun. And then you drew your sword, and lifted it up, and I shouted, "Ailixond! No!" What were you trying to do?'

The woman was moaning, and reciting a rapid gabble

under her breath; her skirts tumbled across Arpalond's legs, Caiblin was struggling with her. She wailed softly, 'No! No! Let me go!'

Aleizon Ailix Ayndra went on. 'When I saw you in Diamoon's chamber in the palace, when you came down in a whirlwind and set the room on fire – and then when I was sick from stabbing, and you came . . . why do you bring fire? What were you doing on the water? When you said to me, *when the time comes, I'll be there*, Ailixond, what did you mean?'

'Exorcise him!' hissed Caiblin.

'I cannot!' squealed the woman.

'You sit there, you speak to me, so sweet, just as you used to be, but Ailixond, I do not think you show your true face now to me. There are rebels in Gaba, Sulakon has raised his banner against me, I saw you walking on the water – Ailixond, what manner of devil are you? Why were you with a horse in the forest? Was it you that Diamoon summoned?'

The woman screamed aloud. Arpalond did not move. His sightless ears caught the whisper of a sword as it left its scabbard. Aleizon Ailix Ayndra spoke in a high piercing voice. 'By Chainaron in the north, by Asharil in the south, by Hastarokl in the east and Hayburad in the west, by Shumar in the heaven and Maishis in the earth, by the father that begot me and the mother that gave me birth: I conjure thee, I conjure thee, by blood and the wind I breathe, I conjure thee – I conjure thee – show me thy face – or– '

Caiblin cried out, a heavy body fell to the floor, someone ran away down the passage as the door crashed back against the wall.

'What in gods' name– ' said Aleizon Ailix Ayndra, and then shrieked, 'Arpalond!'

'Put your sword up! Put your sword up!'

'What?'

'I can hear it. For gods' sake, put it up, I'm blind.'

'Very well.' He heard it return to the sheath. 'Caiblin, what is the matter? Are you hurt?'

'No more than winded, my lord. She has a kick like a mule.'

'Who has? Mistress Diamoon?'

321

'Yes.' Caiblin got to his feet and leant against the wall.

'Arpalond,' said Aleizon Ailix Ayndra. 'So you were the blind harpist at the crossroads! However did you come here? Did you come through Pozal t'Ill?'

'Not at all. Lady Siriane found me a ship to take me to Magarrla, just after you left the city. I have sung for my supper from Mirkitya to Haramin. I suppose you must have often made such a journey, but for me, why, I never knew what it was to travel without family or household, pleading with wagon-drivers for rides, being fed bowls of stew and left-over bread at the back doors of kitchens . . . catching vermin . . . I have learnt a multitude of songs too: would you like to hear one or two?'

'Why, yes! Come in here. Can you see?'

'I can tell the blaze of the sun in the sky at noon. Lamps are too weak for me. My right eye is stone blind already. In another year I shall be entirely in the dark. Is that a chair? Thank you.'

'You have come alone like this all the way from Magarrla? What possessed you?'

'No one molests a blind man. I wanted to make one last journey to the north before I settle in one place to write my history.'

'Your history?'

'Yes, the Acts of Lord Ailixond. You must remember how long I have been collecting material for it. I thought, an I visited you here, your people could help me find some documents in your archives. I know what it is that I want, but I must have readers to look them out for me.'

'You could have come with an escort.'

'No! I had a dream of being a blind harpist. Let me pursue it!'

'You do play the harp very well.'

'I have had a lot of practice since my eyes became too weak to read when I was alone.'

'And you came all this way when you can discern nothing at all?'

'No more than glows and shadows. In this light, nothing. I confess I recall the hills and dales of this land, and it saddens me that I cannot discern them any longer; I must be content with smelling the grass in the wind. And the faces of the people ... my lord, will you permit me?' His hand moved toward her face.

'You wish to see with your fingers,' she said.

'Yes.'

'As you will.' She moved her chair within easy reach of him, and sat still. His fingertips traced the line of her chin, the bridge of her nose, the lines around her closed eyes; slipped down her cheek, and came to rest in the hollow of her throat. She did not move. Her breathing was deep and uneasy.

He said softly, 'There are all sorts of strange rumours afoot in the town.'

'I know.'

'You know what they say.'

'Yes ... you must know too by now. How long were you there outside the door?'

'Long enough.'

She shook her head so that her hair brushed his hand.

'You must tell me what you think about it,' he said.

'What I think? Why, Arpalond–' Her voice caught in her throat. She said abruptly, 'I think that I have gone mad, but no one has the courage to tell me so,' and buried her head in his lap.

'Break it down,' said Caiblin, and stood aside. The slave raised his axe, measured the distance, and buried it in the panel of the door. The wood splintered in all directions as he pulled it out and swung again. In four blows the door was in ruins. Caiblin reached through to the bolt, undid it and stepped inside. The two beds were rumpled, the table scattered with dishes full of ashes, a charcoal brazier was still alight in the middle of the floor with all sorts of stained rags spread around it, but there was not a box or a bag or a living being in the room. It had been left locked from the inside. He cursed in Haraminharn tongue. 'To the stables!'

'Mistress Diamoon! Mistress, what are you doing? Are you leaving?'

'Master Firumin, I must go. I cannot stay here another hour, else it will be the end of me!' The steward had got

323

hold of Diamoon's arm. She tried to shake him off. 'Sir, release me.'

'No,' said Firumin.

'Sir, let go, else I shall strike you.'

'You cannot go!' said the steward. 'My lord needs you! Mistress, do not go, now more than ever we need you!'

'You do not need me. I have done enough evil here. I have raised that which I cannot put down. I must go make amends in another part. I tell you, release me, before I strike you!'

'Mistress! Mistress!' called a thin female voice behind them. Firumin looked round, which was enough for Diamoon; in a moment he found his arm snapped back behind him so sharply that he yelled, and then he was flying through the air. The shattering blow to his head thundered in company with horses' hooves; in a few moments the throbbing pain had overtaken the sound. He struggled to his knees and felt his head, only to cry out as soon as his fingers touched the side of it.

Caiblin found him there, moaning, stumbling through the frozen straw of the stableyard. He did not need to ask him what had happened. 'Firumin. Come inside.'

'We have almost four thousand men, all ready to leave in three days now. An the rebels are more than that, most of them are not trained, nor does it seem that they have many weapons beyond billhooks and slings. I only wish we had some news from Safi.'

Aleizon Ailix Ayndra passed the pipe to Daior-deor. He drew on it before he replied. 'Does not Lord Arpalond know what has been happening in Safi?'

'He has not been in Safi for months. Besides, he says he has no concern in the politics of the present day. He came here to look for old records of the time of the conquest and before.'

'Indeed? I believed he must be on a secret mission, that he came in disguise.'

'No mission beyond that of his own imagination,' Ayndra said calmly. She tipped ashes from the dead pipe and refilled it from the crumbled resin by her side. 'I would have lent Diamoon to him to help him in his quest, an she'd not disappeared.'

'He'll stay behind when we go into the field, then.'

'No. I think he wishes to travel with us. I never expected to see so many volunteers for a campaign in the dead of winter.'

'You are very well beloved here, my lord.'

'In spite of everything.' She looked up at him as she fitted her mouth to the open top of the pipe.

He grinned as she was enveloped in a blue cloud of smoke. 'In spite of everything,' he said.

The western upland stretched out in a glittering plain under the flawless sky, its whiteness broken only here and there by clumps of trees distorted by the constant wind, dry-stone walls half buried in snowdrifts, cottages whose thatched roofs came down almost to the ground on either side and whose smokeholes sat cold and empty for fear of the armies. The King's quartermasters gave out biscuit and salt meat to anyone who came asking for it; many of the refugees turned back in their tracks and joined the fat dark snake crawling over the frozen land towards their ravaged hamlets. It was a slow harsh journey, with the wind sending icy spicules skittering over the ground like handfuls of dry sand on a beach, and nothing but salt pork boiled in melted snow for supper. People slept piled together for warmth, or bedded down between the draught oxen if they could. The King's scouts reported that the enemy were no more numerous than they were, that many of them were wild men out of Pozal t'Ill who went about robbing every house they came upon, that the mass of them were still encamped around the mud walls of Gaba. The vanguard was some thirty miles, or two days' march at the army's encumbered pace, from the town when they saw a great blot of smoke in the icy-clear distance, and knew that for the besieged they were too late. In a couple of hours they reached the escarpment at the edge of the shallow valley of the Ullbi river, and the sack of Gaba was laid clear to their eyes. Aleizon Ailix Ayndra ordered the wagons to make a defensive square behind the crest of the slope, and the infantry and camp-followers to stay within it, while she took the cavalry out to look at the enemy. The town was still on fire; the farsighted could detect little knots of people scattering on the tracks leading

325

away from it, some pursuing and others pursued, some beyond fleeing anywhere now.

'A tragedy for the town, but a gift to us,' she said. 'I feared they'd take the town, then shut themselves up in it and we'd have to siege them in turn; but it seems they have nothing but rapine in mind. Let us break up into bands and go harass them a little, and in the end we shall draw them up on the hillside and our main body will put paid to them there. Can you see banners anywhere, flags? Can you see Sulakon's banner?'

'I can see somewhat on the walls, over the gate, my lord . . . no, there is too much smoke, I cannot tell what it is.'

'Make sure you are content with skirmishing. We are not ready for a pitched battle now. Next day, or the day after, we will draw them to battle. Then we shall be a sledgehammer; now we are a swarm of wasps. And take the banners, scatter them about. I want that they should know who has come after them.'

Daior-deor had been awarded Selanor's place as chief infantry commander, since Gerrin was as he always had been at the head of the cavalry; but he left Daiket in charge of the camp and joined Sassafrange's troop to go out looking for the enemy. The S'Thurrulan was wearing a felt mask he had made himself; he claimed that it eased the snow-glare in his eyes and concealed his nose, which he seemed to believe an infallibly attractive target. When Daior-deor saw it he told Senkur to go and fetch a black banner. 'Else they will take us for a pack of highwaymen, no more.'

'Who?' said Sassafrange. 'Are 'ighwaymen?' He took a swig from a flask.

'You, sir, you look like a brigand in that mask.'

'Yah! I're brigand, you're pirate. Issa teeth. Before, sir, y'always look liker boy; now are look liker pirate.' He handed the flask to Daior-deor, who swallowed and passed it on. Sassafrange laughed. 'Are dring li' pirate too!'

'We may all be pirates before long,' his captain returned. 'Are all ready? Forward!'

The valley which looked so level from above was as lumpy as an ancient mattress on the ground, a maze of false hills piled out of snow, concealed walls and unexpected drops; ideal country for skirmishing. Daior-deor directed his little company along the most secretive routes, towards the maleficent cloud that still billowed over the sacked city. Twice they came upon parties of refugees crouching in abandoned farmyards; mostly they ran away screaming before they could come up on them to tell them that they were friendly and that they should go up on the hill for food and shelter. After the second encounter he told his men to proceed with care, for the next group they tripped over might not be so harmless. A little while later he smelt woodsmoke, and then a distinct whiff of roasting meat. 'Hush! Now let us see if we can ambush them. Leave the horses here . . . softly, now.' Voices floated in the current of aromas; mostly local dialect, he could not tell whether of the forest or the uplands, but one or two very clear in Safic. The snow crunched under his hands and knees as he lifted his head; and then he froze. The other was hacking a leg off the sheep carcass roasting over the fire; he pulled it free and bit into the blackened skin with a white flash of teeth. He was muffled up in a dark blue cloak but the black hair, the straight nose, the eyes . . .'

'Yayi-i! Chusa! Chusa! Chusa!'

'Haramin!'

The leg of mutton fell into the ashes as its owner whipped out a long sword. The rest of his men were already running. He met the first of the Haraminharn and went straight past his guard; in two slashes the man was dead and the blue cloak leaping up the far slope towards the tethered horses. An arrow thrummed past Daior-deor's head and one of the enemy threw up his arms with a yell; Sassafrange gave a joy-cry. Daior-deor broke out of his paralysis and scrambled to his feet. 'That one! Shoot that one!'

The S'Thurrulan snarled at him and fitted another arrow to his string, but the other had severed his horse's tether with one blow of his sword and was already away. Sassafrange shot the tardiest of his followers and lowered his bow with a sigh of satisfaction. He gave Daior-deor a snide look. 'Wha'happen you, sir? A long time you aren' in a battle perhaps?'

The rest of their party was converging on the remains of the sheep, rejoicing at the prospect of fresh meat. 'No,' said

Daior-deor. Sassafrange shrugged, and hung his bow over his shoulder again to trudge towards the fire. Daior-deor pulled his glove off and looked at the purple scar on his hand. Did he imagine that it itched? He scratched it anyway.

'Sir! Look what we have! Sir!' Senkur was struggling through the snow, waving a broken-shafted red banner. He spread it out to display the golden emblem. 'Look, sir!'

'O. Yes,' said Daior-deor. He recalled himself to his responsibilities.

'Sir,' said Senkur. 'Are you well, sir?'

'A goose has walked over my grave. Let us take this meat and go back to the King. I'll be bound she'll give you a gold sol for that banner. Was it you that found it?'

He must have looked distracted when Senkur came up, for the summoner kept at his side all the way back to the camp, even after Aleizon Ailix Ayndra had given him the predicted gold sol; she had apparently done for half a dozen of the enemy by her own efforts, but they had not got near any banner. 'Was it Sulakon himself that you came upon? It must have been one of his captains at least.' It was almost dark; they were standing on the skyline in front of a line of flags, trying to discern whether the enemy were making camp beside the city or were moving off and in what direction.

'I do not know who it was,' said Daior-deor.

'I wonder if we should send him a herald and challenge him to a pitched battle.'

'You wish for a pitched battle?'

'Yes!' she exclaimed. 'And I want it now. God curse it! I will challenge him. A formal challenge, he cannot refuse it, however poor and disorganised his forces. I should have put him out of the way years ago! I cannot wait any longer!' She took off at a run, shouting for her heralds. Daior-deor drew the sign of blessing, secretly, under his cloak.

'Look at that miserable excuse for phalanx! They cannot even dress their line now, how will they be half an hour into the action? We shall eat them up! Daior, you are so silent; have you had an evil dream of this conflict?'

'No, my lord, not at all.'

328

'My lord, the priests are here, they wish to bless our men. Will you allow it?'

'Ay, must they do it?'

'The Deliverers are crying out for it, my lord.'

'Then I suppose I must let them have it. Tell them to make it rapid. Ikindur, what is it?'

'My lord.' The man was out of breath, dirty, and exhausted; he stood blinking at her out of a sunburned face. 'Where have you been?' she said. 'The rest of your hobilars came back days ago.'

'I was lost, my lord. But after I lost them, I found . . . the enemy . . . a great army marching toward us . . .'

'But the enemy are here. They are drawing up their battle line at this very moment. Look!'

'O, my lord.' The man looked ready to weep. 'It is another enemy, then. Not them at all. They had . . . a purple banner, with a sword, or something on it, I did not get close, there were thousands of them.'

'What? Where were they? Where were they going?'

'I know not, my lord, I was lost, I rode away north, I did not know . . . only when I came upon our trail, that we had left behind, then I followed it . . . and caught up . . . is that the enemy?'

'Another army?' Gerrin exclaimed.

'I've had no food for three days,' Ikindur said faintly.

'What sort of army?' Ayndra demanded. 'A Safic army?'

'They had phalanx. I saw them marching. And horsemen. All in mail. Helmets and shields. And packhorses, I never saw so many in all my days, more than the summer fair in Raq'min.'

'Purple banners!' She scratched her head. 'Lakkanar had a purple banner; but he's dead, and left no heirs . . .' Ikindur swayed on his feet. She told one of the trumpeters to take him back to the camp and give him a hot meal, then find out all else that he knew. 'Gods' teeth! We have been so slack these last days. I have been slack, thinking all the danger was here under my eyes. Whoever uses a purple banner?'

'My lord! The enemy are nearly out in their line.'

'And so are we, Daiket, never worry. Why do you not go and take up your place. Daior, I am going to go and ride

329

along in front of the line before we engage; will you come with me?' She was fully armed, save for her helmet; Firumin had sat up half the night burnishing all her mail until it was like a mirror. 'Daior, say something.'

'I'll come with you, my lord.'

She appeared in front of the line as the priests were completing their aspersions. Sulakon's forces were drawn up on the other side of the stretch of open ground above the valley which they had chosen so that it should be a fair fight, no advantage of ground to either side. When they saw her, the enemy started to shout and bang on their shields, and a couple of horsemen dashed out in front of their line; the soldiers of Haramin shouted in reply. In the racket there was no space for exhortatory speeches; she rode up and down the line with her sword held high. 'Look! There he is, my beloved half-brother. Who is that by his side? Gods' dog, I wish my eyes were better. Can you see?'

'It looks like– ' said Daior-deor, and broke off.

She pulled up Tarap dead in his tracks. 'Can *you* see him?' she said.

'I saw him yesterday! That was who we took the banner from!'

'You took the – aah!' She screamed aloud and struck her forehead with her mailed fist. 'That's Takarem! It's not Ailixond, it's his goddamned nephew! Takarem! I have lost my mind! I saw him in the forest, gods' teeth, when you were burning that woman I met him and I talked to him and I thought – aah! God in heaven, I deserve to die!'

'No!' cried Daior-deor. 'You cannot die!'

'I shall die fighting, that's for sure. You thought you saw him?'

'I saw him before, in Safi, when you were ill, he was going to kiss you when I knocked the lamp over.'

'Takarem?'

'No, Ailixond.'

'You saw– ?' She lowered her hand. 'O, Daior,' she said gently.

'You are not mad,' he said. 'I care not what they say about you.'

'Daior.' The black horse crowded up against him and in the sight of two armies she put her arm round his neck. 'I'm sane now, that's for certain.' She kissed his mouth. 'They're going to places now, we must go.' The black horse had been shifting uneasily all the while; as soon as she touched his sides with her spurs, he was off like an arrow. The soldiers cheered. Daior-deor did not catch up with her till she was at the head of her cavalry squadron; a couple of message-riders just beat him to it. 'My lord! Message from Captain Gerrin! The enemy, they're coming up over the hill!'

'What enemy?'

'Over there, my lord, look!'

She looked. The whiteness of the far horizon was disrupted by a dark shimmer, a prickle, as it might be horses or men or swarming phalanx points. She did not even utter an oath. 'Go to your places as assigned,' she said. 'We shall engage with this our enemy that face us proximately. The other is far away, and we do not even know that they will attack us. Let us take Lord Sulakon and then we will defeat the others. We must fight now. That is my order to all of you. Do you understand? Trumpeter! Sound the advance! Where is my shield, my helmet? Quick! Phalanx forward, advance — sound for it!' As her armour-bearer came running up with her helmet and the new shield with the waves of Safi enamelled on it, she saw Daior-deor. 'Daior! What are you doing? You are supposed to be in the line!'

'Who is going to guard your back?' he said.

She was hastening into her helmet, fumbling the chin-strap; she cursed. 'All these men will guard my back! Daior, I need you down there, go!' Still he lingered. She finished with the helmet and pushed her arm into the straps of the shield while the black horse danced in place. 'That is an order! Go!'

'My lord.' He crowded his horse up against her and looked right into her eyes. She did not flinch, she pulled the last buckle tight and seized his hand. 'Your men are advancing without you.' The winter light showed up all the lines in her face.

'All right.' He did not let go of her hand. She did it for him.

'You damn fool!' she said. 'Now go! And Daior — remember, that stands to the death have never been part of your contract.'

331

'Contract—'

'Neither for love nor for money. Now go!' She kicked her spurs into the side of his mount. It reared, and bounded away.

He was halfway to his proper place before he had a chance to look back: one helmet among dozens under the banners. The trumpets were sounding and the phalanxmen were advancing at a slow march while Sulakon's men moved towards them. He fell into his place just before the leftmost battalion. Senkur ran up beside him. He said, 'Sir!' Then he saw the glittering tracks of the tears on his master's face, and trotted silently beside him.

Aleizon Ailix Ayndra rounded on her own messengers. 'I want you to find out who it is over there and whose side they are on,' she said calmly. 'An they are ours, tell them to hurry and join us. An they are Sulakon's, then kill any of them you lay hands on, but for god's sake let me know which it is!'

They saluted and galloped away. She turned her attention to the battlefield as the phalanx points swung down into the attack position. The cavalry began to go forward at a walk so as to maintain the dressing of the line. A flight of arrows sang through the air, and she heard cries from the enemy side: Sassafrange's men were doing their work. The stretch of untrodden snow between the two ranks of sarissas grew narrower and narrower. 'Haramin! Haramin!' The strange army in the distance seemed to be coming closer with abnormal speed, but still too far to distinguish the banners. The two lines of phalanx rolled into each other with an almighty crash and the familiar riot of battle began; her light-armed troops ran between the files with a long knife in each hand, ducking in under the close-packed spears to stab the men who bore them, others were spitted on the enemy's weapons and held up by the press around them, each side tried to get its spears swinging from side to side or at least to dig the butts into the ground, but Sulakon's cavalry were still holding back; she could hear their chant, two syllables, it must be, 'Safi! Safi! Safi!' Her own people should be shouting that, not, 'Haramin!' but what did it matter? Gods' blood, the strange army were coming on at a rate, and they were purple banners, purple, purple . . .

'My lord! It's Lord Polem! Lord Polem's leading an army against us!'

'Polem?' she said. For a long moment she was without words. She looked at the battlefield. 'Polem! So much for love and affection.' She drew her sword and held it up. 'Gentlemen!' she cried. 'We are besieged from all sides. We have only one hope, that we can destroy Lord Sulakon and drive his men away in disorder before Lord Polem reaches us, and then he may forsake his rebellion ... are you ready?' They shouted in reply. She said to her trumpeter, 'Sound the charge; then sound the general assault, and keep on sounding it till you have no more reason. Are you ready?' She lifted her sword above her head and looked back along the wedge of horsemen whose point she was. 'CHARGE!'

They rammed straight into the side of Sulakon's phalanx, crashing through the light-armed hillmen beside it; as soon as his men heard the trumpet signal they too charged, and in moments the two lines had dissolved into a bloody mêlée around the two opposed blocks of phalanx. The King's blue and black banners were seen among the spears, moving slower all the time, then halted, then collapsing, tumbling into the whirlpool, rising again, falling ... falling ...

White feathery bars of cloud crossed the pale blue sky. They looked very still and far away and nothing moved beyond them, in the deeper blue, where even more distant skeins of cloud lay, like teasings of wool in the sky. Some time after she started looking at them a ragged black thing passed across her field of vision, then it returned to stillness. After a while two more black things passed and one gave a harsh cry. Another such cry sounded close at hand. She turned her head to look at it and realised that a heavy weight pinned her lower body and legs to the ground. The ragged thing, it was a crow, hopped over another black mound that obstructed her view to the side. She squinted at it, then raised her arms to push herself upright, but one was trapped in her shield which lay half under her dead horse's head. The black mound was Tarap's belly and he was lying on her legs. She moved her free arm over, pulled the gauntlet off with her teeth and blew on the clumsy fingers until she

333

could feel her way out of the buckles on the shield straps. The crow perched on Tarap's head and began to pick at his eyes. Hooves sounded and she lay still. Out of the corner of her eye she saw two riders pass, dragging a third figure between them. The third was screaming; it frightened the crow which fluttered away, but it, or another, soon returned. Someone must have ripped Tarap's belly open and the guts had tumbled out; she was lying in a pool of them, congealed blood smeared her hand. Surely the appalling pain was due to her trapped legs. She could not even move them to see if they were broken. She decided to try turning over, if that would make it any easier. She was lying in the middle of a field of filthy snow and corpses, bathed in the luminous low light of late afternoon. More horsemen passed at a distance; they did not look like hers. As she wormed over on to her belly she felt a stabbing pain in her side and a rush of hot liquid; she put her hand there. It came away warm and wet with brilliant blood. She pulled the soaked folds of her cloak away. The shining mail was coated in red and black blood and pressed and mangled into a great hole; like the one that Getaleen had made, but many times bigger. 'Ah,' she said. It went on bleeding as she got to all fours, tried to stand on her numb legs, and fell over again; she bundled her cloak up over it, undid her sword belt and buckled it over the soaked wool so as to press it into the hole. Then she began to crawl forward among the litter of bodies, until she found a dead phalanxman lying on top of his pike. She opened the joint linking the two sections, removed the one with the blade and jammed it into the snow; hand over hand she climbed up it until she was standing. Now she could see that there were a few others wandering over this plain of desolation, one or two couples bearing bodies away, but mostly bent figures looking for jewels and money among the dead. None of them paid any attention to her. After a while she discerned the place where her camp was; the wagons were still there, or some of them at least. No one seemed to be fighting any more. She pulled up her half-pike and set out on the laborious journey towards them.

Ogo crouched under the baggage wagon with his bundle of goods by his side. Fortunate that it had not been seized in the mad rush to escape once it was clear that the King was dead and Lord Polem intended to seize the victory; unfortunate that he had not had time to find a horse, or someone who would take him on theirs. Polem's men might decide to come and loot the camp – not knowing that its own people had already looted it as best they could – at any time; or had they gone off in hot pursuit of the mercenary captain and the remnants of the cavalry? Perhaps they would not come back at all. Perhaps they would come back and kill everyone they found. Perhaps if they found him they would at least put him in a cart to go somewhere; else he would have to cross this deserted land on foot, and in the depth of winter too, with no more than a bit of salt pork and some weevilly biscuits. He should have run away with the rest of them; now he had not so much as a travelling companion, and Yunnil and the children left behind in Raq'min with who knew what to follow. It might be best to stay in the camp this night at least, and make a fire to keep warm; but then someone might see the smoke, and come and kill him . . . or offer to take him to Raq'min . . . his thoughts chased one another like gnats over a summer pond while the short winter daylight seeped away. When he saw that the western sky was turning gold he started to shuffle out from under the cart, and then he saw someone coming and ducked back under it. The helmet showed that it was a soldier; no red cloak, not an officer; a half-pike, a phalanxman? No, the pike was being used as a staff, not a weapon. He backed behind the wheel, watching. The someone was sick, or wounded, from the way they walked; the first wagon they reached, they fell against it, dropping the pike and gasping for breath. As they tipped their face up he saw who it was. He waited, still, until she was by the next cart; she fell down on all fours, clutching her stomach and gasping in pain. He scrambled out into view. 'My lord!'

'What? Ogo!' The tormented lines of her face dissolved into a smile. 'Ogo! Why are you here? You must run away!'

He knelt down beside her. 'No! I'll stay with you, my lord. They've all run away, but I'll stay with you!'

'No,' she said. 'Look.' She pulled the improvised dressing away from her wound and heard him gasp. 'Yes,' she said. 'Ogo, I shall die soon. They will come looking for me and cut my head off. Did they not, this would carry me off in a sixday with the flesh-rot. A deep belly wound, I cannot live. I will not live. Ogo, I shall kill myself before they find me. You cannot stay.' She was trying to take her helmet off. He helped her. 'I thank you,' she said. Her face was the colour of death but her eyes were still warm when she smiled. 'Now run away.'

'No!'

'Yes!' She held up the Royal Ring, still linked to her lord's bracelet by a fine chain. 'Do you see this? I command you to go, Ogo, now!' She reached for her other bracelet, pulled out the pin that closed the clasp, snapped it open and pressed it with both hands into his. 'Take it, go away and sell it. Go back to Raq'min. Find Yunnil. Bless your children, give them names. If you're on the far side of the hill by dark you can make a fire and they'll not find you. Go quickly now, I beg you. In the name of all these years.'

She watched him till he was out of sight among the snows. Twice he stopped and looked back. Twice she waved him on. If there was a third time, she could no longer see him. The long white clouds had turned orange and mauve with the glory of the sunset. She raised herself to her feet with the aid of the wheel she was leaning against; a big red blotch marked where she had sat in the snow. Other blotches joined it as she shuffled along to a place where two wagons were jammed together. She could prop herself against them, facing the sunset, and if she stiffened quickly she would not fall down. The rent in her mailshirt made it easy to slip the knife up under her ribs. She made sure that her feet were firmly settled, and pushed; and watched the light expand until it filled her eyes.

'We found her horse, my lord. We looked at every body on the battlefield, but she's not there.'

'Is she not? Then you'll damn well find her! It is not enough to say that you saw her go down, that you believe her dead. One does not know her dead till – what was that? Say it out loud, sir, let us all hear it.'

'I said, well my lord, a witch – will her body not, not wither away–'

'It will not! She is no more a witch than I am. Now get on

336

and find her and bring her here to me. You found Lord Sulakon fast enough.'

The officers tramped out. Polem huffed and went into the tent next door, where Sulakon's body lay wrapped in a tarpaulin on a trestle table. He pulled the cloth back to look at the former Regent's face. 'How did he die?'

'He was stabbed, sir. He was wearing plate-mail sewn on leather, they slipped a stiletto between the plates. It was still in him when we found him.'

'Stabbed in the back! Know you who might have done it?'

The guards looked at him in silence. Finally one of them said hopefully, 'The witch?'

'Who knows, my lord?'

'Who indeed?' said Polem. The lines engraved on Sulakon's face showed the familiar aspect of harshness and pride. Someone had put a couple of copper coins over his eyes. He twitched the cover up again. 'Have him properly laid out, so that everyone can come and see him and make sure that he is dead. This table will do.'

In the morning light the camp of Haramin was still deserted. Tilts flapped in the wind on the abandoned wagons. 'Why have they not come here to scavenge?'

'The barbarians scavenged it already.'

'They are afraid of the witch's curse on her things.'

'There's nothing here.'

'Wait! Look over there!'

'Ssh! Creep up quietly. Do not let her see us!'

'Is that her?'

'Yes, yes, no one else has hair like that!'

'She does not move.'

'Ssh! It's her craft.'

Little by little, as the wind ruffled her hair and she remained dead still, they dared to approach, until they stood in a circle round her. Her blue eyes stared forward and the white-gold hair waved softly over her forehead. There was blood all around her feet, frozen now overnight. Finally a crow hopped over the wagon, settled on her head and made to peck at one of the staring eyes. Then the captain finally swatted at it and as it cawed and flapped away they knew that she was dead. They made a stretcher out of a wagon tilt and four of them carried her away. They laid her out next to Sulakon but nothing would close her eyes.

'Where is her other lord's bracelet?' Polem asked.

'She only had the one on when we found her, my lord.'

He stood there gazing at the corpse. One by one the others slipped away, till there were only the two guards on the door. Her hands were crossed on her breast, over the knife they had found sunk in it. They had cleaned the blood off her armour but there was no way to mend the gaping blackened hole in her side. After so much spite and passion her face was entirely serene.

Polem picked up her right hand and tugged at the Royal Ring. It was held by the chain. He undid the bracelet, snapped it open, and pulled the ring off with it; broke the chain, and put the ring on his own finger. He held it up to look at the white eye of the jewel. The discarded bracelet lay like a dead crab on the floor.

'Which is the road to Safi?' Polem said.